Less Than One

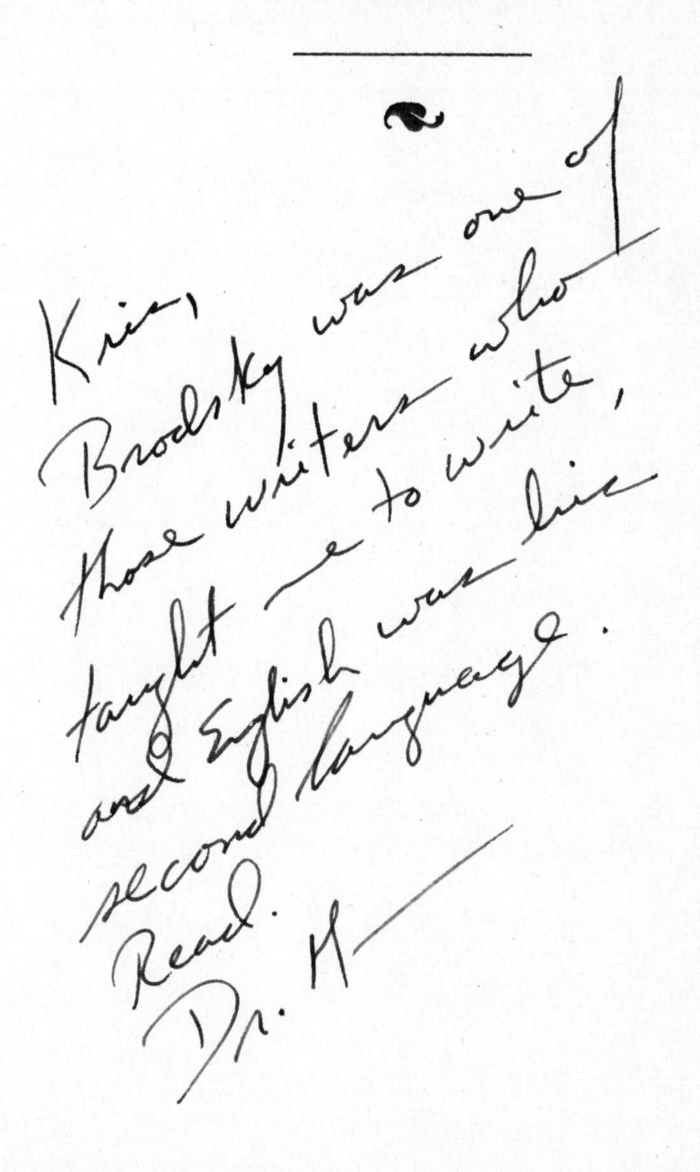

BY JOSEPH BRODSKY

Elegy for John Donne and Other Poems

Selected Poems

A Part of Speech

Less Than One

To Urania

Marbles

Watermark

On Grief and Reason

So Forth

JOSEPH BRODSKY

LESS THAN ONE

SELECTED ESSAYS

Farrar Straus Giroux

NEW YORK

Farrar, Straus and Giroux
18 West 18th Street, New York 10011

Distributed in Canada by Douglas & McIntyre Ltd.
Printed in the United States of America
Published in 1986 by Farrar, Straus and Giroux
First paperback edition, 1987

Portions of this book have appeared, in somewhat different form, in *The New York Review of Books*, *The New York Times*, *The New York Times Book Review*, *Parnassus: Poetry in Review*, *Stand*, *Vanity Fair*, and *Vogue*; "Flight from Byzantium" originally appeared in *The New Yorker.*

"The Keening Muse," originally published as the introduction to *Anna Akhmatova: Poems*, selected and translated by Lyn Coffin, is reprinted with the permission of W. W. Norton and Company, Inc. Copyright © 1983 by Lyn Coffin. "The Child of Civilization," originally published as the introduction to *Fifty Poems by Osip Mandelstam*, translated by Bernard Meares, is reprinted with the permission of Persea Books. Introduction copyright © 1977 by Joseph Brodsky. "The Sound of the Tide," originally published as the introduction to *Poems of the Caribbean* by Derek Walcott, illustrations by Romare Bearden, is reprinted with the permission of Limited Editions Book Club. Introduction copyright © 1983 by Joseph Brodsky.

The Library of Congress has cataloged the hardcover edition as follows:
Brodsky, Joseph, 1940–
Less than one : selected essays / Joseph Brodsky.—1st ed.
p. cm.
1. Poetry, Modern—20th century—History and criticism—Addresses, essays, lectures. 2. Russian literature—History and criticism—Addresses, essays, lectures. I. Title.
PN1271.B76 1986
809.1'04
85-15900

Paperback ISBN-13: 978-0-374-52055-7
Paperback ISBN-10: 0-374-52055-0

www.fsgbooks.com

26 25 24 23 22

The author wishes to express his gratitude to the John and Catherine MacArthur Foundation for its five years of generous support.

In memory of my mother and my father

In memory of Carl Ray Proffer

Contents

And the heart doesn't die when one thinks it should.

CZESLAW MILOSZ, *"Elegy for N.N."*

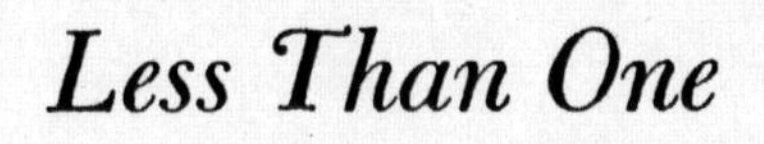

Less Than One

Less Than One

As failures go, attempting to recall the past is like trying to grasp the meaning of existence. Both make one feel like a baby clutching at a basketball: one's palms keep sliding off.

I remember rather little of my life and what I do remember is of small consequence. Most of the thoughts I now recall as having been interesting to me owe their significance to the time when they occurred. If any do not, they have no doubt been expressed much better by someone else. A writer's biography is in his twists of language. I remember, for instance, that when I was about ten or eleven it occurred to me that Marx's dictum that "existence conditions consciousness" was true only for as long as it takes consciousness to acquire the art of estrangement; thereafter, consciousness is on its own and can both condition and ignore existence. At that age, this was surely a discovery—but one hardly worth recording, and surely it had been better stated by others. And does it really matter who first cracked the mental cuneiform of which "existence conditions consciousness" is a perfect example?

So I am writing all this not in order to set the record

straight (there is no such record, and even if there is, it is an insignificant one and thus not yet distorted), but mostly for the usual reason why a writer writes—to give or to get a boost from the language, this time from a foreign one. The little I remember becomes even more diminished by being recollected in English.

For the beginning I had better trust my birth certificate, which states that I was born on May 24, 1940, in Leningrad, Russia, much as I abhor this name for the city which long ago the ordinary people nicknamed simply "Peter"—from Petersburg. There is an old two-liner:

The sides of people
Are rubbed by Old Peter.

In the national experience, the city is definitely Leningrad; in the growing vulgarity of its content, it becomes Leningrad more and more. Besides, as a word, "Leningrad" to a Russian ear already sounds as neutral as the word "construction" or "sausage." And yet I'd rather call it "Peter," for I remember this city at a time when it didn't look like "Leningrad"—right after the war. Gray, pale-green façades with bullet and shrapnel cavities; endless, empty streets, with few passersby and light traffic; almost a starved look with, as a result, more definite and, if you wish, nobler features. A lean, hard face with the abstract glitter of its river reflected in the eyes of its hollow windows. A survivor cannot be named after Lenin.

Those magnificent pockmarked façades behind which—among old pianos, worn-out rugs, dusty paintings in heavy bronze frames, leftovers of furniture (chairs least of all) consumed by the iron stoves during the siege—a faint life was beginning to glimmer. And I remember, as I passed these façades on my way to school, being completely absorbed in imagining what was going on in those rooms with the old, billowy wallpaper. I must say that from these façades and porticoes—classical, modern, eclectic, with their columns, pilasters, and plastered heads of mythic animals or people—from their ornaments and caryatids holding up the balconies, from the torsos in the niches of their entrances, I have learned more about the history of our world than I subsequently have from any book. Greece, Rome, Egypt—all of them were there, and all were chipped by artillery shells during the bombardments. And from the gray, reflecting river flowing down to the Baltic, with an occasional tugboat in the midst of it struggling against the current, I have learned more about infinity and stoicism than from mathematics and Zeno.

All that had very little to do with Lenin, whom, I suppose, I began to despise even when I was in the first grade—not so much because of his political philosophy or practice, about which at the age of seven I knew very little, but because of his omnipresent images which plagued almost every textbook, every class wall, postage stamps, money, and what not, depicting the man at various ages and stages of his life. There was baby Lenin, looking like a cherub in his blond curls. Then Lenin in his twenties and thirties, bald and uptight, with that meaningless expression on his face which could be mistaken for anything, preferably a sense of purpose. This face in some way haunts every Russian and suggests some sort of standard for human appearance because it is utterly lacking in character. (Perhaps because there is nothing specific in that face it suggests many possibilities.) Then there was an oldish Lenin, balder, with his wedge-like beard, in his three-piece dark suit, sometimes smiling, but most often addressing the "masses" from the top of an armored car or from the podium of some party congress, with a hand outstretched in the air.

There were also variants: Lenin in his worker's cap, with a carnation pinned to his lapel; in a vest, sitting in his study, writing or reading; on a lakeside stump, scribbling his April Theses, or some other nonsense, al fresco. Ultimately, Lenin in a paramilitary jacket on a garden bench next to Stalin, who was the only one to surpass Lenin in the ubiquitousness of his printed images. But Stalin was then alive, while Lenin was dead and, if only because of that, "good" because he belonged to the past—i.e., was sponsored by both history and nature. Whereas Stalin was sponsored only by nature, or the other way around.

I think that coming to ignore those pictures was my first lesson in switching off, my first attempt at estrangement. There were more to follow; in fact, the rest of my life can be viewed as a nonstop avoidance of its most importunate aspects. I must say, I went quite far in that direction; perhaps too far. Anything that bore a suggestion of repetitiveness became compromised and subject to removal. That included phrases, trees, certain types of people, sometimes even physical pain; it affected many of my relationships. In a way, I am grateful to Lenin. Whatever there was in plenitude I immediately regarded as some sort of propaganda. This attitude, I think, made for an awful acceleration through the thicket of events, with an accompanying superficiality.

I don't believe for a moment that all the clues to character are to be found in childhood. For about three generations Russians have been living in communal apartments and cramped rooms, and our parents made love while we pretended to be asleep. Then there was a war, starvation, absent or mutilated fathers, horny mothers, official lies at school and unofficial ones at home. Hard winters, ugly clothes, public exposé of our wet sheets in summer camps, and citations of such matters in front of others. Then the red flag would flutter on the mast of the camp. So what? All this militarization of childhood, all the menacing idiocy, erotic tension (at ten we all lusted for our female teachers) had not affected our ethics much, or our aesthetics—or our ability to love and suffer. I recall these things not because I think that they are the keys to the subconscious, or certainly not out of nostalgia for my childhood. I recall them because I have never done so before, because I want some of those things to stay—at least on paper. Also, because looking backward is more rewarding than its opposite. Tomorrow is just less attractive than yesterday. For some reason, the past doesn't radiate such immense monotony as the future does. Because of its plenitude, the future is propaganda. So is grass.

The real history of consciousness starts with one's first lie. I happen to remember mine. It was in a school library when I had to fill out an application for membership. The fifth blank was of course "nationality." I was seven years old and knew very well that I was a Jew, but I told the attendant that I didn't know. With dubious glee she suggested that I go home and ask my parents. I never returned to that library, although I did become a member of many others which had the same application forms. I wasn't ashamed of being a Jew, nor was I scared of admitting it. In the class ledger our names, the names of our parents, home addresses, and nationalities were registered in full detail, and from time to time a teacher would "forget" the ledger on the desk in the classroom during breaks. Then, like vultures, we would fall upon those pages; everyone in my class knew that I was a Jew. But seven-year-old boys don't make good anti-Semites. Besides, I was fairly strong for my age, and the fists were what mattered most then. I was ashamed of the word "Jew" itself—in Russian, "*yevrei*"—regardless of its connotations.

A word's fate depends on the variety of its contexts, on the frequency of its usage. In printed Russian "*yevrei*" appears nearly as seldom as, say, "mediastinum" or "gennel" in American English. In fact, it also has something like the status of a four-letter word or like a name for VD. When one is seven one's vocabulary proves sufficient to acknowledge this word's rarity, and it is utterly unpleasant to identify oneself with it; somehow it goes against one's sense of prosody. I remember that I always felt a lot easier with a Russian equivalent of "kike"—"*zhyd*" (pronounced like André Gide): it was clearly offensive and thereby meaningless, not loaded with allusions. A one-syllable word can't do much in Russian. But when suffixes are applied, or endings, or prefixes, then feathers fly. All this is not to say that I suffered as a Jew at that tender age; it's simply to say that my first lie had to do with my identity.

Not a bad start. As for anti-Semitism as such, I didn't care much about it because it came mostly from teachers: it seemed innate to their negative part in our lives; it had to be coped with like low marks. If I had been a Roman Catholic, I would have wished most of them in Hell. True, some teachers were better than others; but since all were masters of our immediate lives, we didn't bother to distinguish. Nor did they try to distinguish among their little slaves, and even the most ardent anti-Semitic remarks bore an air of impersonal inertia. Somehow, I never was capable of taking seriously any verbal assault on me, especially from people of such a disparate age group. I guess the diatribes my parents used to deliver against me tempered me very well. Besides, some teachers were Jews themselves, and I dreaded them no less than I did the pure-blooded Russians.

This is just one example of the trimming of the self that —along with the language itself, where verbs and nouns change places as freely as one dares to have them do so— bred in us such an overpowering sense of ambivalence that in ten years we ended up with a willpower in no way superior to a seaweed's. Four years in the army (into which men were drafted at the age of nineteen) completed the process of total surrender to the state. Obedience would become both first and second nature.

If one had brains, one would certainly try to outsmart the system by devising all kinds of detours, arranging shady deals with one's superiors, piling up lies and pulling the strings of one's semi-nepotic connections. This would become a full-time job. Yet one was constantly aware that the web one had woven was a web of lies, and in spite of the degree of success or your sense of humor, you'd despise yourself. That is the ultimate triumph of the system: whether you beat it or join it, you feel equally guilty. The national belief is—as the proverb has it—that there is no Evil without a grain of Good in it and presumably vice versa.

Ambivalence, I think, is the chief characteristic of my nation. There isn't a Russian executioner who isn't scared of turning victim one day, nor is there the sorriest victim who would not acknowledge (if only to himself) a mental ability to become an executioner. Our immediate history has provided well for both. There is some wisdom in this. One might even think that this ambivalence *is* wisdom, that life itself is neither good nor bad, but arbitrary. Perhaps our literature stresses the good cause so remarkably because this cause is challenged so well. If this emphasis were simply doublethink, that would be fine; but it grates on the instincts. This kind of ambivalence, I think, is precisely that "blessed news" which the East, having little else to offer, is about to impose on the rest of the world. And the world looks ripe for it.

The world's destiny aside, the only way for a boy to fight his imminent lot would be to go off the track. This was hard to do because of your parents, and because you yourself were quite frightened of the unknown. Most of all, because it made you different from the majority, and you got it with your mother's milk that the majority is right. A certain lack of concern is required, and unconcerned I was. As I remember my quitting school at the age of fifteen, it wasn't so much a conscious choice as a gut reaction. I simply couldn't stand certain faces in my class—of some of my classmates, but mostly of teachers. And so one winter morning, for no apparent reason, I rose up in the middle of the session and made my melodramatic exit through the school gate, knowing clearly that I'd never be back. Of the emotions overpowering me at that moment, I remember only a general disgust with myself for being too young and letting so many things boss me around. Also, there was that vague but happy sensation of escape, of a sunny street without end.

The main thing, I suppose, was the change of exterior. In a centralized state all rooms look alike: the office of my school's principal was an exact replica of the interrogation chambers I began to frequent some five years later. The same wooden panels, desks, chairs—a paradise for carpenters. The same portraits of our founders, Lenin, Stalin, members of the Politburo, and Maxim Gorky (the founder of Soviet literature) if it was a school, or Felix Dzerzhinsky (the founder of the Soviet Secret Police) if it was an interrogation chamber.

Often, though, Dzerzhinsky—"Iron Felix" or "Knight of the Revolution," as propaganda has it—would decorate the principal's wall as well, because the man had glided into the system of education from the heights of the KGB. And those stuccoed walls of my classrooms, with their blue horizontal stripe at eye level, running unfailingly across the whole country, like the line of an infinite common denominator: in halls, hospitals, factories, prisons, corridors of communal apartments. The only place I didn't encounter it was in wooden peasant huts.

This decor was as maddening as it was omnipresent, and how many times in my life would I catch myself peering mindlessly at this blue two-inch-wide stripe, taking it sometimes for a sea horizon, sometimes for an embodiment of nothingness itself. It was too abstract to mean anything. From the floor up to the level of your eyes a wall covered with rat-gray or greenish paint, and this blue stripe topping it off; above it would be the virginally white stucco. Nobody ever asked why it was there. Nobody could have answered. It was just there, a border line, a divider between gray and white, below and above. They were not colors themselves but hints of colors, which might be interrupted only by alternating patches of brown: doors. Closed, half open. And through the half-open door you could see another room with the same distribution of gray and white marked by the blue stripe. Plus a portrait of Lenin and a world map.

It was nice to leave that Kafkaesque cosmos, although even then—or so it seems—I sort of knew that I was trading six for half a dozen. I knew that any other building I was going to enter would look the same, for buildings are where we are doomed to carry on anyhow. Still, I felt that I had to go. The financial situation in our family was grim: we existed mostly on my mother's salary, because my father, after being discharged from the navy in accordance with some seraphic ruling that Jews should not hold substantial military ranks, had a hard time finding a job. Of course, my parents would have managed without my contribution; they would have preferred that I finish school. I knew that, and yet I told myself that I had to help my family. It was almost a lie, but this way it looked better, and by that time I had already learned to like lies for precisely this "almost-ness" which sharpens the outline of truth: after all, truth ends where lies start. That's what a boy learned in school and it proved to be more useful than algebra.

2

Whatever it was—a lie, the truth, or, most likely, their mixture—that caused me to make such a decision, I am immensely grateful to it for what appears to have been my first free act. It was an instinctive act, a walkout. Reason had very little to do with it. I know that, because I've been walking out ever since, with increasing frequency. And not necessarily on account of boredom or of feeling a trap gaping; I've been walking out of perfect setups no less often than out of dreadful ones. However modest the place you happen to occupy, if it has the slightest mark of decency, you can be sure that someday somebody will walk in and claim it for himself or, what is worse, suggest that you share it. Then you either have to fight for that place or leave it. I happened to prefer the latter. Not at all because I couldn't fight, but rather out of sheer disgust with myself: managing to pick something that attracts others denotes a certain vulgarity in your choice. It doesn't matter at all that you came across the place first. It is even worse to get somewhere first, for those who follow will always have a stronger appetite than your partially satisfied one.

Afterward I often regretted that move, especially when I saw my former classmates getting on so well inside the system. And yet I knew something that they didn't. In fact, I was getting on too, but in the opposite direction, going somewhat further. One thing I am especially pleased with is that I managed to catch the "working class" in its truly proletarian stage, before it began to undergo a middle-class conversion in the late fifties. It was a real "proletariat" that I dealt with at the factory where, at the age of fifteen, I began to work as a milling machine operator. Marx would recognize them instantly. They—or rather "we"—all lived in communal apartments, four or more people in one room, often with three generations all together, sleeping in shifts, drinking like sharks, brawling with each other or with neighbors in the communal kitchen or in a morning line before the communal john, beating their women with a moribund determination, crying openly when Stalin dropped dead, or at the movies, and cursing with such frequency that a normal word, like "airplane," would strike a passerby as something elaborately obscene—becoming a gray, indifferent ocean of heads or a forest of raised hands at public meetings on behalf of some Egypt or other.

The factory was all brick, huge, straight out of the industrial revolution. It had been built at the end of the nineteenth century, and the population of "Peter" referred to it as "the Arsenal": the factory produced cannons. At the time I began to work there, it was also producing agricultural machinery and air compressors. Still, according to the seven veils of secrecy which blanket almost everything in Russia that has to do with heavy industry, the factory had its code name, "Post Office Box 671." I think, though, that secrecy was imposed not so much to fool some foreign intelligence service as to maintain a kind of paramilitary discipline, which was the only device for guaranteeing any stability in production. In either case, failure was evident.

The machinery was obsolete; 90 percent of it had been taken from Germany as reparations after World War II. I remember that whole cast-iron zoo full of exotic creatures bearing the names Cincinnati, Karlton, Fritz Werner, Siemens & Schuckert. Planning was hideous; every once in a while a rush order to produce some item would mess up your flickering attempt to establish some kind of working rhythm, a procedure. By the end of a quarter (i.e., every third month), when the plan was going up in smoke, the administration would issue the war cry mobilizing all hands on one job, and the plan would be subjected to a storm attack. Whenever something broke down, there were no spare parts, and a bunch of usually semi-drunk tinkers would be called in to exercise their sorcery. The metal would arrive full of craters. Virtually everyone would have a hangover on Mondays, not to mention the mornings after paydays.

Production would decline sharply the day after a loss by the city or national soccer team. Nobody would work, and everybody discussed the details and the players, for along with all the complexes of a superior nation, Russia has the great inferiority complex of a small country. This is mostly the consequence of the centralization of national life. Hence the positive, "life-affirming" drivel of the official newspapers and radio even when describing an earthquake; they never give you any information about victims but only sing of other cities' and republics' brotherly care in supplying the stricken area with tents and sleeping bags. Or if there is a cholera epidemic, you may happen to learn of it only while reading about the latest success of our wondrous medicine as manifested in the invention of a new vaccine.

The whole thing would have looked absurd if it were not for those very early mornings when, having washed my breakfast down with pale tea, I would run to catch the streetcar and, adding my berry to the dark-gray bunch of human grapes hanging on the footboard, would sail through the pinkish-blue, watercolor-like city to the wooden doghouse of my factory's entrance. It had two guards checking our badges and its façade was decorated with classical veneered pilasters. I've noticed that the entrances of prisons, mental hospitals, and concentration camps are done in the same style: they all bear a hint of classicistic or baroque porticoes. Quite an echo. Inside my shop, nuances of gray were interwoven under the ceiling, and the pneumatic hoses hissed quietly on the floor among the mazout puddles glittering with all the colors of the rainbow. By ten o'clock this metal jungle was in full swing, screeching and roaring, and the steel barrel of a would-be antiaircraft gun soared in the air like the disjointed neck of a giraffe.

I have always envied those nineteenth-century characters who were able to look back and distinguish the landmarks of their lives, of their development. Some event would mark a point of transition, a different stage. I am talking about writers; but what I really have in mind is the capacity of certain types of people to rationalize their lives, to see things separately, if not clearly. And I understand that this phenomenon shouldn't be limited to the nineteenth century. Yet in my life it has been represented mostly by literature. Either because of some basic flaw of my mind or because of the fluid, amorphous nature of life itself, I have never been capable of distinguishing any landmark, let alone a buoy. If there is anything like a landmark, it is that which I won't be able to acknowledge myself—i.e., death. In a sense, there never was such a thing as childhood. These categories—childhood, adulthood, maturity—seem to me very odd, and if I use them occasionally in conversation I always regard them mutely, for myself, as borrowed.

I guess there was always some "me" inside that small and, later, somewhat bigger shell around which "everything" was happening. Inside that shell the entity which one calls

"I" never changed and never stopped watching what was going on outside. I am not trying to hint at pearls inside. What I am saying is that the passage of time does not much affect that entity. To get a low grade, to operate a milling machine, to be beaten up at an interrogation, or to lecture on Callimachus in a classroom is essentially the same. This is what makes one feel a bit astonished when one grows up and finds oneself tackling the tasks that are supposed to be handled by grownups. The dissatisfaction of a child with his parents' control over him and the panic of an adult confronting a responsibility are of the same nature. One is neither of these figures; one is perhaps less than "one."

Certainly this is partly an outgrowth of your profession. If you are in banking or if you fly an aircraft, you know that after you gain a substantial amount of expertise you are more or less guaranteed a profit or a safe landing. Whereas in the business of writing what one accumulates is not expertise but uncertainties. Which is but another name for craft. In this field, where expertise invites doom, the notions of adolescence and maturity get mixed up, and panic is the most frequent state of mind. So I would be lying if I resorted to chronology or to anything that suggests a linear process. A school is a factory is a poem is a prison is academia is boredom, with flashes of panic.

Except that the factory was next to a hospital, and the hospital was next to the most famous prison in all of Russia, called the Crosses.* And the morgue of that hospital was where I went to work after quitting the Arsenal, for I had the idea of becoming a doctor. The Crosses opened its cell doors to me soon after I changed my mind and started to

* The Crosses has 999 cells.

write poems. When I worked at the factory, I could see the hospital over the wall. When I cut and sewed up corpses at the hospital, I would see prisoners walking in the courtyard of the Crosses; sometimes they managed to throw their letters over the wall, and I'd pick them up and mail them. Because of this tight topography and because of the shell's enclosure, all these places, jobs, convicts, workers, guards, and doctors have merged into one another, and I don't know any longer whether I recall somebody walking back and forth in the flatiron-shaped courtyard of the Crosses or whether it is me walking there. Besides, both the factory and the prison were built at approximately the same time, and on the surface they were indistinguishable; one looked like a wing of the other.

So it doesn't make sense to me to try to be consecutive here. Life never looked to me like a set of clearly marked transitions; rather, it snowballs, and the more it does, the more one place (or one time) looks like another. I remember, for instance, how in 1945 my mother and I were waiting for a train at some railway station near Leningrad. The war was just over, twenty million Russians were decaying in makeshift graves across the continent, and the rest, dispersed by war, were returning to their homes or what was left of their homes. The railway station was a picture of primeval chaos. People were besieging the cattle trains like mad insects; they were climbing on the roofs of cars, squeezing between them, and so on. For some reason, my eye caught sight of an old, bald, crippled man with a wooden leg, who was trying to get into car after car, but each time was pushed away by the people who were already hanging on the footboards. The train started to move and the old man hopped along. At one point he managed to grab a handle of one of the cars, and then I saw a woman in the doorway lift a kettle and pour boiling water straight on the old man's bald crown. The man fell—the Brownian movement of a thousand legs swallowed him and I lost sight of him.

It was cruel, yes, but this instance of cruelty, in its own turn, merges in my mind with a story that took place twenty years later when a bunch of former collaborators with the German occupation forces, the so-called *Polizei,* were caught. It was in the papers. There were six or seven old men. The name of their leader was naturally Gurewicz or Ginzburg—i.e., he was a Jew, however unthinkable it is to imagine a Jew collaborating with Nazis. They all got various sentences. The Jew, naturally, got capital punishment. I was told that on the morning of the execution he was taken from the cell, and while being led into the courtyard of the prison where the firing squad was waiting, he was asked by the officer in charge of the prison guard: "Ah, by the way, Gurewicz [or Ginzburg], what's your last wish?" "Last wish?" said the man. "I don't know . . . I'd like to take a leak . . ." To which the officer replied: "Well, you'll take a leak later." Now, to me both stories are the same; yet it is even worse if the second story is pure folklore, although I don't think it is. I know hundreds of similar tales, perhaps more than hundreds. Yet they merge.

What made my factory different from my school wasn't what I'd been doing inside each, not what I'd been thinking in the respective periods, but the way their façades looked, what I saw on my way to class or to the shop. In the last analysis, appearances are all there is. The same idiotic lot befell millions and millions. Existence as such, monotonous in itself, has been reduced to uniform rigidity by the centralized state. What was left to watch were faces, weather, buildings; also, the language people used.

I had an uncle who was a member of the Party and who was, as I realize now, an awfully good engineer. During the war he built bomb shelters for the Party *Genossen*; before and after it he built bridges. Both still stand. My father always ridiculed him while quarreling about money with my mother, who would cite her engineer-brother as an example of solid and steady living, and I disdained him more or less automatically. Still, he had a magnificent library. He didn't read much, I think; but it was—and still is—a mark of chic for the Soviet middle class to subscribe to new editions of encyclopedias, classics, and so on. I envied him madly. I remember once standing behind his chair, peering at the back of his head and thinking that if I killed him all his books would become mine, since he was then unmarried and had no children. I used to take books from his shelves, and even fashioned a key to a tall bookcase behind whose glass sat four huge volumes of a prerevolutionary edition of *Man and Woman*.

This was a copiously illustrated encyclopedia, to which I still consider myself indebted for my basic knowledge of how the forbidden fruit tastes. If, in general, pornography is an inanimate object that causes an erection, it is worth noting that in the puritanical atmosphere of Stalin's Russia, one could get turned on by the one hundred percent innocent Socialist Realist painting called *Admission to the Komsomol*, which was widely reproduced and which decorated almost every classroom. Among the characters depicted in this painting was a young blond woman sitting on a chair with her legs crossed in such a way that two or three inches of her thigh were visible. It wasn't so much that bit of her thigh as its contrast to the dark brown dress she wore that drove me crazy and pursued me in my dreams.

It was then that I learned to disbelieve all the noise about the subconscious. I think that I never dreamed in symbols—I always saw the real thing: bosom, hips, female underwear. As to the latter, it had an odd significance for us boys at that time. I remember how during a class, somebody would crawl under a row of desks all the way up to the teacher's desk, with a single purpose—to look under her dress to check what color underpants she was wearing that day. Upon completing his expedition, he would announce in a dramatic whisper to the rest of the class, "Lilac."

In short, we were not troubled much by our fantasies—we had too much reality to deal with. I've said somewhere else that Russians—at least my generation—never resort to shrinks. In the first place, there are not so many of them. Besides, psychiatry is the state's property. One knows that to have a psychiatric record isn't such a great thing. It might backfire at any moment. But in any case, we used to handle our problems ourselves, to keep track of what went on inside our heads without help from the outside. A certain advantage of totalitarianism is that it suggests to an individual a kind of vertical hierarchy of his own, with consciousness at the top. So we oversee what's going on inside ourselves; we almost report to our consciousness on our instincts. And then we punish ourselves. When we realize that this punishment is not commensurate with the swine we have discovered inside, we resort to alcohol and drink our wits out.

I think this system is efficient and consumes less cash. It

is not that I think suppression is better than freedom; I just believe that the mechanism of suppression is as innate to the human psyche as the mechanism of release. Besides, to think that you are a swine is humbler and eventually more accurate than to perceive yourself as a fallen angel. I have every reason to think so because in the country where I spent thirty-two years, adultery and moviegoing are the only forms of free enterprise. Plus Art.

All the same, I felt patriotic. This was the normal patriotism of a child, a patriotism with a strong militaristic flavor. I admired planes and warships, and nothing was more beautiful to me than the yellow and blue banner of the air force, which looked like an open parachute canopy with a propeller in the center. I loved planes and until quite recently followed developments in aviation closely. With the arrival of rockets I gave up, and my love became a nostalgia for propjets. (I know I am not the only one: my nine-year-old son once said that when he grew up he would destroy all turbojets and reintroduce biplanes.) As for the navy, I was a true child of my father and at the age of fourteen applied for admission to a submarine academy. I passed all the exams, but because of the fifth paragraph —nationality—didn't get in, and my irrational love for navy overcoats with their double rows of gold buttons, resembling a night street with receding lights, remained unrequited.

Visual aspects of life, I am afraid, always mattered to me more than its content. For instance, I fell in love with a photograph of Samuel Beckett long before I'd read a line of his. As for the military, prisons spared me the draft, so that my affair with the uniform forever remained platonic. In my view, prison is a lot better than the army. In the first place, in prison nobody teaches you to hate that distant "potential" enemy. Your enemy in prison isn't an abstraction; he is concrete and palpable. That is, you are always palpable to your enemy. Perhaps "enemy" is too strong a word. In prison you are dealing with an extremely domesticated notion of enemy, which makes the whole thing quite earthly, mortal. After all, my guards or neighbors were not any different from my teachers or those workers who humiliated me during my apprenticeship at the factory.

My hatred's center of gravity, in other words, wasn't dispersed into some foreign capitalist nowhere; it wasn't even hatred. The damned trait of understanding and thus forgiving everybody, which started while I was in school, fully blossomed in prison. I don't think I hated even my KGB interrogators: I tended to absolve even them (good-for-nothing, has a family to feed, etc.). The ones I couldn't justify at all were those who ran the country, perhaps because I'd never got close to any of them. As enemies go, in a cell you have a most immediate one: lack of space. The formula for prison is a lack of space counterbalanced by a surplus of time. This is what really bothers you, that you can't win. Prison is a lack of alternatives, and the telescopic predictability of the future is what drives you crazy. Even so, it is a hell of a lot better than the solemnity with which the army sics you on people on the other side of the globe, or nearer.

Service in the Soviet Army takes from three to four years, and I never met a person whose psyche wasn't mutilated by its mental straitjacket of obedience. With the exception, perhaps, of musicians who play in military bands and two distant acquaintances of mine who shot themselves in

1956, in Hungary, where both were tank commanders. It is the army that finally makes a citizen of you; without it you still have a chance, however slim, to remain a human being. If there is any reason for pride in my past, it is that I became a convict, not a soldier. Even for having missed out on the military lingo—the thing that worried me most—I was generously reimbursed with the criminal argot.

Still, warships and planes were beautiful, and every year there were more of them. In 1945, the streets were full of "Studebekker" trucks and jeeps with a white star on their doors and hoods—the American hardware we had got on lend-lease. In 1972, we were selling this kind of thing *urbi et orbi* ourselves. If the standard of living during that period improved 15 to 20 percent, the improvement in weaponry production could be expressed in tens of thousands of percent. It will continue to go up, because it is about the only real thing we have in that country, the only tangible field for advancement. Also because military blackmail, i.e., a constant increase in the production of armaments which is perfectly tolerable in the totalitarian setup, may cripple the economy of any democratic adversary that tries to maintain a balance. Military buildup isn't insanity: it's the best tool available to condition the economy of your opposite number, and in the Kremlin they've realized that full well. Anyone seeking world domination would do the same. The alternatives are either unworkable (economic competition) or too scary (actually using military devices).

Besides, the army is a peasant's idea of order. There is nothing more reassuring for an average man than the sight of his cohorts parading in front of Politburo members standing on top of the Mausoleum. I guess it never occurred to any of them that there is an element of blasphemy in standing on top of a holy relic's tomb. The idea, I guess, is that of a continuum, and the sad thing about these figures on top of the Mausoleum is that they really join the mummy in defying time. You either see it live on TV or as a poor-quality photograph multiplied in millions of copies of the official newspapers. Like the ancient Romans who related themselves to the center of the Empire by making the main street in their settlements always run north-south, so the Russians check the stability and predictability of their existence by those pictures.

When I was working at the factory, we would go for lunch breaks into the factory yard; some would sit down and unwrap their sandwiches, others would smoke or play volleyball. There was a little flower bed surrounded by the standard wooden fence. This was a row of twenty-inch-high planks with two-inch spaces between them, held together by a transverse lath made of the same material, painted green. It was covered with dust and soot, just like the shrunken, withered flowers inside the square-shaped bed. Wherever you went in that empire, you would always find this fence. It comes prefabricated, but even when people make it with their own hands, they always follow the prescribed design. Once I went to Central Asia, to Samarkand; I was all warmed up for those turquoise cupolas and the inscrutable ornaments of madrasahs and minarets. They were there. And then I saw that fence, with its idiotic rhythm, and my heart sank, the Orient vanished. The small-scale, comb-like repetitiveness of the narrow palings immediately annihilated the space—as well as the time—between the factory yard and Kubla Khan's ancient seat.

There is nothing more remote from these planks than

nature, whose green color their paint idiotically suggests. These planks, the governmental iron of railings, the inevitable khaki of the military uniform in every passing crowd on every street in every city, the eternal photographs of steel foundries in every morning paper and the continuous Tchaikovsky on the radio—these things would drive you crazy unless you learned to switch yourself off. There are no commercials on Soviet TV; there are pictures of Lenin, or so-called photo-études of "spring," "autumn," etc., in the intervals between the programs. Plus "light" bubbling music which never had a composer and is a product of the amplifier itself.

At that time I didn't know yet that all this was a result of the age of reason and progress, of the age of mass production; I ascribed it to the state and partly to the nation itself, which would go for anything that does not require imagination. Still, I think I wasn't completely wrong. Should it not be easier to exercise and distribute enlightenment and culture in a centralized state? A ruler, theoretically, has better access to perfection (which he claims anyhow) than a representative. Rousseau argued this. Too bad it never worked in Russia. This country, with its magnificently inflected language capable of expressing the subtlest nuances of the human psyche, with an incredible ethical sensitivity (a good result of its otherwise tragic history), had all the makings of a cultural, spiritual paradise, a real vessel of civilization. Instead, it became a drab hell, with a shabby materialist dogma and pathetic consumerist gropings.

My generation, however, was somewhat spared. We emerged from under the postwar rubble when the state was too busy patching its own skin and couldn't look after us very well. We entered schools, and whatever elevated rubbish we were taught there, the suffering and poverty were visible all around. You cannot cover a ruin with a page of *Pravda.* The empty windows gaped at us like skulls' orbits, and as little as we were, we sensed tragedy. True, we couldn't connect ourselves to the ruins, but that wasn't necessary: they emanated enough to interrupt laughter. Then we would resume laughing, quite mindlessly—and yet it would be a resumption. In those postwar years we sensed a strange intensity in the air; something immaterial, almost ghostly. And we were young, we were kids. The amount of goods was very limited, but not having known otherwise, we didn't mind it. Bikes were old, of prewar make, and the owner of a soccer ball was considered a bourgeois. The coats and underwear that we wore were cut out by our mothers from our fathers' uniforms and patched drawers: exit Sigmund Freud. So we didn't develop a taste for possessions. Things that we could possess later were badly made and looked ugly. Somehow, we preferred ideas of things to the things themselves, though when we looked in mirrors we didn't much like what we saw there.

We never had a room of our own to lure our girls into, nor did our girls have rooms. Our love affairs were mostly walking and talking affairs; it would make an astronomical sum if we were charged for mileage. Old warehouses, embankments of the river in industrial quarters, stiff benches in wet public gardens, and cold entrances of public buildings—these were the standard backdrops of our first pneumatic blisses. We never had what are called "material stimuli." Ideological ones were a laughable matter even for kindergarten kids. If somebody sold himself out, it wasn't for the sake of goods or comfort: there were none. He was selling out because of inner want and he knew that himself. There were no supplies, there was sheer demand.

If we made ethical choices, they were based not so much on immediate reality as on moral standards derived from fiction. We were avid readers and we fell into a dependence on what we read. Books, perhaps because of their formal element of finality, held us in their absolute power. Dickens was more real than Stalin or Beria. More than anything else, novels would affect our modes of behavior and conversations, and 90 percent of our conversations were about novels. It tended to become a vicious circle, but we didn't want to break it.

In its ethics, this generation was among the most bookish in the history of Russia, and thank God for that. A relationship could have been broken for good over a preference for Hemingway over Faulkner; the hierarchy in that pantheon was our real Central Committee. It started as an ordinary accumulation of knowledge but soon became our most important occupation, to which everything could be sacrificed. Books became the first and only reality, whereas reality itself was regarded as either nonsense or nuisance. Compared to others, we were ostensibly flunking or faking our lives. But come to think of it, existence which ignores the standards professed in literature is inferior and unworthy of effort. So we thought, and I think we were right.

The instinctive preference was to read rather than to act. No wonder our actual lives were more or less a shambles. Even those of us who managed to make it through the very thick woods of "higher education," with all its unavoidable lip—and other members'—service to the system, finally fell victim to literature-imposed scruples and couldn't manage any longer. We ended up doing odd jobs, menial or editorial—or something mindless, like carving tombstone inscriptions, drafting blueprints, translating technical texts, accounting, bookbinding, developing X-rays. From time to time we would pop up on the threshold of one another's apartment, with a bottle in one hand, sweets or flowers or snacks in the other, and spend the evening talking, gossiping, bitching about the idiocy of the officials upstairs, guessing which one of us would be the first to die. And now I must drop the pronoun "we."

Nobody knew literature and history better than these people, nobody could write in Russian better than they, nobody despised our times more profoundly. For these characters civilization meant more than daily bread and a nightly hug. This wasn't, as it might seem, another lost generation. This was the only generation of Russians that had found itself, for whom Giotto and Mandelstam were more imperative than their own personal destinies. Poorly dressed but somehow still elegant, shuffled by the dumb hands of their immediate masters, running like rabbits from the ubiquitous state hounds and the even more ubiquitous foxes, broken, growing old, they still retained their love for the nonexistent (or existing only in their balding heads) thing called "civilization." Hopelessly cut off from the rest of the world, they thought that at least that world was like themselves; now they know that it is like others, only better dressed. As I write this, I close my eyes and almost see them standing in their dilapidated kitchens, holding glasses in their hands, with ironic grimaces across their faces. "There, there . . ." They grin. "*Liberté, Egalité, Fraternité* . . . Why does nobody add Culture?"

Memory, I think, is a substitute for the tail that we lost for good in the happy process of evolution. It directs our movements, including migration. Apart from that there is something clearly atavistic in the very process of recollection, if only because such a process never is linear. Also, the more one remembers, the closer perhaps one is to dying.

If this is so, it is a good thing when your memory stumbles. More often, however, it coils, recoils, digresses to all sides, just as a tail does; so should one's narrative, even at the risk of sounding inconsequential and boring. Boredom, after all, is the most frequent feature of existence, and one wonders why it fared so poorly in the nineteenth-century prose that strived so much for realism.

But even if a writer is fully equipped to imitate on paper the subtlest fluctuations of the mind, the effort to reproduce the tail in all its spiral splendor is still doomed, for evolution wasn't for nothing. The perspective of years straightens things to the point of complete obliteration. Nothing brings them back, not even handwritten words with their coiled letters. Such an effort is doomed all the more if this tail happens to lag behind somewhere in Russia.

But if the printed words were only a mark of forgetfulness, that would be fine. The sad truth is that words fail reality as well. At least it's been my impression that any experience coming from the Russian realm, even when depicted with photographic precision, simply bounces off the English language, leaving no visible imprint on its surface. Of course the memory of one civilization cannot, perhaps should not, become a memory of another. But when language fails to reproduce the negative realities of another culture, the worst kind of tautologies result.

History, no doubt, is bound to repeat itself: after all, like men, history doesn't have many choices. But at least one should have the comfort of being aware of what one is falling a victim to when dealing with the peculiar semantics prevailing in a foreign realm such as Russia. One gets done in by one's own conceptual and analytic habits—e.g., using language to dissect experience, and so robbing one's mind of the benefits of intuition. Because, for all its beauty, a distinct concept always means a shrinkage of meaning, cutting off loose ends. While the loose ends are what matter most in the phenomenal world, for they interweave.

These words themselves bear witness that I am far from accusing the English language of insufficiency; nor do I lament the dormant state of its native speakers' psyche. I merely regret the fact that such an advanced notion of Evil as happens to be in the possession of Russians has been denied entry into consciousness on the grounds of having a convoluted syntax. One wonders how many of us can recall a plain-speaking Evil that crosses the threshold, saying: "Hi, I'm Evil. How are you?"

If all this, nonetheless, has an elegiac air, it is owing rather to the genre of the piece than to its content, for which rage would be more appropriate. Neither, of course, yields the meaning of the past; elegy at least doesn't create a new reality. No matter how elaborate a structure anyone may devise for catching his own tail, he'll end up with a net full of fish but without water. Which lulls his boat. And which is enough to cause dizziness or to make him resort to an elegiac tone. Or to throw the fish back.

* * *

Once upon a time there was a little boy. He lived in the most unjust country in the world. Which was ruled by creatures who by all human accounts should be considered degenerates. Which never happened.

And there was a city. The most beautiful city on the face of the earth. With an immense gray river that hung over its distant bottom like the immense gray sky over that river. Along that river there stood magnificent palaces with such beautifully elaborated façades that if the little boy was standing on the right bank, the left bank looked like the imprint of a giant mollusk called civilization. Which ceased to exist.

Early in the morning when the sky was still full of stars the little boy would rise and, after having a cup of tea and an egg, accompanied by a radio announcement of a new record in smelted steel, followed by the army choir singing a hymn to the Leader, whose picture was pinned to the wall over the little boy's still warm bed, he would run along the snow-covered granite embankment to school.

The wide river lay white and frozen like a continent's tongue lapsed into silence, and the big bridge arched against the dark blue sky like an iron palate. If the little boy had two extra minutes, he would slide down on the ice and take twenty or thirty steps to the middle. All this time he would be thinking about what the fish were doing under such heavy ice. Then he would stop, turn 180 degrees, and run back, nonstop, right up to the entrance of the school. He would burst into the hall, throw his hat and coat off onto a hook, and fly up the staircase and into his classroom.

It is a big room with three rows of desks, a portrait of the Leader on the wall behind the teacher's chair, a map with two hemispheres, of which only one is legal. The little boy takes his seat, opens his briefcase, puts his pen and notebook on the desk, lifts his face, and prepares himself to hear drivel.

1976

The Keening Muse

When her father learned that his daughter was about to publish a selection of her poems in a St. Petersburg magazine, he called her in and told her that although he had nothing against her writing poetry, he'd urge her "not to befoul a good respected name" and to use a pseudonym. The daughter agreed, and this is how "Anna Akhmatova" entered Russian literature instead of Anna Gorenko.

The reason for this acquiescence was neither uncertainty about the elected occupation and her actual gifts nor anticipation of the benefits that a split identity can provide a writer. It was done simply for the sake of "maintaining appearances," because among families belonging to the nobility—and the Gorenkos were one—the literary profession was generally regarded as somewhat unseemly and befitting those of more humble origins who didn't have a better way of making a name.

Still, the father's request was a bit of an overstatement. After all, the Gorenkos weren't princes. But then again the family lived in Tsarskoe Selo—Tsar's Village—which was the summer residence of the imperial family, and this sort of topography could have influenced the man. For his seventeen-year-old daughter, however, the place had a different significance. Tsarskoe was the seat of the Lyceum in whose gardens a century ago "carelessly blossomed" young Pushkin.

As for the pseudonym itself, its choice had to do with the maternal ancestry of Anna Gorenko, which could be traced back to the last khan of the Golden Horde: to Achmat Khan, descendant of Jenghiz Khan. "I am a Jenghizite," she used to remark not without a touch of pride; and for a Russian ear "Akhmatova" has a distinct Oriental, Tatar to be precise, flavor. She didn't mean to be exotic, though, if only because in Russia a name with a Tatar overtone meets not curiosity but prejudice.

All the same, the five open *a*'s of Anna Akhmatova had a hypnotic effect and put this name's carrier firmly at the top of the alphabet of Russian poetry. In a sense, it was her first successful line; memorable in its acoustic inevitability, with its *Ah* sponsored less by sentiment than by history. This tells you a lot about the intuition and quality of the ear of this seventeen-year-old girl who soon after her first publication began to sign her letters and legal papers as Anna Akhmatova. In its suggestion of identity derived from the fusion of sound and time, the choice of the pseudonym turned out to be prophetic.

Anna Akhmatova belongs to the category of poets who have neither genealogy nor discernible "development." She is the kind of poet that simply "happens"; that arrives in the world with an already established diction and his/her own unique sensibility. She came fully equipped, and she never resembled anyone. What was perhaps more significant is that none of her countless imitators was ever capable of producing a convincing Akhmatova pastiche either; they'd end up resembling one another more than her.

This suggests that Akhmatova's idiom was a product of something less graspable than an astute stylistic calculation and leaves us with the necessity of upgrading the second part of Buffon's famous equation to the notion of "self."

Apart from the general sacred aspects of the said entity, its uniqueness in the case of Akhmatova was further secured by her actual physical beauty. She looked positively stunning. Five feet eleven, dark-haired, fair-skinned, with pale gray-green eyes like those of snow leopards, slim and incredibly lithe, she was for half a century sketched, painted, cast, carved, and photographed by a multitude of artists starting with Amedeo Modigliani. As for the poems dedicated to her, they'd make more volumes than her own collected works.

All this goes to show that the visible part of that self was quite breathtaking; as for the hidden one being a perfect match, there is testimony to it in her writing, which blends both.

This blend's chief characteristics are nobility and restraint. Akhmatova is the poet of strict meters, exact rhymes, and short sentences. Her syntax is simple and free of subordinate clauses whose gnomic convolutions are responsible for most of Russian literature; in fact, in its simplicity, her syntax resembles English. From the very threshold of her career to its very end she was always perfectly clear and coherent. Among her contemporaries, she is a Jane Austen. In any case, if her sayings were dark, it wasn't due to her grammar.

In an era marked by so much technical experimentation in poetry, she was blatantly non-avant-garde. If anything, her means were visually similar to what prompted that wave of innovations in Russian poetry, as everywhere else, at the turn of the century: to the Symbolists' quatrains, ubiquitous as grass. Yet this visual resemblance was maintained by Akhmatova deliberately: through it she sought not the simplification of her task but a worsening of the odds. She simply wanted to play the game straight, without bending or inventing the rules. In short, she wanted her verse to maintain appearances.

Nothing reveals a poet's weaknesses like classical verse, and that's why it's so universally dodged. To make a couple of lines sound unpredictable without producing a comic effect or echoing someone else is an extremely perplexing affair. This echo aspect of strict meters is most nagging, and no amount of oversaturating the line with concrete physical detail sets one free. Akhmatova sounds so independent because from the outset she knew how to exploit the enemy.

She did it by a collage-like diversification of the content. Often within just one stanza she'd cover a variety of seemingly unrelated things. When a person talks in the same breath about the gravity of her emotion, gooseberry blossoms, and pulling the left-hand glove onto her right hand—that compromises the breath—which is, in the poem, its meter—to the degree that one forgets about its pedigree. The echo, in other words, gets subordinated to the discrepancy of objects and in effect provides them with a common denominator; it ceases to be a form and becomes a norm of locution.

Sooner or later this always happens to the echo as well as to the diversity of things themselves—in Russian verse it was done by Akhmatova; more exactly, by that self which bore her name. One can't help thinking that while its inner part hears what, by means of rhyme, the language itself suggests about the proximity of those disparate objects, the outer one literally sees that proximity from the vantage point of her actual height. She simply couples what has been already joined: in the language and in the circumstances of her life, if not, as they say, in heaven.

Hence the nobility of her diction, for she doesn't lay claim to her discoveries. Her rhymes are not assertive, the meter is not insistent. Sometimes she'd drop a syllable or two in a stanza's last or penultimate line in order to create the effect of a choked throat, or that of unwitting awkwardness caused by emotional tension. But that would be as far as she'd go, for she felt very much at home within the confines of classical verse, thereby suggesting that her raptures and revelations don't require an extraordinary formal treatment, that they are not any greater than those of her predecessors who used these meters before.

This, of course, wasn't exactly true. No one absorbs the past as thoroughly as a poet, if only out of fear of inventing the already invented. (This is why, by the way, a poet is so often regarded as being "ahead of his time," which keeps itself busy rehashing clichés.) So no matter what a poet may plan to say, at the moment of speech he always knows that he inherits the subject. The great literature of the past humbles one not only through its quality but through its topical precedence as well. The reason why a good poet speaks of his own grief with restraint is that, as regards grief, he is a Wandering Jew. In this sense, Akhmatova was very much a product of the Petersburg tradition in Russian poetry, the founders of which, in their own turn, had behind them European classicism as well as its Roman and Greek origins. In addition, they, too, were aristocrats.

If Akhmatova was reticent, it was at least partly because she was carrying the heritage of her predecessors into the art of this century. This obviously was but an homage to them, since it was precisely that heritage which made her this century's poet. She simply regarded herself, with her raptures and revelations, as a postscript to their message, to what they recorded about their lives. The lives were tragic, and so was the message. If the postscript looks dark, it's because the message was absorbed fully. If she never screams or showers her head with ashes, it's because they didn't.

Such were the cue and the key with which she started. Her first collections were tremendously successful with both the critics and the public. In general, the response to a poet's work should be considered last, for it is a poet's last consideration. However, Akhmatova's success was in this respect remarkable if one takes into account its timing, especially in the case of her second and third volumes: 1914 (the outbreak of World War I) and 1917 (the October Revolution in Russia). On the other hand, perhaps it was precisely this deafening background thunder of world events that rendered the private tremolo of this young poet all the more discernible and vital. In that sense again, the beginning of this poetic career contained a prophecy of the course it came to run for half a century. What increases the sense of prophecy is that for a Russian ear at the time the thunder of world events was compounded by the incessant and quite meaningless mumbling of the Symbolists. Eventually these two noises shrunk and merged into the threatening incoherent drone of the new era against which Akhmatova was destined to speak for the rest of her life.

Those early collections (*Evening*, *Rosary*, and *White Flock*) dealt mostly with the sentiment which is *de rigueur* for early collections; with that of love. The poems in those books had a diary-like intimacy and immediacy; they'd describe no more than one actual or psychological event and were short—sixteen to twenty lines at best. As such they could be committed to memory in a flash, as indeed they were—and still are—by generations and generations of Russians.

Still, it was neither their compactness nor their subject matter that made one's memory desire to appropriate them; those features were quite familiar to an experienced reader. The news came in the form of a sensibility which manifested itself in the author's treatment of her theme. Betrayed, tormented by either jealousy or guilt, the wounded heroine of these poems speaks more frequently in self-reproach than in anger, forgives more eloquently than accuses, prays rather than screams. She displays all the emotional subtlety and psychological complexity of nineteenth-century Russian prose and all the dignity that the poetry of the same century taught her. Apart from these, there is also a great deal of irony and detachment which are strictly her own and products of her metaphysics rather than shortcuts to resignation.

Needless to say, for her readership those qualities seem to come in both handy and timely. More than any other art, poetry is a form of sentimental education, and the lines that Akhmatova readers learned by heart were to temper their hearts against the new era's onslaught of vulgarity. The comprehension of the metaphysics of personal drama betters one's chances of weathering the drama of history. This is why, and not because of the epigrammatic beauty of her lines only, the public clung to them so unwittingly. It was an instinctive reaction; the instinct being that of self-preservation, for the stampede of history was getting more and more audible.

Akhmatova in any case heard it quite clearly. The intensely personal lyricism of *White Flock* is tinged with the note that was destined to become her imprimatur: the note of controlled terror. The mechanism designed to keep in check emotions of a romantic nature proved to be as effective when applied to mortal fears. The latter was increasingly intertwined with the former until they resulted in emotional tautology, and *White Flock* marks the beginning of this process. With this collection, Russian poetry hit "the real, non-calendar twentieth century" but didn't disintegrate on impact.

Akhmatova, to say the least, seemed better prepared for this encounter than most of her contemporaries. Besides, by the time of the Revolution she was twenty-eight years old: that is, neither young enough to believe in it nor too old to justify it. Furthermore, she was a woman, and it would be equally unseemly for her to extol or condemn the event. Nor did she decide to accept the change of social order as an invitation to loosen her meter and associative chains. For art doesn't imitate life if only for fear of clichés. She remained true to her diction, to its private timbre, to refracting rather than reflecting life through the prism of the individual heart. Except that the choice of detail whose role in a poem previously was to shift attention from an emotionally pregnant issue presently began to be less and less of a solace, overshadowing the issue itself.

She didn't reject the Revolution: a defiant pose wasn't for her either. Using latter-day locution, she internalized it. She simply took it for what it was: a terrible national upheaval which meant a tremendous increase of grief per individual. She understood this not only because her own share went too high but first and foremost through her very craft. The poet is a born democrat not thanks to the precariousness of his position only but because he caters to the entire nation and employs its language. So does tragedy, and hence their affinity. Akhmatova, whose verse always gravitated to the vernacular, to the idiom of folk song, could identify with the people more thoroughly than those who were pushing at the time their literary or other programs: she simply recognized grief.

Moreover, to say that she identified with the people is to introduce a rationalization which never took place because of its inevitable redundancy. She was a part of the whole, and the pseudonym just furthered her class anonymity. In addition, she always disdained the air of superiority present in the word "poet." "I don't understand these big words," she used to say, "poet, billiard." This wasn't humility; this was the result of the sober perspective in which she kept her existence. The very persistence of love as the theme of her poetry indicates her proximity to the average person. If she differed from her public it was in that her ethics weren't subject to historical adjustment.

Other than that, she was like everybody else. Besides, the times themselves didn't allow for great variety. If her poems weren't exactly the *vox populi*, it's because a nation never speaks with one voice. But neither was her voice that of the *crème de la crème*, if only because it was totally devoid of the populist nostalgia so peculiar to the Russian intelligentsia. The "we" that she starts to use about this time in self-defense against the impersonality of pain inflicted by history was broadened to this pronoun's linguistic limits not by herself but by the rest of the speakers of this language. Because of the quality of the future, this "we" was there to stay and the authority of its user to grow.

In any case, there is no psychological difference between Akhmatova's "civic" poems of World War I and the revolutionary period, and those written a good thirty years later during World War II. Indeed, without the date underneath them, poems like "Prayer" could be attributed to virtually any moment of Russian history in this century which justifies that particular poem's title. Apart from the sensitivity of her membrane, though, this proves that the quality of history for the last eighty years has somewhat simplified the poet's job. It did so to the degree that a poet would spurn a line containing a prophetic possibility and prefer a plain description of a fact or sensation.

Hence the nominative character of Akhmatova's lines in general and at that period in particular. She knew not only that the emotions and perceptions she dealt with were fairly common but also that time, true to its repetitive nature, would render them universal. She sensed that history, like its objects, has very limited options. What was more important, however, was that those "civic" poems were but fragments borne by her general lyrical current, which made their "we" practically indistinguishable from the more frequent, emotionally charged "I." Because of their overlapping, both pronouns were gaining in verisimilitude.

Since the name of the current was "love," the poems about the homeland and the epoch were shot through with almost inappropriate intimacy; similarly, those about sentiment itself were acquiring an epic timbre. The latter meant the current's widening.

Later in her life, Akhmatova always resented attempts by critics and scholars to confine her significance to her love poetry of the teens of this century. She was perfectly right, because the output of the subsequent forty years outweighs her first decade both numerically and qualitatively. Still, one can understand those scholars and critics, since after 1922 until her death in 1966 Akhmatova simply couldn't publish a book of her own, and they were forced to deal with what was available. Yet perhaps there was another reason, less obvious or less comprehended by those scholars and critics, that they were drawn to the early Akhmatova.

Throughout one's life, time addresses man in a variety of languages: in those of innocence, love, faith, experience, history, fatigue, cynicism, guilt, decay, etc. Of those, the language of love is clearly the *lingua franca*. Its vocabulary absorbs all the other tongues, and its utterance gratifies a subject, however inanimate it may be. Also, by being thus uttered, a subject acquires an ecclesiastical, almost sacred denomination, echoing both the way we perceive the objects of our passions and the Good Book's suggestion as to what God is. Love is essentially an attitude maintained by the infinite toward the finite. The reversal constitutes either faith or poetry.

Akhmatova's love poems, naturally, were in the first place just poems. Apart from anything else, they had a terrific novelistic quality, and a reader could have had a wonderful time explicating the various tribulations and trials of their heroine. (Some did just that, and on the basis of those poems, the heated public imagination would have their author "romantically involved" with Alexander Blok—the poet of the period—as well as with His Imperial Majesty himself, although she was a far better poet than the former and a good six inches taller than the latter.) Half self-portrait, half mask, their poetic persona would augment an actual drama with the fatality of theater, thus probing both her own and pain's possible limits. Happier states would be subjected to the same probing. Realism, in short, was employed as the means of transportation to a metaphysical destination. Still, all this would have amounted to animating the genre's tradition were it not for the sheer quantity of poems dealing with the said sentiment.

That quantity denies both biographical and Freudian approaches, for it overshoots the addressees' concreteness and renders them as pretexts for the author's speech. What art and sexuality have in common is that both are sublimations of one's creative energy, and that denies them hierarchy. The nearly idiosyncratic persistence of the early Akhmatova love poems suggests not so much the recurrence of passion as the frequency of prayer. Correspondingly, different though their imagined or real protagonists are, these poems display a considerable stylistic similarity because love as content is in the habit of limiting formal patterns. The same goes for faith. After all, there are only so many adequate manifestations for truly strong sentiments; which, in the end, is what explains rituals.

It is the finite's nostalgia for the infinite that accounts for the recurrence of the love theme in Akhmatova's verse, not the actual entanglements. Love indeed has become for her a language, a code to record time's messages or, at least, to convey their tune; she simply heard them better this way. For what interested this poet most was not her own life but precisely time and the effects of its monotone on the human psyche and on her own diction in particular. If she later resented attempts to reduce her to her early writing, it was not because she disliked the status of the habitually love-sick girl: it was because her diction and, with it, the code, subsequently changed a great deal in order to make the monotone of the infinite more audible.

In fact, it was already quite distinct in *Anno Domini MCMXXI*—her fifth and technically speaking last collection. In some of its poems, that monotone merges with the author's voice to the point that she has to sharpen the concreteness of detail or image in order to save them, and by the same token her own mind, from the inhuman neutrality of the meter. Their fusion, or rather the former's subordination to the latter, came later. In the meantime, she was trying to save her own notions of existence from being overtaken by those supplied to her by prosody: for prosody knows more about time than a human being would like to reckon with.

Close exposure to this knowledge, or more accurately to this memory of time restructured, results in an inordinate mental acceleration that robs insights that come from the actual reality of their novelty, if not of their gravity. No poet can ever close this gap, but a conscientious one may lower his pitch or muffle his diction so as to downplay his estrangement from real life. This is done sometimes for purely aesthetic purposes: to make one's voice less theatrical, less *bel canto*–like. More frequently, though, the purpose of this camouflage is, again, to retain sanity, and Akhmatova, a poet of strict meters, was using it precisely to that end. But the more she did so, the more inexorably her voice was approaching the impersonal tonality of time itself, until they merged into something that makes one shudder trying to guess—as in her *Northern Elegies* —who is hiding behind the pronoun "I."

What happened to pronouns was happening to other parts of speech, which would peter out or loom large in the perspective of time supplied by prosody. Akhmatova was a very concrete poet, but the more concrete the image, the more extemporary it would become because of the accompanying meter. No poem is ever written for its story line's sake only, just as no life is lived for the sake of an obituary. What is called the music of a poem is essentially time restructured in such a way that it brings this poem's content into a linguistically inevitable, memorable focus.

Sound, in other words, is the seat of time in the poem, a background against which its content acquires a stereoscopic quality. The power of Akhmatova's lines comes from her ability to convey the music's impersonal epic sweep, which more than matched their actual content, especially from the twenties on. The effect of her instrumentation upon her themes was akin to that of somebody used to being put against the wall being suddenly put against the horizon.

The above should be kept very much in mind by the foreign reader of Akhmatova, since that horizon vanishes in translations, leaving on the page absorbing but one-dimensional content. On the other hand, the foreign reader may perhaps be consoled by the fact that this poet's native audience also has been forced to deal with her work in a very misrepresented fashion. What translation has in common with censorship is that both operate on the basis of the "what's possible" principle, and it must be noted that linguistic barriers can be as high as those erected by the state. Akhmatova, in any case, is surrounded by both and it's only the former that shows signs of crumbling.

Anno Domini MCMXXI was her last collection: in the forty-four years that followed she had no book of her own. In the postwar period there were, technically speaking, two slim editions of her work, consisting mainly of a few reprinted early lyrics plus genuinely patriotic war poems and doggerel bits extolling the arrival of peace. These last ones were written by her in order to win the release of her son from the labor camps, in which he nonetheless spent eighteen years. These publications in no way can be regarded as her own, for the poems were selected by the editors of the state-run publishing house and their aim was to convince the public (especially those abroad) that Akhmatova was alive, well, and loyal. They totaled some fifty pieces and had nothing in common with her output during those four decades.

For a poet of Akhmatova's stature this meant being buried alive, with a couple of slabs marking the mound. Her going under was a product of several forces, mostly that of history, whose chief element is vulgarity and whose immediate agent is the state. Now, by MCMXXI, which means 1921, the new state could already be at odds with Akhmatova, whose first husband, poet Nikolai Gumilyov, was executed by its security forces, allegedly on the direct order of the state's head, Vladimir Lenin. A spin-off of a didactic, eye-for-eye mentality, the new state could expect from Akhmatova nothing but retaliation, especially given her reputed tendency for an autobiographical touch.

Such was, presumably, the state's logic, furthered by the destruction in the subsequent decade and a half of her entire circle (including her closest friends, poets Vladimir Narbut and Osip Mandelstam). It culminated in the arrests of her son, Lev Gumilyov, and her third husband, art-historian Nikolai Punin, who soon died in prison. Then came World War II.

Those fifteen years preceding the war were perhaps the darkest in the whole of Russian history; undoubtedly they were so in Akhmatova's own life. It's the material which this period supplied, or more accurately the lives it subtracted, that made her eventually earn the title of the Keening Muse. This period simply replaced the frequency of poems about love with that of poems in memoriam. Death, which she would previously evoke as a solution for this or that emotional tension, became too real for any emotion to matter. From a figure of speech it became a figure that leaves you speechless.

If she proceeded to write, it's because prosody absorbs death, and because she felt guilty that she survived. The pieces that constitute her "Wreath for the Dead" are simply attempts to let those whom she outlived absorb or at least join prosody. It's not that she tried to "immortalize" her dead: most of them were the pride of Russian literature already and thus had immortalized themselves enough. She simply tried to manage the meaninglessness of existence, which suddenly gaped before her because of the destruction of the sources of its meaning, to domesticate the reprehensible infinity by inhabiting it with familiar shadows. Besides, addressing the dead was the only way of preventing speech from slipping into a howl.

The elements of howl, however, are quite audible in other Akhmatova poems of the period and later. They'd appear either in the form of idiosyncratic excessive rhyming or as a non sequitur line interjected in an otherwise coherent narrative. Nevertheless, the poems dealing directly with someone's death are free of anything of this sort, as though the author doesn't want to offend her addressees with her emotional extremes. This refusal to exploit the ultimate opportunity to impose herself upon them echoes, of course, the practice of her lyric poetry. But by continuing to address the dead as though they were alive, by not adjusting her diction to "the occasion," she also refuses the opportunity to exploit the dead as those ideal, absolute interlocutors that every poet seeks and finds either in the dead or among angels.

As a theme, death is a good litmus test for a poet's ethics. The "in memoriam" genre is frequently used to exercise self-pity or for metaphysical trips that denote the subconscious superiority of survivor over victim, of majority (of the alive) over minority (of the dead). Akhmatova would have none of that. She particularizes her fallen instead of generalizing about them, since she writes for a minority with which it's easier for her to identify in any case. She simply continues to treat them as individuals whom she knew and who, she senses, wouldn't like to be used as the point of departure for no matter how spectacular a destination.

Naturally enough, poems of this sort couldn't be published, nor could they even be written down or retyped. They could only be memorized by the author and by some seven other people, since she didn't trust her own memory. From time to time, she'd meet a person privately and would ask him or her to recite quietly this or that selection as a means of inventory. This precaution was far from being excessive: people would disappear forever for smaller things than a piece of paper with a few lines on it. Besides, she feared not so much for her own life as for that of her son, who was in a camp and whose release she desperately tried to obtain for eighteen years. A little piece of paper with a few lines on it could cost a lot, and more to him than to her, who could lose only hope and, perhaps, mind.

The days of both, however, would have been numbered had the authorities found her *Requiem*, a cycle of poems describing the ordeal of a woman whose son is arrested and who waits under prison walls with a parcel for him and scurries about the thresholds of state offices to find out about his fate. Now, this time around she was autobiographical indeed, yet the power of *Requiem* lies in the fact that Akhmatova's biography was all too common. This requiem mourns the mourners: mothers losing sons, wives turning widows, sometimes both, as was the author's case. This is a tragedy where the chorus perishes before the hero.

The degree of compassion with which the various voices of *Requiem* are rendered can be explained only by the author's Orthodox faith; the degree of understanding and forgiveness which accounts for this work's piercing, almost unbearable lyricism, only by the uniqueness of her heart, her self, and this self's sense of time. No creed would help to understand, much less forgive, let alone survive this double widowhood at the hands of the regime, this fate of her son, these forty years of being silenced and ostracized. No Anna Gorenko would be able to take it. Anna Akhmatova did, and it's as though she knew what was in store when she took this pen name.

At certain periods of history it is only poetry that is capable of dealing with reality by condensing it into something graspable, something that otherwise couldn't be retained by the mind. In that sense, the whole nation took up the pen name of Akhmatova—which explains her popularity and which, more importantly, enabled her to speak for the nation as well as to tell it something it didn't know. She was, essentially, a poet of human ties: cherished, strained, severed. She showed these evolutions first through the prism of the individual heart, then through the prism of history, such as it was. This is about as much as one gets in the way of optics anyway.

These two perspectives were brought into sharp focus through prosody, which is simply a repository of time within language. Hence, by the way, her ability to forgive—because forgiveness is not a virtue postulated by creed but a property of time in both its mundane and metaphysical senses. This is also why her verses are to survive whether published or not: because of the prosody, because they are charged with time in both those senses. They will survive because language is older than state and because prosody always survives history. In fact, it hardly needs history; all it needs is a poet, and Akhmatova was just that.

1982

Pendulum's Song

Constantine Cavafy was born in Alexandria, Egypt, in 1863, and died there seventy years later of throat cancer. The uneventfulness of his life would have made the strictest of New Critics happy. Cavafy was the ninth child of a well-to-do mercantile family, whose prosperity went into rapid decline with the death of his father. At the age of nine the future poet went to England, where Cavafy and Sons had its branches, and he returned to Alexandria at sixteen. He was brought up in the Greek Orthodox religion. For a while he attended the Hermes Lyceum, a business school in Alexandria, and some sources tell us that while there he was more interested in classical and historical studies than in the art of commerce. But this may be merely a cliché in the biography of a poet.

In 1882, when Cavafy was nineteen, an anti-European outbreak took place in Alexandria which caused a great deal of bloodshed (at least according to that century's standards), and the British retaliated with a naval bombardment of the city. Since Cavafy and his mother had left for Constantinople not long before, he missed his chance to witness perhaps the only historic event to take place in Alexandria during his lifetime. He spent three subsequent years in Constantinople—important years for his development. It was in Constantinople that the historical diary, which he had been keeping for several years, stopped—at the entry marked "Alexander." Here also he allegedly had his first homosexual experience. At twenty-eight Cavafy got his first job, as a temporary clerk at the Department of Irrigation in the Ministry of Public Works. This provisional position turned out to be fairly permanent: he held it for the next thirty years, occasionally making some extra money as a broker on the Alexandrian Stock Exchange.

Cavafy knew ancient and modern Greek, Latin, Arabic, French; he read Dante in Italian and he wrote his first poems in English. But if there were any literary influences —and in *Cavafy's Alexandria* Edmund Keeley sees some of the English Romantics—they ought to be confined to that stage of Cavafy's poetic development which the poet himself dismissed from the "canon" of his work, as Keeley defines it. As for the later period, Cavafy's treatment of what were known during Hellenic times as mime-jambs (or simply "mime") and his use of the epitaph are so much his own that Keeley is correct in sparing us the haze of the *Palatine Anthology*.

The uneventfulness of Cavafy's life extends to his never having published a book of his poems. He lived in Alexandria, wrote poems (occasionally printing them in *feuilles volantes*, as pamphlets or broadsheets in a severely limited edition), talked in cafés to local or visiting literati, played cards, bet on horses, visited homosexual brothels, and sometimes attended church.

I believe that there are at least five editions of Cavafy's poetry in English. The most successful renderings are those by Rae Dalven* and Messrs. Edmund Keeley and Philip Sherrard.† The hardcover version of the latter is bilingual. Since there is little or no cooperation in the world of translation, translators sometimes duplicate others' efforts without knowing it. But a reader may benefit from such duplication and, in a way, the poet may benefit too. In this case, at least, he does, although there is a great deal of similarity between the two books in the goal they set themselves of straightforward rendering. Judged by this goal, Keeley and Sherrard's versions are certainly superior. It is lucky though that less than half of Cavafy's work is rhymed, and it is mostly his early poems.

Every poet loses in translation, and Cavafy is not an exception. What is exceptional is that he also gains. He gains not only because he is a fairly didactic poet, but also because, starting as early as 1900–1910, he began to strip his poems of all poetic paraphernalia—rich imagery, similes, metric flamboyance, and, as already mentioned, rhymes. This is the economy of maturity, and Cavafy resorts to deliberately "poor" means, to using words in their primary meanings as a further move toward economy. Thus he calls emeralds "green" and describes bodies as being "young and beautiful." This technique comes out of Cavafy's realization that language is not a tool of cognition but one of assimilation, that the human being is a natural bourgeois and uses lan-

* *The Complete Poems of Cavafy* (Harcourt Brace Jovanovich, 1966).
† *C. P. Cavafy: Collected Poems*, edited by George Savadis (Princeton University Press, 1975).

guage for the same ends as he uses housing or clothing. Poetry seems to be the only weapon able to beat language, using language's own means.

Cavafy's use of "poor" adjectives creates the unexpected effect of establishing a certain mental tautology, which loosens the reader's imagination, whereas more elaborate images or similes would capture that imagination or confine it to their accomplishments. For these reasons a translation of Cavafy is almost the next logical step in the direction the poet was moving—a step which Cavafy himself could have wished to take.

Perhaps he didn't need to take it: his handling of metaphor alone was sufficient for him to have stopped where he did or even earlier. Cavafy did a very simple thing. There are two elements which usually constitute a metaphor: the object of description (the "tenor," as I. A. Richards called it), and the object to which the first is imagistically, or simply grammatically, allied (the "vehicle"). The implication which the second part usually contains provides the writer with the possibility of virtually endless development. This is the way a poem works. What Cavafy did, almost from the very beginning of his career as a poet, was to jump straight to the second part: for the rest of that career he developed and elaborated upon its implicit notions without bothering to return to the first part, assumed as self-evident. The "vehicle" was Alexandria; the "tenor" was life.

2

Cavafy's Alexandria is subtitled "Study of a Myth in Progress." Although the phrase "myth in progress" was coined by George Seferis, "study of a metaphor in progress" would do just as well. Myth is essentially an attribute of the pre-Hellenic period, and the word "myth" seems an unhappy choice if we take into consideration Cavafy's own view of all the hackneyed approaches to Greek themes—myth- and hero-making, nationalistic fervor, etc.—taken by numerous men of letters, Cavafy's compatriots as well as foreigners.

Cavafy's Alexandria is not exactly Yoknapatawpha County, nor is it Tilbury Town or Spoon River. It is, first of all, a squalid and desolate place in that stage of decline when the routine character of decay weakens the very sentiment of regret. In a way, the opening of the Suez Canal in 1869 did more to dim Alexandria's luster than had Roman domination, the emergence of Christianity, and the Arab conquest together: most of the shipping, the main source of Alexandria's commercial existence, was shunted to Port Said. Cavafy, though, could view this as a distant echo of the time, eighteen centuries earlier, when the last ships of Cleopatra escaped by the same route after losing the battle of Actium.

He called himself a historical poet, and Keeley's book, in its turn, represents some sort of archaeological undertaking. We should keep in mind, however, that the word "history" is equally applicable to the endeavors of nations and to private lives. In both cases it consists of memory, record, and interpretation. *Cavafy's Alexandria* is a kind of upward-reaching archaeology because Keeley is dealing with the layers of an imagined city; he proceeds with the greatest care, knowing that such layers are apt to be intermingled. Keeley distinguishes clearly at least five of them: the literal city, the metaphoric city, the sensual city, mythical Alexandria, and the world of Hellenism. He finally draws a chart indicating into which category each poem falls. This book is as marvelous a guide to the imagined Alexandria as E. M. Forster's is to the real one. (Forster's book was dedicated to Cavafy, and Forster was the first to introduce Cavafy to the English reader.)

Keeley's findings are helpful, so is his method; and if one disagrees with some of his conclusions, this is because the phenomenon is, and was, still larger than his findings can suggest. Comprehension of its size, however, rests on Keeley's fine performance as a translator of Cavafy's work. If Keeley doesn't say certain things in this book, it is largely because he has *done* them in translation.

One of the main characteristics of historical writing—and especially of classical history—is, inevitably, stylistic ambiguity caused either by an abundance of contradictory evidence or by firm contradictory evaluations of that evidence. Herodotus and Thucydides themselves, not to mention Tacitus, sometimes sound like latter-day paradoxicalists. In other words, ambiguity is an inevitable by-product of the struggle for objectivity in which, since the Romantics, every more or less serious poet has been involved. We know that as a stylist Cavafy was already moving in this direction; we know also his affection for history.

By the turn of the century Cavafy had acquired that objective, although properly ambiguous, dispassionate tone that he was to employ for the next thirty years. His sense of history, more precisely his reading tastes, took hold of him and supplied him with a mask. Man is what he reads, and poets even more so. Cavafy in this respect is a library of the Greek, Roman, and Byzantine (Psellus, above all). In particular, he is a compendium of documents and inscriptions pertaining to the Greco-Roman interplay during the last three centuries B.C. and the first four centuries A.D. It is the neutral cadences of the former and the highly formal pathos of the latter that are responsible for the emergence of Cavafy's stylistic idiom, for this cross between a record and an epitaph. This type of diction, whether it is applied to his "historical poems" or to properly lyrical matters, creates an odd effect of genuineness, saving his raptures and reveries from verbosity, staining the plainest utterances with reticence. Under Cavafy's pen, sentimental clichés and conventions become—very much like his "poor" adjectives—a mask.

It is always unpleasant to draw boundaries when you are dealing with a poet, but Keeley's archaeology requires it. Keeley introduces us to Cavafy at about the time that the poet found his voice and his theme. By then Cavafy was already over forty and had made up his mind about many things, especially about the literal city of Alexandria, where he had decided to stay. Keeley is very persuasive about the difficulty of this decision for Cavafy. With the exception of six or seven unrelated poems, the "literal" city does not come to the surface in Cavafy's 220-poem canon. What emerges first are the "metaphoric" and mythical cities. This only proves Keeley's point, because utopian thought, even when, as in Cavafy's case, it turns toward the past, usually implies the unbearable character of the present. The more squalid and desolate the place, the stronger one's desire becomes to enliven it. What prevents us from saying that there was something extremely Greek about Cavafy's decision to remain in Alexandria (as if he had chosen to go along with Fate, which had put him there, to go along with

Parkos) is Cavafy's own distaste for mythologizing; also, perhaps, the realization on the reader's part that every choice is essentially a flight from freedom.

Another possible explanation for Cavafy's decision to stay is that he did not like himself enough to think that he deserved better. Whatever his reason, his imagined Alexandria exists as vividly as the literal city. Art is an alternate form of existence, though the emphasis in this statement falls on the word "existence," the creative process being neither an escape from reality nor a sublimation of it. At any rate, Cavafy's was not a case of sublimation, and his treatment of the entire sensual city in his work is proof of that.

He was a homosexual, and his frank treatment of this theme was advanced not only by the standards of his time, as Keeley suggests, but by present standards as well. Relating his thought to attitudes traditionally found in the eastern Mediterranean is of little or no help; the difference between the Hellenic world and the actual society in which the poet lived was too great. If the moral climate of the actual city suggested techniques of camouflage, recollections of Ptolemaic grandeur should have required some sort of boastful exaggeration. Neither strategy was acceptable to Cavafy because he was, first and foremost, a poet of contemplation and because both attitudes are more or less equally incompatible with the very sentiment of love.

Ninety percent of the best lyric poetry is written post-coitum, as was Cavafy's. Whatever the subject of his poems, they are always written in retrospect. Homosexuality as such enforces self-analysis more than heterosexuality does. I believe that the homosexual concept of sin is much more elaborate than the heterosexual concept: heterosexuals are, to say the least, provided with the possibility of instant redemption through marriage or other forms of socially acceptable constancy. Homosexual psychology, like the psychology of any minority, is overtly one of nuance and ambivalence: it capitalizes on one's vulnerability to the extent of producing a mental U-turn after which the offensive can be launched. In a way, homosexuality is a form of sensual maximalism which absorbs and consumes both the rational and the emotional faculties of a person so completely that T. S. Eliot's old friend, "felt thought," is likely to be the result. The homosexual's notion of life might, in the end, have more facets than that of his heterosexual counterpart. Such a notion, theoretically speaking, provides one with the ideal motive for writing poetry, though in Cavafy's case this motive is no more than a pretext.

What matter in art are not one's sexual affiliations, of course, but what is made of them. Only a superficial or partisan critic would label Cavafy's poems simply "homosexual," or reduce them to examples of his "hedonistic bias." Cavafy's love poems were undertaken in the same spirit as his historical poems. Because of his retrospective nature, one even gets the feeling that the "pleasures"—one of the words Cavafy uses most frequently to refer to the sexual encounters he is recalling—were "poor" almost in the same way that the literal Alexandria, as Keeley describes it, was a poor leftover of something grandiose. More often than not, the protagonist of these lyric poems is a solitary, aging person who despises his own features, which have been disfigured by that very time which has altered so many other things that were central to his existence.

The only instrument that a human being has at his disposal for coping with time is memory, and it is his unique, sensual historical memory that makes Cavafy so distinctive. The mechanics of love imply some sort of bridge between the sensual and the spiritual, sometimes to the point of deification; the notion of an afterlife is implicit not only in our couplings but also in our separations. Paradoxically enough, Cavafy's poems, in dealing with that Hellenic "special love," and touching *en passant* upon conventional broodings and longings, are attempts—or rather recognized failures—to resurrect once-loved shadows. Or: photographs.

Criticism of Cavafy tends to domesticate his perspective, taking his hopelessness for detachment, his absurdity for irony. Cavafy's love poetry is not "tragic" but terrifying, for while tragedy deals with the *fait accompli*, terror is the product of the imagination (no matter where it is directed, toward the future or toward the past). His sense of loss is much more acute than his sense of gain simply because separation is a more lasting experience than being together. It almost looks as though Cavafy was more sensual on paper than in reality, where guilt and inhibitions alone provide strong restraints. Poems like "Before Time Altered Them" or "Hidden Things" represent a complete reversal of Susan Sontag's formula "Life is a movie; death is a photograph." To put it another way, Cavafy's hedonistic bias, if such it is, is biased itself by his historical sense, since history, among other things, implies irreversibility. Alternatively, if Cavafy's historical poems had not been hedonistically slanted, they would have turned into mere anecdotes.

* * *

One of the best examples of the way this dual technique works is the poem about Kaisarion, Cleopatra's fifteen-year-old son, nominally the last king of the Ptolemaic line, who was executed by the Romans in "conquered Alexandria" by the order of the Emperor Octavian. After finding Kaisarion's name in some history book one evening, the narrator plunges into fantasies of this young boy and "fashions him freely" in his mind, "so completely" that, by the end of the poem, when Kaisarion is put to death, we perceive his execution almost as a rape. And then the words "conquered Alexandria" acquire an extra dimension: the torturing recognition of personal loss.

Not so much by combining as by equating sensuality and history, Cavafy tells his readers (and himself) the classic Greek story of Eros, ruler of the world. In Cavafy's mouth it sounds convincing, all the more so because his historical poems are preoccupied with the decline of the Hellenic world, the situation which he, as an individual, reflects in miniature, or in mirrors. As if unable to be precise in his handling of the miniature, Cavafy builds us a large-scale model of Alexandria and the adjacent Hellenic world. It is a fresco, and if it seems fragmentary, this is partly because it reflects its creator, but largely because the Hellenic world at its nadir was fragmented both politically and culturally. With the death of Alexander the Great it began to crumble, and wars, skirmishes, and the like kept tearing it apart for centuries after, the way contradictions tear one's mind. The only force which held these motley, cosmopolitan pieces together was *magna lingua Grecae*; Cavafy could say the same about his own life. Perhaps the most uninhibited voice we hear in Cavafy's poetry is when in a tone of heightened, intense fascination he lists the beauties of the Hellenic way of life—Hedonism, Art, Sophistic philosophy, and "especially our great Greek language."

3

It was not the Roman conquest that brought an end to the Hellenic world; it was the day Rome itself fell to Christianity. The interplay between the pagan and Christian worlds in Cavafy's poetry is the only one of his themes that is not sufficiently covered in Keeley's book. It is easy to understand why, however, since this theme deserves a book to itself. To reduce Cavafy to a homosexual who felt uneasy about Christianity would be simplistic. For that matter, he felt no cozier with paganism. He was perceptive enough to know that he had been born with the mixture of both in his veins—born, too, into this mixture. If he felt the tension, it was not the fault of either one but of both: his was not a question of split loyalty. Ostensibly, at least, he was a Christian; he always wore a cross, attended church on Good Friday, and received the last rites. Profoundly, too, he was perhaps a Christian: his most vigorous ironies were directed against one of the main vices of Christianity—pious intolerance. But what matters to us as readers, of course, is not Cavafy's church affiliation but the way in which he handled the mixture of two religions—and Cavafy's way was neither Christian nor pagan.

At the end of the pre-Christian era (although people, whether they are warned about the coming Messiah or about the impending holocaust, do not count their time backward) Alexandria was a marketplace of creeds and ideologies, among them Judaism, local Coptic cults, Neoplatonism, and, of course, newly arrived Christianity. Polytheism and monotheism were familiar issues in this city, site of the first real academy in the history of our civilization—Mouseion. By juxtaposing one faith with another we certainly take them out of their context, and the context was precisely what mattered to the Alexandrians, until the day came when they were told that what mattered was choosing one of them. They didn't like doing so, and neither does Cavafy. When Cavafy uses the words "paganism" and "Christianity" we should keep in mind, as he did, that they are approximations, conventions, common denominators, and that numerators are what civilization is all about.

In his historical poems Cavafy uses what Keeley calls "common" metaphors, i.e., metaphors based on political symbolism (as in the poems "Darius" and "Waiting for the Barbarians"); and this is another reason why Cavafy almost gains in translation. Politics itself is a kind of meta-language, a mental uniform, and unlike most modern poets, Cavafy is very good at unbuttoning it. The "canon" contains seven poems about Julian the Apostate—quite a few considering the brevity (three years) of Julian's reign as emperor. There must be some reason for Cavafy's interest in Julian, and Keeley's interpretation does not seem adequate. Julian was brought up as a Christian, but when he took the throne he tried to re-establish paganism as the state religion. Although the very idea of a state religion suggests Julian's Christian streak, he went about the matter in a quite different fashion: he did not persecute the Christians, nor did he try to convert them. He merely deprived Christianity of state support and sent his sages to dispute publicly with Christian priests.

In these verbal sparring matches, the priests were often losers, partly because of dogmatic contradictions in the teachings of that time and partly because the priests were usually less prepared for a debate than their opponents, since they simply assumed their Christian dogma to be superior. At any rate, Julian was tolerant of what he called "Galileanism," whose Trinity he regarded as a backward blend of Greek polytheism and Judaic monotheism. The only thing Julian did which could be viewed as persecution was to demand the return of certain pagan temples seized by Christians during the rule of Julian's predecessors and to forbid Christian proselytizing in the schools. "Those who vilify the gods should not be allowed to teach youths and interpret the works of Homer, Hesiod, Demosthenes, Thucydides and Herodotus, who worshipped those gods. Let them, in their own Galilean churches, interpret Matthew and Luke."

Not yet having their own literature and, on the whole, not having much with which to counter Julian's arguments, the Christians attacked him for the very tolerance with which he treated them, calling him Herod, a carnivorous scarecrow, an arch-liar who, with devilish cunning, does not persecute openly and so deceives the simpleminded. Whatever it was that Julian was really after, Cavafy evidently was interested in the way this Roman emperor handled the problem. Cavafy, it seems, saw Julian as a man who tried to preserve the two metaphysical possibilities, not by making a choice, but by creating links between them that would make the best of both. This is surely a rational attitude for one to take on spiritual issues, but Julian was after all a politician. His attempt was a heroic one, considering both the scope of the problem and its possible outcomes. Risking the charge of idealization, one is tempted to call Julian a great soul obsessed with the recognition that neither paganism nor Christianity is sufficient by itself and that, taken separately, neither can exercise man's spiritual capacity to the fullest. There are always tormenting leftovers, always the sense of a certain partial vacuum, causing, at best, a sense of sin. The fact is that man's spiritual restlessness is not satisfied by either font, and there is no doctrine which, without incurring condemnation, one may speak of as combining both, except, perhaps, stoicism or existentialism (which might be viewed as a form of stoicism, sponsored by Christianity).

A sensual and, by implication, a spiritual extremist cannot be satisfied by this solution, but he can resign himself to it. What matters in any resignation, however, is not so much *to* what as *from* what one is resigning. It adds greater scope to Cavafy's poetry to realize that he did not choose between paganism and Christianity but was swinging between them like a pendulum. Sooner or later, though, a pendulum realizes the limitations imposed upon it by its box. Unable to reach beyond its walls, the pendulum nevertheless gets some glimpses of the outer realm and recognizes that it is subservient and that the directions in which it is forced to swing are preordained, that they are governed by time in—if not for—its progress.

Hence that implacable note of ennui which makes Cavafy's voice with its hedonistic-stoic tremolo sound so haunting. What makes it even more haunting is our realization that we are on this man's side, that we recognize his situation, even if it is only in a poem that deals with the assimilation of a pagan into a pious Christian regime. I have in mind the poem "If Actually Dead" about Apollonius of Tyana, the pagan prophet who lived only thirty years later than Christ, was known for miracles, cured people, left no record of his death, and, unlike Christ, could write.

1975

A Guide to a Renamed City

To possess the world in the form of images is, precisely, to reexperience the unreality and remoteness of the real.
Susan Sontag, *On Photography*

In front of the Finland Station, one of five railroad terminals through which a traveler may enter or leave this city, on the very bank of the Neva River, there stands a monument to a man whose name this city presently bears. In fact, every station in Leningrad has a monument to this man, either a full-scale statue in front of or a massive bust inside the building. But the monument before the Finland Station is unique. It's not the statue itself that matters here, because Comrade Lenin is depicted in the usual quasi-romantic fashion, with his hand poking into the air, supposedly addressing the masses; what matters is the pedestal. For Comrade Lenin delivers his oration standing on the top of an armored car. It's done in the style of early Constructivism, so popular nowadays in the West, and in general the very idea of carving an armored car out of stone smacks of a certain psychological acceleration, of the sculptor being a bit ahead of his time. As far as I know, this is the only monument to a man on an armored car that exists in the world. In this respect alone, it is a symbol of a new society. The old society used to be represented by men on horseback.

And appropriately enough, a couple of miles downstream, on the opposite bank of the river, there stands a monument to a man whose name this city bore from the day of its foundation: to Peter the Great. This monument is known universally as the "Bronze Horseman," and its immobility matches only the frequency with which it has been photographed. It's an impressive monument, some twenty feet tall, the best work of Etienne-Maurice Falconet, who was recommended by both Diderot and Voltaire to Catherine the Great, its sponsor. Atop the huge granite rock dragged here from the Karelian Isthmus, Peter the Great looms on high, restraining with his left hand the rearing horse that symbolizes Russia, and stretching his right hand to the north.

Since both men are responsible for the name of the place, it's quite tempting to compare not their monuments alone but their immediate surroundings, too. On his left, the man on the armored car has the quasi-classicistic building of the local Party Committee and the infamous "Crosses"—the biggest penitentiary in Russia. On his right, there is the Artillery Academy; and, if you follow the direction in which his hand points, the tallest post-revolutionary building on the left bank of the river—Leningrad's KGB headquarters. As for the "Bronze Horseman," he too has a military institution on his right—the Admiralty; on his left, however, there is the Senate, now the State Historical Archive, and his hand points across the river to the university which he built and where the man on the armored car later got some of his education.

So this two-hundred-and-seventy-six-year-old city has two names, maiden and alias, and by and large its inhabitants tend to use neither. When it comes to their mail or identity papers, they certainly write "Leningrad," but in a normal conversation they would rather call it simply "Peter." This choice of name has very little to do with their politics; the point is that both "Leningrad" and "Petersburg" are a bit cumbersome phonetically, and anyway, people are inclined to nickname their habitats—it's a further degree of domestication. "Lenin" certainly won't do, if only because this was the last name of the man (and an alias at that); whereas "Peter" seems to be the most natural choice. For one thing, the city already has been called that for two centuries. Also, the presence of Peter I's spirit is still much more palpable here than the flavor of the new epoch. On top of that, since the real name of the Emperor in Russian is Pyotr, "Peter" suggests a certain foreignness and sounds congenial—for there is something distinctly foreign and alienating in the atmosphere of the city: its European-looking buildings, perhaps its location itself, in the delta of that northern river which flows into the hostile open sea. In other words, on the edge of so familiar a world.

Russia is a very continental country; its land mass constitutes one-sixth of the world's firmament. The idea of building a city on the edge of the land, and furthermore proclaiming it the capital of the nation, was regarded by Peter I's contemporaries as ill conceived, to say the least. The womb-warm, and traditional to the point of idiosyncrasy, claustrophobic world of Russia proper was shivering badly under the cold, searching Baltic wind. The opposition to Peter's reforms was formidable, not least because the lands of the Neva delta were really bad. They were lowlands, and swamps; and, in order to build on them, the ground would have to be strengthened. There was plenty of timber around but no volunteers to cut it, much less to drive the piles into the ground.

But Peter I had a vision of the city, and of more than the city: he saw Russia with her face turned to the world. In the context of his time, this meant to the West, and the city was destined to become—in the words of a European writer who visited Russia then—a window on Europe. Actually, Peter wanted a gate, and he wanted it ajar. Unlike both his predecessors and his successors on the Russian throne, this six-and-a-half-foot-tall monarch didn't suffer from the traditional Russian malaise—an inferiority complex toward Europe. He didn't want to imitate Europe: he wanted Russia to *be* Europe, in much the same way as he was, at least partly, a European himself. Since his childhood many of his intimate friends and companions, as well as the principal enemies with whom he warred, were Europeans; he spent more than a year working, traveling, and literally living in Europe; he visited it frequently afterward. For him, the West wasn't terra incognita. A man of sober mind, though of frightful drinking habits, he regarded every country where he had set his foot—his own included—as but a continuation of space. In a way, geography was far more real for him than history, and his most beloved directions were north and west.

In general, he was in love with space, and with the sea in particular. He wanted Russia to have a navy, and with his own hands this "Czar-carpenter," as he was called by contemporaries, built its first boat (currently on display at the Navy Museum), using the skills he had acquired while working in the Dutch and British shipyards. So his vision of this city was quite particular. He wanted it to be a harbor for the Russian fleet, a fortress against the Swedes, who beset these shores for centuries, the northern stronghold of his nation. At the same time, he thought of this city becoming the spiritual center of the new Russia: the center of reason, of the sciences, of education, of knowledge. For him, these were the elements of vision, and conscious goals, not the by-products of the military drive of the subsequent epochs.

When a visionary happens also to be an emperor, he acts ruthlessly. The methods to which Peter I resorted, to carry out his project, could be at best defined as conscription. He taxed everything and everyone to force his subjects to fight the land. During Peter's reign, a subject of the Russian crown had a somewhat limited choice of being either drafted into the army or sent to build St. Petersburg, and it's hard to say which was deadlier. Tens of thousands found their anonymous end in the swamps of the Neva delta, whose islands enjoyed a reputation similar to that of today's Gulag. Except that in the eighteenth century you knew what you were building and also had a chance in the end to receive the last rites and a wooden cross on the top of your grave.

Perhaps there was no other way for Peter to ensure the execution of the project. Save for wars, Russia until his reign hardly knew centralization and never acted as an overall entity. The universal coercion exercised by the future Bronze Horseman to get his project done united the nation for the first time and gave birth to the Russian totalitarianism whose fruits taste no better than did the seeds. Mass had invited a mass solution, and neither by education nor by Russian history itself was Peter prepared for anything else. He dealt with the people in exactly the same fashion as he dealt with the land for his would-be capital. Carpenter and navigator, this ruler used only one instrument while designing his city: a ruler. The space unrolling before him was utterly flat, horizontal, and he had every reason to treat it like a map, where a straight line suffices. If anything curves in this city, it's not because of specific planning but because he was a sloppy draftsman whose finger would slide occasionally off the edge of the ruler, and the pencil followed this slip. So did his terrified subordinates.

This city really rests on the bones of its builders as much as on the wooden piles that they drove into the ground. So does, to a degree, nearly any other place in the Old World; but then history takes good care of unpleasant memories. St. Petersburg happens to be too young for soothing mythology; and every time a natural or premeditated disaster takes place, you can spot in a crowd a pale, somewhat starved, ageless face with its deep-set, white, fixed eyes, and hear the whisper: "I tell you, this place is cursed!" You'll shudder, but a moment later, when you try to take another look at the speaker, the face is gone. In vain, your eyes will search the slowly milling crowds, the traffic creeping along: you will see nothing except the indifferent passersby and, through the slanted veil of rain, the magnificent features of the great imperial buildings. The geometry of this city's architectural perspectives is perfect for losing things forever.

But on the whole the sentiment about nature returning someday to reclaim its usurped property, yielded once under human assault, has its logic here. It derives from the long history of floods that have ravaged this city, from the city's palpable, physical proximity to the sea. Even though the trouble never goes beyond the Neva's jumping out of her granite straitjacket, the very sight of those massive leaden wads of clouds rushing in on the city from the Baltic makes the inhabitants weary with anxieties that are always there anyway. Sometimes, especially in the late fall, this kind of weather with its gushing winds, pouring rain, and the Neva tipping over the embankments lasts for weeks. Even though nothing changes, the mere time factor makes you think that it's getting worse. On such days, you recall that there are no dikes around the city and that you are literally surrounded by this fifth column of canals and tributaries; that you are practically living on an island, one of the 101 of them; that you saw in that movie—or was it in your dream?—that gigantic wave which et cetera, et cetera; and then you turn on the radio for the next forecast. Which usually sounds affirmative and optimistic.

But the main reason for this sentiment is the sea itself. Oddly enough, for all the naval might that Russia has amassed today, the idea of the sea is still somewhat alien to the general population. Both folklore and the official propaganda treat this theme in a vague, if positive, romantic fashion. For the average person, the sea is associated most of all with the Black Sea, vacations, the south, resorts, perhaps palm trees. The most frequent epithets encountered in songs and poems are "wide," "blue," "beautiful." Sometimes you might get "rugged," but it doesn't jar with the rest of the context. The notions of freedom, open space, of getting the hell out of here, are instinctively suppressed and consequently surface in the reverse forms of fear of water, fear of drowning. In these terms alone, the city in the Neva delta is a challenge to the national psyche and justly bears the name of "foreigner in his own fatherland" given to it by Nikolai Gogol. If not a foreigner, then at least a sailor. In a way, Peter I achieved his goal: this city became a harbor, and not only literally; metaphysically, too. There is no other place in Russia where thoughts depart so willingly from reality: it is with the emergence of St. Petersburg that Russian literature came into existence.

However true it might be that Peter was planning to have a new Amsterdam, the result has as little in common with that Dutch city as does its former namesake on the shores of the Hudson. But what went, in the latter, up, in the former was spread horizontally; the scope, however, was the same. For the width of the river alone demanded a different scale of architecture.

In the epochs following Peter's, they started to build, not separate buildings but whole architectural ensembles, or, more precisely, architectural landscapes. Untouched till then by European architectural styles, Russia opened the sluices and the baroque and classicism gushed into and inundated the streets and embankments of St. Petersburg. Organ-like forests of columns sprang high and lined up on the palatial façades ad infinitum in their miles-long Euclidian triumph. For the last half of the eighteenth and the first quarter of the nineteenth century, this city became a real safari for the best Italian and French architects, sculptors, and decorators. In acquiring its imperial look, this city was scrupulous to the very last detail: the granite revetment of the rivers and canals, the elaborate character of every curl on their cast-iron grilles, speak for themselves. So does the decor of the inner chambers in the palaces and country residences of the Czar's family and the nobility, the decor whose variety and exquisiteness verge on obscenity. And yet whatever the architects took for the standard in their work—Versailles, Fontainebleau, and so on—the outcome was always unmistakably Russian, because it was more the overabundance of space that dictated to the builder where to put what on another wing, and in what style it ought to be done, than the capricious will of his often ignorant but immensely rich client. When you look at the Neva's panorama opening from the Trubetzkoy bastion of the Peter and Paul fortress, or at the Grand Cascade by the Gulf of Finland, you get the odd sensation that it's not Russia trying to catch up with European civilization but a blown-up projection of the latter through a *laterna magica* onto an enormous screen of space and waters that takes place.

In the final analysis, the rapid growth of the city and of its splendor should be attributed first of all to the ubiquitous presence of water. The twelve-mile-long Neva branching right in the center of the town, with its twenty-five large and small coiling canals, provides this city with such a quantity of mirrors that narcissism becomes inevitable. Reflected every second by thousands of square feet of running silver amalgam, it's as if the city were constantly being filmed by its river, which discharges its footage into the Gulf of Finland, which, on a sunny day, looks like a depository of these blinding images. No wonder that sometimes this city gives the impression of an utter egoist preoccupied solely with its own appearance. It is true that in such places you pay more attention to façades than to faces; but the stone is incapable of self-procreation. The inexhaustible, maddening multiplication of all these pilasters, colonnades, porticoes hints at the nature of this urban narcissism, hints at the possibility that at least in the inanimate world water may be regarded as a condensed form of time.

But perhaps more than by its canals and rivers, this extremely "premeditated city," as Dostoevsky termed it, has been reflected in the literature of Russia. For water can talk about surfaces only, and exposed ones at that. The depiction of both the actual and mental interior of the city, of its impact on the people and their inner world, became the main subject of Russian literature almost from the very day of this city's founding. Technically speaking, Russian literature was born here, on the shores of the Neva. If, as the saying goes, all Russian writers "came out of Gogol's 'Overcoat,'" it's worth remembering then that this overcoat was ripped off that poor civil servant's shoulders nowhere else but in St. Petersburg, at the very beginning of the nineteenth century. The tone, however, was set by Pushkin's "The Bronze Horseman," whose hero, a clerk in some department, upon losing his beloved to a flood, accuses the mounted statue of the Emperor of negligence (no dikes) and goes insane when he sees the enraged Peter on his horse jumping off the pedestal and rushing in pursuit to trample him, an offender, into the ground. (This could be, of course, a simple tale about a little man's rebellion against arbitrary power, or one about persecution mania, subconscious versus superego, and so forth, were it not for the magnificence of the verses themselves—the best ever written in praise of this city, with the exception of those by Osip Mandelstam, who was literally stamped into the ground of the empire a century after Pushkin was killed in a duel.)

At any rate, by the beginning of the nineteenth century, St. Petersburg was already the capital of Russian letters, a fact that had very little to do with the actual presence of the court here. After all, the court sat in Moscow for centuries and yet almost nothing came out of there. The reason for this sudden outburst of creative power was again mostly geographical. In the context of the Russian life in those days, the emergence of St. Petersburg was similar to the discovery of the New World: it gave pensive men of the time a chance to look upon themselves and the nation as though from outside. In other words, this city provided them with the possibility of objectifying the country. The notion of criticism being most valid when conducted from without enjoys a great deal of popularity even today. Then, enhanced by the alternative—at least visually—utopian character of the city, it instilled those who were the first to take quill in their hands with a sense of the almost unquestionable authority of their pronouncements. If it's true that every writer has to estrange himself from his experience to be able to comment upon it, then the city, by rendering this alienating service, saved them a trip.

Coming from the nobility, gentry, or clergy, all these writers belonged, to use an economic stratification, to the middle class: the class which is almost solely responsible for the existence of literature everywhere. With two or three exceptions, all of them lived by the pen, i.e., meagerly enough to understand without exegesis or bewilderment the plight of those worse off as well as the splendor of those at the top. The second attracted their attention far less if only because the chances of moving up were far smaller. Consequently, we have a pretty thorough, almost stereoscopic picture of the inner, real St. Petersburg, for it is the poor who constitute the main body of reality; the little man is always universal. Furthermore, the more perfect his immediate surroundings are, the more jarring and incongruous he looks. No wonder that all of them—the retired officers, impoverished widows, robbed civil servants, hungry journalists, humiliated clerks, tubercular students, and so forth—seen against the impeccable utopian background of classicistic porticoes, haunted the imagination of writers and flooded the very first chapters of Russian prose.

Such was the frequency with which these characters appeared on paper and such was the number of people who put them there, such was their mastery of their material and such was the material itself—words—that in no time something strange began to happen to the city. The process of recognizing these incurably semantic reflections, loaded with moral judgment, became a process of identification with them. As often happens to a man in front of a mirror, the city began to fall into dependence on the three-dimensional image supplied by literature. Not that the adjustments it was making were not enough (they weren't!); but with the insecurity innate to any narcissist, the city started to peer more and more intently at that looking glass which the Russian writers were carrying—to paraphrase Stendhal—through the streets, courtyards, and shabby apartments of its population. Occasionally, the reflected would even try to correct or simply smash the reflection, which was all the easier to accomplish since nearly all the authors were residing in the city. Toward the middle of the nineteenth century, these two things merged: Russian literature caught up with reality to the extent that today when you think of St. Petersburg you can't distinguish the fictional from the real. Which is rather odd for a place only two hundred and seventy-six years old. The guide will show you today the building of the Third Section of the police, where Dostoevsky was tried, as well as the house where his character Raskolnikov killed that old money-lending woman with an ax.

The role of nineteenth-century literature in shaping the image of the city was all the more crucial because this was the century when St. Petersburg's palaces and embassies grew into the bureaucratic, political, business, military, and in the end industrial center of Russia. Architecture began to lose its perfect—to the degree of being absurd—abstract character and worsened with every new building. This was dictated as much by the swing toward functionalism (which is but a noble name for profit making) as by general aesthetic degradation. Save for Catherine the Great, Peter's successors had little in the way of vision, nor did they share his. Each of them tried to promulgate his version of Europe, and did so quite thoroughly; but in the nineteenth century Europe wasn't worth imitating. From reign to reign the decline was more and more evident; the only thing that saved the face of new ventures was the necessity to adjust them to those of their great predecessors. Today, of course, even the barrack-like style of the Nicholas I epoch may warm a brooding aesthete's heart, for it conveys well the spirit of the time. But on the whole, this Russian execution of the Prussian military ideal of society, together with the cumbersome apartment buildings squeezed between the classical ensembles, produces rather a disheartening effect. Then came the Victorian wedding cakes and hearses; and, by the last quarter of the century, this city that started as a leap from history into the future began to look in some parts like a regular Northern European bourgeois.

Which was the name of the game. If the literary critic Belinsky was exclaiming in the thirties of the past century: "Petersburg is more original than all American cities, because it is a new city in an old country; consequently it is a new hope, the marvelous future of this country!" then a quarter of a century later Dostoevsky could reply sardonically: "Here is the architecture of a huge modern hotel —its efficiency incarnate already, its Americanism, hundreds of rooms; it's clear right away that we too have railroads, we too suddenly became a business-like people."

"Americanism" as an epithet applied to the capitalist era in St. Petersburg's history is perhaps a bit farfetched; but the visual similarity to Europe was indeed quite startling. And it was not the façades of the banks and joint-stock companies only that matched in their elephantine solidity their counterparts in Berlin and London; the inner decor of a place like the Elyseev Brothers food store (which is still intact and functioning well, if only because there is not much to expand with today) could easily bear comparison with Fauchon in Paris. The truth is that every "ism" operates on a mass scale that mocks national identity; capitalism wasn't an exception. The city was booming; manpower was arriving from all ends of the empire; the male population outnumbered the female two to one, prostitution was thriving, orphanages overflowed; the water in the harbor boiled because of the ships exporting Russian grain, just as it boils today as the ships bring grain to Russia from abroad. It was an international city, with large French, German, Dutch, and English colonies, not to speak of diplomats and merchants. Pushkin's prophecy, put into his Bronze Horseman's mouth: "All flags will come to us as guests!" received its literal incarnation. If in the eighteenth century the imitation of the West didn't run deeper than the makeup and the fashions of the aristocracy ("These Russian monkeys!" cried a French nobleman after attending a ball in the Winter Palace, "how quickly they've adapted!

They're outdoing our court!"), then the St. Petersburg of the nineteenth century with its *nouveau riche* bourgeoisie, high society, demimonde, etc., became Western enough to afford even a degree of contempt toward Europe.

However, this contempt, displayed mostly in literature, had very little to do with the traditional Russian xenophobia, often manifested in the form of an argument as to the superiority of Orthodoxy to Catholicism. It was rather a reaction of the city to itself, a reaction of professed ideals to mercantile reality; of aesthete to bourgeois. As for this business of Orthodoxy versus Western Christianity, it never got very far, since the cathedrals and churches were designed by the same architects who built the palaces. So unless you step into their vaults, there is no way of determining what denomination these houses of prayer are, unless you pay attention to the form of the cross on the cupola; and there are practically no onion domes in this city. Still, in that contempt, there was something of a religious nature.

Every criticism of the human condition suggests the critic's awareness of a higher plane of regard, of a better order. Such was the history of Russian aesthetics that the architectural ensembles of St. Petersburg, churches included, were—and still are—perceived as the closest possible incarnation of such an order. In any case, a man who has lived long enough in this city is bound to associate virtue with proportion. This is an old Greek idea; but set under the northern sky, it acquires the peculiar authority of an embattled spirit and, to say the least, makes an artist very conscious of form. This kind of influence is especially clear in the case of Russian or, to name it by its birthplace, Petersburgian poetry. For two and a half centuries this school, from Lomonosov and Derzhavin to Pushkin and his pleiad (Baratynsky, Vyazemsky, Delvig), to the Acmeists—Akhmatova and Mandelstam in this century—has existed under the very sign under which it was conceived: the sign of classicism.

Yet less than fifty years separate Pushkin's paean to the city in "The Bronze Horseman" and Dostoevsky's utterance in *Notes from Underground*: "It's an unhappy lot to habitate Petersburg, the most abstract and the most premeditated place in the world." The brevity of such a span can be explained only by the fact that the pace of this city's development wasn't actually a pace: it was acceleration from the start. The place whose population in 1700 was zero had reached one and a half million by 1900. What would take a century elsewhere was here squeezed into decades. Time acquired a mythic quality because the myth was that of creation. Industry was booming and smokestacks rose around the city like a brick echo of its colonnades. The Imperial Russian Ballet under the direction of Petipa starred Anna Pavlova and in barely two decades developed its concept of ballet as a symphonic structure—a concept which was destined to conquer the world. About three thousand ships flying foreign and Russian flags bustled annually into St. Petersburg harbor, and more than a dozen political parties would convene in 1906 on the floor of the would-be Russian parliament called the Duma, which in Russian means "thought" (its achievements, in retrospect, make its sound in English—"Dooma"—seem particularly ominous). The prefix "St." was disappearing—gradually but justly—from the name of the city; and, with the outbreak of World War I, due to anti-German sentiment, the name itself was Russified, and "Petersburg" became "Petrograd." The once perfectly graspable idea of the city shone less and less through the thickening web of economics and civic demagoguery. In other words, the city of the Bronze Horseman galloped into its future as a regular metropolis in giant strides, treading on the heels of its little men and pushing them forward. And one day a train arrived at the Finland Station, and a little man emerged from the carriage and climbed onto the top of an armored car.

This arrival was a disaster for the nation but a salvation for the city. For its development came to a full stop, as did the economic life of the whole country. This city froze as if in total mute bewilderment before the impending era, unwilling to attend it. If anything, Comrade Lenin deserves his monuments here for sparing St. Petersburg both ignoble membership in the global village and the shame of becoming the seat of his government: in 1918 he moved the capital of Russia back to Moscow.

The significance of this move alone could equate Lenin with Peter. However, Lenin himself would hardly approve of naming the city after him if only because the total amount of time he spent there was about two years. Had it been up to him, he would have preferred Moscow or any other place in Russia proper. Besides, he didn't care much for the sea: he was a man of the terra firma, and a city dweller at that. And if he felt uncomfortable in Petrograd, it was partly because of the sea, although it wasn't the flood which he was mindful of, but the British Navy.

There were perhaps only two things he had in common with Peter I: knowledge of Europe and ruthlessness. But while Peter, with his variety of interests, boisterous energy, and the amateurishness of his grand designs, was either an up- or outdated version of a Renaissance man,

Lenin was very much a product of his time: a narrow-minded revolutionary with a typical petit bourgeois, monomaniacal desire for power, which is in itself an extremely bourgeois concept.

So Lenin went to Petersburg because that's where he thought it was: power. For that he would go to any other place if he thought that place had it (and, in fact, he did: while living in Switzerland he tried the same thing in Zurich). In short, he was one of the first men for whom geography is a political science. But the point is that Petersburg never, even during its most reactionary period under Nicholas I, was a center of power. Every monarchy rests on the traditional feudal principle of willing submission or resignation to the rule of one, backed by the church. After all, either of these—submission or resignation—is an act of will, as much as casting a ballot is. Whereas Lenin's main idea was the manipulation of will itself, the control over minds; and that was news to Petersburg. For Petersburg was merely the seat of imperial rule, and not the mental or political locus of the nation—since the national will can't be localized by definition. An organic entity, society generates the forms of its organization the way trees generate their distance from one another, and a passerby calls that a "forest." The concept of power, alias state control over the social fabric, is a contradiction in terms and reveals a woodcutter. The city's very blend of architectural grandeur with a web-like bureaucratic tradition mocked the idea of power. The truth about palaces, especially about winter ones, is that not all of their rooms are occupied. Had Lenin stayed longer in this city, his idea of statehood might have grown a bit more humble. But from the age of thirty, he lived for nearly sixteen years abroad, mostly in Germany and Switzerland, nourishing his political theories. He returned to Petersburg only once, in 1905, for three months, in an attempt to organize workers against the czarist government, but was soon forced abroad, back to his café politicking, chess playing, and Marx reading. It couldn't help him to get less idiosyncratic: failure seldom broadens perspectives.

In 1917, in Switzerland, upon learning from a passerby about the Czar's abdication, Lenin with a group of his followers boarded a sealed train provided by the German General Staff, which relied on these gentlemen to do a fifth-column job behind the Russian lines, and went to Petersburg. The man who stepped down from the train in 1917 at the Finland Station was forty-seven years old, and this was presumably his last gamble: he had to win or face the charge of treason. Except for 12 million in German marks, his only luggage was the dream of world socialist revolution which, once started in Russia, would produce a chain reaction, and another dream of becoming head of the Russian state in order to execute this first dream. On the sixteen-year-long, bumpy journey to the Finland Station, the two dreams merged into a somewhat nightmarish concept of power; but climbing onto that armored car, he didn't know that only one of those things was destined to come true.

So it wasn't so much his coming to Petersburg to grab power as it was the idea of power which grabbed him long ago that was carrying Lenin now to Petersburg. What's rendered in the history books as the Great October Socialist Revolution was, in fact, a plain *coup d'état*, and a bloodless one at that. Following the signal—a blank-fire shot of the cruiser *Aurora*'s bow gun—a platoon of the newly formed

Red Guards walked into the Winter Palace and arrested a bunch of ministers of the Provisional Government idling there, vainly trying to take care of Russia after the Czar's abdication. The Red Guards didn't meet any resistance; they raped half of the female unit guarding the palace and looted its chambers. At that, two Red Guardsmen were shot and one drowned in the wine cellars. The only shooting that ever took place in the Palace Square, with bodies falling and the searchlight crossing the sky, was Sergei Eisenstein's.

It's perhaps in reference to the modesty of that October 25 night enterprise that the city has been termed in official propaganda "the cradle of the Revolution." And a cradle it remained, an empty cradle, and quite enjoyed this status. To a degree, the city escaped the revolutionary carnage. "God forbid us to see," said Pushkin, "the Russian debacle, meaningless and merciless," and Petersburg didn't see it. The civil war raged all around and across the country, and a horrible crack went through the nation, splitting it into two mutually hostile camps; but here, on the shores of the Neva, for the first time in two centuries, quiet reigned and the grass started to shoot up through the cobblestones of emptied squares and the slates of sidewalks. Hunger took its toll, and so did the Cheka (the maiden name of the KGB); but other than that, the city was left to itself and to its reflections.

As the country, with its capital returned to Moscow, retreated to its womblike, claustrophobic, and xenophobic condition, Petersburg, having nowhere to withdraw to, came to a standstill—as though photographed in its nineteenth-century posture. The decades that followed the civil war didn't change it much: there were new buildings but mostly in the industrial outskirts. Besides, the general housing policy was that of so-called condensation, i.e., putting the deprived in with the well-off. So if a family had a three-room apartment all to itself, it had to squeeze into one room in order to let other families move into the other rooms. The city's interiors thus became more Dostoevskian than ever, while the façades peeled off and absorbed dust, this suntan of epochs.

Quiet, immobilized, the city stood watching the passage of seasons. Everything can change in Petersburg except its weather. And its light. It's the northern light, pale and diffused, one in which both memory and eye operate with unusual sharpness. In this light, and thanks to the directness and length of the streets, a walker's thoughts travel farther than his destination, and a man with normal eyesight can make out at a distance of a mile the number of the approaching bus or the age of the tail following him. In his youth, at least, a man born in this city spends as much time on foot as any good Bedouin. And it's not because of the shortage or the price of cars (there is an excellent system of public transportation), or because of the half-mile-long queues at the food stores. It's because to walk under this sky, along the brown granite embankments of this immense gray river, is itself an extension of life and a school of farsightedness. There is something in the granular texture of the granite pavement next to the constantly flowing, departing water that instills in one's soles an almost sensual desire for walking. The seaweed-smelling head wind from the sea has cured here many hearts oversaturated with lies, despair, and powerlessness. If that is what conspires to enslave, the slave may be excused.

This is the city where it's somehow easier to endure loneliness than anywhere else: because the city itself is lonely. A strange consolation comes from the notion that these stones have nothing to do with the present and still less with the future. The farther the façades go into the twentieth century, the more fastidious they look, ignoring these new times and their concerns. The only thing that makes them come to terms with the present is the climate, and they feel most at home in the foul weather of late fall or of premature spring and its showers mixed with snow and its impetuous disoriented squalls. Or—in the dead of winter, when the palaces and mansions loom over the frozen river in their heavy snow trimmings and shawls like old imperial dignitaries, sunk up to their eyebrows in massive fur coats. When the crimson ball of the setting January sun paints their tall Venetian windows with liquid gold, a freezing man crossing the bridge on foot suddenly sees what Peter had in mind when he erected these walls: a giant mirror for a lonely planet. And, exhaling steam, he feels almost pity for those naked columns with their Doric hairdos as though captured and driven into this merciless cold, into this knee-high snow.

The lower the thermometer falls, the more abstract the city looks. Minus 25 Centigrade is cold enough, but the temperature keeps falling as though, having done away with people, river, and buildings, it aims for ideas, for abstract concepts. With the white smoke floating above the roofs, the buildings along the embankments more and more resemble a stalled train bound for eternity. Trees in parks and public gardens look like school diagrams of human lungs with black caverns of crows' nests. And always in the distance, the golden needle of the Admiralty's spire tries, like a reversed ray, to anesthetize the content of the clouds. And there is no way of telling who looks more incongruous against such a background: the little men of today or their mighty masters scurrying along in black limousines stuffed with bodyguards. To say the least, both feel quite uncomfortable.

Even in the late thirties, when local industries finally began to catch up with the pre-revolutionary level of production, the population hadn't sufficiently increased; it was fluctuating somewhere near the two million mark. In fact, the percentage of long-standing families (those who had lived in Petersburg for two generations or more) was constantly dropping because of the civil war, emigration in the twenties, purges in the thirties. Then came World War II and the nine-hundred-day-long siege, which took nearly one million lives as much through bombardments as through starvation. The siege is the most tragic page in the city's history, and I think it was then that the name "Leningrad" was finally adopted by the inhabitants who survived, almost as a tribute to the dead; it's hard to argue with tombstone carvings. The city suddenly looked much older; it was as though History had finally acknowledged its existence and decided to catch up with this place in her usual morbid way: by piling up bodies. Today, thirty-three years later, however repainted and stuccoed, the ceilings and façades of this unconquered city still seem to preserve the stain-like imprints of its inhabitants' last gasps and last gazes. Or perhaps it's just bad paint and bad stucco.

Today, the population of this city is around five million; and at eight o'clock in the morning, the overcrowded trams, buses, and trolleys rumble across the numerous bridges carrying the barnacles of humanity to their factories and offices. The housing policy has changed from "condensation" to building new structures on the outskirts whose style resembles everything else in the world and is known popularly as "barrackko." It's a big credit to the present city fathers that they preserved the main body of the city virtually untouched. There are no skyscrapers, no braiding speedways here. Russia has an architectural reason to be grateful for the existence of the Iron Curtain, for it helped her to retain a visual identity. These days when you receive a postcard it takes a while to figure out whether it's been mailed from Caracas, Venezuela, or Warsaw, Poland.

It's not that the city fathers wouldn't like to immortalize themselves in glass and concrete; but somehow they don't dare. For all their worth, they, too, fall under the spell of the city, and the furthest they go is to erect here and there a modern hotel where everything is done by foreign (Finnish) builders—with the exception, of course, of telephone and electric wiring: the latter is subject to Russian know-how only. As a rule, these hotels are designated to service only foreign tourists, often the Finns themselves, owing to the proximity of their country to Leningrad.

The population amuses itself in nearly one hundred movie houses and a dozen drama, opera, and ballet theaters; there are also two huge soccer stadiums and the city supports two professional soccer teams and one ice-hockey team. In general, sports are endorsed substantially by officialdom, and it's widely known here that the most enthusiastic ice-hockey fan lives in the Kremlin. But the main pastime in Leningrad, as everywhere in Russia, is "the bottle." In terms of alcohol consumption, this city is the window on Russia indeed, and a wide-open one at that. At nine o'clock in the morning, a drunk is more frequently seen than a taxi. In the wine section of the grocery stores, you always find a couple of men with that idle but searching expression on their faces: they are looking for "a third" with whom to share both the price and the content of a bottle. The price shared at the cashier's, the content—in the nearest doorway. In the semidarkness of those entrances, reigns, at its highest, the art of dividing a pint of vodka into three equal parts without any remainder. Strange, unexpected, but sometimes lifelong friendships originate here, as well as the most grisly crimes. And while propaganda condemns alcoholism orally and in print, the state continues to sell vodka and increases the prices because "the bottle" is the source of the state's biggest revenue: its cost is five kopecks and it's sold to the population for five rubles. Which means a profit of 9,900 percent.

But drinking habits are no rarity among those who live by the sea. The most characteristic features of Leningraders are: bad teeth (because of lack of vitamins during the siege), clarity in pronunciation of sibilants, self-mockery, and a degree of haughtiness toward the rest of the country. Mentally, this city is still the capital; and it is in the same relation to Moscow as Florence is to Rome or Boston is to Washington. Like some of Dostoevsky's characters, Leningrad derives pride and almost a sensual pleasure from being "unrecognized," rejected; and yet it's perfectly aware that, for everyone whose mother tongue is Russian, the city is more real than anywhere else in the world where this language is heard.

For there is the second Petersburg, the one made of verses and of Russian prose. That prose is read and reread and the verses are learned by heart, if only because in Soviet schools children are made to memorize them if they want to graduate. And it's this memorization which secures the city's status and place in the future—as long as this language exists—and transforms the Soviet schoolchildren into the Russian people.

The school year usually is over by the end of May, when the White Nights arrive in this city, to stay throughout the whole month of June. A white night is a night when the sun leaves the sky for barely a couple of hours—a phenomenon quite familiar in the northern latitudes. It's the most magic time in the city, when you can write or read without a lamp at two o'clock in the morning, and when the buildings, deprived of shadows and their roofs rimmed with gold, look like a set of fragile china. It's so quiet around that you can almost hear the clink of a spoon falling in Finland. The transparent pink tint of the sky is so light that the pale-blue watercolor of the river almost fails to reflect it. And the bridges are drawn up as though the islands of the delta have unclasped their hands and slowly begun to drift, turning in the mainstream, toward the Baltic. On such nights, it's hard to fall asleep, because it's too light and because any dream will be inferior to this reality. Where a man doesn't cast a shadow, like water.

1979

In the Shadow of Dante

Unlike life, a work of art never gets taken for granted: it is always viewed against its precursors and predecessors. The ghosts of the great are especially visible in poetry, since their words are less mutable than the concepts they represent.

A significant part, therefore, of every poet's endeavor involves polemics with these shadows whose hot or cold breath he senses on his neck, or is led to sense by the industry of literary criticism. "Classics" exert such tremendous pressure that at times verbal paralysis is the result. And since the mind is more able to produce a negative view of the future than to handle such a prospect, the tendency is to perceive the situation as terminal. In such cases natural ignorance or even bogus innocence seems blessed, because it permits one to dismiss all such specters as nonexistent, and to "sing" (in *vers libre*, preferably) merely out of a sense of one's own physical stage presence.

To consider any such situation terminal, however, usually reveals not so much lack of courage as poverty of imagination. If a poet lives long enough, he learns how to handle such dry spells (regardless of their origins), using them for his own ends. The unbearableness of the future is easier to face than that of the present if only because human foresight is much more destructive than anything that the future can bring about.

Eugenio Montale is now eighty-one years old and has left behind many futures—his own as well as others'. Only two things in his biography could be considered spectacular: one is that he served as an infantry officer in the Italian Army during World War I. The second is that he won the Nobel Prize for Literature in 1975. Between these events one might have found him studying to become an opera singer (he had a promising *bel canto*), opposing the Fascist regime—which he did from the start, and which eventually cost him his post as curator in the Vieusseux Library in Florence—writing articles, editing little magazines, covering musical and other cultural events for about three decades for the "third page" of *Il Corriere della Sera*, and, for sixty years, writing poetry. Thank God that his life has been so uneventful.

Ever since the Romantics, we have been accustomed to the biographies of poets whose startling careers were sometimes as short as their contributions. In this context, Montale is a kind of anachronism, and the extent of his contribution to poetry has been anachronistically great. A contemporary of Apollinaire, T. S. Eliot, Mandelstam, he belongs more than chronologically to that generation. Each of these writers wrought a qualitative change in his respective literature, as did Montale, whose task was much the hardest.

While it is usually chance that brings the English-speaking poet to read a Frenchman (Laforgue, say), an Italian does so out of a geographical imperative. The Alps, which used to be civilization's one-way route north, are now a two-way highway for all sorts of literary isms! Ghost-wise, that crowds (clouds) one's operation enormously. For any Italian poet to take a new step, he must lift up the load amassed by the traffic of the past and the present; and it is the load of the present that was, perhaps, a lighter thing for Montale to handle.

With the exception of this French proximity, the situation in Italian poetry during the first two decades of this century was not much different from that of other European literature. By that I mean that there was an aesthetic inflation caused by the absolute domination of the poetics of Romanticism (whether in its naturalistic or symbolist version). The two principal figures on the Italian poetic scene at that time—the "*prepotenti*" Gabriele D'Annunzio and Marinetti—did little more than manifest that inflation, each in his own way. While D'Annunzio carried inflated harmony to its extreme (and supreme) conclusion, Marinetti and the other Futurists were striving for the opposite, to dismember that harmony. In both cases it was a war of means against means; i.e., a conditioned reaction which marked a captive aesthetics, a sensibility. It now seems clear that it took three poets from the next generation, Giuseppe Ungaretti, Umberto Saba, and Eugenio Montale, to make the Italian language yield a modern lyric.

In spiritual odysseys there are no Ithacas, and even speech is but a means of transportation. A metaphysical realist with an evident taste for extremely condensed imagery, Montale managed to create his own poetic idiom through the juxtaposition of what he called the "aulic"—the courtly—and the "prosaic"; an idiom which as well could be defined as "*amaro stile nuovo*" (in contrast to Dante's formula, which reigned in Italian poetry for more than six centuries). The most remarkable aspect of Montale's achievement is that he managed to pull forward despite the grip of the *dolce stile nuovo.* In fact, far from trying to loosen this grip, Montale constantly refers to or paraphrases the great Florentine both in imagery and vocabulary. His allusiveness is partially responsible for the charges of obscurity that critics occasionally level against him. But references and paraphrases are the natural elements of any civilized discourse (free—or "freed"—of them, discourse is but gesturing), especially within the Italian cultural tradition. Michelangelo and Raphael, to cite only two instances, were both avid interpreters of *La Divina Commedia.* One of the purposes of a work of art is to create dependents; the paradox is that the more indebted the artist, the richer he is.

The maturity that Montale displayed in his very first book —*Ossi di Seppia,* published in 1925—makes it more difficult to account for his development. Already here he has subverted the ubiquitous music of the Italian hendecasyllabics, assuming a deliberately monotonous intonation that is occasionally made shrill by the addition of feet or is muted by their omission—one of the many techniques he employs in order to avoid prosodic inertia. If one recalls Montale's immediate predecessors (and the flashiest figure among them is certainly D'Annunzio), it becomes clear that stylistically Montale is indebted to nobody—or to everybody he bounces up against in his verse, for polemic is one form of inheritance.

This continuity through rejection is evident in Montale's use of rhyme. Apart from its function as a kind of linguistic echo, a sort of homage to the language, a rhyme lends a sense of inevitability to the poet's statement. Advantageous as it is, the repetitive nature of a rhyme scheme (or for that matter, of any scheme) creates the danger of overstatement, not to mention the distancing of the past from the reader. To prevent this, Montale often shifts from rhymed to unrhymed verse within the same poem. His objection to stylistic excess is clearly an ethical as well as an aesthetic one—proving that a poem is a form of the closest possible interplay between ethics and aesthetics.

This interplay, lamentably, is precisely what tends to vanish in translation. Still, despite the loss of his "vertebrate compactness" (in the words of his most perceptive critic, Glauco Cambon), Montale survives translation well. By lapsing inevitably into a different tonality, translation—because of its explanatory nature—somehow catches up with the original by clarifying those things which could be regarded by the author as self-evident and thus elude the native reader. Though much of the subtle, discreet music is lost, the American reader has an advantage in understanding the meaning, and would be less likely to repeat in English an Italian's charges of obscurity. Speaking of the present collection, one only regrets that the footnotes do not include indications of the rhyme scheme and metric patterns of the poems. After all, a footnote is where civilization survives.

Perhaps the term "development" is not applicable to a poet of Montale's sensitivity, if only because it implies a linear process; poetic thinking always has a synthesizing quality and employs—as Montale himself expresses it in one of his poems—a kind of "bat-radar" technique, i.e., when thought operates in a 360-degree range. Also, at any given time a poet is in possession of an entire language; his preference for an archaic word, for instance, is dictated by his subject matter or his nerves rather than by a preconceived stylistic program. The same is true of syntax, stanzaic design, and the like. For sixty years Montale has managed to sustain his poetry on a stylistic plateau, the altitude of which one senses even in translation.

New Poems is, I believe, Montale's sixth book to appear in English. But unlike previous editions, which aspired to give a comprehensive idea of the poet's entire career, this volume contains only poems written during the last decade, coinciding thus with Montale's most recent (1971) collection—*Satura.* And though it would be senseless to view them as the ultimate word of the poet, still—because of their author's age and their unifying theme, the death of his wife—each conveys to some extent an air of finality. For death as a theme always produces a self-portrait.

In poetry, as in any other form of discourse, the addressee matters no less than the speaker. The protagonist of the *New Poems* is preoccupied with the attempt to estimate the distance between himself and his "interlocutor" and then to figure out the response "she" would have made had she been present. The silence into which his speech necessarily has been directed harbors, by implication, more in the way of answers than human imagination can afford—a fact which endows Montale's "her" with undoubted superiority. In this respect Montale resembles neither T. S. Eliot nor Thomas Hardy, with whom he has been frequently compared, but rather the Robert Frost of the "New Hampshire period," with his idea that woman was created out of man's rib (a nickname for heart), neither to be loved nor to be loving, nor to be judged, but to be "a judge of thee."

Unlike Frost, however, Montale is dealing with a form of superiority that is a *fait accompli*—superiority *in absentia*—and this stirs in him not so much a sense of guilt as a feeling of disjunction: his persona in these poems has been exiled into "outer time."

This is, therefore, love poetry in which death plays approximately the same role it does in *La Divina Commedia* or in Petrarch's sonnets to Madonna Laura: the role of a guide. But here quite a different person is moving along familiar lines; his speech has nothing to do with sacred anticipation. What Montale displays in *New Poems* is that tenaciousness of imagination, that urge to outflank death, which might enable a person, upon arriving in the domain of shadows and finding "Kilroy was here," to recognize his own handwriting.

Yet there is no morbid fascination with death, no falsetto in these poems; what the poet is talking about here is the absence which lets itself be felt in exactly the same nuances of language and feeling as those which "she" once used to manifest "her" presence—the language of intimacy. Hence the extremely private tone of the poems: in their metrics and in their choice of detail. This voice, of a man speaking—often muttering—to himself, is generally the most conspicuous characteristic of Montale's poetry. But this time the personal note is enforced by the fact that the poet's persona is talking about things only the real he and the real she had knowledge of—shoehorns, suitcases, the names of hotels where they used to stay, mutual acquaintances, books they had both read. Out of this sort of realia, and out of the inertia of intimate speech, emerges a private mythology which gradually acquires all the traits appropriate to any mythology, including surrealistic visions, metamorphoses, and the like. In this mythology, instead of some female-breasted sphinx, there is the image of "her," minus her glasses: this is the surrealism of subtraction, and this subtraction, affecting either subject matter or tonality, is what gives unity to this collection.

Death is always a song of "innocence," never of experience. And from the beginning of his career Montale shows his preference for song over confession. Although less explicit than the latter, a song is less repeatable; as is loss. Over the course of a lifetime, psychological acquisitions become more real than real estate. There is nothing more moving than an alienated man resorting to elegy:

With my arm in yours I have descended at least
a million stairs,
and now that you aren't here, a void opens at
each step.
Even so our long journey has been brief.
Mine continues still, though I've no more use
for connections, bookings, traps,
and the disenchantment of him who believes
that the real is what one sees.

I have descended millions of stairs with my arm
in yours,
not, of course, that with four eyes one might
see better.
I descended them because I knew
that even though so bedimmed
yours were the only true eyes.

Other considerations aside, this reference to a continuing solitary descent of stairs echoes something in *La Divina Commedia.* "Xenia I" and "Xenia II," as well as "Diary of 71" and "Diary of 72," the poems that make up the present volume, are full of references to Dante. Sometimes a reference consists of a single word, sometimes an entire poem is an echo—like No. 13 of "Xenia I," which echoes the conclusion of the twenty-first Song in the *Purgatorio*, the most stunning scene in the whole *Cantica.* But what marks Montale's poetic and human wisdom is his rather bleak, almost exhausted, falling intonation. After all, he is speaking to a woman with whom he has spent many years: he knows her well enough to realize that she would not appreciate a tragic tremolo. He knows, certainly, that he is speaking into silence; the pauses that punctuate his lines suggest the closeness of that void, which is made somewhat familiar—if not actually inhabited—because of his belief that "she" might be somewhere out there. And it is the sense of her presence that keeps him from resorting to expressionistic devices, elaborate imagery, high-pitched catch-phrases, and so forth. She who died would resent verbal flamboyance as well. Montale is old enough to know that the classically "great" line, however immaculate its conception, flatters the audience and by and large is self-serving, whereas he is perfectly aware toward whom and where his speech is directed.

In such an absence, art grows humble. For all our cerebral progress, we are still greatly subject to relapse into the Romantic (and, hence, Realistic as well) notion that "art imitates life." If art does anything of this kind, it undertakes to reflect those few elements of existence which transcend "life," extend it beyond its terminal point—an undertaking which is frequently mistaken for art's or the artist's own groping for immortality. In other words, art "imitates" death rather than life; i.e., it imitates that realm of which life supplies no notion: realizing its own brevity, art tries to domesticate the longest possible version of time. After all, what distinguishes art from life is the ability of the former to produce a higher degree of lyricism than is possible within any human interplay. Hence poetry's affinity with—if not the very invention of—the notion of afterlife.

New Poems provides an idiom which is qualitatively new. It is largely Montale's own idiom, but some of it derives from the act of translation, whose limited means only increase the original austerity. The cumulative effect of this book is startling, not so much because the psyche portrayed in *New Poems* has no previous record in world literature, as because it makes clear that such a mentality could not be expressed in English as its original language. The question "why" may only obscure the reason, since even in Montale's native Italian such a mentality is strange enough to earn him the reputation of an exceptional poet.

Poetry after all in itself is a translation; or, to put it another way, poetry is one of the aspects of the psyche rendered in language. It is not so much that poetry is a form of art as that art is a form to which poetry often resorts. Essentially, poetry is the articulation of perception, the translation of that perception into the heritage of language—language is, after all, the best available tool. But for all the value of this tool in ramifying and deepening perceptions—revealing sometimes more than was originally intended, which, in the happiest cases, merges with the perceptions—every more or less experienced poet knows how much is left out or has suffered because of it.

This suggests that poetry is somehow also alien or resistant to language, be it Italian, English, or Swahili, and that the human psyche because of its synthesizing nature is infinitely superior to any language we are bound to use (having somewhat better chances with inflected ones). To say the least, if the psyche had its own tongue, the distance between it and the language of poetry would be approximately the same as the distance between the latter and conversational Italian. Montale's idiom shortens both trips.

New Poems ought to be read and reread a number of times, if not for the sake of analysis, the function of which is to return a poem to its stereoscopic origins—the way it existed in the poet's mind—then for the fugitive beauty of this subtle, muttering, and yet firm stoic voice, which tells us that the world ends with neither a bang nor a whimper but with a man talking, pausing, and then talking again. When you have had such a long life, anticlimax ceases to be just another device.

The book is certainly a monologue; it couldn't be otherwise when the interlocutor is absent, as is nearly always the case in poetry. Partly, however, the idea of monologue as a principal device springs from the "poetry of absence," another name for the greatest literary movement since Symbolism—a movement which came into existence in Europe, and especially in Italy, in the twenties and thirties—"Hermeticism." The following poem, which opens the present collection, is testimony to the main postulates of the movement and is itself its triumph. (*Tu* in Italian is the familiar form of "you.")

The Use of "Tu"

Misled by me
the critics assert that my "tu"
is an institution, that were it not
for this fault of mine, they'd have known
that the many in me are one,
even though multiplied by the mirrors.
The trouble is that once caught in the net
the bird doesn't know if he is himself
or one of his too many duplicates.

Montale joined the Hermetic movement in the late thirties while living in Florence, where he moved in 1927 from his native Genoa. The principal figure in Hermeticism at that time was Giuseppe Ungaretti, who took the aesthetics of Mallarmé's "*Un Coup de Dés*" perhaps too much to heart. However, in order to comprehend the nature of Hermeticism fully it is worthwhile to take into account not only those who ran this movement, but also who ran the whole Italian show—and that was Il Duce. To a large degree, Hermeticism was a reaction of the Italian intelligentsia to the political situation in Italy in the third and fourth decades of this century and could be viewed as an act of cultural self-defense—linguistic self-defense, in the case of poetry—against Fascism. At least, to overlook this aspect of Hermeticism would be as much a simplification as frequently overstressing this aspect is.

Although the Italian regime was far less carnivorous toward art than were its Russian and German counterparts, the sense of its incompatibility with the traditions of Italian culture was much more apparent and intolerable than in those countries. It is almost a rule that in order to survive under totalitarian pressure art should develop density in direct proportion to the magnitude of that pressure. The whole history of Italian culture supplied part of the required substance; the rest of the job fell to the Hermeticists, little though their name implied it. What could be more odious for those who stressed literary asceticism, compactness of language, emphasis on the word and its alliterative powers, sound versus—or, rather, over—meaning, and the like, than the propaganda verbosities and state-sponsored versions of Futurism?

Montale has the reputation of being the most difficult poet of this school and he is certainly more difficult—in the sense of being more complex—than Ungaretti or Salvatore Quasimodo. But for all the overtones, reticence, merging of associations, or hints of associations in his work, its hidden references, substitutions of general statements for microscopic detail, elliptical speech, etc., it was he who wrote "*La primavera Hitleriana*" ("The Hitler Spring"), which begins:

The dense white cloud of the mayflies crazily
whirls around the pallid street lamps and over the
parapets
spread on the ground a blanket on which the foot
grates as on sprinkled sugar . . .

This image of the foot grating on the dead mayflies as on sprinkled sugar conveys such a toneless, deadpan unease and horror that when some fourteen lines below he says:

. . . and the water continues to eat at the
shoreline, and no one is any more blameless
(*Translated by Maurice English*)

it sounds like lyricism. Little in these lines recalls Hermeticism, that ascetic variant of Symbolism. Reality was calling for a more substantial response, and World War II brought with it a "de-Hermetization." Still, the "Hermeticist" label became glued to Montale's back, and he has, ever since, been considered an "obscure" poet. But whenever one hears of obscurity, it is time to stop and ponder one's notion of clarity, for it usually rests on what is already known or preferred, or, in the worst cases, remembered. In this sense, the more obscure, the better. In this sense, too, the obscure poetry of Montale still carries on a defense of culture, this time against a much more ubiquitous enemy:

> The man of today has inherited a nervous system which cannot withstand the present conditions of life. While waiting for the man of tomorrow to be born, the man of today reacts to the altered conditions not by standing up to them or by endeavoring to resist their blows, but by turning into a mass.

This passage is taken from *Poet in Our Time*, a collection of Montale's prose pieces which he himself calls a "collage of notes." The pieces are excerpted from essays, reviews, interviews, etc., published at different times and in different places. The importance of this book goes far beyond the sidelights it casts on the poet's own progress, if it does that at all. Montale seems to be the last person to disclose his inner processes of thought, let alone the "secrets of his craft." A private man, he prefers to make the public life the subject of his scrutiny, rather than the reverse. *Poet in Our Time* is a book concerned precisely with the results of such scrutiny, and its emphasis falls on "Our Time" rather than on "Poet."

Both the lack of chronology and the harsh lucidity of language in these pieces supply this book with an air of diagnosis or of verdict. The patient or the accused is the civilization which "believes it is walking while in fact it is being carried along by a conveyor belt," but since the poet realizes that he is himself the flesh of this civilization's flesh, neither cure nor rehabilitation is implied. *Poet in Our Time* is, in fact, the disheartened, slightly fastidious testament of a man who doesn't seem to have inheritors other than the "hypothetical stereophonic man of the future incapable even of thinking about his own destiny." This particular vision surely sounds backward in our track-taped present, and it betrays the fact that a European is speaking. It is hard, however, to decide which one of Montale's visions is more frightening—this one or the following, from his "*Piccolo Testamento*," a poem which easily matches Yeats's "Second Coming":

> *. . . only this iris can I*
> *leave you as testimony*
> *of a faith that was much disputed*
> *of a hope that burned more slowly*
> *than a hard log in the fireplace.*
> *Conserve its powder in your compact*
> *when every lamplight spent*
> *the sardana becomes infernal*
> *and a shadowy Lucifer descends on a prow*
> *of the Thames or Hudson or Seine*
> *thrashing bituminous wings half-*
> *shorn from the effort to tell you: It's time*
>
> (*Translated by Cid Corman*)

Still, a good thing about testaments is that they imply a future. Unlike philosophers or social thinkers, a poet ponders the future out of professional concern for his audience or awareness of art's mortality. The second reason plays a bigger part in *Poet in Our Time* because "the content of art is diminishing, just as the difference between individuals is diminishing." The pages in this collection that do not sound either sarcastic or elegiac are those that deal with the art of letters:

> There remains the hope that the art of the word, an incurably semantic art, will sooner or later make its repercussions felt even in those arts which claim to have freed themselves from every obligation toward the identification and representation of truth.

This is about as affirmative as Montale can be with respect to the art of letters, which he does not spare, however, the following comment:

> To belong to a generation which can no longer believe in anything may be a cause of pride for anyone convinced of the ultimate nobility of this emptiness or of some mysterious need for it, but it does not excuse anyone who wants to transform this emptiness into a paradoxical affirmation of life simply in order to give himself a style . . .

It is a tempting and dangerous thing to quote Montale because it easily turns into a full-time occupation. Italians have their way with the future, from Leonardo to Marinetti. Still, this temptation is due not so much to the aphoristic quality of Montale's statements or even to their prophetic quality as to the tone of his voice, which alone makes one trust his utterances because it is so free of anxiety. There is a certain air of recurrence to it, kindred to water coming ashore or the invariable refraction of light in a lens. When one lives as long as he has, "the provisional encounters between the real and the ideal" become frequent enough for the poet both to develop a certain familiarity with the ideal and to be able to foretell the possible changes of its features. For the artist, these changes are perhaps the only sensible measurements of time.

There is something remarkable about the almost simultaneous appearance of these two books; they seem to merge. In the end, *Poet in Our Time* makes the most appropriate illustration of the "outer time" inhabited by the persona of the *New Poems.* Again, this is a reversal of *La Divina Commedia*, where this world was understood as "that realm." "Her" absence for Montale's persona is as palpable as "her" presence was for Dante's. The repetitive nature of existence in this afterlife now is, in its turn, kindred to Dante's circling among those "who died as men before their bodies died." *Poet in Our Time* supplies us with a sketch—and sketches are always somewhat more convincing than oils—of that rather overpopulated spiral landscape of such dying yet living beings.

This book doesn't sound very "Italian," although the old civilization contributes a great deal to the accomplishment of this old man of letters. The words "European" and "international" when applied to Montale also look like tired euphemisms for "universal." Montale is one writer whose mastery of language stems from his spiritual autonomy; thus, both *New Poems* and *Poet in Our Time* are what books used to be before they became mere books: chronicles of souls. Not that the latter need any. The last of the *New Poems* goes as follows:

To Conclude

I charge my descendants (if I have
any) on the literary plane,
which is rather improbable, to make
a big bonfire of all that concerns
my life, my actions, my non-actions.
I'm no Leopardi, I leave
little behind me to be burnt,
and it's already too much to live
by percentages. I lived at the rate
of five per cent; don't increase
the dose. And yet
it never rains but it pours.

1977

On Tyranny

Illness and death are, perhaps, the only things that a tyrant has in common with his subjects. In this sense alone a nation profits from being run by an old man. It's not that one's awareness of one's own mortality necessarily enlightens or makes one mellow, but the time spent by a tyrant pondering, say, his metabolism is time stolen from the affairs of state. Both domestic and international tranquillities are in direct proportion to the number of maladies besetting your First Secretary of the Party, or your President-for-Life. Even if he is perceptive enough to learn that additional art of callousness inherent in every illness, he is usually quite hesitant to apply this acquired knowledge to his palace intrigues or foreign policies, if only because he instinctively gropes for the restoration of his previous healthy condition or simply believes in full recovery.

In the case of a tyrant, time to think of the soul is always used for scheming to preserve the status quo. This is so because a man in his position doesn't distinguish between the present, history, and eternity, fused into one by the state propaganda for both his and the population's convenience. He clings to power as any elderly person does to his pension or savings. What sometimes appears as a purge in the top ranks is perceived by the nation as an attempt to sustain the stability for which this nation opted in the first place by allowing the tyranny to be established.

The stability of the pyramid seldom depends on its pinnacle, and yet it is precisely the pinnacle that attracts our attention. After a while a spectator's eye gets bored with its intolerable geometrical perfection and all but demands changes. When changes come, however, they are always for the worse. To say the least, an old man fighting to avoid disgrace and discomfort, which are particularly unpleasant at his age, is quite predictable. Bloody and nasty as he may appear to be in that fight, it affects neither the pyramid's inner structure nor its external shadow. And the objects of his struggle, the rivals, fully deserve his vicious treatment, if only because of the tautology of their ambition in view of the difference in age. For politics is but geometrical purity embracing the law of the jungle.

Up there, on the head of the pin, there is room only for one, and he had better be old, since old men never pretend they are angels. The aging tyrant's sole purpose is to retain his position, and his demagoguery and hypocrisy do not tax the minds of his subjects with the necessity of belief or textual proliferation. Whereas the young upstart with his true or false zeal and dedication always ends up raising the level of public cynicism. Looking back on human history we can safely say that cynicism is the best yardstick of social progress.

For new tyrants always introduce a new blend of hypocrisy and cruelty. Some are more keen on cruelty, others on hypocrisy. Think of Lenin, Hitler, Stalin, Mao, Castro, Qaddafi, Khomeini, Amin, and so on. They always beat their predecessors in more ways than one, and give a new twist to the arm of the citizen as well as to the mind of the spectator. For an anthropologist (an extremely aloof one at that) this kind of development is of great interest, for it widens one's notion of the species. It must be noted, however, that the responsibility for the aforesaid processes lies as much with technological progress and the general growth of population as with the particular wickedness of a given dictator.

Today, every new sociopolitical setup, be it a democracy or an authoritarian regime, is a further departure from the spirit of individualism toward the stampede of the masses. The idea of one's existential uniqueness gets replaced by that of one's anonymity. An individual perishes not so much by the sword as by the penis, and, however small a country is, it requires, or becomes subjected to, central planning. This sort of thing easily breeds various forms of autocracy, where tyrants themselves can be regarded as obsolete versions of computers.

But if they were only the obsolete versions of computers, it wouldn't be so bad. The problem is that a tyrant is capable of purchasing new, state-of-the-art computers and aspires to man them. Examples of obsolete forms of hardware running advanced forms are the Führer resorting to the loudspeaker, or Stalin using the telephone monitoring system to eliminate his opponents in the Politburo.

People become tyrants not because they have a vocation for it, nor do they by pure chance either. If a man has such a vocation, he usually takes a shortcut and becomes a family tyrant, whereas real tyrants are known to be shy and not terribly interesting family men. The vehicle of a tyranny is a political party (or military ranks, which have a structure similar to that of the party), for in order to get to the top of something you need to have something that has a vertical topography.

Now, unlike a mountain or, better still, a skyscraper, a party is essentially a fictitious reality invented by the mentally or otherwise unemployed. They come to the world and find its physical reality, skyscrapers and mountains, fully occupied. Their choice, therefore, is between waiting for an opening in the old system and creating a new, alternative one of their own. The latter strikes them as the more expedient way to proceed, if only because they can start right away. Building a party is an occupation in itself, and an absorbing one at that. It surely doesn't pay off immediately; but then again the labor isn't that hard and there is a great deal of mental comfort in the incoherence of the aspiration.

In order to conceal its purely demographic origins, a party usually develops its own ideology and mythology. In general, a new reality is always created in the image of an old one, aping the existing structures. Such a technique, while obscuring the lack of imagination, adds a certain air of authenticity to the entire enterprise. That's why, by the way, so many of these people adore realistic art. On the whole, the absence of imagination is more authentic than its presence. The droning dullness of a party program and the drab, unspectacular appearance of its leaders appeal to the masses as their own reflection. In the era of overpopulation, evil (as well as good) becomes as mediocre as its subjects. To become a tyrant, one had better be dull.

And dull they are, and so are their lives. Their only rewards are obtained while climbing: seeing rivals outdone, pushed away, demoted. At the turn of the century, in the heyday of political parties, there were the additional pleasures of, say, putting out a haywire pamphlet, or escaping police surveillance; of delivering a fervent oration at a clandestine congress or resting at the party's expense in the Swiss Alps or on the French Riviera. Now all that is gone: burning issues, false beards, Marxist studies. What's left is the waiting game of promotion, endless red tape, paper work, and a search for reliable pals. There isn't even the thrill of watching your tongue, for it's surely devoid of anything worth the attention of your fully bugged walls.

What gets one to the top is the slow passage of time, whose only comfort is the sense of authenticity it gives to the undertaking: what's time-consuming is real. Even within the ranks of the opposition, party advancement is slow; as for the party in power, it has nowhere to hurry, and after half a century of domination is itself capable of distributing time. Of course, as regards ideals in the Victorian sense of the word, the one-party system isn't very different from a modern version of political pluralism. Still, to join the only existing party takes more than an average amount of dishonesty.

Nevertheless, for all your cunning, and no matter how crystal-clear your record is, you are not likely to make it to the Politburo before sixty. At this age life is absolutely irreversible, and if one grabs the reins of power, he unclenches his fists only for the last candle. A sixty-year-old man is not likely to try anything economically or politically risky. He knows that he has a decade or so to go, and his joys are mostly of a gastronomical and a technological nature: an exquisite diet, foreign cigarettes, and foreign cars. He is a status quo man, which is profitable in foreign affairs, considering his steadily growing stockpile of missiles, and intolerable inside the country, where to do nothing means to worsen the existing condition. And although his rivals may capitalize on the latter, he would rather eliminate them than introduce any changes, for one always feels a bit nostalgic toward the order that brought one to success.

The average length of a good tyranny is a decade and a half, two decades at most. When it's more than that, it invariably slips into a monstrosity. Then you may get the kind of grandeur that manifests itself in waging wars or internal terror, or both. Blissfully, nature takes its toll, resorting at times to the hands of the rivals just in time; that is, before your man decides to immortalize himself by doing something horrendous. The younger cadres, who are not so young anyway, press from below, pushing him into the blue yonder of pure Chronos. Because after reaching the top of the pinnacle that is the only way to continue. However, more often than not, nature has to act alone and encounter a formidable opposition from both the Organs of State Security and the tyrant's personal medical team. Foreign doctors are flown in from abroad to fish your man out from the depths of senility to which he has sunk. Sometimes they succeed in their humanitarian mission (for their governments are themselves deeply interested in the preservation of the status quo), enough to enable the great man to reiterate the death threat to their respective countries.

In the end both give up; Organs perhaps less willingly than doctors, for medicine has less in the way of a hierarchy which stands to be affected by the impending changes. But even the Organs finally get bored with their master, whom they are going to outlive anyway, and as the bodyguards turn their faces sideways, in slips death with scythe, hammer, and sickle. The next morning the population is awakened not by the punctual roosters but by waves of Chopin's *Marche Funèbre* pouring out of the loudspeakers. Then comes the military funeral, horses dragging the gun carriage, preceded by a detachment of soldiers carrying on small scarlet cushions the medals and orders that used to adorn the coat of the tyrant like the chest of a prize-winning dog. For this is what he was: a prize- and race-winning dog. And if the population mourns his demise, as often happens, its tears are the tears of bettors who lost: the nation mourns its lost time. And then appear the members of the Politburo, shouldering the banner-draped coffin: the only denominator that they have in common.

As they carry their dead denominator, cameras chirr and click, and both foreigners and the natives peer intently at the inscrutable faces, trying to pick out the successor. The deceased may have been vain enough to leave a political testament, but it won't be made public anyway. The decision is to be made in secrecy, at a closed—that is, to the population—session of the Politburo. That is, clandestinely. Secretiveness is an old party hang-up, an echo of its demographic origin, of its glorious illegal past. And the faces reveal nothing.

They do it all the more successfully because there is nothing to reveal. For it's simply going to be more of the same. The new man will differ from the old man only physically. Mentally and otherwise he is bound to be the exact replica of the corpse. This is perhaps the biggest secret there is. Come to think of it, the party's replacements are the closest thing we've got to resurrection. Of course, repetition breeds boredom, but if you repeat things in secret there is still room for fun.

The funniest thing of all, however, is the realization that

any one of these men can become a tyrant. That what causes all this uncertainty and confusion is just that the supply exceeds the demand. That we are dealing not with the tyranny of an individual but with the tyranny of a party that simply has put the production of tyrants on an industrial footing. Which was very shrewd of this party in general and very apt in particular, considering the rapid surrender of individualism as such. In other words, today the "who-is-going-to-be-who" guessing game is as romantic and antiquated as that of bilboquet, and only freely elected people can indulge in playing it. The time is long since over for the aquiline profiles, goatees or shovel-like beards, walrus or toothbrush mustaches; soon it will be over even for eyebrows.

Still, there is something haunting about these bland, gray, undistinguished faces: they look like everyone else, which gives them an almost underground air; they are similar as blades of grass. The visual redundance provides the "government of the people" principle with an additional depth: with the rule of nobodies. To be governed by nobodies, however, is a far more ubiquitous form of tyranny, since nobodies look like everybody. They represent the masses in more ways than one, and that's why they don't bother with elections. It's a rather thankless task for the imagination to think of the possible result of the "one man, one vote" system in, for example, the one-billion-strong China: what kind of a parliament that could produce, and how many tens of millions would constitute a minority there.

The upsurge of political parties at the turn of the century was the first cry of overpopulation, and that's why they score so well today. While the individualists were poking fun at them, they capitalized on depersonalization, and presently the individualists quit laughing. The goal, however, is neither the party's own nor some particular bureaucrat's triumph. True, they turned out to be ahead of their time; but time has a lot of things ahead, and above all, a lot of people. The goal is to accommodate their numerical expansion in the non-expanding world, and the only way to achieve it is through the depersonalization and bureaucratization of everybody alive. For life itself is a common denominator; that's enough of a premise for structuring existence in a more detailed fashion.

And a tyranny does just that: structures your life for you. It does this as meticulously as possible, certainly far better than a democracy does. Also, it does it for your own sake, for any display of individualism in a crowd may be harmful: first of all for the person who displays it; but one should care about those next to him as well. This is what the party-run state, with its security service, mental institutions, police, and citizens' sense of loyalty, is for. Still, all these devices are not enough: the dream is to make every man his own bureaucrat. And the day when such a dream comes true is very much in sight. For bureaucratization of individual existence starts with thinking politics, and it doesn't stop with the acquisition of a pocket calculator.

So if one still feels elegiac at the tyrant's funeral, it's mostly for autobiographical reasons, and because this departure makes one's nostalgia for "the good old days" even more concrete. After all, the man was also a product of the old school, when people still saw the difference between what they were saying and what they were doing. If he doesn't deserve more than a line in history, well, so much the better: he just didn't spill enough of his subjects' blood for a paragraph. His mistresses were on the plump side and few. He didn't write much, nor did he paint or play a musical instrument; he didn't introduce a new style in furniture either. He was a plain tyrant, and yet leaders of the greatest democracies eagerly sought to shake his hand. In short, he didn't rock the boat. And it's partly thanks to him that as we open our windows in the morning, the horizon there is still not vertical.

Because of the nature of his job, nobody knew his real thoughts. It's quite probable that he didn't know them himself. That would do for a good epitaph, except that there is an anecdote the Finns tell about the will of their President-for-Life Urho Kekkonnen which begins as follows: "If I die . . ."

1980

The Child of Civilization

For some odd reason, the expression "death of a poet" always sounds somewhat more concrete than "life of a poet." Perhaps this is because both "life" and "poet," as words, are almost synonymous in their positive vagueness. Whereas "death"—even as a word—is about as definite as a poet's own production, i.e., a poem, the main feature of which is its last line. Whatever a work of art consists of, it runs to the finale which makes for its form and denies resurrection. After the last line of a poem nothing follows except literary criticism. So when we read a poet, we participate in his or his works' death. In the case of Mandelstam, we participate in both.

A work of art is always meant to outlast its maker. Paraphrasing the philosopher, one could say that writing poetry, too, is an exercise in dying. But apart from pure linguistic necessity, what makes one write is not so much a concern for one's perishable flesh as the urge to spare certain things of one's world—of one's personal civilization—one's own non-semantic continuum. Art is not a better, but an alternative existence; it is not an attempt to escape reality but the opposite, an attempt to animate it. It is a spirit seeking flesh but finding words. In the case of Mandelstam, the words happened to be those of the Russian language.

For a spirit, perhaps, there is no better accommodation: Russian is a very inflected language. What this means is that the noun could easily be found sitting at the very end of the sentence, and that the ending of this noun (or adjective, or verb) varies according to gender, number, and case. All this provides any given verbalization with the stereoscopic quality of the perception itself, and (sometimes) sharpens and develops the latter. The best illustration of this is Mandelstam's handling of one of the main themes of his poetry, the theme of time.

There is nothing odder than to apply an analytic device to a synthetic phenomenon; for instance, to write in English about a Russian poet. Yet in dealing with Mandelstam it wouldn't be much easier to apply such a device in Russian either. Poetry is the supreme result of the entire language, and to analyze it is but to diffuse the focus. It is all the more true of Mandelstam, who is an extremely lonely figure in the context of Russian poetry, and it is precisely the density of his focus that accounts for his isolation. Literary criticism is sensible only when the critic operates on the same plane of both psychological and linguistic regard. The way it looks now, Mandelstam is bound for a criticism coming strictly "from below" in either language.

The inferiority of analysis starts with the very notion of theme, be it a theme of time, love, or death. Poetry is, first of all, an art of references, allusions, linguistic and figurative parallels. There is an immense gulf between *Homo sapiens* and *Homo scribens*, because for the writer the notion of theme appears as a result of combining the above techniques and devices, if it appears at all. Writing is literally an existential process; it uses thinking for its own ends, it consumes notions, themes, and the like, not vice versa. What dictates a poem is the language, and this is the voice of the language, which we know under the nicknames of Muse or Inspiration. It is better, then, to speak not about the theme of time in Mandelstam's poetry, but about the presence of time itself, both as an entity and as a theme, if only because time has its seat within a poem anyway, and it is a caesura.

It is because we know this full well that Mandelstam, unlike Goethe, never exclaims "O moment, stay! Thou art so very fair!" but merely tries to extend his caesura. What is more, he does it not so much because of this moment's particular fairness or lack of fairness; his concern (and subsequently his technique) is quite different. It was the sense of an oversaturated existence that the young Mandelstam was trying to convey in his first two collections, and he chose the portrayal of overloaded time as his medium. Using all the phonetic and allusory power of words themselves, Mandelstam's verse in that period expresses the slowing-down, viscous sensation of time's passage. Since he succeeds (as he always does), the effect is that the reader realizes that the words, even their letters—vowels especially—are almost palpable vessels of time.

On the other hand, his is not at all that search for bygone days with its obsessive gropings to recapture and to reconsider the past. Mandelstam seldom looks backward in a poem; he is all in the present—in this moment, which he makes continue, linger beyond its own natural limit. The past, whether personal or historical, has been taken care of by the words' own etymology. But however un-Proustian his treatment of time is, the density of his verse is somewhat akin to the great Frenchman's prose. In a way, it is the same total warfare, the same frontal attack—but in this case, an attack on the present, and with resources of a different nature. It is extremely important to note, for instance, that in almost every case when Mandelstam happens to deal with this theme of time, he resorts to a rather heavily caesuraed verse which echoes the hexameter either in its beat or in its content. It is usually an iambic pentameter lapsing into alexandrine verse, and there is always a paraphrase or a direct reference to either of Homer's epics. As a rule, this kind of poem is set somewhere by the sea, in late summer, which directly or indirectly evokes the ancient Greek background. This is partly because of Russian poetry's traditional regard for the Crimea and the Black Sea as the only available approximation of the Greek world, of which these places—Taurida and Pontus Euxinus—used to be the outskirts. Take, for instance, poems like "The stream of the golden honey was pouring so slow . . . ," "Insomnia. Homer. Tautly swelling sails . . . ," and "There are orioles in woods and lasting length of vowels," where there are these lines:

> *. . . Yet nature once a year*
> *Is bathed in lengthiness as in Homeric meters.*
> *Like a caesura that day yawns . . .*

The importance of this Greek echo is manifold. It might seem to be a purely technical issue, but the point is that the alexandrine verse is the nearest kin to hexameter, if only in terms of using a caesura. Speaking of relatives, the mother of all Muses was Mnemosyne, the Muse of Memory, and a poem (be it a short one or an epic) must be memorized in order to survive. Hexameter was a remarkable mnemonic device, if only because of being so cumbersome and different from the colloquial speech of any audience, Homer's included. So by referring to this vehicle of memory within another one—i.e., within his alexandrine verse—Mandelstam, along with producing an almost physical sensation of time's tunnel, creates the effect of a play within a play, of a caesura within a caesura, of a pause within a pause. Which is, after all, a form of time, if not its meaning: if time does not get stopped by that, it at least gets focused.

Not that Mandelstam does this consciously, deliberately. Or that this is his main purpose while writing a poem. He does it offhandedly, in subordinate clauses, while writing (often about something else), *never* by writing to make this point. His is not topical poetry. Russian poetry on the whole is not very topical. Its basic technique is one of beating around the bush, approaching the theme from various angles. The clear-cut treatment of the subject matter, which is so characteristic of poetry in English, usually gets exercised within this or that line, and then a poet moves on to something else; it seldom makes for an entire poem. Topics and concepts, regardless of their importance, are but material, like words, and they are always there. Language has names for all of them, and the poet is the one who masters language.

Greece was always there, so was Rome, and so were the biblical Judea and Christianity. The cornerstones of our civilization, they are treated by Mandelstam's poetry in approximately the same way time itself would treat them: as a unity—and *in* their unity. To pronounce Mandelstam an adept at either ideology (and especially at the latter) is not only to miniaturize him but to distort his historical perspective, or rather his historical landscape. Thematically, Mandelstam's poetry repeats the development of our civilization: it flows north, but the parallel streams in this current mingle with each other from the very beginning. Toward the twenties, the Roman themes gradually overtake the Greek and biblical references, largely because of the poet's growing identification with the archetypal predicament of "a poet versus an empire." Still, what created this kind of attitude, apart from the purely political aspects of the situation in Russia at the time, was Mandelstam's own estimate of his work's relation to the rest of contemporary literature, as well as to the moral climate and the intellectual concerns of the rest of the nation. It was the moral and the mental degradation of the latter which were suggesting this imperial scope. And yet it was only a thematic overtaking, never a takeover. Even in "Tristia," the most Roman poem, where the author clearly quotes from the exiled Ovid, one can trace a certain Hesiodic patriarchal note, implying that the whole enterprise was being viewed through a somewhat Greek prism.

TRISTIA

I've mastered the great craft of separation
amidst the bare unbraided pleas of night,
those lingerings while oxen chew their ration,
the watchful town's last eyelid's shutting tight.
And I revere that midnight rooster's descant
when shouldering the wayfarer's sack of wrong
eyes stained with tears were peering at the distance
and women's wailings were the Muses' song.

Who is to tell when hearing "separation"
what kind of parting this may resonate,
foreshadowed by a rooster's exclamation
as candles twist the temple's colonnade;
why at the dawn of some new life, new era
when oxen chew their ration in the stall
that wakeful rooster, a new life's towncrier,
flaps its torn wings atop the city wall.

And I adore the worsted yarn's behavior:
the shuttle bustles and the spindle hums;
look how young Delia, barefooted, braver
than down of swans, glides straight into your arms!
Oh, our life's lamentable coarse fabric,
how poor the language of our joy indeed.
What happened once, becomes a worn-out matrix.
Yet, recognition is intensely sweet!

So be it thus: a small translucent figure
spreads like a squirrel pelt across a clean
clay plate; a girl bends over it, her eager
gaze scrutinizes what the wax may mean.
To ponder Erebus, that's not for our acumen.
To women, wax is as to men steel's shine.
Our lot is drawn only in war; to women
it's given to meet death while they divine.

(*Translated by Joseph Brodsky*)

Later, in the thirties, during what is known as the Voronezh period, when all those themes—including Rome and Christianity—yielded to the "theme" of bare existential horror and a terrifying spiritual acceleration, the pattern of interplay, of interdependence between those realms, becomes even more obvious and dense.

It is not that Mandelstam was a "civilized" poet; he was rather a poet for and of civilization. Once, on being asked to define Acmeism—the literary movement to which he belonged—he answered: "nostalgia for a world culture." This notion of a world culture is distinctly Russian. Because of its location (neither East nor West) and its imperfect history, Russia has always suffered from a sense of cultural inferiority, at least toward the West. Out of this inferiority grew the ideal of a certain cultural unity "out there" and a subsequent intellectual voracity toward anything coming from that direction. This is, in a way, a Russian version of Hellenicism, and Mandelstam's remark about Pushkin's "Hellenistic paleness" was not an idle one.

The mediastinum of this Russian Hellenicism was St. Petersburg. Perhaps the best emblem for Mandelstam's attitude toward this so-called world culture could be that strictly classical portico of the St. Petersburg Admiralty decorated with reliefs of trumpeting angels and topped with a golden spire bearing a silhouette of a clipper at its tip. In order to understand his poetry better, the English-speaking reader perhaps ought to realize that Mandelstam was a Jew who was living in the capital of Imperial Russia, whose dominant religion was Orthodoxy, whose political structure was inherently Byzantine, and whose alphabet had been devised by two Greek monks. Historically speaking, this organic blend was most strongly felt in Petersburg, which became Mandelstam's "familiar as tears" eschatological niche for the rest of his not-that-long life.

It was long enough, however, to immortalize this place, and if his poetry was sometimes called "Petersburgian," there is more than one reason to consider this definition both accurate and complimentary. Accurate because, apart from being the administrative capital of the empire, Petersburg was also the spiritual center of it, and in the beginning of the century the strands of that current were merging there the way they do in Mandelstam's poems. Complimentary because both the poet and the city profited in meaning by their confrontation. If the West was Athens, Petersburg in the teens of this century was Alexandria. This "window on Europe," as Petersburg was called by some gentle souls of the Enlightenment, this "most invented city," as it was defined later by Dostoevsky, lying at the latitude of Vancouver, in the mouth of a river as wide as the Hudson between Manhattan and New Jersey, was and is beautiful with that kind of beauty which happens to be caused by madness—or which tries to conceal this madness. Classicism never had so much room, and the Italian architects who kept being invited by successive Russian monarchs understood this all too well. The giant, infinite, vertical rafts of white columns from the façades of the embankments' palaces belonging to the Czar, his family, the aristocracy, embassies, and the *nouveaux riches* are carried by the reflecting river down to the Baltic. On the main avenue of the empire—Nevsky Prospect—there are churches of all creeds. The endless, wide streets are filled with cabriolets, newly introduced automobiles, idle, well-dressed crowds, first-class boutiques, confectioneries, etc. Immensely wide squares with mounted statues of previous rulers and triumphal columns taller than Nelson's. Lots of publishing houses, magazines, newspapers, political parties (more than in contemporary America), theaters, restaurants, gypsies. All this is surrounded by the brick Birnam

Wood of the factories' smoking chimneys and covered by the damp, gray, widespread blanket of the Northern Hemisphere's sky. One war is lost, another—a world war—is impending, and you are a little Jewish boy with a heart full of Russian iambic pentameters.

In this giant-scale embodiment of perfect order, iambic beat is as natural as cobblestones. Petersburg is a cradle of Russian poetry and, what is more, of its prosody. The idea of a noble structure, regardless of the quality of the content (sometimes precisely *against* its quality, which creates a terrific sense of disparity—indicating not so much the author's but the verse's own evaluation of the described phenomenon), is utterly local. The whole thing started a century ago, and Mandelstam's usage of strict meters in his first book, *Stone*, is clearly reminiscent of Pushkin, and of his pleiad. And yet, again, it is not a result of some conscious choice, nor is it a sign of Mandelstam's style being predetermined by the preceding or contemporary processes in Russian poetry.

The presence of an echo is the primal trait of any good acoustics, and Mandelstam merely made a great cupola for his predecessors. The most distinct voices underneath it belong to Derzhavin, Baratynsky, and Batyushkov. To a great extent, however, he was acting very much on his own in spite of any existing idiom—especially the contemporary one. He simply had too much to say to worry about his stylistic uniqueness. But this overloaded quality of his otherwise regular verse was what made him unique.

Ostensibly, his poems did not look so different from the work of the Symbolists, who were dominating the literary scene: he was using fairly regular rhymes, a standard stanzaic design, and the length of his poems was quite ordinary—from sixteen to twenty-four lines. But by using these humble means of transportation he was taking his reader much farther than any of those cozy-because-vague metaphysicists who called themselves Russian Symbolists. As a movement, Symbolism was surely the last great one (and not only in Russia); yet poetry is an extremely individualistic art, it resents isms. The poetic production of Symbolism was as voluminous and seraphic as the enrollment and postulates of this movement were. This soaring upward was so groundless that graduate students, military cadets, and clerks felt tempted, and by the turn of the century the genre was compromised to the point of verbal inflation, somewhat like the situation with free verse in America today. Then, surely, devaluation as reaction came, bearing the names of Futurism, Constructivism, Imagism, and so forth. Still, these were isms fighting isms, devices fighting devices. Only two poets, Mandelstam and Tsvetaeva, came up with a qualitatively new content, and their fate reflected in its dreadful way the degree of their spiritual autonomy.

In poetry, as anywhere else, spiritual superiority is always disputed at the physical level. One cannot help thinking it was precisely the rift with the Symbolists (not entirely without anti-Semitic overtones) which contained the germs of Mandelstam's future. I am not referring so much to Georgi Ivanov's sneering at Mandelstam's poem in 1917, which was then echoed by the official ostracism of the thirties, as to Mandelstam's growing separation from any form of mass production, especially linguistic and psychological. The result was an effect in which the clearer a voice gets, the more dissonant it sounds. No choir likes it, and the aesthetic isolation acquires physical dimensions. When a man creates a world of his own, he becomes a foreign body against which all laws are aimed: gravity, compression, rejection, annihilation.

Mandelstam's world was big enough to invite all of these. I don't think that, had Russia chosen a different historical path, his fate would have been that much different. His world was too autonomous to merge. Besides, Russia went the way she did, and for Mandelstam, whose poetic development was rapid by itself, that direction could bring only one thing—a terrifying acceleration. This acceleration affected, first of all, the character of his verse. Its sublime, meditative, caesuraed flow changed into a swift, abrupt, pattering movement. His became a poetry of high velocity and exposed nerves, sometimes cryptic, with numerous leaps over the self-evident with somewhat abbreviated syntax. And yet in this way it became more a song than ever before, not a bardlike but a birdlike song, with its sharp, unpredictable turns and pitches, something like a goldfinch tremolo.

And like that bird, he became a target for all kinds of stones generously hurled at him by his motherland. It is not that Mandelstam opposed the political changes taking place in Russia. His sense of measure and his irony were enough to acknowledge the epic quality of the whole undertaking. Besides, he was a paganistically buoyant person, and, on the other hand, whining intonations were completely usurped by the Symbolist movement. Also, since the beginning of the century, the air was full of loose talk about a redivision of the world, so that when the Revolution came, almost everyone took what had occurred for what was desired. Mandelstam's was perhaps the only sober response to the events which shook the world and made so many thoughtful heads dizzy:

> *Well, let us try the cumbersome, the awkward,*
> *The screeching turning of the wheel . . .*
> (*from "The Twilight of Freedom"*)

But the stones were already flying, and so was the bird. Their mutual trajectories are fully recorded in the memoirs of the poet's widow, and they took two volumes. These books are not only a guide to his verse, though they are that too. But any poet, no matter how much he writes, expresses in his verse, physically or statistically speaking, at most one-tenth of his life's reality. The rest is normally shrouded in darkness; if any testimony by contemporaries survives, it contains gaping voids, not to mention the differing angles of vision that distort the object.

The memoirs of Osip Mandelstam's widow take care precisely of that, of those nine-tenths. They illuminate the darkness, fill in the voids, eliminate the distortion. The net result is close to a resurrection, except that everything that killed the man, outlived him, and continues to exist and gain popularity is also reincarnated, reenacted in these pages. Because of the material's lethal power, the poet's widow re-creates these elements with the care used in defusing a bomb. Because of this precision and because of the fact that through his verse, by the acts of his life, and by the quality of his death somebody called forth great prose, one would instantly understand—even without knowing a single line by Mandelstam—that it is indeed a great poet being recalled in these pages: because of the quantity and energy of the evil directed against him.

Still, it is important to note that Mandelstam's attitude toward a new historical situation wasn't at all that of outright hostility. On the whole he regarded it as just a harsher form of existential reality, as a qualitatively new challenge. Ever since the Romantics we have had this notion of a poet throwing down the glove to his tyrant. Now if there ever was such a time at all, this sort of action is utter nonsense today: tyrants do not make themselves available for such a tête-à-tête any longer. The distance between us and our masters can be reduced only by the latter, which seldom happens. A poet gets into trouble because of his linguistic, and, by implication, his psychological superiority, rather than because of his politics. A song is a form of linguistic disobedience, and its sound casts a doubt on a lot more than a concrete political system: it questions the entire existential order. And the number of its adversaries grows proportionally.

It would be a simplification to think that it was the poem against Stalin which brought about Mandelstam's doom. This poem, for all its destructive power, was just a byproduct of Mandelstam's treatment of the theme of this not-so-new era. For that matter, there's a much more devastating line in the poem called "Ariosto" written earlier the same year (1933): "Power is repulsive as are the barber's fingers . . ." There were plenty of others, too. And yet I think that by themselves these mug-slapping comments wouldn't invite the law of annihilation. The iron broom that was walking across Russia could have missed him if he were merely a political poet or a lyrical poet spilling here and there into politics. After all, he got his warning and he could have learned from that as many others did. Yet he didn't because his instinct for self-preservation had long since yielded to his aesthetics. It was the immense intensity of lyricism in Mandelstam's poetry which set him apart from his contemporaries and made him an orphan of his epoch, "homeless on an all-union scale." For lyricism is the ethics of language and the superiority of this lyricism to anything that could be achieved within human interplay, of whatever denomination, is what makes for a work of art and lets it survive. That is why the iron broom, whose purpose was the spiritual castration of the entire populace, couldn't have missed him.

It was a case of pure polarization. Song is, after all, restructured time, toward which mute space is inherently hostile. The first has been represented by Mandelstam; the second chose the state as its weapon. There is a certain terrifying logic in the location of that concentration camp where Osip Mandelstam died in 1938: near Vladivostok, in the very bowels of the state-owned space. This is about as far as one can get from Petersburg inside Russia. And here is how high one can get in poetry in terms of lyricism (the poem is in memory of a woman, Olga Vaksel, who reportedly died in Sweden, and was written while Mandelstam was living in Voronezh, where he was transferred from his previous place of exile near the Ural Mountains after having a nervous breakdown). Just four lines:

. . . And stiff swallows of round eyebrows (a)
flew (b) from the grave to me
to tell me they've rested enough in their (a)
cold Stockholm bed (b).

Imagine a four-foot amphibrach with alternating (*a b a b*) rhyme.

This strophe is an apotheosis of restructuring time. For one thing, language is itself a product of the past. The return of these stiff swallows implies both the recurrent character of their presence and of the simile itself, either as an intimate thought or as a spoken phrase. Also, "flew . . . to me" suggests spring, returning seasons. "To tell me they've rested enough," too, suggests past: past imperfect because not attended. And then the last line makes a full circle because the adjective "Stockholm" exposes the hidden allusion to Hans Christian Andersen's children's story about the wounded swallow wintering in the mole's hole, then recovering and flying home. Every schoolboy in Russia knows this story. The conscious process of remembering turns out to be strongly rooted in the subconscious memory and creates a sensation of sorrow so piercing, it's as if this is not a suffering man we hear but the very voice of his wounded psyche. This kind of voice surely clashes with everything, even with its medium's—i.e., poet's—life. It is like Odysseus tying himself to a mast against the call of his soul; this—and not only the fact that Mandelstam is married—is why he is so elliptical here.

He worked in Russian poetry for thirty years, and what he did will last as long as the Russian language exists. It will certainly outlast the present and any subsequent regime in that country, because of both its lyricism and its profundity. Quite frankly, I don't know anything in the poetry of the world comparable to the revelatory quality of these four lines from his "Verses on the Unknown Soldier," written just a year prior to his death:

An Arabian mess and a muddle,
The light of speeds honed into a beam—
And with its slanted soles,
A ray balances on my retina . . .

There is almost no grammar here but it is not a modernistic device, it is a result of an incredible psychic acceleration, which at other times was responsible for the breakthroughs of Job and Jeremiah. This honing of speeds is as much a self-portrait as an incredible insight into astrophysics. What he heard at his back "hurrying near" wasn't any "wingèd chariot" but his "wolf-hound century," and he ran till there was space. When space ended, he hit time.

Which is to say, us. This pronoun stands not only for his Russian- but also for his English-speaking readers. Perhaps more than anyone in this century, he was a poet of civilization: he contributed to what had inspired him. One may even argue that he became a part of it long before he met death. Of course he was a Russian, but not any more so than Giotto was an Italian. Civilization is the sum total of different cultures animated by a common spiritual numerator, and its main vehicle—speaking both metaphorically and literally—is translation. The wandering of a Greek portico into the latitude of the tundra is a translation.

His life, as well as his death, was a result of this civilization. With a poet, one's ethical posture, indeed one's very temperament, is determined and shaped by one's aesthetics. This is what accounts for poets finding themselves invariably at odds with the social reality, and their death rate indicates the distance which that reality puts between itself and civilization. So does the quality of translation.

A child of a civilization based on the principles of order and sacrifice, Mandelstam incarnated both; and it is only fair to expect from his translators at least a semblance of parity. The rigors involved in producing an echo, formidable though they may seem, are in themselves an homage to that nostalgia for the world culture which drove and fashioned the original. The formal aspects of Mandelstam's verse are not the product of some backward poetics but, in effect, columns of the aforesaid portico. To remove them is not only to reduce one's own "architecture" to heaps of rubble and shacks: it is to lie about what the poet has lived and died for.

Translation is a search for an equivalent, not for a substitute. It requires stylistic, if not psychological, congeniality. For instance, the stylistic idiom that could be used in translating Mandelstam is that of the late Yeats (with whom he has much in common thematically as well). The trouble of course is that a person who can master such an idiom—if such a person exists—will no doubt prefer to write his own verse anyway and not rack his brains over translation (which doesn't pay that well besides). But apart from technical skills and even psychological congeniality, the most crucial thing that a translator of Mandelstam should possess or else develop is a like-minded sentiment for civilization.

Mandelstam is a formal poet in the highest sense of the word. For him, a poem begins with a sound, with "a sonorous molded shape of form," as he himself called it. The absence of this notion reduces even the most accurate rendition of his imagery to a stimulating read. "I alone in

Russia work from the voice, while all round the unmitigated muck scribbles," says Mandelstam of himself in his "Fourth Prose." This is said with the fury and dignity of a poet who realized that the source of his creativity conditioned its method.

It would be futile and unreasonable to expect a translator to follow suit: the voice one works from and by is bound to be unique. Yet the timbre, pitch, and pace reflected in the verse's meter are approachable. It should be remembered that verse meters in themselves are kinds of spiritual magnitudes for which nothing can be substituted. They cannot be replaced even by each other, let alone by free verse. Differences in meters are differences in breath and in heartbeat. Differences in rhyming pattern are those of brain functions. The cavalier treatment of either is at best a sacrilege, at worst a mutilation or a murder. In any case, it is a crime of the mind, for which its perpetrator—especially if he is not caught—pays with the pace of his intellectual degradation. As for the readers, they buy a lie.

Yet the rigors involved in producing a decent echo are too high. They excessively shackle individuality. Calls for the use of an "instrument of poetry in our own time" are too strident. And translators rush to find substitutes. This happens primarily because such translators are themselves usually poets, and their own individuality is dearest of all to them. Their conception of individuality simply precludes the possibility of sacrifice, which is the primary feature of mature individuality (and also the primary requirement of any—even a technical—translation). The net result is that a poem of Mandelstam's, both visually and in its texture, resembles some witless Neruda piece or one from Urdu or Swahili. If it survives, this is due to the oddity of its imagery, or of its intensity, acquiring in the eyes of the reader a certain ethnographic significance. "I don't see why Mandelstam is considered a great poet," said the late W. H. Auden. "The translations that I've seen don't convince me of it."

Small wonder. In the available versions, one encounters an absolutely impersonal product, a sort of common denominator of modern verbal art. If they were simply bad translations, that wouldn't be so bad. For bad translations, precisely because of their badness, stimulate the reader's imagination and provoke a desire to break through or abstract oneself from the text: they spur one's intuition. In the cases at hand this possibility is practically ruled out: these versions bear the imprint of self-assured, insufferable stylistic provincialism; and the only optimistic remark one can make regarding them is that such low-quality art is an unquestionable sign of a culture extremely distant from decadence.

Russian poetry on the whole, and Mandelstam in particular, does not deserve to be treated as a poor relation. The language and its literature, especially its poetry, are the best things that that country has. Yet it is not concern for Mandelstam's or Russia's prestige that makes one shudder at what has been done to his lines in English: it is rather a sense of plundering the English-language culture, of degrading its own criteria, of dodging the spiritual challenge. "O.K.," a young American poet or reader of poetry may conclude after perusing these volumes, "the same thing goes on over there in Russia." But what goes on over there is not at all the same thing. Apart from her metaphors, Russian poetry has set an example of moral purity and firmness, which to no small degree has been reflected in the preservation of so-called classical forms without any damage to content. Herein lies her distinction from her Western sisters, though in no way does one presume to judge whom this distinction favors most. However, it is a distinction, and if only for purely ethnographic reasons, that quality ought to be preserved in translation and not forced into some common mold.

A poem is the result of a certain necessity: it is inevitable, and so is its form. "Necessity," as the poet's widow Nadezhda Mandelstam says in her "Mozart and Salieri" (which is a must for everyone interested in the psychology of creativity), "is not a compulsion and is not the curse of determinism, but is a link between times, if the torch inherited from forebears has not been trampled." Necessities of course cannot be echoed; but a translator's disregard for forms which are illumined and hallowed by time is nothing but stamping out that torch. The only good thing about the theories put forth to justify this practice is that their authors get paid for stating their views in print.

As though it is aware of the fragility and treachery of man's faculties and senses, a poem aims at human memory. To that end, it employs a form which is essentially a mnemonic device allowing one's brain to retain a world—and simplifying the task of retaining it—when the rest of one's frame gives up. Memory usually is the last to go, as if it were trying to keep a record of the going itself. A poem thus may be the last thing to leave one's drooling lips. Nobody expects a native English speaker to mumble at that moment verses of a Russian poet. But if he mumbles something by Auden or Yeats or Frost he will be closer to Mandelstam's originals than current translators are.

In other words, the English-speaking world has yet to

hear this nervous, high-pitched, pure voice shot through with love, terror, memory, culture, faith—a voice trembling, perhaps, like a match burning in a high wind, yet utterly inextinguishable. The voice that stays behind when its owner is gone. He was, one is tempted to say, a modern Orpheus: sent to hell, he never returned, while his widow dodged across one-sixth of the earth's surface, clutching the saucepan with his songs rolled up inside, memorizing them by night in the event they were found by Furies with a search warrant. These are our metamorphoses, our myths.

1977

Nadezhda Mandelstam (1899–1980) An Obituary

Of the eighty-one years of her life, Nadezhda Mandelstam spent nineteen as the wife of Russia's greatest poet in this century, Osip Mandelstam, and forty-two as his widow. The rest was childhood and youth. In educated circles, especially among the literati, being the widow of a great man is enough to provide an identity. This is especially so in Russia, where in the thirties and in the forties the regime was producing writers' widows with such efficiency that in the middle of the sixties there were enough of them around to organize a trade union.

"Nadya is the most fortunate widow," Anna Akhmatova used to say, having in mind the universal recognition coming to Osip Mandelstam at about that time. The focus of this remark was, understandably, her fellow poet, and right though she was, this was the view from the outside. By the time this recognition began to arrive, Mme Mandelstam was already in her sixties, her health extremely precarious and her means meager. Besides, for all the universality of that recognition, it did not include the fabled "one-sixth of the entire planet," i.e., Russia itself. Behind her were already two decades of widowhood, utter deprivation, the Great (obliterating any personal loss) War, and the daily fear of being grabbed by the agents of State Security as a wife of an enemy of the people. Short of death, anything that followed could mean only respite.

I met her for the first time precisely then, in the winter of 1962, in the city of Pskov, where together with a couple of friends I went to take a look at the local churches (the finest, in my view, in the empire). Having learned about our intentions to travel to that city, Anna Akhmatova suggested we visit Nadezhda Mandelstam, who was teaching English at the local pedagogical institute, and gave us several books for her. That was the first time I heard her name: I didn't know that she existed.

She was living in a small communal apartment consisting of two rooms. The first room was occupied by a woman whose name, ironically enough, was Nyetsvetaeva (literally: Non-Tsvetaeva), the second was Mme Mandelstam's. It was eight square meters large, the size of an average American bathroom. Most of the space was taken up by a cast-iron twin-sized bed; there were also two wicker chairs, a wardrobe chest with a small mirror, and an all-purpose bedside table, on which sat plates with the leftovers of her supper and, next to the plates, an open paperback copy of *The Hedgehog and the Fox*, by Isaiah Berlin. The presence of this red-covered book in this tiny cell, and the fact that she didn't hide it under the pillow at the sound of the doorbell, meant precisely this: the beginning of respite.

The book, as it turned out, was sent to her by Akhmatova, who for nearly half the century remained the closest friend of the Mandelstams: first of both of them, later of Nadezhda alone. Twice a widow herself (her first husband, the poet Nikolai Gumilyov, was shot in 1921 by the Cheka—the maiden name of the KGB; the second, the art historian Nikolai Punin, died in a concentration camp belonging to the same establishment), Akhmatova helped Nadezhda Mandelstam in every way possible, and during the war years literally saved her life by smuggling Nadezhda into Tashkent, where some of the writers had been evacuated, and by sharing with her the daily rations. Even with her two husbands killed by the regime, with her son languishing in the camps for eighteen years, Akhmatova was somewhat better off than Nadezhda Mandelstam, if only because she was recognized, however reluctantly, as a writer, and was allowed to live in Leningrad and Moscow. For the wife of an enemy of the people big cities were simply off limits.

For decades this woman was on the run, darting through the back waters and provincial towns of the big empire, settling down in a new place only to take off at the first sign of danger. The status of nonperson gradually became her second nature. She was a small woman, of slim build, and with the passage of years she shriveled more and more, as though trying to turn herself into something weightless, something easily pocketed in the moment of flight. Similarly, she had virtually no possessions: no furniture, no art objects, no library. The books, even foreign books, never stayed in her hands for long: after being read or glanced through they would be passed on to someone else—the way it ought to be with books. In the years of her utmost affluence, at the end of the sixties and the beginning of the seventies, the most expensive item in her one-room apartment on the outskirts of Moscow was a cuckoo clock on the kitchen wall.

A thief would be disillusioned here; so would those with a search warrant.

In those "affluent" years following the publication in the West of her two volumes of memoirs* that kitchen became the place of veritable pilgrimages. Nearly every other night the best of what survived or came to life in the post-Stalin era in Russia gathered around the long wooden table, which was ten times bigger than the bedstead in Pskov. It almost seemed that she was about to make up for decades of being a pariah. I doubt, though, that she did, and somehow I remember her better in that small room in Pskov, or sitting on the edge of a couch in Akhmatova's apartment in Leningrad, where she would come from time to time illegally from Pskov, or emerging from the depth of the corridor in Shklovsky's apartment in Moscow, where she perched before she got a place of her own. Perhaps I remember that more clearly because there she was more in her element as an outcast, a fugitive, "the beggar-friend," as Osip Mandelstam calls her in one of his poems, and that is what she remained for the rest of her life.

There is something quite breathtaking in the realization that she wrote those two volumes of hers at the age of sixty-five. In the Mandelstam family it is Osip who was the writer; she wasn't. If she wrote anything before those volumes, it was letters to her friends or appeals to the Supreme Court. Nor is hers the case of someone reviewing a long and eventful life in the tranquillity of retirement. Because her

* Translated as *Hope Against Hope* and *Hope Abandoned* (both published by Atheneum, in 1970 and 1973, and translated by Max Hayward).

sixty-five years were not exactly normal. It's not for nothing that in the Soviet penal system there is a paragraph specifying that in certain camps a year of serving counts for three. By this token, the lives of many Russians in this century came to approximate in length those of biblical patriarchs—with whom she had one more thing in common: devotion to justice.

Yet it wasn't this devotion to justice alone that made her sit down at the age of sixty-five and use her time of respite for writing these books. What brought them into existence was a recapitulation, on the scale of one, of the same process that once before had taken place in the history of Russian literature. I have in mind the emergence of great Russian prose in the second half of the nineteenth century. That prose, which appears as though out of nowhere, as an effect without traceable cause, was in fact simply a spin-off of the nineteenth century's Russian poetry. It set the tone for all subsequent writing in Russian, and the best work of Russian fiction can be regarded as a distant echo and meticulous elaboration of the psychological and lexical subtlety displayed by the Russian poetry of the first quarter of that century. "Most of Dostoevsky's characters," Anna Akhmatova used to say, "are aged Pushkin heroes, Onegins and so forth."

Poetry always precedes prose, and so it did in the life of Nadezhda Mandelstam, and in more ways than one. As a writer, as well as a person, she is a creation of two poets with whom her life was linked inexorably: Osip Mandelstam and Anna Akhmatova. And not only because the first was her husband and the second her lifelong friend. After all, forty years of widowhood could dim the happiest memories (and in the case of this marriage they were few and far between, if only because this marriage coincided with the economic devastation of the country, caused by revolution, civil war, and the first five-year plans). Similarly, there were years when she wouldn't see Akhmatova at all, and a letter would be the last thing to confide to. Paper, in general, was dangerous. What strengthened the bond of that marriage as well as of that friendship was a technicality: the necessity to commit to memory what could not be committed to paper, i.e., the poems of both authors.

In doing so in that "pre-Gutenberg epoch," in Akhmatova's words, Nadezhda Mandelstam certainly wasn't alone. However, repeating day and night the words of her dead husband was undoubtedly connected not only with comprehending them more and more but also with resurrecting his very voice, the intonations peculiar only to him, with a however fleeting sensation of his presence, with the realization that he kept his part of that "for better or for worse" deal, especially its second half. The same went for the poems of the physically often absent Akhmatova, for, once set in motion, this mechanism of memorization won't come to a halt. The same went for other authors, for certain ideas, for ethical principles—for everything that couldn't survive otherwise.

And gradually those things grew on her. If there is any substitute for love, it's memory. To memorize, then, is to restore intimacy. Gradually the lines of those poets became her mentality, became her identity. They supplied her not only with the plane of regard or angle of vision; more importantly, they became her linguistic norm. So when she set out to write her books, she was bound to gauge—by that time already unwittingly, instinctively—her sentences against theirs. The clarity and remorselessness of her pages, while reflecting the character of her mind, are also inevitable stylistic consequences of the poetry that had shaped that mind. In both their content and style, her books are but a postscript to the supreme version of language which poetry essentially is and which became her flesh through learning her husband's lines by heart.

To borrow W. H. Auden's phrase, great poetry "hurt" her into prose. It really did, because those two poets' heritage could be developed or elaborated upon only by prose. In poetry they could be followed only by epigones. Which has happened. In other words, Nadezhda Mandelstam's prose was the only available medium for the language itself to avoid stagnation. Similarly, it was the only medium available for the psyche formed by those poets' use of language. Her books, thus, were not so much memoirs and guides to the lives of two great poets, however superbly they performed these functions; these books elucidated the consciousness of the nation. Of the part of it, at least, that could get a copy.

Small wonder, then, that this elucidation results in an indictment of the system. These two volumes by Mme Mandelstam indeed amount to a Day of Judgment on earth for her age and for its literature—a judgment administered all the more rightfully since it was this age that had undertaken the construction of earthly paradise. A lesser wonder, too, that these memoirs, the second volume especially, were not liked on either side of the Kremlin Wall. The authorities, I must say, were more honest in their reaction than the intelligentsia: they simply made possession of these books an offense punishable by law. As for the intelligentsia, especially in Moscow, it went into actual turmoil over Nadezhda Mandelstam's charges against many of its illustrious and not so illustrious members of virtual complicity with the regime, and the human flood in her kitchen significantly ebbed.

There were open and semi-open letters, indignant resolutions not to shake hands, friendships and marriages collapsing over whether she was right or wrong to consider this or that person an informer. A prominent dissident declared, shaking his beard: "She shat on our entire generation"; others would rush to their dachas and lock themselves up there, to tap out antimemoirs. This was already the beginning of the seventies, and some six years later these same people would become equally split over Solzhenitsyn's attitude toward the Jews.

There is something in the consciousness of literati that cannot stand the notion of someone's moral authority. They resign themselves to the existence of a First Party Secretary, or of a Führer, as to a necessary evil, but they would eagerly question a prophet. This is so, presumably, because being told that you are a slave is less disheartening news than being told that morally you are a zero. After all, a fallen dog shouldn't be kicked. However, a prophet kicks the fallen dog not to finish it off but to get it back on its feet. The resistance to those kicks, the questioning of a writer's assertions and charges, come not from the desire for truth but from the intellectual smugness of slavery. All the worse, then, for the literati when the authority is not only moral but also cultural—as it was in Nadezhda Mandelstam's case.

I'd like to venture here one step further. By itself reality isn't worth a damn. It's perception that promotes reality to meaning. And there is a hierarchy among perceptions (and, correspondingly, among meanings), with the ones acquired through the most refined and sensitive prisms sitting at the top. Refinement and sensitivity are imparted to such a prism by the only source of their supply: by culture, by civilization, whose main tool is language. The evaluation of reality made through such a prism—the acquisition of which is one goal of the species—is therefore the most accurate, perhaps even the most just. (Cries of "Unfair!" and "Elitist!" that may follow the aforesaid from, of all places, the local campuses must be left unheeded, for culture is "elitist" by definition, and the application of democratic principles in the sphere of knowledge leads to equating wisdom with idiocy.)

It's the possession of this prism supplied to her by the best Russian poetry of the twentieth century, and not the uniqueness of the size of her grief, that makes Nadezhda Mandelstam's statement about her piece of reality unchallengeable. It's an abominable fallacy that suffering makes for greater art. Suffering blinds, deafens, ruins, and often kills. Osip Mandelstam was a great poet *before* the revolution. So was Anna Akhmatova, so was Marina Tsvetaeva. They would have become what they became even if none of the historical events that befell Russia in this century had taken place: because they were *gifted.* Basically, talent doesn't need history.

Would Nadezhda Mandelstam have become what she became had it not been for the Revolution and all the rest that followed? Probably not, for she met her future husband in 1919. But the question itself is immaterial; it leads us into the murky domains of the law of probability and of historical determinism. After all, she became what she became not because of what took place in Russia in this century but rather in spite of it. A casuist's finger will surely point out that from the point of view of historical determinism "in spite of" is synonymous with "because." So much then for historical determinism, if it gets so mindful about the semantics of some human "in spite of."

For a good reason, though. For a frail woman of sixty-five turns out to be capable of slowing down, if not averting in the long run, the cultural disintegration of a whole nation. Her memoirs are something more than a testimony to her times; they are a view of history in the light of conscience and culture. In that light history winces, and an individual realizes his choice: between seeking that light's source and committing an anthropological crime against himself.

She didn't mean to be so grand, nor did she simply try to get even with the system. For her it was a private matter, a matter of her temperament, of her identity and what had shaped that identity. As it was, her identity had been shaped by culture, by its best products: her husband's poems. It's them, not his memory, that she was trying to keep alive. It's to them, and not to him, in the course of forty-two years that she became a widow. Of course she loved him, but love itself is the most elitist of passions. It acquires its stereoscopic substance and perspective only in the context of culture, for it takes up more space in the mind than it does in the bed. Outside of that setting it falls flat into one-dimensional fiction. She was a widow to culture, and I think she loved her husband more at the end than on the day they got married. That is probably why readers of her books find them so haunting. Because of that, and because the status of the modern world vis-à-vis civilization also can be defined as widowhood.

If she lacked anything, it was humility. In that respect she was quite unlike her two poets. But then they had their art, and the quality of their achievements provided them with enough contentment to be, or to pretend to be, humble. She was terribly opinionated, categorical, cranky, disagreeable, idiosyncratic; many of her ideas were half-baked or developed on the basis of hearsay. In short, there was a great deal of one-upwomanship in her, which is not surprising given the size of the figures she was reckoning with in reality and later in imagination. In the end, her intolerance drove a lot of people away, but that was quite all right with her, because she was getting tired of adulation, of being liked by Robert McNamara and Willy Fisher (the real name of Colonel Rudolf Abel). All she wanted was to die in her bed, and, in a way, she looked forward to dying, because "up there I'll again be with Osip." "No," replied Akhmatova, upon hearing this. "You've got it all wrong. Up there it's now me who is going to be with Osip."

Her wish came true, and she died in her bed. Not a small thing for a Russian of her generation. There undoubtedly will surface those who will cry that she misunderstood her epoch, that she lagged behind the train of history running into the future. Well, like nearly every other Russian of her generation, she learned only too well that that train running into the future stops at the concentration camp or at the gas chamber. She was lucky that she missed it, and we are lucky that she told us about its route. I saw her last on May 30, 1972, in that kitchen of hers, in Moscow. It was late afternoon, and she sat, smoking, in the corner, in the deep shadow cast by the tall cupboard onto the wall. The shadow was so deep that the only things one could make out were the faint flicker of her cigarette and the two piercing eyes. The rest—her smallish shrunken body under the shawl, her hands, the oval of her ashen face, her gray, ashlike hair—all were consumed by the dark. She looked like a remnant of a huge fire, like a small ember that burns if you touch it.

1981

The Power of the Elements

Along with air, earth, water, and fire, money is the fifth natural force a human being has to reckon with most often. This is one, if not the main, reason why today, one hundred years after Dostoevsky's death, his novels preserve their relevance. Given the modern world's economic vector, i.e., that of general impoverishment and leveling of living standards, this writer can be regarded as a prophetic phenomenon. For the best way to avoid mistakes in dealing with the future is to perceive it through the prism of poverty or guilt. As it was, Dostoevsky used both lenses.

In her diary, a fervent admirer of the writer, Elizaveta Stackenschneider, a St. Petersburg socialite whose house in the seventies and eighties of the last century was a veritable salon for literati, suffragettes, politicians, artists, etc., writes about Dostoevsky in 1880, i.e., a year before his death:

> . . . but he is a petit bourgeois, yes, a petit bourgeois. Not of the gentry, nor of the clergy, not a merchant, nor an odd ball, like an artist or scholar, but precisely a petit bourgeois. And yet this petit bourgeois is the most profound thinker and a writer of genius . . . Now he frequents the houses of the aristocracy and even those of the high nobility, and of course he

> bears himself with dignity, and yet the petit bourgeois in him trickles through. It can be spotted in certain traits, surfacing in private conversation, but most of all, in his works . . . in his depiction of big capital he will always regard 6,000 rubles as a vast amount of money.

Now this, of course, is not entirely accurate: a great deal more than six thousand rubles flies into Nastasya Filippovna's fireplace in *The Idiot.* On the other hand, in one of the most heartbreaking scenes in world literature—the scene no reader's conscience survives intact—Captain Snegiryov from *The Brothers Karamazov* stamps no more than two hundred rubles into a snowdrift. The point, however, is that those six thousand rubles (at present the equivalent of $20,000) could buy a year of decent living at the time.

What Mme Stackenschneider, a product of her epoch's social stratification, calls petit bourgeois is known today as middle class, as defined in terms of annual income and not social affiliation. In other words, the said amount means neither great riches nor screaming poverty, but a tolerable human condition: a condition that makes one human. Six thousand rubles is the monetary expression of a moderate, normal existence, and if it takes a petit bourgeois to comprehend this fact, hail to the petit bourgeois.

For a normal, human-like existence is what the majority of the human race aspires to. A writer who regards six thousand rubles as a vast amount of money operates, therefore, on the same physical and psychological plane as the majority of people; i.e., he deals with life on its own general terms, since, like every natural process, human life gravitates toward moderation. Conversely, a writer who belongs to the upper echelon of society or to its lower depths will invariably produce a somewhat distorted picture of existence, for, in either case, he would regard it at too sharp an angle. Criticism of society (which is a nickname for life) from either above or below may produce a great read; but it's only an inside job that can supply you with moral imperatives.

Furthermore, a middle-class writer's own position is precarious enough to make him view what goes on below with considerable keenness. Alternatively, the situation above, due to its physical proximity, lacks in celestial appeal. Numerically, to say the least, a middle-class writer deals with a greater variety of plights, increasing, by the same token, the size of his audience. In any case, this is one way to account for the wide readership enjoyed by Dostoevsky, as well as by Melville, Balzac, Hardy, Kafka, Joyce, Faulkner. It looks as if the equivalent of six thousand rubles ensures great literature.

The point is, however, that it is far harder to come into this money than to come into millions or to stay penniless, for there are simply more contenders for the norm than for extremes. Acquisition of the said amount, as well as of a half or a tenth of it, involves far greater convolutions of the human psyche than any get-rich scheme or any form of asceticism. In fact, the smaller the amount involved, the more one spends emotionally to acquire it. It's obvious then why Dostoevsky, for whose operation the intricacies of the human psyche were lock and stock, viewed six thousand rubles as a vast amount of money. To him, it meant a vast amount of human investment, a vast amount of nuance, a vast amount of literature. In short, it was not so much real as metaphysical money.

Almost without exception, all his novels are about people in narrow circumstances. This kind of material itself guarantees absorbing reading. However, what turned Dostoevsky into a great writer was neither the inevitable intricacy of his subject matter nor even the unique profundity of his mind and his capacity for compassion; it was the tool or, rather, the texture of the material he was using, i.e., the Russian language.

As intricacies go, this language, where nouns frequently find themselves sitting smugly at the very end of the sentence, whose main power lies not in the statement but in its subordinate clause, is extremely accommodating. This is not your analytical language of "either/or"—this is the language of "although." Like a banknote into change, every stated idea instantly mushrooms in this language into its opposite, and there is nothing its syntax loves to couch more than doubt and self-deprecation. Its polysyllabic nature (the average length of a Russian word is three to four syllables) reveals the elemental, primeval force of the phenomena covered by a word a lot better than any rationalization possibly could, and a writer sometimes, instead of developing his thought, stumbles and simply revels in the word's euphonic contents, thereby sidetracking his issue in an unforeseen direction. And in Dostoevsky's writing we witness an extraordinary friction, nearly sadistic in its intensity, between the metaphysics of the subject matter and that of the language.

He made the most of Russian's irregular grammar. His sentences have a feverish, hysterical, idiosyncratic pace and their lexical content is an all but maddening fusion of belles-lettres, colloquialisms, and bureaucratese. True, he never wrote at leisure. Much like his characters, he worked to make ends meet: there were always either creditors or a deadline. Still, for a man beset with deadlines, he was extraordinarily digressive, and those digressions, I venture to say, were prompted more by the language than by the requirements of a plot. Reading him simply makes one realize that stream of consciousness springs not from consciousness but from a word which alters or redirects one's consciousness.

No, he was not a victim of the language; but his treatment of the human psyche was by far too inquisitive for the Russian Orthodox he claimed to be, and it is syntax rather than the creed that is responsible for the quality of that treatment. Every writing career starts as a personal quest for sainthood, for self-betterment. Sooner or later, and as a rule quite soon, a man discovers that his pen accomplishes a lot more than his soul. This discovery very often creates an unbearable schism within an individual and is, in part, responsible for the demonic reputation literature enjoys in certain witless quarters. Basically, it's just as well, for the seraphim's loss nearly always is the mortal's gain. Besides, either extreme, in itself, is quite boring, and in a work of a good writer we always hear a dialogue of the spheres with the gutter. If it doesn't destroy the man or his manuscript (as in the case of Gogol's Part II of *Dead Souls*), this schism is precisely what creates a writer, whose job therefore becomes making his pen catch up with his soul.

This is what Dostoevsky was all about, except that his pen was pushing his soul beyond the confines of his creed, Russian Orthodoxy. For to be a writer means invariably to be a Protestant or, to say the least, to employ the Protestant conception of man. While either in Russian Orthodoxy or in Roman Catholicism man is judged by the Almighty or

His Church, in Protestantism it is the man who subjects himself to a personal equivalent of the Last Judgment. In doing so, he is far more merciless toward himself than the Deity, or even than the Church, if only because he knows himself better (so he thinks) than does either, and is unwilling or, to be precise, unable to forgive. Since no writer writes for his parish alone, a literary character and his deeds should be given a fair trial. The more thorough the investigation, the greater the verisimilitude, and verisimilitude is what a writer is, in the first place, after. In literature, Grace doesn't count for much; that's why Dostoevsky's holy man stinks.

Of course, he was a great defender of the "good cause," the cause of Christianity. But come to think of it, there hardly ever was a better devil's advocate. From classicism, he took the principle that before you come forth with your argument, however right or righteous you may feel, you have to list all the arguments of the opposite side. And it is not that in the process of listing them one is being swayed by the opposite side; it is simply that the listing itself is a mightily absorbing process. One may not in the end drift away from one's original stance, but after having exhausted all the arguments on behalf of evil, one utters the creed's dictums with nostalgia rather than with fervor. This, in its own way, also fosters the case of verisimilitude.

But it is not for the sake of verisimilitude only that this writer's heroes bare their souls with an almost Calvinistic tenacity before the reader. There is something else that forces Dostoevsky to turn their lives inside out and undo every fold and wrinkle of their mental dirty linen; and it is not the quest for truth either. For the results of his inquisition show more than truth; they reveal the very fabric of life, and that this fabric is shabby. The force that drives him to do it is the omnivorousness of his language which eventually comes to a point where it cannot be satisfied with God, man, reality, guilt, death, infinity, salvation, air, earth, water, fire, money; and then it takes on itself.

1980

*The Sound of the Tide**

Because civilizations are finite, in the life of each of them comes a moment when centers cease to hold. What keeps them at such times from disintegration is not legions but languages. Such was the case with Rome, and before that, with Hellenic Greece. The job of holding at such times is done by the men from the provinces, from the outskirts. Contrary to popular belief, the outskirts are not where the world ends—they are precisely where it unravels. That affects a language no less than an eye.

Derek Walcott was born on the island of Saint Lucia, in the parts where "the sun, tired of empire, declines." As it does, however, it heats up a far greater crucible of races and cultures than any melting pot north of the equator. The realm this poet comes from is a real genetic Babel; English, however, is its tongue. If at times Walcott writes in Creole patois, it's not to flex his stylistic muscle or to enlarge his audience but as a homage to what he spoke as a child—before he spiraled the tower.

Poets' real biographies are like those of birds, almost identical— their real data are in the way they sound. A poet's biography is in his vowels and sibilants, in his meters, rhymes, and metaphors. Attesting to the miracle of exis-

* This piece originally appeared as the introduction to *Poems of the Caribbean* by Derek Walcott (Limited Editions Club, 1983).

tence, the body of one's work is always in a sense a gospel whose lines convert their writer more radically than his public. With poets, the choice of words is invariably more telling than the story line; that's why the best of them dread the thought of their biographies being written. If Walcott's origins are to be learned, the pages of this selection are the best guide. Here's what one of his characters tells about himself, and what may well pass for the author's self-portrait:

> *I'm just a red nigger who love the sea,*
> *I had a sound colonial education,*
> *I have Dutch, nigger, and English in me,*
> *and either I'm nobody, or I'm a nation.*

This jaunty four-liner informs us about its writer as surely as does a song—saving you a look out the window—that there is a bird. The dialectal "love" tells us that he means it when he calls himself "a red nigger." "A sound colonial education" may very well stand for the University of the West Indies, from which Walcott graduated in 1953, although there is a lot more to this line, which we'll deal with later. To say the least, we hear in it both scorn for the very locution typical of the master race and the pride of the native in receiving that education. "Dutch" is here because by blood Walcott is indeed part Dutch and part English. Given the nature of the realm, though, one thinks not so much about blood as about languages. Instead of—or along with—"Dutch" there could have been French, Hindu, Creole patois, Swahili, Japanese, Spanish of some Latin American denomination, and so forth—anything that one heard in the cradle or in the streets. The main thing is, there was English.

The way this third line arrives at "English in me" is remarkable in its subtlety. After "I have Dutch," Walcott throws in "nigger," sending the whole line into a jazzy downward spin, so that when it swings up to "and English in me" we get a sense of terrific pride, indeed of grandeur, enhanced by this syncopatic jolt between "English" and "in me." And it's from this height of "having English," to which his voice climbs with the reluctance of humility and yet with certitude of rhythm, that the poet unleashes his oratorial power in "either I'm nobody, or I'm a nation." The dignity and astonishing vocal power of this statement are in direct proportion to both the realm in whose name he speaks and the oceanic infinity that surrounds it. When you hear such a voice, you know; the world unravels. This is what the author means when he says that he "love the sea."

For the almost forty years that Walcott has been at it, at this loving the sea, critics on both its sides have dubbed him "a West Indian poet" or "a black poet from the Caribbean." These definitions are as myopic and misleading as it would be to call the Saviour a Galilean. This comparison is appropriate if only because every reductive tendency stems from the same terror of the infinite; and when it comes to an appetite for the infinite, poetry often bests creeds. The mental as well as spiritual cowardice, obvious in these attempts to render this man a regional writer, can be further explained by the unwillingness of the critical profession to admit that the great poet of the English language is a black man. It can also be attributed to completely busted helixes or bacon-lined retinae. Still, its most benevolent explanation is, of course, a poor knowledge of geography.

For the West Indies is a huge archipelago, about five

times as big as the Greek one. If poetry is to be defined by the subject matter alone, Mr. Walcott would have ended up with material five times superior to that of the bard who wrote in the Ionian dialect and who, too, loved the sea. Indeed, if there is a poet Walcott seems to have a lot in common with, it's nobody English but rather the author of the *Iliad* and the *Odyssey*, or else the author of *On the Nature of Things.* For Walcott's descriptive powers are truly epic; what saves his lines from the corresponding tedium, though, is the shortage of the realm's actual history and the quality of his ear for the English language, whose sensibility in itself is a history.

Quite apart from the matter of his own unique gifts, Walcott's lines are so resonant and stereoscopic precisely because this "history" is eventful enough: because language itself is an epic device. Everything this poet touches mushrooms with reverberations and perspectives, like magnetic waves whose acoustics are psychological, whose implications are echo-like. Of course, in that realm of his, in the West Indies, there is plenty to touch—the natural kingdom alone provides a great deal of fresh material. But here's an example of how this poet deals with the most *de rigueur* of all poetic subjects—with the moon—which he makes speak for itself:

Slowly my body grows a single sound,
slowly I become
a bell,
an oval, disembodied vowel,
I grow, an owl,
an aureole, white fire.

(*from "Metamorphoses, I/Moon"*)

And here's how he himself speaks *about* this most unpalpable poetic subject—or rather, here's what makes him speak about it:

> *a moon ballooned up from the Wireless Station. O*
> *mirror, where a generation yearned*
> *for whiteness, for candour, unreturned.*
>
> (*from* Another Life)

The psychological alliteration that almost forces the reader to see both of the Moon's *o*'s suggests not only the recurrent nature of this sight but also the repetitive character of looking at it. A human phenomenon, the latter is of a greater significance to this poet, and his description of those who do the looking and of their reasons for it astonishes the reader with its truly astronomical equation of black ovals to the white one. One senses here that the Moon's two *o*'s have mutated via the two *l*'s in "ballooned" into the two *r*'s of "O mirror," which, true to their consonant virtue, stand for "*r*esisting *r*eflection"; that the blame is being put neither on nature nor on people but on language and time. It's the redundance of these two, and not the author's choice, that is responsible for this equation of black and white—which takes better care of the racial polarization this poet was born to than all his critics with their professed impartiality are capable of.

To put it simply, instead of reductive racial self-assertion, which no doubt would have endeared him to both his foes and his champions, Walcott identifies himself with that "disembodied vowel" of the language which both parts of his equation share. The wisdom of this choice is, again, not so much his own as the wisdom of his language—

better still, the wisdom of its letter: of black on white. He is simply a pen that is aware of its movement, and it is this self-awareness that forces his lines into their graphic eloquence:

> *Virgin and ape, maid and malevolent Moor,*
> *their immortal coupling still halves our world.*
> *He is your sacrificial beast, bellowing, goaded,*
> *a black bull snarled in ribbons of its blood.*
> *And yet, whatever fury girded*
> *on that saffron-sunset turban, moon-shaped sword*
> *was not his racial, panther-black revenge*
> *pulsing her chamber with raw musk, its sweat,*
> *but horror of the moon's change,*
> *of the corruption of an absolute,*
> *like a white fruit*
> *pulped ripe by fondling but doubly sweet.*
>
> (*from "Goats and Monkeys"*)

This is what "sound colonial education" amounts to; this is what having "English in me" is all about. With equal right, Walcott could have claimed having in him Greek, Latin, Italian, German, Spanish, Russian, French: because of Homer, Lucretius, Ovid, Dante, Rilke, Machado, Lorca, Neruda, Akhmatova, Mandelstam, Pasternak, Baudelaire, Valéry, Apollinaire. These are not influences—they are the cells of his bloodstream, no less so than Shakespeare or Edward Thomas are, for poetry is the essence of world culture. And if world culture feels more palpable among urine-stunted trees through which "a mud path wriggles like a snake in flight," hail to the mud path.

And so Walcott's lyric hero does. Sole guardian of the

civilization grown hollow in the center, he stands on this mud path watching how "the fish plops, making rings/ that marry the wide harbour" with "clouds curled like burnt-out papers at their edges" above it, with "telephone wires singing from pole to pole / parodying perspective." In his keensightedness this poet resembles Joseph Banks, except that by setting his eyes on a plant "chained in its own dew" or on an object, he accomplishes something no naturalist is capable of—he animates them. To be sure, the realm needs it, not any less so than does the poet in order to survive there. In any case, the realm pays back, and hence lines like:

> *Slowly the water rat takes up its reed pen*
> *and scribbles leisurely, the egret*
> *on the mud tablet stamps its hieroglyph* . . .

This is more than naming things in the garden—this is also a bit later. Walcott's poetry is Adamic in the sense that both he and his world have departed from Paradise—he, by tasting the fruit of knowledge; his world, by political history.

"Ah brave third world!" he exclaims elsewhere, and a lot more goes into this exclamation than simple anguish or exasperation. This is a comment of language upon a greater than purely local failure of nerves and imagination; a semantic reply to the meaningless and abundant reality, epic in its shabbiness. Abandoned, overgrown airstrips, dilapidated mansions of retired civil servants, shacks covered with corrugated iron, single-stack coastal vessels coughing like "relics out of Conrad," four-wheeled corpses escaped from their junkyard cemeteries and rattling their bones past condominium pyramids, helpless or corrupt politicos and young ignoramuses trigger-happy to replace them and babbling revolutionary garbage, "sharks with well-pressed fins / ripping we small fry off with razor grins"; a realm where "you bust your brain before you find a book," where if you turn on the radio, you may hear the captain of a white cruise boat insisting that a hurricane-stricken island reopen its duty-free shop no matter what, where "the poor still poor, whatever arse they catch," where one sums up the deal the realm got by saying "we was in chains, but chains made us unite, / now who have, good for them, and who blight, blight," and where "beyond them the firelit mangrove swamps, / ibises practicing for postage stamps."

Whether accepted or rejected, the colonial heritage remains a mesmerizing presence in the West Indies. Walcott seeks to break its spell neither by plunging "into incoherence of nostalgia" for a nonexistent past nor by eking himself a niche in the culture of departed masters (into which he wouldn't fit in the first place because of the scope of his talent). He acts out of the belief that language is greater than its masters or its servants, that poetry, being its supreme version, is therefore an instrument of self-betterment for both; i.e., that it is a way to gain an identity superior to the confines of class, race, or ego. This is just plain common sense; this is also the most sound program of social change there is. But then poetry is the most democratic art —it always starts from scratch. In a sense, a poet is indeed like a bird that chirps no matter what twig it alights on, hoping there is an audience, even if it's only the leaves.

About these "leaves"—lives—mute or sibilant, faded or

immobile, about their impotence and surrender, Walcott knows enough to make you look sideways from the page containing:

Sad is the felon's love for the scratched wall,
beautiful the exhaustion of old towels,
and the patience of dented saucepans
seems mortally comic . . .

And you resume the reading only to find:

. . . I know how profound is the folding of
a napkin
by a woman whose hair will go white . . .

For all its disheartening precision, this knowledge is free of modernistic despair (which often only disguises one's shaky sense of superiority) and is conveyed in tones as level as its source. What saves Walcott's lines from hysterical pitch is his belief that:

. . . time that makes us objects, multiplies
our natural loneliness . . .

which results in the following "heresy":

. . . God's loneliness moves in His smallest
creatures.

No "leaf," neither up here nor in the tropics, would like to hear this sort of thing, and that's why they seldom clap to this bird's song. Even a greater stillness is bound to follow after:

All of the epics are blown away with leaves,
blown with careful calculations on brown paper,
these were the only epics: the leaves . . .

The absence of response has done in many a poet, and in so many ways, the net result of which is that infamous equilibrium—or tautology—between cause and effect: silence. What prevents Walcott from striking a more than appropriate, in his case, tragic pose is not his ambition but his humility, which binds him and these "leaves" into one tight book: ". . . yet who am I . . . under the heels of the thousand / racing towards the exclamation of their single name, / Sauteurs! . . ."

Walcott is neither a traditionalist nor a modernist. None of the available -isms and the subsequent -ists will do for him. He belongs to no "school": there are not so many of them in the Caribbean, save those of fish. One would feel tempted to call him a metaphysical realist, but then realism is metaphysical by definition, as well as the other way around. Besides, that would smack of prose. He can be naturalistic, expressionistic, surrealistic, imagistic, hermetic, confessional—you name it. He simply has absorbed, the way whales do plankton or a paintbrush the palette, all the stylistic idioms the North could offer; now he is on his own, and in a big way.

His metric and genre versatility is enviable. In general, however, he gravitates to a lyrical monologue and to a narrative. That, and the tendency to write in cycles, as well as his verse plays, again suggest an epic streak in this poet, and perhaps it's time to take him up on that. For almost forty years his throbbing and relentless lines kept arriving in the English language like tidal waves, coagulating into an archipelago of poems without which the map of modern literature would effectively match wallpaper. He gives us more than himself or "a world"; he gives us a sense of infinity embodied in the language as well as in the ocean which is always present in his poems: as their background or foreground, as their subject, or as their meter.

To put it differently, these poems represent a fusion of two versions of infinity: language and ocean. The common parent of these two elements is, it must be remembered, time. If the theory of evolution, especially that part of it that suggests we all came from the sea, holds any water, then both thematically and stylistically Derek Walcott's poetry is the case of the highest and most logical evolvement of the species. He was surely lucky to be born at this outskirt, at this crossroads of English and the Atlantic where both arrive in waves only to recoil. The same pattern of motion—ashore, and back to the horizon—is sustained in Walcott's lines, thoughts, life.

Open this book and see ". . . the grey, iron harbour / open on a sea-gull's rusty hinge," hear how ". . . the sky's window rattles / at gears raked into reverse," be warned that "At the end of the sentence, rain will begin. / At the rain's edge, a sail . . ." This is the West Indies, this is that realm which once, in its innocence of history, mistook the lantern of a caravel for a light at the end of a tunnel and paid for that dearly—it was a light at the tunnel's entrance. This sort of thing happens often, to archipelagoes as well as to individuals; in this sense, every man is an island. If, nevertheless, we must register this experience as West Indian and call this realm the West Indies, let's do so, but let's also clarify that we have in mind the place discovered by Columbus, colonized by the British, and immortalized by Walcott. We may add, too, that giving a place a status of lyrical reality is a more imaginative as well as a more generous act than discovering or exploiting something that was created already.

1983

A Poet and Prose

The tradition of dividing literature into poetry and prose dates from the beginnings of prose, since it was only in prose that such a distinction could be made. Ever since, poetry and prose have customarily been regarded as separate areas—or, better yet, spheres—of literature wholly independent of each other. To say the least, "prose poems," "rhythmical prose," and the like indicate a derivative mentality, a polarized rather than integral perception of literature as a phenomenon. Curiously enough, such a view of things has by no means been imposed upon us by criticism from without. This view is, above all, the fruit of the guild approach to literature taken by literati themselves.

The concept of equality is extrinsic to the nature of art, and the thinking of any man of letters is hierarchical. Within this hierarchy poetry occupies a higher position than prose, and the poet, in principle, is higher than the prose writer. This is true not so much because poetry is in fact older than prose, but because a poet in narrow circumstances can sit down and produce a piece; whereas in similar straits a prose writer would hardly give thought to a poem. Even if the prose writer has what it takes to write a decent verse text, he knows full well that poetry pays a lot worse, and more slowly than prose.

With few exceptions, all the more or less eminent writers of recent times have paid their dues to verse. Some, like Nabokov, for example, have tried to the very end to convince themselves and those around them that even if they were not primarily poets, they were poets all the same. Most of them, however, after once yielding to the temptation of poetry, never addressed themselves to it again except as readers; still, they remained deeply grateful for the lessons in laconism and harmony it taught them. In twentieth-century literature the only case of an outstanding prose writer becoming a great poet is that of Thomas Hardy. In general, however, it can be said that the prose writer without active experience in poetry is prone to prolixity and grandiloquence.

What does a writer of prose learn from poetry? The dependence of a word's specific gravity on context, focused thinking, omission of the self-evident, the dangers that lurk within an elevated state of mind. And what does the poet learn from prose? Not much: attention to detail, the use of common parlance and bureaucratese, and, in rare instances, compositional know-how (the best teacher of which is music). All three of these, however, can be gleaned from the experience of poetry itself (especially from Renaissance poetry), and theoretically—but only theoretically—a poet can get along without prose.

And only theoretically can he get along without writing prose. Need or a reviewer's ignorance, not to mention ordinary correspondence, will sooner or later force him to write in run-on lines, "like everyone else." But apart from these, a poet has other reasons, which we will attempt to examine here. In the first place, one fine day a poet may simply get an urge to write something in prose. (The inferiority complex that the prose writer suffers vis-à-vis the poet doesn't automatically imply the poet's superiority complex vis-à-vis the prose writer. The poet often deems the latter's work much more serious than his own, which he may not even always regard as work.) Moreover, there are subjects that can be treated only in prose. A narrative involving more than three characters resists almost every poetic form except the epos. Reflections on historical themes, as well as childhood remembrances (in which the poet indulges to the same degree as ordinary mortals do), in turn look more natural in prose. *The History of the Pugachev Rebellion, The Captain's Daughter**—what could be more gratifying subjects for romantic poems! And especially in the era of Romanticism . . . However, what happens in the end is that the novel in verse is replaced more and more often by "verses from a novel."† No one knows how much poetry loses when a poet turns to prose; it is quite certain, though, that prose profits from it greatly.

The prose works of Marina Tsvetaeva explain this better than anything else. To paraphrase Clausewitz, prose for Tsvetaeva was nothing but the continuation of poetry by other means (which, in fact, is what prose historically is). Everywhere—in her diary entries, essays on literature, fictionalized reminiscences—that is just what we encounter: the resetting of the methodology of poetic thinking into a prose text, the growth of poetry into prose. Tsvetaeva's

* Prose works by Pushkin.

† Allusions to Pushkin's novel in verse, *Eugene Onegin*, and to the poems concluding Pasternak's novel, *Doctor Zhivago*.

sentence is constructed not so much in accordance with the principle of subject followed by predicate as through the use of specifically poetic technology: sound association, root rhyme, semantic enjambment, etc. That is, the reader is constantly dealing not with a linear (analytic) development but with a crystalline (synthesizing) growth of thought. Perhaps no better laboratory can be found for analyzing the psychology of poetic creation, inasmuch as all stages of the process are shown at extremely close range, verging on the starkness of caricature.

"Reading," says Tsvetaeva, "is complicity in the creative process." This most certainly is the statement of a poet; Leo Tolstoy would not have said such a thing. In this statement a sensitive or at least a reasonably alert ear can distinguish a note of despair, greatly muffled by authorial (and feminine at that) pride, coming specifically from a poet sorely fatigued by the ever-widening rift—growing with each additional line—between author and audience. And in the poet's turning to prose, that *a priori* "normal" form of communication with a reader, there is always a touch of slackening tempo, shifting gear, trying to make oneself clear, to explain things. For without complicity in the creative process there is no comprehension: what is comprehension if not complicity? As Whitman said: "Great poetry is possible only if there are great readers." In turning to prose, and dismantling almost every other word of it into component parts, Tsvetaeva shows her reader what a word, a thought, a phrase consists of; she tries, often against her own will, to draw the reader closer to her: to make him equally great.

There is still another explanation of the methodology of Tsvetaeva's prose. Since the day that the narrative genre first came into being, every form of it—short story, tale, novel—has dreaded one thing: the charge of being unconvincing. Hence either a striving for realism, or structural mannerisms. In the final analysis, every writer strives for the same thing: to regain or hold back time past or current. Toward this end a poet has at his disposal caesura, unaccented feet, dactylic endings; a prose writer has nothing of the kind. Turning to prose, Tsvetaeva quite unconsciously transfers to it the dynamics of poetic language—essentially the dynamics of song—which is in itself a form of restructured time. (If only because a verse line is short; each word in it, frequently each syllable, is subjected to a double or triple semantic burden. A multiplicity of meanings presupposes a corresponding number of attempts to comprehend, that is, several takes; and what is a *take* if not a unit of time?) Tsvetaeva, however, is not particularly concerned about how convincing the language of her prose is: whatever the topic of her narrative, its technology remains the same. Furthermore, her narrative in a strict sense is plotless and is held together mainly by the energy of monologue. But all the same, unlike professional prose writers and other poets who have resorted to prose, she does not submit to the genre's aesthetic inertia: she imposes her own technology on it, she imposes herself. This is not a result of an obsession with her own self, the belief generally held; instead it comes from an obsession with intonation, which is far more important to her than either poem or story.

Verisimilitude in a narrative may be a result of complying with the genre's requirements; the same effect may also be ascribed to the timbre of the voice that does the narrating. In the latter case both the plausibility of the story line and the story line itself recede into the background of the listener's consciousness (i.e., into parentheses), as the author's dues paid to the proprieties of the genre. What stand outside the parentheses are the timbre of the voice and its intonation. To create this effect on the stage requires supplementary gestures; on paper—that is, in prose—it is achieved by the device of dramatic arrhythmia, which is most often brought about by interspersing nominative sentences among a mass of complex ones. In this alone one can see elements of borrowing from poetry. Yet Tsvetaeva, who doesn't have to borrow anything from anyone, starts with the utmost structural compactness of language and ends with it as well. The degree of linguistic expressiveness of her prose, given the minimal use of typographical means, is remarkable. Let us recall the author's stage direction describing Casanova in her play *Casanova's End*: "Not starlike—tsarlike" (*Ne barstvenen—tsarstvenen*). Let us now try to imagine what space this would have taken in Chekhov. At the same time, this is not a result of intentional economy—of paper, words, or effort—but a by-product of the poet's instinctive laconism.

Extending poetry into prose, Tsvetaeva does not obliterate the boundary existing between them in the popular consciousness; instead, she shifts it into hitherto syntactically inaccessible linguistic spheres—upward. And prose, where the danger of a stylistic dead end is much greater than in poetry, only benefits from this shift: there, in the rarefied air of her syntax, Tsvetaeva imparts to it an acceleration that leads to a change in the very notion of inertia. "Telegraphic style," "stream of consciousness," "the art of subtext," and so forth, bear no relation to the above. The works of her contemporaries, not to mention authors of subsequent decades whose production begs for such definitions, can be read seriously mainly for nostalgic reasons, or else for literary history (which is about the same) considerations. The literature created by Tsvetaeva is a literature of "supertext"; if her consciousness "streams," it follows a channel of ethics. The only way in which her style approaches the telegraphic is through her principal punctuation mark, the dash, identifying proximity of phenomena as well as leaps across the self-evident. That dash does serve one more purpose, though: it crosses out a great deal in Russian literature of the twentieth century.

2

"Marina often begins a poem on high C," Anna Akhmatova said. The same thing can be said, to a certain degree, about Tsvetaeva's intonation in prose as well. Such was the character of her voice that her speech almost always begins at the other end of the octave, in the highest register, at its uppermost limit, after which only descent or, at best, a plateau is conceivable. However, the timbre of her voice was so tragic that it ensured a sensation of rising no matter how long the sound lasted. This tragic quality was not exactly a product of her life experience; it existed prior to it. Her experience only coincided with it, responded to it, like an echo. This timbre is already clearly distinguishable in her *Juvenilia* (a collection of lyrics written between 1913 and 1915):

> *Lines of my poetry, so early written*
> *That I knew not I was a poet yet . . .*

This, already, is not so much an accounting as a discounting of oneself. Her life experience could do nothing but follow the voice, permanently lagging behind it, for the voice was overtaking events—after all, it had the speed of sound. On the whole, experience always lags behind anticipation.

Yet the issue here is not only that of experience lagging behind anticipation; it is a question of the differences between art and reality. One of them is that in art, owing to the properties of the material itself, it is possible to attain a degree of lyricism that has no physical equivalent in the real world. Nor, in the same way, does there exist in the real world an equivalent of the tragic in art, which (the tragic) is the reverse of lyricism—or the stage that follows it. No matter how dramatic a person's direct experience is, it is always exceeded by the experience of an instrument. Yet a poet is a combination of an instrument and a human being in one person, with the former gradually taking over the latter. The sensation of this takeover is responsible for timbre; the realization of it, for destiny.

Perhaps this may partly explain why a poet turns to prose, especially to autobiographical prose. In Tsvetaeva's case, it is certainly not an attempt to reset history—too late for that; it is, rather, a withdrawal from reality into prehistory, into childhood. However, this is not the "when-nothing-is-known-yet" childhood of a certified memoirist. It is the "when-everything-is-already-known" but "nothing-has-begun-yet" childhood of the mature poet caught up in the middle of her life by a brutal era. Autobiographical prose—prose in general—in this case is just a breather. Like any respite, it is lyrical and temporary. (This sensation—of respite and its accompanying qualities—is quite evident in most of her essays on literature, along with the strong autobiographical element. Because of it, her essays prove to be "literature within literature" to a much greater extent than all modern "textual criticism of text.") In essence, all of Tsvetaeva's prose, except for her diary entries, is retrospective, for only after taking a glance backward is it possible to pause for breath.

The role of detail in this kind of prose thus becomes similar to the role of the very flow of the prose itself, slackened in comparison with poetic speech. This role is purely therapeutic; it is the role of a straw at which we all know who clutches. The more detailed the description, the more obvious the need for the straw. In general: the more a work of this kind is constructed in the "Turgenev mode," the more avant-garde are the author's own "modifiers" of time, place, and manner. Even the punctuation takes on an added burden. Thus, a period that completes a narrative denotes its physical end, a boundary, a precipice plummeting into reality, into nonliterature. The unavoidability and proximity of this precipice, which are controlled by the narrative itself, make the author's striving for perfection within the allotted bounds ten times as great and, in part, even simplifies his task, forcing him to discard everything superfluous.

The discarding of the superfluous is in itself the first cry of poetry—the beginning of the predominance of sound over reality, of essence over existence: the source of tragic consciousness. Along this path Tsvetaeva went farther than anyone in Russian and, it would seem, world literature. In Russian literature, at least, she has occupied a place extremely apart from all—including the most remarkable—of her contemporaries, fenced off from them by a wall built of discarded excess. The only one who proves to be near her—and precisely as a prose writer—is Osip Mandelstam. The parallel relationship between Tsvetaeva and Mandelstam as prose writers is indeed remarkable. Mandelstam's *The Noise of Time* and *The Egyptian Stamp* can be put on a par with Tsvetaeva's *Autobiographical Prose*; his essays in *On Poetry* and "A Conversation about Dante" with her literary essays; and Mandelstam's *Journey to Armenia* and "Fourth Prose" with Tsvetaeva's *Pages from a Diary*. The stylistic similarity—plotlessness, retrospectivity, linguistic and metaphorical density—is clearly even greater than the similarity of genre and theme, although Mandelstam is somewhat more traditional.

It would be a mistake, however, to try to explain this closeness of style and genre by the similarity of the two authors' biographies or by the general climate of the era. Biographies are never known in advance, just as "climate" and "era" are strictly transitory notions. The basic element of similarity between the prose works of Tsvetaeva and Mandelstam is their purely linguistic oversaturation perceived as emotional oversaturation and quite often reflecting it. In the "thickness" of writing, density of images, sentence dynamics, they are so close that it is possible to suspect if not blood ties then cliquishness, adherence to the same *ism*. But while Mandelstam was in fact an Acmeist, Tsvetaeva never belonged to any group, and even the bravest of her critics never ventured so far as to attach a label to her. The key to the similarity between Tsvetaeva and Mandelstam in prose lies in the same place as the reason for their difference as poets: in their relation to language, or more precisely, in the degree of their dependence on the same.

Poetry is not "the best words in the best order"; for language it is the highest form of existence. In purely technical terms, of course, poetry amounts to arranging words with the greatest specific gravity in the most effective and externally inevitable sequence. Ideally, however, it is language negating its own mass and the laws of gravity; it is language's striving upward—or sideways—to that beginning where the Word was. In any case, it is movement of language into pre- (supra-) genre realms, that is, into the spheres from which it sprang. The seemingly most artificial forms for organizing poetic language—terza rima, sestinas, decimas, and so forth—are in fact nothing more than a natural, reiterative, fully detailed elaboration of the echo that followed the original Word. Consequently, Mandelstam, outwardly a more formal poet than Tsvetaeva, needed prose that spared him from echo, from the power of repeated sound, not a whit less than she did, with her extrastanzaic—on the whole, extraverse—thinking, and with her principal strength lying in the subordinate clause, in word-root dialectics.

Any uttered word requires some sort of continuation. It can be continued in various ways: logically, phonetically, grammatically, in rhyme. This is the way a language develops, and if not logic, then phonetics indicates that language needs development. For what has been uttered is never the end but the edge of speech, which—owing to the existence of time—is always followed by something. And what follows is always more interesting than what has already been said—and no longer on account of time but, rather, in spite of it. Such is the logic of speech, and such is the basis of Tsvetaeva's poetics. She never has enough space: either in a poem or in prose. Even her most scholarly-sounding essays are always like elbows protruding from a small room. A poem is constructed on the principle of the complex sentence; prose consists of grammatical enjambments: that is how she escapes tautology. (For invention in prose plays the same role with respect to reality as rhyme in a poem.) The most awful thing about service to the Muses is precisely that it does not tolerate repetition—either of metaphor, subject, or device. In everyday life, to tell the same joke two or three times is not a crime. One cannot, however, allow oneself to do that on paper; language forces you to take the next step—at least stylistically. Not for the sake of your inner well-being, of course (though subsequently it does prove to be for its sake as well), but for the sake of language's own stereoscopic (-phonic) well-being. A cliché is a safety valve by means of which art protects itself from the danger of degeneration.

The more often a poet takes this next step, the more isolated a position he finds himself in. The process of elimination, in the final analysis, usually turns against a person who overuses the method. And if we were not speaking of Tsvetaeva, it might be possible to see in a poet's turning to prose a kind of literary *nostalgie de la boue*, a desire to merge with the (writing) mass, to become, at last, "like everyone else." We are considering, however, a poet who knew from the very beginning what she was headed for, or—where language led. We are dealing with the author of the lines: "A poet starts his speaking from afar. / The speaking takes the speaker far . . ."* We are dealing with the author of "The Pied Piper." Prose for Tsvetaeva is by no means a refuge; it is not a form of emancipation—either psychological or stylistic. For her, prose is a witting expansion of her sphere of isolation, that is, of the possibilities of language.

3

This is, in fact, the sole direction in which a self-respecting writer can move. (In essence, all existing art is already a cliché: precisely because it *already* exists.) And insofar as literature is the linguistic equivalent of thinking, Tsvetaeva, taken extraordinarily far by speech, proves to be the most interesting thinker of her time. Any generalized description of any person's views, especially if they have been expressed in artistic form, inevitably tends toward caricature; any attempt to approach analytically a phenomenon whose nature is synthetic is doomed by definition. Nonetheless, without running any particular risk one can define Tsvetaeva's system of views as a philosophy of discomfort, as a plea for the cause not so much of borderline situations as of existence on the edge. This position can be called neither stoic—since it was dictated above all by reasons of an aesthetico-linguistic nature—nor existentialist—since it is precisely the denial of reality that makes up its substance. On a philosophical level there is no evidence of her having either forerunners or successors. As for contemporaries, if it were not for the absence of documentary evidence, it would

* Opening lines of "The Poet" (1923).

be natural to assume a thorough knowledge of Lev Shestov's works. There is no such evidence, alas; or the sum of it is quite insignificant. The only Russian thinker (or rather, ponderer) whose influence on her work—though only in its early stage—Marina Tsvetaeva openly acknowledged is Vasily Rozanov. But if indeed there was such influence, it should be recognized as strictly stylistic, however, since there is nothing more polar to Rozanov's lack of discrimination than the brutal, at times almost Calvinistic, spirit of personal responsibility that pervades the work of the mature Tsvetaeva.

Many things determine consciousness besides being* (the prospect of nonbeing, in particular). One of them is language. The self-pitilessness that makes one think of Calvin (and whose obverse is Tsvetaeva's often unwarranted generosity in evaluating the work of her fellow writers) is not only the product of upbringing, but is—and this first of all—the reflection or continuation of the professional relationship between the poet and her language. With regard to upbringing, however, it is important to remember that Tsvetaeva's was trilingual, with Russian and German predominant. Certainly, it was not a matter of choice: her native tongue was Russian. But a child who reads Heine in the original becomes instructed, willingly or not, in deductive "seriousness and honor/ in the West, from an alien family."† Bearing an outwardly strong resemblance to the striving for truth, the striving for precision is by nature linguistic; that is, it is rooted in language, has its source in the word. The process of elimination mentioned above,

* Karl Marx: "Being [existence] determines consciousness."
† From Mandelstam's poem "To the German Tongue" (1932).

the need to discard the superfluous—which has reached, or rather been brought to, the level of instinct—is one of the means through which this striving is pursued. In the case of a poet, this striving often takes on an idiosyncratic quality, inasmuch as to the poet phonetics and semantics are, with few exceptions, identical.

This identity imparts to consciousness so much acceleration that it carries its possessor beyond the parentheses of any *polis* a lot sooner and farther than suggested by this or that energetic Plato. But that is not all. Any emotion that accompanies this imaginary or—more frequently—real relocation is edited by that identity; and the form—as well as the very fact—of the expression of that emotion proves to be aesthetically dependent on the said identity. In a more general sense, ethics slip into a dependence on aesthetics. A remarkable feature of Tsvetaeva's work is precisely the absolute independence of her moral valuations that exists along with such a phenomenally heightened linguistic sensitivity. One of the best examples of the struggle between ethical principle and linguistic determinism is her 1932 essay "The Poet and Time": it is a duel in which no one is killed and both parties are victorious. This essay, one of the most crucial for an understanding of Tsvetaeva's work, affords one of the most trenchant examples of a semantic frontal attack on the positions occupied in our consciousness by abstract categories (in this instance, on the idea of time). An indirect gain achieved by such maneuvers is that the literary language receives training in breathing the rarefied atmosphere of abstract concepts, while the latter acquire the flesh of phonetics and morality.

Represented on a graph, Tsvetaeva's work would exhibit a curve—nay, a straight line—rising at almost a right angle because of her constant endeavor to raise the pitch a note higher, an idea higher. (Or, more precisely, an octave and faith higher.) She always carries everything she has to say to its conceivable and expressible end. In either her verse or her prose nothing remains hanging in the air or leaves a feeling of ambivalence. Tsvetaeva is that unique case in which the paramount spiritual experience of an epoch (in this instance, the sense of ambivalence, of the contradictoriness of the nature of human existence) served not as the object of expression but as its means; whereupon it was transformed into the material of art. That a poet resorts to prose, which creates the illusion of a more consistent development of thought than poetry does, is in itself a kind of indirect proof that the paramount spiritual experience is not so paramount; that experiences of a higher nature are possible, and that a reader can be taken by the hand by prose and delivered to where he would otherwise have to be shoved by a poem.

This last consideration—the notion of concern for the reader—should be taken into account if merely because it is our only chance to squeeze Tsvetaeva into the tradition of Russian literature, with its main tendency toward consoling, toward justifying (on the highest level, if possible) reality and the existing order of things in general. Or else, it turns out that the "gray wolf" who keeps looking to the "thick woods of Eternity" no matter how much time you feed it, the mouthpiece or the ear of the voice of "heavenly truth versus earthly truth," i.e., Tsvetaeva, who cares for nothing in between, really stands all alone in Russian literature, very, very much off by herself. An unwillingness to accept reality, motivated not only by ethics but by aesthetics as well, is something unusual in Russian literature.

This, of course, can be attributed to the quality of reality itself, within the Russian homeland and without; but the problem undoubtedly lies elsewhere. Most likely, the problem is that the new semantics required new phonetics, and Tsvetaeva provided it. In her, Russian letters found a dimension that hitherto had not been intrinsic to it: she demonstrated language's own self-interest in tragic subject matter. In this dimension justification or acceptance of reality is out of the question if only because the existing order of things is tragic in purely phonetic terms. According to Tsvetaeva, the very sound of speech is prone to the tragical and, in a way, even profits from it: as in a lament. No wonder, then, that for a literature so steeped in didactical positivism that the expression "to begin with well-wishing but end with 'Ashes to ashes'" is considered a formula for deviation from the norm, Tsvetaeva's work proved to be something novel, with all the ensuing personal consequences. Tsvetaeva's biography differs favorably only from the biographies of those of her contemporaries who perished earlier.

But what was a novelty for letters was not one for the national psyche. Of the entire pleiad of great twentieth-century Russian poets, with the exception of Nikolai Klyuev, Tsvetaeva stands closest to folklore, and the style of the lament provides one of the keys to understanding her work. Leaving aside the decorative, not to say drawing-room, aspect of folklore, which was so successfully elaborated by, again, Klyuev, Tsvetaeva was compelled by force of circumstance to resort to that device which is the essential element of folklore: unaddressed speech. In both her verse and her prose we constantly hear a monologue—not the monologue of a heroine, but a monologue as a consequence of having no one to talk to.

The characteristic feature of this kind of speech is that the speaker is also the listener. Folklore—a shepherd's song—is speech intended for the self, for itself: the ear heeds the mouth. Thus, through self-audition language achieves self-cognition. But no matter how or through what one accounts for the genealogy of Tsvetaeva's poetics, the degree of responsibility placed on the reader's consciousness by its fruits exceeded—and exceeds to this day—the degree of the Russian reader's preparedness to accept this responsibility (with the demand for which the difference between folklore and authored literature presumably starts). Even protected by the armor of dogma or by the no less sturdy armor of absolute cynicism, he proves defenseless against the intensity of art lighting up his conscience. The inevitability of the presumably ruinous effect that this entails is understood more or less equally by both the shepherds and the flock itself, and to this day Tsvetaeva's collected works do not exist either outside or inside the country in the language of whose people she wrote. Theoretically, the dignity of a nation degraded politically cannot be seriously wounded by obliterating its cultural heritage. Russia, however, in contrast to nations blessed with a legislative tradition, elective institutions, and so forth, is in a position to understand herself only through literature, and to retard the literary process by disposing of or treating as nonexistent the works of even a minor author is tantamount to a genetic crime against the future of the nation.

Whatever the reasons that moved Tsvetaeva to turn to prose and regardless of how much Russian poetry consequently lost, one can only be grateful to Providence that such a turn took place. Moreover, poetry has in fact hardly lost; if it did lose something with respect to form, it remained true to itself in terms of energy and essence, i.e., it preserved its substance. Every author expands upon—even by means of repudiating—the postulates, the idioms, the aesthetics of his predecessors. Turning to prose, Tsvetaeva was expanding upon herself—she was a reaction to her own self. Her isolation was not premeditated but enforced, imposed from without: by the logic of language, by historical circumstances, by the quality of her contemporaries. By no means is she an esoteric poet—no more passionate voice ever sounded in Russian poetry of the twentieth century. Besides, esoteric poets don't write prose. The fact that she ended up, nevertheless, out of the mainstream of Russian literature was only for the better. Thus, a star, in a poem by her beloved Rilke translated by her no less beloved Pasternak, like the light in the window "of the last house at the parish's edge," only expands the parishioners' conception of the size of the parish.

(Translated by Barry Rubin)

1979

Footnote to a Poem

On February 7, 1927, in Bellevue, outside Paris, Marina Tsvetaeva finished "*Novogodnee*" ("New Year's Greetings"), in many respects a landmark not only in her own work but in Russian poetry as a whole. In terms of genre, the poem can be regarded as an elegy—that is, the most fully developed genre in poetry; and this classification would be proper were it not for certain attendant circumstances, one being that this is an elegy on the death of a poet.

Every "on the death of" poem, as a rule, serves not only as a means for an author to express his sentiments occasioned by a loss but also as a pretext for more or less general speculations on the phenomenon of death per se. In mourning his loss (be it the beloved, a national hero, a close friend, or a guiding light), an author by the same token frequently mourns—directly, obliquely, often unwittingly—himself, for the tragic timbre is always autobiographical. In other words, any "on the death of" poem contains an element of self-portrait. This element is all the more inevitable if the object of mourning happens to be a fellow writer with whom the author was linked by bonds—real or imaginary—too strong for the author to avoid the temptation of identifying with the poem's subject. In his struggle to resist such temptation the author is hampered by his sense of professional guild-like association, by the theme of death's own somewhat exalted status, and, finally, by the strictly personal, private experience of loss: something has been taken away from him; therefore, he must bear some relation to it. It may be that the only shortcoming of these wholly natural and otherwise respectable sentiments is that we learn more about the author and his attitude toward his own possible demise than about what actually happened to the other person. On the other hand, a poem is not a news report, and often a poem's tragic music alone informs us of what is happening more precisely than a detailed description can. Nevertheless, it is difficult, sometimes simply awkward, to combat the feeling that the writer is situated in regard to his subject as a spectator is to the stage, and that his own reaction (tears, not applause) is of greater consequence to him than the horror of what is taking place; that at best he simply occupies a seat in the front row of the orchestra.

Such are the costs of the genre, and from Lermontov to Pasternak Russian poetry bears witness to their inevitability. The only exception, perhaps, is Prince Vyazemsky and his "In Memoriam," written in 1837. Very likely, the inevitability of these costs, of this, in the end, self-mourning, at times bordering on self-admiration, can and even must be explained by the fact that the addressees were always, specifically, fellow writers; that the tragedy was occurring within native Russian literature, and self-pity was the reverse side of presumptuousness and an outgrowth of the sense of loneliness that increases with the passing of any poet and is, in any case, intrinsic to a writer. If, however, the subject was the demise of a preeminent figure belonging to another culture (the death of Byron or Goethe, for example), its very "foreignness" seemed to give added stimulus to the most general, abstract kind of discussion, viz.: of the role of the "bard" in the life of society, of art in general, of, as Akhmatova put it, "ages and peoples." Emotional distance in these cases engendered a didactic diffuseness, and some Byron or Goethe was not easily distinguishable from a Napoleon or from Italian Carbonari. The element of self-portrait in these instances naturally disappeared; for, paradoxical as it may seem, death, in spite of all its properties as a common denominator, did not lessen the distance between the author and the mourned "bard," but, on the contrary, increased it, as though an elegist's ignorance regarding the circumstances of the life of a particular "Byron" extended as well to the essence of that "Byron's" death. In other words, death, in its turn, was perceived as something foreign, alien—which may be perfectly justified as circumstantial evidence of its—death's—inscrutability. Especially since the inscrutability of a phenomenon or, at least, the feeling of mistrust toward the results of cognition is what constitutes the ethos of the age of Romanticism, in which the tradition of poems "on the death of a poet" originates, and by whose poetics it is still colored.

Tsvetaeva's "*Novogodnee*" has much less in common with this tradition and these poetics than does the virtual hero of the poem, Rainer Maria Rilke. As possibly the only thread connecting Tsvetaeva with Romanticism in this poem one ought to consider the fact that for Tsvetaeva "German is more native than Russian," i.e., that German was, on a par with Russian, the language of her childhood, which coincided with the end of the last century and the beginning of the present one, with all the consequences that nineteenth-century German literature entailed for a child. This thread is, to be sure, more than just a connective—which is something we shall dwell on again later. For a start, let us note that it was precisely her knowledge of German that Tsvetaeva had to thank for her relation to Rilke, whose death, thus, delivered an indirect blow—across the whole of her life—to her childhood.

For no other reason than that a child's attachment to a language (which is not native but *more native*) culminates in adulthood as reverence for poetry (i.e., the form of that language's highest degree of maturity), an element of self-portraiture in "*Novogodnee*" seems inevitable. "*Novogodnee,*" however, is more than a self-portrait, just as Rilke to Tsvetaeva is more than a poet. (Just as a poet's death is something more than a human loss. Above all, it is a drama of language as such: that of inadequacy of linguistic experience vis-à-vis existential experience.) Even irrespective of Tsvetaeva's personal feelings toward Rilke—extremely powerful ones that underwent an evolution from platonic love and stylistic dependence to an awareness of a certain equality—even irrespective of these feelings, the death of the great German poet created a situation in which Tsvetaeva could not confine herself to an attempt at a self-portrait. In order to understand—or even not understand—what had happened, she had to extend the limits of the genre and step up from the orchestra, as it were, onto the stage.

"*Novogodnee*" is above all a confession. In this regard one feels inclined to mention that Tsvetaeva is an extremely candid poet, quite possibly the most candid in the history of Russian poetry. She makes no secret of anything, least of all of her aesthetic and philosophical credos, which are scattered about her verse and prose with the frequency of a first person singular pronoun. The reader, therefore, turns out to be more or less prepared for Tsvetaeva's manner of speech in "*Novogodnee*"—the so-called lyrical monologue. What he is not at all prepared for, however, no matter how many times he may reread "*Novogodnee*," is the intensity of the monologue, the purely linguistic energy of this confession. And the point is not at all that "*Novogodnee*" is a poem, that is, a form of narration that requires, by definition, maximum condensation of speech, sharpening of the maximum focus. The point is that Tsvetaeva confesses not to a priest but to a poet. And on her scale of ranks a poet is higher than a priest to roughly the same degree as man, in standard theology, is higher than the angels, since the latter were not created in the image and likeness of the Almighty.

Paradoxical and blasphemous as it may seem, in the dead Rilke Tsvetaeva found what every poet seeks: the supreme listener. The widespread belief that a poet always writes for someone is only half justified and is fraught with numerous confusions. The best answer to the question "Whom do you write for?" was given by Igor Stravinsky: "For myself and for a hypothetical alter ego." Consciously or unconsciously, every poet in the course of his career engages in a search for an ideal reader, for that alter ego, since a poet seeks not recognition but understanding. Baratynsky long ago consoled Pushkin in a letter, saying that one shouldn't be particularly surprised "if the Hussars don't read us anymore." Tsvetaeva goes even further, and in her poem "Homesickness" she declares:

Nor shall I crave my native speech,
its milky call that comes in handy.
It makes no difference in which
tongue passers-by won't comprehend me.
(*Translated by Joseph Brodsky*)

This type of attitude toward things inevitably leads to a narrowing of the circle, which by no means always signifies an improvement in the quality of readers. A writer, however, is a democrat by definition, and the poet always hopes for some parallelism between the processes taking place in his own work and those in the consciousness of the reader. But the further a poet goes in his development, the greater—unintentionally—his demands are on an audience, and the narrower that audience is. The situation oftentimes ends with the reader becoming the author's projection, which scarcely coincides with any living creature at all. In those instances, the poet directly addresses either the angels, as Rilke does in the *Duino Elegies*, or another poet—especially one who is dead, as Tsvetaeva addresses Rilke. In both instances what takes place is a monologue, and in both instances it assumes an absolute quality, for the author addresses his words to nonexistence, to Chronos.

For Tsvetaeva, whose verse is distinctive for its almost pathological need to say, to think, to carry all things to their logical end, this was by no means a new destination. What turned out to be new—with the death of Rilke—was the fact that it turned out to be inhabited and for the poet in Tsvetaeva this could not but be of interest. To be sure, "*Novogodnee*" is the result of a particular emotional outburst; but Tsvetaeva is a maximalist, and the vector of her emotional movements is known in advance. Nevertheless, it is impossible to call Tsvetaeva a poet of extremes, if only because an extreme—whether deductive, emotional, or linguistic—is merely the point where, for her, a poem starts. "Going through life is not the same as walking across a field"* or "Odysseus returned full of space and time"† could never have been used as last lines in a poem of Tsvetaeva's; a poem of hers would have begun with these lines. Tsvetaeva is a poet of extremes only in the sense that for her an "extreme" is not so much the end of the known world as the beginning of the unknowable one. The technique of allusion, circumlocution, half-statement, or omission is characteristic of this poet to only a minute degree. Even less attributable to her is the use of the highest achievements of the rhythmic school, psychologically comforting to the reader with their lulling metrical pattern. Oversaturated with stresses, the harmony of Tsvetaeva's verse line is unpredictable; she leans more toward trochees and dactyls than toward the certitude of the iamb. The beginnings of her lines tend to be trochaic rather than stressed, the endings mournful, dactylic. It's hard to find another poet who has made such skillful and abundant use of caesura and truncated feet. In terms of form, Tsvetaeva is significantly more interesting than any of her contemporaries, including the Futurists, and her rhymes are more inventive than Pasternak's. Most importantly, however, her technical achievements have not been dictated by formal explorations but are by-products—that is, natural effects—of speech, for which the most significant thing is its subject.

* The last line of "Hamlet," by Boris Pasternak.

† The last line of "The Stream of Golden Honey Was Pouring . . ." by Osip Mandelstam.

Art, generally speaking, always comes into being as a result of an action directed outward, sideways, toward the attainment (comprehension) of an object having no immediate relationship to art. It is a means of conveyance, a landscape flashing in a window—rather than the conveyance's destination. "If you only knew," said Akhmatova, "what rubbish verse grows from . . ." The farther away the purpose of movement, the more probable the art; and, theoretically, death (anyone's, and a great poet's in particular, for what can be more removed from everyday reality than a great poet or great poetry?) turns into a sort of guarantee of art.

The theme of "Tsvetaeva and Rilke" has been, is, and will continue to be the subject of many investigations. What interests us is the role—or idea—of Rilke as the addressee in "*Novogodnee*," his role as the object of psychic movement and the extent of his responsibility for the by-product of that movement: a poem. Knowing Tsvetaeva's maximalism, one cannot but take note of how natural her choice of this subject is. Apart from the concrete, deceased Rilke, there appears in the poem an image (or idea) of an "absolute Rilke," who has ceased being a body in space and has become a soul—in eternity. This removal is an absolute, maximum removal. The feelings the poem's heroine has—i.e., love—toward their absolute object, a soul, are also absolute. What in addition proves to be absolute are the means of expressing this love: maximum selflessness and maximum candor. All this could not but create a maximum tension of poetic diction.

There is, however, a paradox in the fact that poetic language possesses—as does any language in general—its own particular dynamics, which impart to psychic movement an acceleration that takes the poet much farther than he imagined when he began the poem. Yet this is, in fact, the principal mechanism (temptation, if you will) of creative work; once having come in contact with it (or having succumbed to it), a person once and for all rejects other modes of thought, expression—conveyance. Language propels the poet into spheres he would not otherwise be able to approach, irrespective of the degree of psychic or mental concentration of which he might be capable beyond the writing of verse. And this propulsion takes place with unusual swiftness: with the speed of sound—greater than what is afforded by imagination or experience. As a rule, a poet is considerably older when he finishes a poem than he was at its outset. The maximum range of Tsvetaeva's diction in "*Novogodnee*" takes her much farther than the mere experience of loss could; possibly even farther than the soul of Rilke himself is capable of getting to in its posthumous wanderings. Not only because any thought of someone else's soul, as distinct from the soul itself, is less burdened than that soul by its deeds, but also because a poet, generally speaking, is more generous than an apostle. A poetic "paradise" is not limited to "eternal bliss," and it is not threatened with the overcrowding of a dogmatic paradise. In contrast to the standard Christian paradise that is presented as a kind of last instance, the soul's dead end, poetic paradise is, rather, a peak, and a bard's soul is not so much perfected as left in a continual state of motion. The poetic idea of eternal life on the whole gravitates more toward a cosmogony than toward theology, and what is often put forward as a measure of the soul is not the degree of its perfection essential for achieving likeness and merger with the Creator but rather the physical (metaphysical) duration and distance of its wanderings in time. In principle, the poetic conception of existence eschews any form of finiteness or stasis, including theological apotheosis. In any case, Dante's paradise is much more interesting than the ecclesiastical version of it.

Even if the loss of Rilke served Tsvetaeva only as "An Invitation to a Journey," it would be justified by the otherworldly topography of "*Novogodnee*." But this is not in fact the case, and Tsvetaeva does not replace Rilke the man with the "idea of Rilke" or with the idea of his soul. She would have been incapable of making such a replacement if only because that soul had already been embodied in Rilke's work. (On the whole, the not overly justifiable polarization of soul and body, a practice that is very commonly abused when a person dies, appears all the less convincing when we are dealing with a poet.) In other words, the poet invites the reader to follow his soul during the poet's lifetime, and Tsvetaeva, with regard to Rilke, was first of all a reader. The dead Rilke, consequently, is not particularly different for her from the living one, and she follows him in roughly the same way that Dante followed Virgil, with great justification in the fact that Rilke himself undertook similar journeys in his own work ("Requiem for a Lady Friend"). In brief, the next world has been sufficiently domesticated by the poetic imagination to warrant the assumption that self-pity or curiosity about the otherworldly might have served Tsvetaeva as motivation for "*Novogodnee*." The tragedy of "*Novogodnee*" lies in the separation, in the almost physical rupture of her psychological bond with Rilke, and she sets out on this "journey," not frightened by a Dantean leopard blocking her path, but by an awareness of abandonment, of being no longer able to follow him the way she did during his lifetime—following every line of his. And also—in addition to that abandonment—from a feeling of guilt: I'm alive, whereas he—the better one—is dead. But the love of one poet for another (even of the opposite sex) is not Juliet's love for Romeo: the tragedy lies not in that existence without him is unthinkable but precisely in that such an existence *is* thinkable. And as a consequence of this conceivability, the author's attitude toward herself, still living, is more merciless, more uncompromising. Therefore, when beginning to speak, and—if it ever comes to this—when beginning to speak of oneself, one does so as if confessing, for it is *he*—not a priest or God but another poet—who hears you. Hence the intensity of Tsvetaeva's diction in "*Novogodnee*," since she is addressing someone who, in contrast to God, has absolute pitch.

"*Novogodnee*" begins in typical Tsvetaeva fashion, at the far right—i.e., highest—end of the octave, on high C:

> *S Novym godom—svetom—kraem—krovom!*
> *Happy New Year—World/Light—Edge/Realm—*
> *Haven!*

—with an exclamation directed upward, outward. Throughout the entire poem this tonality, just like the very tenor of this speech, is unvarying: the only possible modification is not a lowering of the register (even in parentheses) but a raising of it. Imbued with this tonality, the device of the nominative sentence in this line creates an ecstatic effect, an effect of emotional soaring. This sensation is intensified by the outwardly synonymic enumeration, like ascending stairs (stages) with each step higher than the previous one. This enumeration, however, is synonymic only with respect to the number of syllables each word has, and Tsvetaeva's sign of equality (or inequality)—the dash—separates them more than a comma would: it thrusts each successive word upward beyond the one preceding it.

What is more, only the word *god* ("year") in *S Novym godom* ("Happy New Year") is used in its literal meaning; all the other words in this line are loaded—overloaded—with associations and figurative meanings. *Svet* ("world," "light") is used in a threefold meaning: first as "world," as in "New World," by analogy with "New Year"—i.e., geographically new. But this geography is the abstract one; Tsvetaeva more likely has in mind here something "at the back of beyond," rather than on the other side of the ocean: a certain outer limit. This understanding of a "new world" as another limit leads to the idea of the "next world," which in fact is the real issue. However, the "next world" is, first of all, *light*; for, owing to the drift of the line and the euphonic superiority (more piercing sound) of *svetom* over *godom*, it is located somewhere literally overhead, above, in the heavens, which are the source of light. The preceding and succeeding dashes, which nearly free the word from semantic obligations, equip *svet* with the entire arsenal of its positive allusions. At any rate, in the concept of "next world" emphasis falls tautologically on the aspect of the light rather than, as usual, of darkness.

Next, from the abstractly geographic *svet* the line acoustically and topographically flies upward toward the short, sob-like *krai* ("edge," "realm"): edge of the world, edge in general, heavenward, to paradise. *S novym . . . kraem* means, apart from everything else, "Happy new realm, happy new boundary, happy crossing of it." The line ends with the coda *s novym krovom* ("Happy new haven"), which is both phonetic and semantic, for the phonic substance of *krovom* is almost identical to that of *godom*. But these two syllables have already been raised a whole octave —eight syllables—above their original sound by *svetom* and *kraem*, and there is no way they can return either to the tonality of the beginning of the line or to its literalness. It's as though *krovom*, from higher up, were looking back upon itself in *godom*, unable to recognize either vowels or consonants. The consonants *kr* in *krovom* belong not so much to the word *krov* itself as to the word *krai*, and partly because of that the semantics of *krov* seems too rarefied: the word has been placed too high up. Its meaning as a refuge at the edge of the world and as a home to come back to, a haven, intertwines with the *krov* that means heaven: the universal heaven of the planet as well as the individual one, the last refuge of the soul.

Essentially, Tsvetaeva uses the trochaic pentameter here like a keyboard, a similarity made greater by the use of dashes instead of commas; the transition from one disyllable to another is achieved by a pianistic rather than a standard grammatical logic, and each successive exclamation, as when keys are pressed, starts up when the sound of the previous one dies out. However unconscious this device may be, it is eminently appropriate to the essence of the image developed in this line—of heaven with its levels accessible first to the eye, and after the eye, only to the spirit.

A strictly emotional impression that the reader gets from this line is the sensation of a pure voice soaring upward and, as it were, renouncing (relinquishing) itself. Yet it should be remembered that the first—if not the only—reader whom the author has in mind here is the very person to whom the poem is addressed: Rilke. Hence, the desire for self-renunciation, the urge to disavow everything worldly—that is, the psychology of confession. Naturally, all this—both the choice of words and the choice of tone—takes place so unwittingly that the concept of "choice" is inapplicable here. For art, especially poetry, differs from any other form of psychological activity precisely because in it everything—form, content, and the very spirit of the work—is picked out by ear.

The above by no means signifies intellectual irresponsibility. Exactly the opposite is the case: rational enterprise—choice, selection—is entrusted to hearing, or (putting it more clumsily but more accurately) is focused into hearing. In a certain sense, at issue is a miniaturization, a computerization of selective, that is, analytical, processes, a transformation or reduction of them to one organ—that of hearing.

But not only analytical functions are relegated by the poet to hearing; the same thing happens with the purely spiritual aspect of creativity. Picked out "by ear" is the very spirit of the work, whose vehicle or transmitter in a poem is its meter, for it is precisely meter that predetermines the tonality of the work. Anyone with some experience in composing verse knows that verse meter is the equivalent of a certain psychological state, at times not of just one state but of several. The poet "picks" his way toward the spirit of a work by means of the meter. Lurking within the use of standard meters is, of course, the danger of mechanical speech, and every poet overcomes that danger in his own way, and the more difficult the process of overcoming, the more detailed—both for himself and for the reader—becomes the picture of a given psychological state. Often the upshot is that the poet begins to perceive meters as animate—inspired in the archaic sense—entities, as certain sacred vessels. This is basically just. Form is even less separable from content in poetry than body is from soul, and what makes the body dear is precisely that it is mortal (in poetry the equivalent of death is mechanicalness of sound or the possibility of slipping into cliché). At any rate, every verse-maker has his own favorite, dominant meters, which could be regarded as his signatures, for they correspond to the most frequently repeated psychological state of the author. Trochees with feminine or—more often—dactylic endings may properly be considered Tsvetaeva's "signature." In the frequency of their use Tsvetaeva probably surpasses even Nekrasov. It's quite possible, however, that both poets resorted to trochaic meters in response to the glut of iambic trimeter and tetrameter common to the works of authors belonging both to the "Harmonic School" and to the Russian Symbolists. Tsvetaeva may have had an added psychological reason: in the Russian trochee one can always hear folklore. This was known by Nekrasov as well; yet his trochees echo with the narrative tone of the *bylina* (epic song), whereas Tsvetaeva's reverberate with lamentations and incantation.

Her involvement with the tradition of the lamentation (or rather the fact that her ear was attuned to it) can be explained by, among other things, the additional possibilities of assonance contained in trisyllabic clausulae, on which the verse line of the lamentation, as a rule, rests. Most likely, it is a question of the poet endeavoring to transmit the psychology of modern man by means of traditional folk poetics. When it works—and for Tsvetaeva it almost always worked—it gives one an impression of linguistic justification for any fracture or dislocation of the modern sensibility; and not only of a linguistic justification but, regardless of the subject, of *a priori* lacrimation. At any rate, it is hard to imagine anything more suitable than the trochee in the case of "*Novogodnee.*"

Tsvetaeva's poetry differs from the production of her contemporaries by virtue of a certain *a priori* tragic note, by a hidden—in a verse—wail. Given that, it should be kept in mind that this note started to sound in the voice of Tsvetaeva not as a result of firsthand tragic experience but as a by-product of her working with language, in particular as a result of her experiments with folklore.

Tsvetaeva in general was extremely prone to stylization: of Russian antiquities (*Tsar-Maiden, Swans' Encampment*, etc.), of the French Renaissance and Romanticism ("Phoenix" [*Casanova's End*], "The Snowstorm"), of German folklore ("The Pied Piper"), and so on. However, regardless of the tradition with which she dealt, regardless of the concrete content, and—what is more important—regardless of the purely intrinsic, emotional reasons that made her resort to this or that cultural mask, every theme was rendered, purely euphonically, in a tragic key. It was, in all likelihood, not only a matter of intuitive (at first) and physical (later on) perception of her own epoch, but of the general tone—background—of Russian poetic diction at the beginning of the century. Every creative process is a reaction to predecessors, and the purely linguistic harmonic stasis of Symbolism needed resolution. Every language, and especially poetic language, always has a vocal future. What

Tsvetaeva produced turned out to be the sought-after vocal way out of the condition of poetic diction, but the pitch of her timbre was so high that a split with both the broad readership and the bulk of the literary profession was inevitable. The new sound carried not merely a new content but a new spirit. Tsvetaeva's voice had the sound of something unfamiliar and frightening to the Russian ear: the unacceptability of the world.

It was not the reaction of a revolutionary or a progressive demanding changes for the better, nor was it the conservatism or snobbery of an aristocrat who remembers better days. On the level of content, it was a question of the tragedy of existence in general, par excellence, outside a temporal context. On the plane of sound, it was a matter of the voice striving in the only direction possible for it: upward. A striving similar to that of the soul toward its source. In the poet's own words, "gravitation from/the earth, above the earth, away from/both the worm and the grain." To this should be added: from one's own self, from one's own throat. The purity (as well as the frequency, for that matter) of this voice's vibration was akin to an echo-signal which is sent into mathematical infinity and finds no reverberation, or, if it does, immediately rejects it. But while acknowledging that this rejection of the world by the voice is indeed a leitmotif of Tsvetaeva's work, it must be noted that her diction was completely devoid of any "etherealness." On the contrary: Tsvetaeva was a poet very much of this world, concrete, surpassing the Acmeists in precision of detail, and in aphoristicness and sarcasm surpassing everybody. More like that of a bird than an angel, her voice always knew above *what* it was elevated, knew what was there, down below (or, more precisely, what—there below—was lacking). Perhaps that is why it kept rising higher and higher, to expand the field of vision, in reality, though, expanding only the diameter of the world within which the sought-after was missing. That's why her trochee in the first line of "*Novogodnee*" takes flight, muffling the short sob with an exclamation point.

There are 193 more lines like this in "*Novogodnee.*" It would take just as much space to analyze any one of them as it did to analyze the first. In principle, this is the way it ought to be, for poetry is the art of condensation, of narrowing things down. The most interesting thing for the scholar—as well as for the reader—is to go "back along the beam," that is, to trace the course of this condensation, to determine at what point in the dispersion common to us all the poet first gets a glimpse of a linguistic denominator. However, no matter how much the scholar is rewarded in the course of such a process, the very process itself is similar to an unraveling of fabric, and we shall try to avoid that possibility. We shall dwell only on several of Tsvetaeva's statements made in the course of the poem that cast light on her attitude toward things in general and on the psychology and methodology of the creative process in particular. Statements of this kind in "*Novogodnee*" are numerous, yet there are even more of the very means of expression—metrical artifices, rhymes, enjambments, sound patterning, and so on—which tell us more about a poet than does his most sincere and broad-beaming declaration.

We needn't look very far for examples if we consider the enjambment extending through the second, third, and fourth lines of "*Novogodnee*":

Pervoe pis'mo tebe na novom
—Nedorozumenie, chto zlachnom—
(Zlachnom—zhvachnom) meste zychnom,
meste zvuchnom
Kak Eolova pustaya bashnya.

The first letter to you in your new
—Mistaken as lush, green—
(Lush [suggests] ruminant) clamorous,
sonorous place
Like Aeolus's empty tower.

This excerpt is a remarkable illustration of the manifold thinking characteristic of Tsvetaeva's oeuvre and her endeavor to consider all. Tsvetaeva is an extremely realistic poet, a poet of the infinite subordinate clause, a poet who does not allow either herself or the reader to take anything on faith.

Her main purpose in these lines is the grounding of the first line's ecstatic charge: "Happy New Year—World—Realm—Haven!" To achieve this she resorts to prosaism, calling the "next world" a "new place." However, she goes beyond normal prosaicizing. The adjective repeated in the phrase "new place" is sufficiently redundant in itself, and that alone would be enough to create an effect of lowering: the redundancy of "new" all by itself compromises "place." But the *a priori* positiveness residing, independent of the author's will, in the expression "new place"—especially as applied to the "next world"—provokes an upsurge of sarcasm in her, and "new place" is equated by the poet with an object of tourist pilgrimage (which is justified by the ubiquity of death as a phenomenon) by means of the epithet *zlachny* ("lush, green"). This is all the more remarkable because *zlachny* undoubtedly came from the Orthodox prayer for the souls of the dead (". . . in green pastures, in blissful realms . . ."). Tsvetaeva, however, puts the prayer book aside, if only because Rilke wasn't Orthodox, and the epithet returns to its own base modern context. The virtual similarity of the "next world" with a resort is intensified by the internal rhyme of the following adjective, *zhvachny* ("ruminant"), which is followed by *zychny* ("clamorous") and *zvuchny* ("sonorous"). The piling up of adjectives is always suspect even in ordinary speech. In a poem it arouses even more suspicion—and not without reason. For the use of *zychny* here marks the beginning of a transition from sarcasm to an overall elegiac tone.

Zychny ("clamorous"), of course, still continues the theme of the crowd, of the marketplace, which was introduced by *zlachny—zhvachny*; but this is already a different function of the mouth, a function of the voice in space reinforced by the last epithet, *zvuchny*. And space itself is expanded by the vision of a solitary tower (Aeolus's) in it. "Empty"—that is, inhabited by the wind, that is, possessing a voice. The "new place/pasture" gradually begins to acquire the features of the "next world."

Theoretically, the lowering effect could have been achieved simply by the enjambment itself (*novom/ . . . meste*). Tsvetaeva used this device—the run-on line—so often that enjambment, in turn, can be considered her signature, her fingerprint. But perhaps, precisely because of the frequency of its use, this device did not satisfy her enough, and she felt the need to "animate" it with parentheses—that minimalized form of lyrical digression. (In general, Tsvetaeva, like no one else, indulged in the use of typographic means of expressing subordinate aspects of speech.)

However, the main reason that prompted her to extend the enjambment over three lines was not so much the danger of cliché hidden (for all the irony of the tone) in the phrase "new place" as the author's dissatisfaction with the commonplaceness of the rhyme *krovom—novom.* She couldn't wait to get even, and a line and a half later she really does get even. But until that happens, the author subjects every word of hers, every thought of hers, to the sharpest rebuke; that is, she comments upon herself. More precisely, though: the ear comments upon the content.

None of Tsvetaeva's contemporaries is so constantly mindful of what has been stated, so prone to keep tabs on himself as she is. Thanks to that feature (of character? eye? ear?), her poems acquire the verisimilitude of prose. They contain—especially those of the mature Tsvetaeva—no poetic *a priority*, nothing which hasn't been questioned. Tsvetaeva's verse is dialectical, but it is the dialectics of dialogue: between meaning and meaning, between meaning and sound. It is as though Tsvetaeva were constantly struggling against the *a priori* authority of poetic speech, constantly trying to "take the buskins off" her verse. The main device, to which she resorts especially often in "*Novogodnee*," is refinement. In the line that follows "Like Aeolus's empty tower," as if she were crossing out what she has already stated, she falls back to the beginning and starts the poem anew:

The first letter to you from yesterday's—
In which, without you, I'll moan myself empty—
Homeland . . .

The poem gathers momentum again, but now along the tracks that were laid by the stylistic features of the preceding lines and by the preceding rhyme. "In which, without you, I'll moan myself empty" wedges itself into the enjambment, thereby not so much emphasizing the author's personal emotion as separating "yesterday's" from "homeland" (here meaning the earth, the planet, the world). This pause between "yesterday's" and "homeland" is seen—heard—no longer by the author but by the poem's addressee, Rilke. At this point Tsvetaeva is looking at the world, herself included, through his eyes now, not through her own; that is, from a distance. This may be the only form of narcissism characteristic of her; and one of her motives for writing "*Novogodnee*" may well have been this temptation: to take a look at herself from a distance. In any case, precisely because she is attempting here to give a picture of the world through the eyes of someone who has left it, Tsvetaeva separates "yesterday's" from "homeland," at the same time paving the way for one of the most transfixing—the first of many—passages in the poem, where she does get even—with herself—for the uneventful rhyme in the first two lines. The subordinate awkwardness of the wedged-in "In which, without you, I'll moan myself empty" is followed by

> *Homeland—now already from one of*
> *The stars . . .*

This is astounding. For it's one thing to take a look at oneself from a distance; ultimately, she was engaged in this in one way or another all her life. To look at yourself through the eyes of Rilke is something else. But in this too, we must suppose, she engaged rather frequently, if we take into account her attitude toward Rilke. To look at herself through the eyes of the deceased Rilke's soul wandering in space, and moreover to see not herself but the world abandoned by *him*—is something that requires a spiritual optic capability which we don't know that anyone has. A reader is not prepared for such a turn of events. To be more precise, the deliberate awkwardness of "in which, without you, I'll moan myself empty" may prepare him for a lot of things, but not for the accelerating dactylism of "Homeland" or much less for the remarkable broken compound rhyme of *odnoi iz* ("one of"). And least of all, of course, does he expect that *odnoi iz* will be followed by that explosively abrupt *Zvyozd* ("the stars"). He is still lulled by the homey-sounding "yesterday's" (*vcherashnei*), he is still lingering over the slightly mannered *iznoyus'* ("I'll moan myself empty"), when he is overwhelmed by the full dynamics and total irrevocability of "Homeland—now already from one of/The stars." After two ruptured enjambments he is least prepared for a third—a traditional one.

It is not altogether improbable that this run-on verse is a bow, a private signal given by Tsvetaeva to Rilke in reply to his elegy to her, written and sent to Tsvetaeva in the summer of the same year, 1926, whose third line also begins with an enjambment containing a star:

O die Verluste ins All, Marina, die stürzenden
Sterne!
Wir vermehren es nicht, wohin wir uns werfen,
zu welchem

Sterne hinzu! Im Ganzen ist immer schon alles
*gezählt.**

It is unlikely that in human consciousness two more divergent concepts exist than "homeland" (read "earth") and "star." Equating them with each other is in itself an act of violence upon consciousness. But the slightly disdainful "one of . . . ," in diminishing both "star" and "homeland," seems to compromise their mutual significance and debases the violated consciousness. In this regard, it is worthwhile to note Tsvetaeva's tactfulness in playing down, here and later on in the poem, her lot as an expatriate and in limiting the meaning of "homeland" and "star" to the context that emerged as a result of Rilke's death, and not as a result of her own peregrinations. Nevertheless, it is hard to rid oneself completely of the impression that the view described here contains an oblique autobiographical element. For the quality of sight—vision—that the author ascribes to her addressee was engendered not only by her psychological attachment to the latter. The center of gravity in any attachment is, as a rule, not its object but the one who has become attached; even if it is a matter of one poet's attachment to another, the main question is: What are *my* poems—to him?

As for the degree of despair over the loss of a loved one, which is expressed in our readiness to swap places with him, the *a priori* impossibility of the realization of such a wish is in itself comforting enough, for it serves as a certain

* Oh, the losses into the All, Marina, the falling/stars! We can't make it larger, wherever we fling, to whatever/star we go! Numbered for all time are the parts of the Whole. (Translated by J. B. Leishman)

emotional limit that spares the imagination further responsibility. Whereas the quality of vision responsible for perceiving "homeland" as "one of the stars" testifies not only to the ability of "*Novogodnee*'s" author to switch the places of subtrahends but also to the ability of her imagination to abandon her hero and to look at even him from afar. For it is not so much Rilke who "sees" his homeland of yesterday as one of the stars, as it is the author of the poem who "sees" Rilke "seeing" all of this. And the question naturally arises: What is the author's own location and how does she happen to be there?

As for the first part of the question, one can be content with a reference to the thirty-eighth line of Gavrila Romanovich Derzhavin's ode "On the Death of Prince Meshchersky" (1779).* As for the second part, the best answer is provided by Tsvetaeva herself, and a little later we'll turn to the quotes. For the moment, though, let us presuppose that the knack of estranging—from reality, from a text, from the self, from thoughts about the self—which may be the first prerequisite for creativity and is peculiar, to a certain degree, to every man of letters, developed in Tsvetaeva's case to the level of instinct. What began as a literary device became a form (nay, norm) of existence. And not only because she was physically estranged from so many things (including motherland, readership, recognition). And not because in her lifetime so many things occurred to which the only response could be distancing, things that demanded distancing. The abovementioned transformation took place because Tsvetaeva

* This line, referring to Prince Meshchersky, who has suddenly died, reads: "Where *is* he?—He's there.—Where there?—We don't know."

the poet was identical to Tsvetaeva the person; between word and deed, between art and existence, there was neither a comma nor even a dash: Tsvetaeva used an equals sign. Hence, it follows that the device is transferred to life, that what develops, instead of craftsmanship, is the soul; that in the end they are the same thing. Up to a certain point, verse plays the role of the soul's tutor; afterward—and fairly soon—it's the other way around. The writing of "*Novogodnee*" took place at a time when the soul no longer had anything to learn from literature, even from Rilke. That's exactly why it became possible for the author of "*Novogodnee*" to get a view of the world through the eyes of a poet who had abandoned this world, but also to take a look at that poet from afar, from the outside—from where that poet's soul had not yet been. In other words, the quality of vision is determined by the metaphysical possibilities of the individual, which, in turn, are a guarantee of infinity—if not a mathematical, then a vocal one.

That is how this poem begins—with a fusion of extreme degrees of despair and estrangement. Psychologically that was more than justified, for the latter is often a direct consequence and expression of the former; especially in the case of someone's death, which precludes the possibility of adequate reaction. (Isn't art, generally speaking, a substitute for this unavailable emotion? And poetic art especially? And if so, isn't the "on the death of a poet" genre of poetry a sort of logical apotheosis and the purpose of poetry: a sacrifice of effect on the altar of cause?) Their interdependence is so obvious that it is difficult at times to avoid identifying despair with estrangement. In any case, let us try not to forget the pedigree of the latter when we talk about

"*Novogodnee*"; estrangement is at the same time both the method and the subject of this poem.

Lest she should slip into pathos (something the development of the "homeland—one of the stars" metaphor might have led to), and also because of her own proclivity for the concrete, for realism, Tsvetaeva devotes the next sixteen lines to a very detailed description of the circumstances in which she learned of Rilke's death. The ecstatic character of the preceding eight lines is offset in this description (in the form of a dialogue with a visitor, Marc Slonim, who suggests she "do a piece" about Rilke) by the literalism of direct speech. The naturalness, the unpredictability of the rhymes that rig out this dialogue, the abruptness of the retorts—impart to this passage the character of a diary entry, almost prosaic verisimilitude. At the same time, the dynamics of the retorts themselves, reinforced partly by their monosyllables as well as by the dialecticism of their content, create an impression of shorthand, of a desire to be done with all these details as soon as possible and to get down to what is most crucial. Striving to achieve a realistic effect, Tsvetaeva employs all sorts of means, the main one being her mixing of lexical planes, which permits her (sometimes in one line) to convey the entire psychological gamut produced by some situation or other. Thus, through the give-and-take with the visitor soliciting the piece from her, she learns about the place where Rilke has died—the sanatorium at Valmont, near Lausanne, whereupon follows the nominative sentence that appears even without the question "Where?" that normally prompts such information:

"In a sanatorium."

And immediately afterward, the author, who has already turned down the request to "do" a piece, that is, who does not wish to bare her emotions in public and therefore conceals them from her interlocutor, adds in parentheses: ("A rented paradise").

This is an important shift from the albeit feverish but nonetheless civil tone of the dialogue: a shift toward vulgarity, almost a marketplace womanish yammer (cf. the standard saying: "A lawyer's a hired conscience"). This specific shift—let us call it a downward estrangement—is triggered not so much by the desire to conceal one's feelings as by the wish to humiliate oneself—and by this debasement defend oneself from those feelings. As if to say, "It's not me, it's somebody else who's suffering. I couldn't have taken it . . ."* Nevertheless, even in this self-flagellation, in this self-denial, in this vulgarity, the poetic tension doesn't slacken, and this is attested by the word "paradise." For the point of the poem is the description of the "next world," the comprehension of which is derived from "this" one. The coarseness of the sensations, however, is evidence not so much of their strength as of their approximateness, and by exclaiming "A rented paradise," the author alludes to her still imperfect conception of the "next world," to the level of comprehension on which she still exists; that is, to the need for further developing the subject, something which, in the first place, is necessitated by the very rapidity of the verse, which is increased by the telegraphic piling up of monosyllables and sentence fragments.

* Akhmatova, "Requiem."

S nastupayushchim! (Rozhdalsya zavtra!)—
Rasskazat', chto sdelala uznav pro . . . ?
Tss . . . Ogovorilas'. Po privychke.
Zhizn' i smert' davno beru v kavychki,
Kak zavedomo pustye splyoty.

Happy forthcoming year! (Born tomorrow!)—
Shall I tell you what I did when I learned of . . . ?
Sh! . . . A slip of the tongue. Out of habit.
I have long put life and death in quotes
Like known-to-be-empty gossip/fabrications.

Throughout the entire poem Tsvetaeva never once uses the phrase "your death." She avoids it even when the line allows it; even though several days after writing "*Novogodnee*" she wrote a short essay with just that title: "Your Death." It is not so much a question of superstitious reluctance to acknowledge death's proprietary right to Rilke—or his to death. The author simply refuses to hammer with her own hands this last psychological nail into the poet's coffin. First of all because such a phrase is the first step toward oblivion, toward domestication—i.e., toward incomprehension—of the catastrophe. And, in addition, because it is impossible to speak of a person's physical death without speaking—because of not knowing—about his physical life. In that case, Rilke's death would have taken on an abstract character against which Tsvetaeva would have rebelled purely as a realist. As a result, death becomes the object of guesswork to the same degree that Rilke's life was its object. That is, the expression "your death" proves to be just as inapplicable and meaningless as "your life." But Tsvetaeva goes a bit further, and here we have the beginning of what we can call an "upward estrangement" and Tsvetaeva's confession.

I have long put life and death in quotes
Like known-to-be-empty gossip/fabrications.

The literal meaning of these lines—and Tsvetaeva should always be taken first of all not figuratively but literally—just as the Acmeists should be, for instance—is as follows: to the author "life" and "death" seem like an unsuccessful attempt by the language to adjust to the phenomenon, and, what is more, an attempt that debases the phenomenon with the sense which usually is invested in these words: "known-to-be-empty gossip/fabrications." That is, the life of So-and-so is not yet Being, with all the consequences that this entails for the death of So-and-so, too. *Splyoty* is either an archaic form for "gossip," or a vernacularism for "plexus" (of circumstances, relationships, etc.); in either case "known-to-be-empty/*a priorily* hollow" is an extremely fitting epithet. The key word here is *davno* ("long"), for it indicates the repetitive, mass character of the *splyoty* ("gossip," "fabrications") that compromises "life" and "death" and makes them inapplicable to Rilke.

Apart from everything else, the lyrical heroine of "*Novogodnee*" is Tsvetaeva herself, the poet; and as poet she gives prejudiced treatment to these two words, which have been emasculated not only by the meaning imparted to them for so long and by so many, but also by her own extremely frequent use of them. And this is precisely what compels her to stop short in the middle and put her finger to her lips:

Sh! . . . A slip of the tongue. Out of habit.

This is one of the many rebellions of the poet against herself that are typical of Tsvetaeva's lyric poems. These rebellions are prompted by the same striving to achieve realistic effects that is responsible for her combining of lexical planes. The purpose of all these devices—or: movements of the soul—is to rid her speech of poetic *a priority*, to demonstrate the presence of common sense. In other words, to make the reader maximally dependent on what has been said. Tsvetaeva doesn't play egalitarian games with the reader: she places herself on his level—lexically, logically, and only far enough to make it possible for him to follow her.

> *Life and death I utter with a hidden*
> *Smirk . . .*

she adds farther on, as if carefully enunciating for the reader the meaning of the previous lines. For the same reasons, and also because at the beginning of the poem a visitor suggests that she "do a piece," Tsvetaeva resorts to the intonation—or mask—of a journalist conducting an interview:

> *Now—how was the trip?*
> *How was the heart tearing and not torn*
> *Apart? As on Orlov trotters,**
> *Not lagging,* you said, *behind eagles,*
> *Was it breathtaking—or more?*
> *Sweeter?*

The euphemistic quality of this "how was the trip?" (to the "new place," i.e., to heaven, paradise, and so forth),

* Bred by Count Orlov, whose name is derived from the Russian word for eagle.

as well as the subsequent periphrasis from Rilke himself, are attempts to contain the emotions about to get out of control several lines earlier as she replies to "Shall I tell you what I did when I learned of . . .":

I did nothing, but something
Was done that does without
Shadow and echo!
Now—how was the trip?

Tsvetaeva resorts here to a graphic interruption emphasizing both a breaking off of the previous intonation and a physical breaking away of the content—upward (in the reader's consciousness) because it is downward (on paper). At this point the poem begins to move only in that direction, and if it stands still at times for lyrical digression or for lowering of tone, it occurs in spheres so high that topographical differentiation seems meaningless. In part, this is what Tsvetaeva herself has in mind when, instead of answering her own question ". . . more?/Sweeter?" she remarks:

No heights are there, or descents
For one who has flown on real Russian
Eagles.

In other words, for a person who has had the experience of living in Russia, who has experienced the metaphysical Russian roller coaster, any landscape, including an otherworldly one, seems ordinary. And further, with the bitterness and pride of the patriot, Tsvetaeva adds:

. . . We have a blood tie with the next world:
Who has ever been to Russia has beheld the
next world
In this one.

This is not flag-waving patriotism or even a liberal variety that, as a rule, is tinged with sardonic tones; it is a metaphysical patriotism. "Who has ever been to Russia has beheld the next world/In this one." These words are prompted by a clear awareness of the tragic nature of human existence as a whole—and by an understanding of Russia as the most perfect approximation of it.

This line totally dispels the idiotic contentions that Tsvetaeva never accepted the Revolution. Of course she didn't: for to "accept" human slaughter, regardless of the ideals in whose name it is carried out, means to become an accomplice and a betrayer of the dead. To "accept" such a thing is tantamount to the assertion that the dead are worse than those who have remained alive. Such an "acceptance" is a position of superiority held by the majority (of the living) with regard to the minority (of the dead)—i.e., the most repulsive form of spiritual debauchery. For any human being who has been brought up on Christian ethical standards, such an "acceptance" is unthinkable, and accusations of political blindness or of failure to understand historical processes, manifested in the refusal to accept these things, turn into praise of the individual for his moral clearsightedness.

"Who has ever been to Russia has beheld the next world/ In this one" is not so far, after all, from "All of you, my native land,/ the King of Heaven traversed/in the guise of a slave, giving his blessing," or from "Russia one must simply believe in."* This line of Tsvetaeva's is evidence that she did something more substantial than not accepting the Revolution: she grasped it fully. As an absolute baring—to the bone—of the core of existence. And this is probably what prompts the use of the verb "has been," which alludes not so much to Rilke's visits to Russia (in 1899 and 1900) as to Tsvetaeva herself, who found herself outside Russia. It is also probable that the exclamation "Smooth switch!" that follows "In this one," that is, the ease of the relocation from this world to the next, is in part an echo of trigger-happy revolutionary justice. And all the more natural is what immediately comes after "switch":

Life and death I utter with a hidden
Smirk—[you]'ll touch it with your own!
Life and death I utter with a footnote,
An asterisk . . .

The accumulating didactic mass of "you'll touch it with your own" finds vent in high lyricism, for the identity of the author's views on "life and death" with those of her addressee is presented here in the form of a certain overlapping of two hidden smiles—this existential kiss, the tenderness of which is euphonically conveyed by the whisper-like *kosnyosh'sya* ("[you]'ll touch"). The omitted personal pronoun *ty* ("you") in "[you]'ll touch it with your own" increases the sensation of intimacy that penetrates the next line as well: "Life and death I utter with a footnote,† / An asterisk"—since "footnote" sounds less dramatic than

* Lines by Fyodor Tyutchev (1803–73).
† *Zhizn' i smert' proiznoshu so snoskoi.*

"quotes" or even "smirk." While still conveying—or developing—the author's feeling that "life and death" are compromised, "footnote" (*snoskoi*), owing to the diminutive, almost hypocoristic quality of its sound, shifts the speech to a purely personal plane and seems to equate the addressee with itself by becoming "an asterisk." For Rilke is already a star or among the stars, and then what follows in parentheses are two and a half lines of pure poetry:

(the night which I plead for:
Instead of a cerebral hemisphere—
A stellar one!)

These parentheses are all the more remarkable because they are, in some sense, a graphic equivalent of the image they enclose. As for the image itself, its additional charm lies in the identification of consciousness with a page consisting solely of footnotes to Rilke—that is, stars. In turn, the archaic word *chayu* ("I plead for") bears within it all possible tenderness and the impossibility of realizing such a desire, so that an immediate change of register is required. Therefore, after the parentheses close we hear speech that is distinguished from the preceding segment by its outwardly businesslike tone. This tone, however, is only a mask; the emotional content is the same as before:

The following, my friend,
Shouldn't be forgotten: that if Russian
Letters are running on now instead of German—
It's not because nowadays, they claim,
Anything will do, that a dead man (beggar) will
wolf anything—
Won't bat an eye! . . .

Camouflaged by the intentional bureaucratic tone of "the following," that content makes itself felt in the very meaning of the passage: its subject is no more and no less than the author's request to Rilke that he forgive her for writing the poem in Russian instead of German. By no means is this request an expression of coyness; Tsvetaeva had been in correspondence with Rilke since 1926 (started, by the way, on Boris Pasternak's initiative), and that correspondence had been conducted in German. The emotional basis of the request lies in the author's awareness that by using Russian—not Rilke's native language—she is distancing herself from the addressee, more than she already was distanced by the fact of his death; and more than she would have been had she taken the trouble of writing in German. Moreover, this request serves the function of creating distance from the "pure poetry" of the preceding lines for which Tsvetaeva virtually reproaches herself. In any case, she realizes that achievements of a purely poetic nature (like the contents of the previous parentheses), in their turn, remove her from Rilke; that she can *get carried away*—she, that is, and not her addressee. In the vulgar bravura of "if Russian/Letters are running on now instead of German . . ." one can detect a note of slight contempt for herself and her work. And then she starts to justify herself in the same jaunty, marketplace tone: "It's not because nowadays, they claim, / Anything will do, that a dead man (beggar) will wolf anything— / Won't bat an eye!" This tone, however, is only a supplementary form of self-flagellation. The raffishness of this ". . . a dead man (beggar) will wolf anything— / Won't bat an eye!"—worsened by a mixture of proverb and folkloric synonym for a deceased person, "blinker" (*zhmurik*)—is present here not as a means of characterizing the addressee but as a touch added to the author's psychological self-portrait: as an illustration of the possible extent of her debasement. Precisely from here, from the very bottom, Tsvetaeva begins her self-defense, yielding a result that is all the more believable the worse the point of departure:

> *—but because the* next *world,*
> *Ours—at thirteen, in Novodevichy [monastery]*
> *I understood—is not tongueless but all-tongues.*

This, again, is staggering, because the preceding lines have not prepared us for anything of the sort. Even a fairly experienced reader of Tsvetaeva, someone accustomed to her stylistic contrasts, often enough finds himself unprepared for these take-offs from the gutters into the empyrean. For in Tsvetaeva's poems the reader encounters not the strategy of the verse-maker but the strategy of ethics—to use her own formulation, art in the light of conscience. On our part let us add: the complete overlapping of art and ethics. It is precisely the logic of conscience (or rather conscientiousness), the logic of guilt for being among the living while her addressee is dead, the awareness that the deceased's oblivion is inevitable and that her own lines are paving the way toward that oblivion—it is precisely all this that prompted her request that she be forgiven for an additional flight from the reality of his—the addressee's—death: for a poem in Russian, or for a *poem* at all. The argument Tsvetaeva makes to vindicate herself—"because the *next* world . . . is not tongueless but all-tongues"—is remarkable above all because it oversteps the psychological threshold at which nearly everyone stops: the interpretation of death as an extralingual experience that rids one of any linguistic pangs. "Not tongueless but all-tongues" goes much further, taking conscience back to its source, where it is relieved of the burden of earthly guilt. These words have a feeling, it seems, of arms stretched wide and the festiveness of a revelation available perhaps only to a child —"at thirteen, in Novodevichy."

Even that argument, however, proves to be insufficient. For those very pangs, the very thoughts about language, recollections of childhood, paraphrases of Rilke himself, ultimately poetry as such with its rhymes and images—everything that reconciles one to reality—seems to the author like a flight, like a distraction from reality:

Am I getting distracted?

Tsvetaeva inquires, looking back at the preceding stanza, but basically at the entire poem as a whole, at her not so much lyrical as guilt-prompted digressions.

On the whole one may observe that Tsvetaeva's strength lies precisely in her psychological realism, in the voice of conscience, pacified by nothing or no one, that resounds in her verse either as a theme or, at least, as a postscript. One of the possible definitions of her creative production is the Russian subordinate clause put at the service of Calvinism. Another variation is: Calvinism in the embrace of this subordinate clause. In any case, no one has demonstrated the congeniality of the said *Weltanschauung* and this grammar in a more obvious way than Tsvetaeva has. Naturally, the severity of the interrelation between an individual and himself possesses a certain aesthetics; but it seems there is no more absorbing, more capacious, and more natural form for self-analysis than the one that is built into the multi-stage syntax of the Russian complex sentence. Enveloped in this form, Calvinism "takes" the individual much farther than he would happen to get had he used Calvinism's native German. So far that what is left of the German is the "best memories," that German becomes the tongue of tenderness:

> *Am I getting distracted? But no such thing*
> *Could happen—to be distracted from you.*
> *Each thought, every,* Du Lieber,
> *Syllable leads to you—no matter what*
> *The subject . . .*

This *Du Lieber* is at once tribute to a feeling of guilt ("Russian / Letters are running on now instead of German") and deliverance from the guilt. Behind it, moreover, there stands a strictly private, intimate, almost physical endeavor to draw nearer to Rilke, to touch him in a way that is natural to him—with the sound of his native tongue. But if this were her only concern, Tsvetaeva, being an extremely versatile poet technically, would not have switched into German; she would have found on her palette other means for expressing those feelings already mentioned. The point is probably that Tsvetaeva has already said *Du Lieber* in Russian at the beginning of the poem: "A man walked in—whoever you like—(beloved— / You)." The repetition of words in verse is in general not recommended; if one repeats words with an *a priori* positive coloring, the risk of tautology is greater than usual. If only for this reason, it was imperative that Tsvetaeva switch into another language, and German played the role here of that *other* language. She uses *Du Lieber* here not so much semantically as phonetically. Above all, because "*Novogodnee*" is not a macaronic poem, and therefore the semantic burden that falls to *Du Lieber* is either too huge or totally insignificant. The first possibility is quite unlikely, for Tsvetaeva utters *Du Lieber* almost *sotto voce* and with the spontaneity of a person for whom "German is more native than Russian." *Du Lieber* is simply that famous "blessed, meaningless word"* pronounced "as our own," and its generalizing blessed and meaningless role is only confirmed by the no less nonspecific atmosphere of its accompanying rhyme: "*o chom by ni byl*" ("no matter what"). Thus, we are left with the second possibility, that is, with pure phonetics. *Du Lieber*, injected into the mass of the Russian text, is first of all a sound—not Russian, but not necessarily German either: like any sound. The sensation to which the use of a foreign word gives rise is one that is first of all directly phonetic and therefore more personal, as it were, more private: the eye or ear reacts before reason. In other words, Tsvetaeva uses *Du Lieber* here in a supralingual rather than in its strictly German meaning.

A shift into another language to illustrate a psychological state is a fairly extreme means and in itself is indicative of that state. But poetry, in essence, is itself a certain *other* language—or a translation from such. The use of the German *Du Lieber* is Tsvetaeva's attempt to approximate the original, which she defines, following what rhymes with *Du Lieber*, in what may be the most significant parentheses in the history of Russian poetry:

* From Mandelstam's poem "In Petersburg we shall meet again."

Each thought, every, Du Lieber,
Syllable leads to you—no matter what
The subject (though German is more native
than Russian
For me, the most native is Angelic!) . . .

This is one of the most significant admissions made by the author in "*Novogodnee*"; and, from the standpoint of intonation, the comma comes not after "me" but after "Russian." It is remarkable that the euphemistic quality of "Angelic" is almost completely removed by the whole context of the poem—by the "next world," where Rilke happens to be, by his immediate surroundings in "that" world. It is also remarkable that "Angelic" testifies not to despair but to the height—almost literal, physical, perhaps—of the spiritual flight precipitated not so much by the presupposed location of the "next world" as by the overall poetic orientation of the author. For "Angelic" is more native to Tsvetaeva *in general* in the same way that German is more native than Russian *in general*: biographically. It is a question of a height that is "more native," i.e., not attainable by either Russian or German: a height that is supralingual, in ordinary parlance—spiritual. Angels, ultimately, communicate in sounds. However, the polemical tone clearly distinguishable in "for me the most native is Angelic" points to the completely nonclerical character of that "Angelic" and to its very indirect relation to bliss; in effect, this is just another variation of Tsvetaeva's celebrated formula: "the voice of heavenly truth—versus earthly truth." The hierarchism of world view reflected in both formulations is an unlimited hierarchism—not limited, at least, by ecclesiastical topography. The "Angelic" she uses here is therefore merely an auxiliary term to designate the height of the *meaning* to which, as she puts it, she shrieks herself.

This height can be expressed only in physical units of space, and the entire remainder of the poem consists of a description of constantly increasing degrees of removal, one of which is in the voice of the author herself. Once again assuming the mask of an interviewer, Tsvetaeva inquires (starting with herself and, as is her habit, immediately discarding herself):

—Haven't you . . . about me at all?—
The surroundings, Rainer, how you're feeling?
Most urgently, most assuredly—
First impression of the universe
(I.e., by the poet in it),
And the last—of the planet
That's been given to you only once—as a whole!

This is already a sufficiently angelic perspective, but Tsvetaeva's understanding of the situation differs from a seraphic interpretation thanks to the absence of the concern on her part for the fate of the soul alone—or, for that matter, for the fate of the body alone (which makes it different from the purely human viewpoint): "To isolate them is to insult them both," she states; no angel would say such a thing.

In "*Novogodnee*" Tsvetaeva illustrates the immortality of a soul which has materialized through bodily activity—creative work—by her use of spatial categories, i.e., bodily ones, and this is what allows her not only to rhyme "poet" with "planet" but to equate them as well: the literal universe with the traditional "universe" of individual consciousness. It is a matter, therefore, of the parting of things that are equal in scope, and what the "interviewer" describes is not the "first impression of the universe . . . by the poet," nor even their separation or meeting, but

—a
Confrontation: a meeting and first
Parting . . .

The reliability of Tsvetaeva's metaphysics comes precisely from the accuracy of her translation of Angelic into police-station parlance, for a "confrontation" is always both a meeting and a parting: both first and last. And what follow this grandiose equation are lines of incredible tenderness and lyricism whose piercing effect is due directly to the ratio between the above-mentioned cosmic spectacle and the insignificance (set off, moreover, in parentheses) of a detail that at once evokes associations both with creative activity and with childhood, and equates their irretrievability.

At your own hand
How did you look (at the trace—on it—of ink)
From your so many (how many?) miles
Endless because beginningless
Height above the crystal level
Of the Mediterranean—and other saucers.

As a variation on the theme of "Thus souls look down from on high . . ."* these lines astonish one not only with the author's perspicacity, which allows her with an equal

* From Tyutchev.

degree of clarity to distinguish both an ink stain on a hand belonging to an "abandoned body" and the crystallinity of "the Mediterranean—and other saucers" (which confirm these saucers' many-mile remove from this particular soul). The most thrilling thing in these lines, concomitant with their perspicacity, is the conception of endlessness as beginninglessness. This entire "landscape of disavowal" is presented in one breath, as though in a glide, by means of a simple compound sentence providing lexical (psychological) identity between the naïvely direct "ink stain" and the abstractness of "endless because beginningless," and through the irony of the "crystal saucers." This is a view from paradise, where (whence) it makes no difference, whence any view is a view downward:

> *and where* else *is one to look,*
> *Leaning one's elbows on the edge of the loge,*
> *From this—if not to that [the next], from that [the next]*
> *If not to the much-suffering this.*

And here Tsvetaeva's view literally "plummets" along with the intonation from the "loge" of paradise to the "orchestra" of reality, to the banality of everyday existence —a banality all the more considerable because it is decorated with the "foreign," French name "Bellevue" (literally: "beautiful view"):

> *In Bellevue I live. A town of nests and branches.*
> *To a guide, having exchanged quick glances:*
> *Belle-vue. A jail whose window fancies*
> *A fine view of chimera-laden Paris,*
> *And a little bit beyond, as far as . . .*
> (*Translated by Joseph Brodsky*)

In this description of her dwelling place, in the "I live" coming after Bellevue, Tsvetaeva for a moment—but only a moment—gives rein to the feeling of the absurdity of everything happening to her. One can hear everything in this phrase: contempt for the place, the feeling of being doomed to stay there, and even—if you will—self-vindication, since: I live. The unbearableness of "In Bellevue I live" is intensified for her in addition because that phrase is the physical embodiment of the incompatibility between her existence and what happened to Rilke. Bellevue for her is the opposite pole of paradise, of the "next world"; perhaps even another version of the "next world," since both poles are fiercely cold and existence there is out of the question. As though refusing to believe her own eyes, refusing to accept the fact of her sojourn in this place, Tsvetaeva chooses its name—Bellevue—as a scapegoat and repeats it aloud twice, balancing on the edge of tautology, on the edge of the absurd. A third repetition of "Bellevue" would verge on hysterics, which Tsvetaeva cannot permit herself in "*Novogodnee*," first of all as a poet: that would mean shifting the poem's center of gravity from Rilke to herself. Instead of that, with mockery (directed more at herself than at the location) in her voice she gives a direct translation of the name, which sounds even more paradoxical because the beautiful view, as she knows, can be obtained not from here but from there, from paradise, from the "loge":

With the elbow on the scarlet velvet,
What a laugh should be for you (and well must
Be for me) from heights where your loge hovers
Bellevues and Belvederes of ours.
(*Translated by Joseph Brodsky*)

That is the ending of the author's one and only description in this poem of her own world, from which "where else is one to look" but to where her hero disappeared (not toward "a chimera-laden Paris/And a little bit beyond, as far as . . .").

And in general this is Tsvetaeva's position regarding any concrete reality, especially regarding her own affairs. Reality for her is always a point of departure, not a point of support or the aim of a journey, and the more concrete it is, the greater, the farther the repulsion. In her verse Tsvetaeva behaves like a classical utopian: the more unbearable the reality, the more aggressive her imagination. With the sole difference, however, that in her case acuity of vision does not depend on the object of contemplation. One may even say that the more ideal—remote—the object, the more scrupulous its depiction, as though distance fosters—develops—the lens of the eye. That is why "Bellevues and Belvederes" are laughable, in the first instance, to *her*—for she is capable of looking at them not only through Rilke's eyes but through her own as well.

And it's right here, naturally—from this end of the universe and from this glance cast cursorily at her own *present*, at herself—that the most unthinkable and inconceivable subject is introduced; the main, strictly personal theme—the author's love for the addressee. Everything preceding is essentially a gigantic exposition, to some extent proportional to the one that in real life too precedes a declaration of strong sentiments. In her elaboration of this topic—or rather, in the process of uttering words of love, Tsvetaeva resorts to means which she has already used in her exposition, specifically, to the spatial expression of qualitative categories (of height, for example). To subject them to a detailed analysis (even despite the presence at times of a significant autobiographical element in them) does not seem expedient in view of the stylistic unity of "*Novogodnee*." It would be just as inexpedient and reprehensible to indulge —on the basis of a poem—in speculation about the "concrete nature" of Tsvetaeva's relations with Rilke. A poem—any poem—is a reality no less significant than the reality presented in space and time. Moreover, the availability of a concrete, physical reality, as a rule, eliminates the need for a poem. Usually it is not reality but precisely irreality that gives occasion for a poem. In particular, the occasion for "*Novogodnee*" was an apotheosis of irreality —both in terms of relations and in the metaphysical sense: Rilke's death. It will therefore be much more sensible to examine the remainder of the poem on the psychological level suggested by the text itself.

The only "reality" important to our understanding of "*Novogodnee*" is the already mentioned correspondence between Tsvetaeva and Rilke that began in 1926 and was broken off in the same year by Rilke's death (from leukemia, in a Swiss sanatorium). Three of Tsvetaeva's letters to Rilke have come down to us (it is possible that there were only three in all, considering the length and intensity of their contents). "*Novogodnee*," therefore, should be regarded as the fourth, and, in any case, the last—though the first sent to the next world instead of Switzerland:

The first letter to you in the new . . .
Place . . .

Being a letter, "*Novogodnee*" naturally contains various references to the contents of previous letters (both Tsvetaeva's to Rilke and Rilke's to Tsvetaeva), on which it seems injudicious to dwell without adducing the letters themselves. Furthermore, these references, allusions, and paraphrases in "*Novogodnee*" more likely serve the aims of the poem itself rather than the aims of a continuing correspondence, since one of the correspondents is dead. The only thing in this correspondence that might be thought to have a direct bearing on the poetics of "*Novogodnee*" was Rilke's "Elegy" dedicated to Tsvetaeva, which he sent to her on June 8, 1926 (from all evidence, immediately after he finished writing it). But except for two or three places (one of which we have already cited at the beginning of this essay) that strike the reader of "*Novogodnee*" as echoing a few lines (the third, twentieth, and forty-fifth) of "Elegy," the similarity between these poems is insignificant, if, of course, we leave aside the common spiritual vector of both authors.

And, finally, one can infer from this correspondence that, all during the time it went on, Tsvetaeva and Boris Pasternak (on whose initiative it began) made various plans to visit Rilke. At first they intended to do this together; later on, when Pasternak's chances of taking part in this trip began to shrink, Tsvetaeva planned to go by herself. In a certain sense, "*Novogodnee*" is the continuation of her plans for this meeting; it is a search for the addressee—though now in pure space, an appointment for a rendezvous we know where. A continuation—if only because the poem is written in private: like a letter. It may also be that "Bellevues and Belvederes of ours," apart from everything else, for all its bitterness and unbearableness, is merely a return address inserted out of inertia—or in blind, senseless hope of an impossible reply.

Whatever the author's feelings may have been that gave rise to this line, Tsvetaeva immediately repudiates it and, as though ashamed of its pettiness, ascribes the emergence of it (and those feelings) to the approaching New Year:

I lose track. Particulars. Noise. Hustle.
The New Year's at hand.

And after this, having allowed the poem to warrant its title, she continues, giving rein to caesura and swinging her trochee, like a pendulum or a drooping head, from side to side:

. . . za chto? S kem choknus'
cherez stol? Chem? Vmesto peny—vaty
klok. Zachem? Nu, b'yot. A pri chom
ya tut?

. . . To what, whom shall
I clink glasses? What with? Wads of cotton
For the foam. What for? Yes, chimes. But what's in
this for me . . . ?

The babel of question marks and the trisyllabic clausula that turns the broken rhyme with "*vaty*" ("cotton") into the coalescent mumble "*aprichomyatut*" ("butwhat'sinthis-forme") create the impression of control being lost, reins slackened, of a transition from organized speech to unconscious lamentation. And although a line lower (but a note higher) Tsvetaeva seems to have a sudden recollection, to restore a likeness of meaning to her words, all of her subsequent discourse is already overpowered by the *a priori* music of a lamentation, which, while not stifling the meaning of the utterance, does subordinate it to its own dynamics:

What am I to do in this night's triumph
With this inner rhyme of Rainer's dying?
That is, if you, such an eye, are dimming,
Life's not life and death's not death. The meaning
Vanishes. When we shall meet, I'll grasp it.
There is neither, but a third, some aspect
Which is new (and, having spread straw even,
What a lark then for the 'twenty-seven,
Coming, and for the departing 'twenty-
Six—to start with you and to be ending
With you). 'Cross this table's boundless island
I shall clink my glass to yours with a silent
Clink . . .

(*Translated by Joseph Brodsky*)

The couplet that opens this excerpt is phenomenal and even in the Tsvetaeva corpus nearly stands alone. It is probably not so much a question of the assonance *Rainer—umer* ("Rainer's dying") per se heard by an ear accustomed to the utterance of this name because of the proximity of the lips—her own—that have uttered this name (and precisely by a Russian ear), as of the fractionalized, discrete dactylism of *vnutrenneyu* ("inner"). The palpability of each vowel in this adjective underscores both the inexorability of the statement and the physiologically internal nature of the word itself. It is no longer a question of internal rhyme but of internal comprehension, of conscious (because of the meaning) and un(supra)conscious (because of the phonetics) spelling/spilling out of everything to the end, to the acoustic limit of the word.

It is important to take notice of both the internal position of *vnutrenneyu* within the line (*S etoi vnutrenneyu rifmoi: Rainer—umer*: "With this inner rhyme of Rainer's dying") and the organizing-subordinating role of the line's five "*r*'s," reinforcing the sensation of internal rhyme, for rather than being taken from the Russian alphabet they seem to derive from the name "Rainer." (It is quite possible that more than a minimal role in the organization of this line —as well as in Tsvetaeva's perception of that poet on the whole—was played by his full name, Rainer Maria Rilke, in which, apart from four "*r*'s," the Russian ear detects all three Russian grammatical genders: masculine, feminine, and neuter. In other words, there is already a definite metaphysical element contained in the very name. For that matter, something that has certainly been drawn from the name and subsequently used for the purposes of the poem is the first syllable of the name "Rainer."* In connection with which Tsvetaeva's ear may be accused of naïveté with no more justification than may folklore. Precisely the inertia of folklore, the unconscious imitation of it, is what has prompted subsequent phrases such as *takoe oko smerklos'* ("you, such an eye, are dimming") and *znachit—tmitsya* ("the meaning vanishes"). This also applies in part to *solomoy zasteliv* ("spreading straw"), not only in the sense of a custom but also in regard to the very nature of the traditional rhyme *solomu—sedmomu* (or *shestomu*) ("straw—seven [or sixth]"); this also applies to "I shall clink my glass to yours with a silent / Clink" and partly to *kabatskim*

* *Rai*—pronounced the same way as the Russian word *rai*, meaning "paradise."

ikhnim ("their barroom sort"), immediately following (although this expression can also be viewed simply as a mannerism). The technique of wailing, lamenting, hysterical babbling is most apparent, however, in the lines "if you, such an eye, are dimming, / Life's not life and death's not death. The meaning / Vanishes." One should not be misled by the rationality associated with the verb *yest'* ("is"), for even if the statements are regarded as formulas, their effectiveness is nullified by the subsequent "The meaning / Vanishes" as well as by the reference to the specific dates in parenthesis.

That parenthesis is a breathtaking lyrical breakthrough of Tsvetaeva's. The generosity of soul invested in

> *. . . What a lark then for the 'twenty-seven,*
> *Coming, and for the departing 'twenty-*
> *Six—to start with you and to be ending*
> *With you).*

is beyond calculation, for it itself is given in the amplest units—in categories of time.

Starting with this envy—almost jealousy—of time, with this sobbing *Kakoye shchast'e* ("what a lark"), which slips (because of the shift to a non-standard stress on the first syllable in *toboi*—"with you") into a vernacular pronunciation of "*o*" as "*aw*" in the next line, Tsvetaeva begins to speak of love almost overtly. The logic of this transition is both simple and touching: time, after all, the year, was luckier than the heroine. And hence the thought of time—all time—in which she is not to be together with "him." The intonation of this parenthesis is the intonation of a lament for one's betrothed. More important, however, is the role of separative force assigned to time, for here one can detect a tendency to objectify and animate time. The truth is that at the heart of every tragedy lies the undesirable version of time; this is most obvious in classical tragedies, where the time (the future) of love is replaced by the time (the future) of death. And the content of the standard tragedy, the reaction of the hero or heroine remaining on stage, is a denial, a protest against an unthinkable prospect.

But no matter how high-pitched such a protest may be, it is always a simplification, a domestication of time. Tragedies, as a rule, are composed by ardent young people when the trail is still hot, or by elders who have substantially forgotten what it was all about, anyway. In 1926 Tsvetaeva was thirty-four, the mother of two children, and the author of several thousand lines of verse. Behind her was the civil war and Russia, love for many, and the death of many, including those she loved. Judging by the parenthesis (as well as by the entire sum of her work, for that matter, starting from 1914–15), she already knew something about time which not many of the classics, the Romantics, or her contemporaries had an inkling of. Namely, that life has much less of a relation to time than death (which is longer), and that from the standpoint of time, death and love are the same: the difference can be discerned only by a human being. That is, in 1926 it was as if Tsvetaeva were on an equal footing with time, and her thought did not try to adjust time to it but was trying to adjust itself to time and its frightening needs. "What a lark then . . . / . . . to start with you, and to be ending / With you" is said in the same tone she would have used to thank time, had time granted her a meeting with Rilke. In other words, the degree of her soul's generosity is but an echo of time's possible generosity toward her—undemonstrated but no less possible on account of that.

Moreover, she also knew something else about Rilke himself. In a letter to Boris Pasternak dealing with their joint plans for a trip to visit Rilke she writes: ". . . and yet I'll tell you that Rilke is overloaded, that he needs nothing, no one . . . Rilke is a hermit . . . The ultimate chill of a possessor comes over me from him, in whose possessions I am included *a priori.* I have nothing to give him: everything's been taken. Yes, yes, despite the ardor of letters, the impeccable ear, and the purity of attunement—he doesn't need me, nor does he need you. He is beyond friends. For me this meeting twists the knife, it's a stab in the heart, yes. Especially since he is right (the chill is not his but that of the protective deity in him!), since I in my best highest strongest most detached hours—am like that myself . . ."

And "*Novogodnee*" is that very best highest strongest most detached hour, and that is why Tsvetaeva yields Rilke to time, with which both poets have too much in common to avoid the semblance of a triangle. Intrinsic to both of them, at least, was a high degree of detachment, which is the main property of time. And the whole poem (as, essentially, her oeuvre in general) is a development, an elaboration of this theme—better still, of this state, i.e., of drawing nearer to time—expressed in the only palpable spatial categories: height, the next world, paradise. To put it more simply, "*Novogodnee*" justifies its title first of all because it is a poem about time, one of whose possible embodiments is love, and another death. Both poets, in any case, associate themselves with eternity, which is merely a fraction of time and not, as is commonly held, vice versa. That is why we hear no resentment in this parenthesis.

What's more, knowing the content of the passage from the letter quoted above, one may assume with certainty that had the projected meeting taken place, the parenthesis would have been retained. Time would have remained the object of jealousy and/or of the author's generosity of soul, for the happiest, i.e., the most detached, love is still inferior to the love for detachment instilled in the poet by time. Time is literally an after-word to everything in the world, and the poet, who constantly deals with the self-generating nature of language, is the first to know this. This equation—of language and time—is precisely that "third, new aspect" which the author hopes to "grasp when we shall meet," on account of which "the meaning vanishes" for her, and, postponing the shedding of the scales, she shifts registers and switches on her vision:

Across the table I look at your cross.
How many spots—out of town, and how
much room
Out of town! And to whom else if not us—
Does a bush beckon? Spots—specifically ours
And no one else's! All the leaves! All the needles!
Spots of yours with me (of yours with you).
(We could have rendezvoused—
Just to chat.) Never mind places! Think of the
months!
And weeks! And rainy suburbs
Without people! And mornings! And everything
altogether
Not yet launched into by nightingales!

The field of vision restricted to a cross on a grave or in the hand underscores the ordinariness—the almost mass character of the described sentiment; and the landscape encompassed by this field is, in turn, an ordinary, middle-class landscape. The neutrality, the semi-legality of suburbia, is the typical background of Tsvetaeva's lyric love poetry. In "*Novogodnee*" Tsvetaeva resorts to it not so much for the sake of lowering the pitch, i.e., for antiromantic reasons, as from the inertia created by her other, longer poems ("Poem of the Hill" and "Poem of the End"). In essence, the addressless and cheerless character of suburbia is universal if only because it corresponds to the intermediate position occupied by a human being himself between total artificiality (the city) and total naturalness (nature). At any rate, an author of modern times, if he wants to be convincing, will not choose either a skyscraper or a glade as a backdrop for his drama or pastoral. It would most likely be a spot out of town, with all three meanings with which Tsvetaeva endows the word "spot": railroad station ("How many spots—out of town"); area, i.e., space ("room / Out of town"); and a trysting place ("Spots—specifically ours / And no one else's!"). The last meaning is made even more specific by the exclamations "All the leaves! All the needles!" in which we see a city dweller in the midst of nature looking for a spot to sit or lie down in. Stylistically, this is still a lamentation, but now the rustic, peasant diction yields at this point to "blue-collar" diction—both in vocabulary and in intonation:

(We could have rendezvoused—
Just to chat.) Never mind places! Think of
the months!

Of course, the idea of a rendezvous or clandestine gathering is explained by the multifacetedness (multifacedness) of Rilke, who is present for the author in everyone and in everything. And of course it is Tsvetaeva herself who hears *mesta* ("places") in *mesyatsakh* ("months"). But the vernacularity of this idiom—"chatting" at a clandestine gathering—and "Think of the months!" shouted out by one of "the unwashed" impart to the physiognomy of the heroine a somewhat more common expression than envisaged by the genre of the poem. Tsvetaeva does this not for democratic reasons, not to enlarge her audience (she never committed that sin), or for the purpose of camouflage—to protect herself from inordinately nosy specialists in dirty linen. She resorts to these "speech masks" solely out of chastity, a chastity that is not so much personal as professional: poetic. She simply tries to lower—and not elevate—the effect created by the expression of strong sentiments, the effect of an avowal. After all, it should not be forgotten that she is addressing someone "also a poet." That's why she resorts to montage—to listing the characteristic elements that make up the background of the standard love scene—which we learn about only from the last line of that list:

> . . . *Never mind places! Think of the months!*
> *And weeks! And rainy suburbs*
> *Without people! And mornings! And everything altogether*
> *Not yet launched into by nightingales!*

Whereupon, however, having already marked by means of these nightingales (inevitable attributes of the standard lyric love poem) the nature of the scene and the space at any point of which this scene could have taken place but didn't, she subjects to doubt the quality of her own eyesight and, consequently, her whole interpretation of space:

> *Probably I see poorly, being in a pit,*
> *Probably you see better, being above . . .*

Still audible here is a pang—self-reproach for the imprecision of her glance? of the heart's churning? of the word in her letter? But her probable aberration and *his* seraphic keensightedness are equated by a line that is staggering precisely for its banality—yet another instance of her "wail of women in all times":

> *Nothing ever worked out between us.*

What makes this wail all the more heartrending is the role of avowal fulfilled by it. It is not merely a "yes" disguised as a "no" by circumstances or by the posturing of the heroine; this is a "no" that overtakes and cancels any possibility of "yes," and therefore the "yes" craving to be pronounced clings to the very denial as the only available form of existence. In other words, "Nothing ever worked out between us" formulates the theme through its denial, and the semantic stress falls on "ever worked out." But no wail is ever the last one; and, most likely, it is precisely because the poem (as well as the situation described in it) ends dramaturgically here that Tsvetaeva, being true to herself, shifts the center of gravity from "ever worked out" to "nothing." For "nothing" defines her and her addressee to a greater degree than anything that might have ever "worked out":

So much, so purely and simply
Nothing, that suits our capacity and size
To such a T—there's no need to enumerate it.
Nothing except—don't expect anything out of
The ordinary . . .

"So much, so purely and simply" is read, at first glance, as something that emotionally develops the preceding line —"Nothing ever worked out between us," for, indeed, the un- or extra-eventful character of the relations between these two poets borders on virginity. In reality, however, this "purely" and especially "simply" relates to "nothing," and the naïveté of these two adverbs, in narrowing the grammatical role of the word they modify to a noun, only increases the vacuum created by means of "nothing." For nothing is a nonsubstantive, and it is precisely in this function that it interests Tsvetaeva here—in the function that suits both of them, her and her hero, so well, in "capacity and size"; i.e., the function that arises as *nichevo* ("nothing," "not-having," "absence") changes into *nichto* ("nothing," "nonbeing," "death"). This *nichevo* is absolute, defies description, is not convertible—into any realia whatsoever, into any concretum at all. It is that degree of not-having and not-possessing wherein envy is roused by what

. . . even a prisoner on death row in chains
Endowed with memory has: those lips!

It is quite likely that such a heightened interest in *nichevo* was motivated by an unconscious translation of the entire construction into German (where "nothing" is much more active grammatically). Most likely, however, it illustrates the author's desire to rid the construction "Nothing ever worked out between us" of its flavor of cliché. Or—to enhance that flavor, to expand the cliché to the proportions of the truth it contains. In any case, the element in this phrase of domesticating the situation is considerably reduced as a result of that concern, and the reader suspects that the entire sentence, and perhaps the whole poem, has been written for the opportunity of uttering this simple formula: "between us . . ."

The remaining fifty-eight lines of the poem are a long postscript, an afterword dictated by the energy of the accelerated verse mass—i.e., by the remaining language, by time that continues beyond the poem. Constantly acting by ear, Tsvetaeva twice tries to end "*Novogodnee*" with the semblance of a final chord. First, in

From the least built-up outskirt—
Happy new place, Rainer, world, Rainer!
Happy furthermost cape of provability—
Happy new eye, Rainer, ear, Rainer!

—where the very name of the poet plays a purely musical role (which, first and foremost, is played by any name, after all), as though it were heard for the first time and is therefore repeated. Or repeated because it is uttered for the last time. But the excessive exclamatory character of the stanza is too contingent on the meter to bring about a resolution; instead, the stanza requires harmonic, if not didactic, development. And Tsvetaeva initiates one more attempt by changing the meter in order to break free from the metrical inertia:

Everything was an obstacle
For you: passion and friend.
Happy new sound, Echo!
Happy new echo, Sound!

But the shift from pentameter to trimeter and from rhymed couplets to alternating rhyme, and, what is more, from feminine to masculine in even lines, creates a perhaps desirable but excessively obvious sensation of abruptness, harshness. This harshness and a concomitant superficial aphoristic quality create the impression that the author is in charge of the situation—which in no way corresponds to reality. The rhythmical contrast of this stanza is so sharp that it not so much performs the role designed for it by the author—to complete the poem—as reminds one of the poem's interrupted music. As if driven back by this stanza, "*Novogodnee*" slows down for a while and then, like a flood sweeping away an unstable dam or a theme interrupted by a cadence, it returns in its full sonority. And indeed, in the opening lines of the concluding part of the poem, immediately following this stanza, the voice of the poet resounds with a startling ring of emancipation; the lyricism of these lines is pure lyricism, not bound either by thematic development (since thematically this passage is an echo of previous ones) or even by considerations about the addressee himself. It is a voice disengaging itself from the poem, nearly detaching itself from the text:

How many times on a classroom chair:
What are the mountains there? What are
the rivers?

Are they lovely, those landscapes without
tourists?
Am I right, Rainer—paradise is mountainous,
Stormy? Not the one of widows' aspirations—
There's not just one paradise, right? Above it there
must be another
Paradise? In terraces? I'm judging by the Tatras—
Paradise cannot but be
An amphitheater. (And the curtain's been
lowered on someone . . .)
Am I right, Rainer, God is a growing
Baobab? Not a Golden Louis—
There's not just one God, right? Above him there
must be yet another
God?

This is again the voice of adolescence, of shedding scales, "at thirteen, in Novodevichy"—or, more precisely, the memory of them through the dulling prism of maturity. That note did not sound in either *The Magic Lantern* or *Evening Album**, except for those poems that talk of separation and in which one can hear—immediately!—the future Tsvetaeva, as though "And passion for breakups entices" were said about her. "How many times on a classroom chair" is, as it were, a recognition of the realized prophecy contained in the helplessness of the tragic notes of her first books, where the diarylike sentimentality and banality are justified if only because they spared her future of their presence. Particularly as this adolescent wit ("What are the mountains there?," "landscapes without tourists," etc.)—

* *Evening Album* (1910) and *The Magic Lantern* (1912): Tsvetaeva's first two collections of verse.

irony in general—becomes in her maturity the only possible form of connecting words, when the subject is the "next world" as the destination of a great and beloved poet: when the subject is concrete death.

For all its harshness (better still: youthful cruelty), this irony is nowhere near possessing youthful logic. "Not the one of widows' aspirations— / There's not just one paradise, right? . . ."—inquires a voice that, for all its fragility, allows the possibility of another point of view: churchgoing, old-womanish, widows'. Having chosen the word "widows'," most likely un- or subconsciously, Tsvetaeva immediately realizes the possible associations it has for herself and at once cuts them away, shifting to an almost sardonic tone: "Above it there must be another/Paradise? In terraces? I'm judging by the Tatras . . ." And now, when it would seem that open derision is inevitable, we suddenly hear this grandiose statement fusing all of Alighieri's efforts into a single phrase:

Paradise cannot but be
An amphitheater . . .

The Czech Tatras, which in Bellevue Tsvetaeva had every reason to recall fondly, gave rise to the ironic "In terraces?" but also demanded a rhyme.* This is a typical example of the organizing role of language in relation to experience: a role that essentially enlightens. Undoubtedly the idea of paradise as a theater had arisen earlier in the poem ("Leaning one's elbows on the edge of the loge"), but there it was presented in an individual and, therefore, tragic key. Pre-

* *Tatram: amfiteatrom* ("Tatras": "amphitheater").

pared with an ironic intonation, however, "amphitheater" neutralizes any emotional coloring and imparts to the image a gigantic, mass (extra-individual) scale. At issue here is no longer Rilke, or even paradise. For "amphitheater," along with its modern, strictly technical meaning, calls forth, above all, associations of antiquity and, in a sense, timelessness.

Apprehensive not so much of the excessively powerful impact that this line might have, as of the author's hubris fed by lucky strikes like this, Tsvetaeva deliberately casts her accomplishment into the banality of the mock-important ("And the curtain's been lowered on someone . . .")—reducing "amphitheater" to "theater." In other words, banality here is used as one of the means in her arsenal that provide the echo of the youthful sentimentality of her early poems requisite for continuing discourse in the key established in "How many times on a classroom chair . . .":

> *Am I right, Rainer, God is a* growing
> *Baobab? Not a Golden Louis—*
> *There's not just one God, right? Above him there*
> *must be yet another*
> *God?*

"Am I right, Rainer . . . ?" is repeated as a refrain, for—she thought that way, as a child, at least; but, in addition, because the repetition of the phrase is the product of despair. And the more obvious the naïveté ("God is a *growing* / Baobab?") of the question, the more palpable—as is often the case with children's Why?'s—the proximity of the hysterics beginning to boil up in the throat of the speaker. At the same time, the subject in question is not atheism or religious quests but the previously mentioned poetic version of eternal life that has more in common with cosmogony than with standard theology. And Tsvetaeva asks Rilke all these questions not at all in expectation of an answer but in order to "set forth a program" (and the less complicated the terminology the better). Moreover, the answer is known to her—if only because the constant possibility, even inevitability, of the subsequent question is also known to her.

The true mover of speech, let us repeat, is the language itself, that is, the liberated verse-mass milling the theme and almost literally splashing up when it hits a rhyme or an image. The only question Tsvetaeva asks here in earnest, i.e., whose answer is not known to her, is the one that follows "Above him there must be another / God?":

How is writing going in the new place?

Actually, this is not so much a question as an indication —like musical notation—of quarter notes and flats of lyricism, an insertion of them into a purely speculative space devoid of musical lineation: into a supravocal existence. The unbearableness and unpronounceableness of this height manifests itself in the already repeated use of the slightly sarcastic "in the new place," in the redonning of the interviewer's mask. The answer, however, surpasses the question in its very timbre alone and comes so very close to the essence of the matter—

Then again, if you are, *verse* is: *for you*
yourself are
Verse!

—that her voice, threatening to crack, requires immediate lowering. This lowering is accomplished in the following line, by means that are so familiar, however, that the effect is diametrically opposite to the one intended; what was intended was irony, what resulted was tragedy:

How is writing going in the sweet life . . .

Because he himself—Rilke—is verse, "writing" becomes a euphemism for existence in general (which, in fact, this word really is), and instead of being condescending, "in the sweet life" becomes compassionate. Not satisfied with this, Tsvetaeva enhances the picture of the "sweet life" through the absence of details typical of the imperfect life, i.e., the earthly one (developed later on in the cycle "Desk"):

How is writing going in the sweet life
Without a desk for your elbow, or brow for
your hand
(Palm).

The mutual necessity of these details raises their absence to the status of mutual absence, equivalent, that is, to a literal absence, to the physical annihilation not only of the effect but of the cause as well—which is, if not one of the possible definitions, then, at any rate, one of the most definite consequences of death. In these two lines Tsvetaeva offers the most capacious formula for the "next world," imparting to nonexistence the quality of an active process. The absence of usual (primary in the interpretation of being as writing) signs of being is not equated with nonbeing but surpasses being in its tangibility. In any case, it is precisely that effect—of negative tangibility—which is achieved by the author through the further qualification of "hand / (Palm)." Absence, in the final analysis, is a crude version of detachment: psychologically it is synonymous with presence in some other place and, in this way, expands the notion of being. In turn, the more significant the absent object, the more signs there are of its existence. This is especially apparent in the case of a poet whose "signs" are the entire phenomenal and speculative world described (comprehended) by him. Here is where the poetic version of "eternal life" originates. Furthermore: the difference between language (art) and reality is specifically that any itemization of whatever no longer is or does not yet exist is an entirely independent reality in itself. That is why nonbeing, i.e., death, consisting utterly and entirely of absence, is nothing but a continuation of language:

> *Rainer, are you pleased with new rhymes?*
> *For, properly interpreting the word*
> *"Rhyme," what—if not a whole row of new*
> *Rhymes—is Death?*

If one takes into account that the concern here is with a poet who addressed the subject of death and being in general with great regularity, then the linguistic reality of the "next world" is materialized into a part of speech, into a grammatical tense. And it is in favor of this time that the author of "*Novogodnee*" rejects the present.

This scholasticism is the scholasticism of grief. The more powerful an individual's thinking, the less comfort it affords its possessor in the event of some tragedy. Grief as experience has two components: one emotional, the other rational. The distinguishing feature of their interrelationship in the case of a highly developed analytical apparatus is that the latter (the apparatus), rather than alleviating the situation of the former, i.e., the emotions, aggravates it. In these cases, instead of being an ally and consoler, the reason of an individual turns into an enemy and expands the radius of the tragedy to an extent unforeseen by its possessor. Thus, at times, the mind of a sick person, instead of painting pictures of recovery, depicts a scene of inevitable demise and thereby cripples his defense mechanisms. The difference between the creative process and the clinical one, however, is that neither the material (in the given instance, language) out of which a work is created nor the conscience of its creator can be given a sedative. In a work of literature, at any rate, an author always pays heed to what he is told by the frightening voice of reason.

The emotional aspect of the grief that forms the content of "*Novogodnee*" is expressed, first of all, in terms of plasticity—in the metrics of this poem, in its caesuras, trochaic openings of lines, in the principle of couplet rhyme, which increases the possibilities of emotional adequacy in a line of verse. The rational side is expressed in the semantics of the poem, which is so patently dominant in the text that it could quite easily be the object of independent analysis. Such a separation, of course—even if it were possible—makes no practical sense; but if one distances oneself from "*Novogodnee*" for a moment and looks at it from the outside, as it were, one may observe that on the level of "pure thought" the poem is more eventful than on the purely verse level. If what is thus accessible to the eye gets translated into simple language, an impression emerges that the author's feelings, under the weight of what has befallen them, rushed to seek consolation from reason, which has taken them extremely far, for reason itself has no one from whom it can seek consolation. With the exception, naturally, of language—which signified a return to the helplessness of feelings. The more rational, in other words, the worse it is—for the author, anyway.

It is precisely on account of its destructive rationalism that "*Novogodnee*" falls outside Russian poetic tradition, which prefers to resolve problems in a key that while not necessarily positive is at least consoling. Knowing to whom the poem is addressed, one might assume that the consistency of Tsvetaeva's logic in "*Novogodnee*" is a tribute to the legendary pedantry of German (and, in general, Western) mentality—a tribute all the more easily paid because "German is more native than Russian." There may be a grain of justice in this; but the rationalism of "*Novogodnee*" is not at all unique in Tsvetaeva's oeuvre. Precisely the opposite is true: it is typical. The only thing, perhaps, that distinguishes "*Novogodnee*" from other poems of the same period is its developed argumentation; whereas in "Poem of the End" or in "The Pied Piper," for example, we are dealing with the reverse phenomenon—an almost hieroglyphic condensation of arguments. (It is even possible that the argumentation in "*Novogodnee*" is so detailed because Russian was somewhat familiar to Rilke, and, as though Tsvetaeva were fearful of the misunderstandings that are especially common when the language barrier is slightly lowered, she intentionally "enunciates" her thoughts. In the end, this letter is the last; it is important to say everything while he has not yet gone "completely," that is, before the onset of oblivion, while life without Rilke has not yet become natural.) In any case, however, we encounter this destructive characteristic of Tsvetaeva's logicality, the premier mark of her authorship.

It might be more reasonable to say that "*Novogodnee*" does not fall outside Russian poetic tradition but expands it. For this poem—"national in form and Tsvetaevan in content"*—extends, or better yet, refines the understanding of "national." Tsvetaeva's thinking is unique only for Russian poetry; for Russian consciousness it is natural, and even preconditioned by Russian syntax. Literature, however, always lags behind individual experience, for it comes about as its result. Moreover, the Russian poetic tradition always balks at disconsolation—not so much because of the possibility of hysterics implicit in disconsolation as because of the Orthodox inertia in justifying the existential order (by any, preferably metaphysical, means). Tsvetaeva, however, is uncompromising as a poet and in the highest degree uncomfortable. The world and many of the things that happen in it all too often lack any sort of justification for her, including a theological one. For art is something more ancient and universal than any faith with which it enters into matrimony, begets children—but with which it does not die. The judgment of art is a judgment more demanding than the Final Judgment. The Russian poetic tradition by the time "*Novogodnee*" was written was still in the grip of feelings for the Orthodox version of Christianity, with which it had been acquainted for only three hundred years. It's only natural that against such a background a poet who cries out, "There's not just one God, right? Above him there must be yet another / God?" proves to be an outcast. The latter circumstance may have played an even greater role in her life than the civil war.

* "National in form and socialist in content," a standard Soviet press definition of a work of art.

One of the basic principles of art is the scrutiny of phenomena with the naked eye, out of context, and without intermediaries. "*Novogodnee*" is essentially one person's tête-à-tête with eternity or—even worse—with the idea of eternity. Tsvetaeva has used the Christian version of eternity here not only terminologically. Even if she had been an atheist, the "next world" would have had concrete ecclesiastical meaning for her: for, having a right to disbelieve in an afterlife for oneself, a person is less willing to deny such a prospect to someone he loved. Furthermore, Tsvetaeva ought to have insisted on "paradise," if only proceeding from the tendency—so typical of her—to dismiss the obvious.

A poet is someone for whom every word is not the end but the beginning of a thought; someone who, having uttered *rai* ("paradise") or *tot svet* ("next world"), must mentally take the subsequent step of finding a rhyme for it. Thus *krai* ("edge/realm") and *otsvet* ("reflection") emerge, and the existence of those whose life has ended is thus prolonged.

Looking in that direction, upward, into the grammatical time and also the grammatical place where "he" is, if only because "he" is not here, Tsvetaeva ends "*Novogodnee*" as all letters end: with the name and address of the addressee:

—So that nothing spills on it I hold it in my
palms.—
Above the Rhone and above the Rarogne,
Above the clear-cut and total separation
To Rainer—Maria—Rilke—into his hands.

(*Translated by Joseph Brodsky*)

"So that nothing spills on it"—rain, perhaps? Overflowing rivers (the Rhone)? Her own tears? Most likely the last, for usually Tsvetaeva omits the subject only in the case of something self-evident—and what could be more self-evident at parting than tears capable of blurring the name of the addressee meticulously inscribed at the end, as though with an indelible pencil on a moist surface. "I hold it in my palms" from a detached viewpoint is a sacrificial gesture and, naturally, is beyond tears. "Above the Rhone" that flows from Lake Geneva, above which Rilke had lived in a sanatorium—that is, almost above his former address; "and above the Rarogne," where he was buried, i.e., above his present address. It is remarkable that Tsvetaeva merges both names acoustically, conveying their sequential order in Rilke's fate. "Above the clear-cut and total separation," the sensation of which is intensified by the reference to the grave site, about which it was said earlier in the poem that it is a place where the poet isn't. And finally, the name of the addressee spelled out in full on the envelope, with the further specification "into his hands" (formerly standard postal terminology for "personal")—as previous letters, no doubt, had also been addressed. This last line would be utterly prosaic (reading it, a postman would spring to his bicycle) were it not for the very name of the poet, which is partly responsible for the previous "you yourself are / Verse!" Apart from its possible effect on the postman, the line returns both the author and the reader to what love for that poet began with. The main element of the line—and of the entire poem as well—is the effort to hold someone back—if only by voice alone calling out a name—from nonbeing; to insist, despite the obviousness of it, upon his full name, to wit, presence, the physical sensation of which is supplemented by the specification "into his hands."

Emotionally and melodically this last stanza creates the impression of a voice that has burst through tears and, cleansed by them, takes off from them. In any case, the voice chokes when reading it aloud. This probably happens because there is nothing for anyone (either the reader or the author) to add to what has already been said; to raise the pitch a note higher is not possible. The art of poetry, apart from its numerous functions, bears witness to the vocal and ethical possibilities of man as a species—if for no other reason than that it drains them dry. For Tsvetaeva, who was always operating at the vocal limit, "*Novogodnee*" served as an opportunity to combine two genres requiring the highest pitch: the love lyric and the funeral lament. It is striking that in the controversy between them the last word rests with the former: "into his hands."

(Translated by Barry Rubin)

1981

Catastrophes in the Air[*]

Il y a des remèdes à la sauvagerie primitive; il n'y en a point à la manie de paraître ce qu'on n'est pas.
Marquis de Custine, *Lettres de Russie*

Because of the volume and quality of Russian fiction in the nineteenth century, it's been widely held that the great Russian prose of that century has automatically, by pure inertia, wandered into our own. From time to time, in the course of our century, here and there one could hear voices nominating this or that writer for the status of the Great Russian Writer, purveyor of the tradition. These voices were coming from the critical establishment and from Soviet officialdom, as well as from the intelligentsia itself, with a frequency of roughly two great writers per decade.

During the postwar years alone—which have lasted, blissfully, so far—a minimum of half a dozen names have filled the air. The forties ended with Mikhail Zoshchenko and the fifties started with the rediscovery of Babel. Then came the thaw, and the crown was temporarily bestowed upon Vladimir Dudintsev for his *Not by Bread Alone*. The

[*] The Biddle Memorial Lecture, delivered at the Solomon R. Guggenheim Museum in New York on January 31, 1984, under the auspices of the Academy of American Poets.

sixties were almost equally shared by Boris Pasternak's *Doctor Zhivago* and by Mikhail Bulgakov's revival. The better part of the seventies obviously belong to Solzhenitsyn; at present what is in vogue is so-called peasant prose, and the name most frequently uttered is that of Valentin Rasputin.

Officialdom, though, it should be noted in all fairness, happens to be far less mercurial in its preferences: for nearly fifty years now it has stuck to its guns, pushing Mikhail Sholokhov. Steadiness paid off—or rather a huge shipbuilding order placed in Sweden did—and in 1965 Sholokhov got his Nobel Prize. Still, for all this expense, for all this muscle of the state on the one hand and agitated fluctuation of the intelligentsia on the other, the vacuum projected by the great Russian prose of the last century into this one doesn't seem to get filled. With every passing year, it grows in size, and now that the century is drawing to its close, there is a growing suspicion that Russia may exit the twentieth century without leaving great prose behind.

It is a tragic prospect, and a Russian native doesn't have to look feverishly around for where to put the blame: the fault is everywhere, since it belongs to the state. Its ubiquitous hand felled the best, and strangled the remaining second-rate into pure mediocrity. Of more far-reaching and disastrous consequence, however, was the state-sponsored emergence of a social order whose depiction or even criticism automatically reduces literature to the level of social anthropology. Even that presumably would be bearable had the state allowed writers to use in their palette either the individual or collective memory of the preceding, i.e., abandoned, civilization: if not as a direct reference, then at least in the guise of stylistic experimentation. With that tabooed, Russian prose quickly deteriorated into the debilitated being's flattering self-portrayal. A caveman began to depict his cave; the only indication that this still was art was that, on the wall, it looked more spacious and better lit than in reality. Also, it housed more animals, as well as tractors.

This sort of thing was called "socialist realism" and nowadays it is universally mocked. But as is often the case with irony, mockery here considerably subtracts from one's ability to grasp how it was possible for a literature to plummet, in less than fifty years, from Dostoevsky to the likes of Bubennov or Pavlenko. Was this dive a direct consequence of a new social order, of a national upheaval that overnight reduced people's mental operation to the level where the consumption of garbage became instinctive? (Enter and exeunt Western observers salivating over the Russians' proclivity to read books while riding public transportation.) Or wasn't there perhaps some flaw in the very literature of the nineteenth century that precipitated that dive? Or was it simply a matter of ups and downs, of a vertical pendulum pertinent to the spiritual climate of any nation? And is it legitimate to ask such questions anyway?

It *is* legitimate, and especially in a country with an authoritarian past and totalitarian present. For unlike the subconscious, the superego is expected to be vocal. To be sure, the national upheaval that took place in Russia in this century has no parallel in the history of Christendom. Similarly, its reductive effect on the human psyche was unique enough to enable the rulers to talk about a "new society" and a "new type of man." But then that was precisely the goal of the whole enterprise: to uproot the species spiritually to the point of no return; for how else can you build a genuinely new society? You start neither with the foundation nor with the roof: you start by making new bricks.

What took place, in other words, was an unprecedented anthropological tragedy, a genetic backslide whose net result is a drastic reduction of human potential. To quibble about it, to use political-science mumbo-jumbo here is misleading and unnecessary. Tragedy is history's chosen genre. Had it not been for literature's own resilience, we wouldn't have known any other. In fact, it is an act of self-preservation on the part of prose to produce a comedy or a *roman à clef*. Yet such was the magnitude of what happened in Russia in this century that all the genres available to prose were, and still are, in one way or another, shot through with this tragedy's mesmerizing presence. No matter which way one turns, one catches the Gorgon-like stare of history.

For literature, unlike its audience, this is both good and bad. The good part comes from the fact that tragedy provides a work of literature with a greater than usual substance and expands its readership by appealing to morbid curiosity. The bad part is that tragedy confines the writer's imagination very much to itself. For tragedy is essentially a didactic enterprise and as such it's stylistically limiting. Personal, let alone national, drama reduces, indeed negates, a writer's ability to achieve the aesthetic detachment imperative for a lasting work of art. The gravity of the matter simply cancels the desire for stylistic endeavor. Narrating a tale of mass extermination, one's not terribly keen to unleash the stream of consciousness; and rightly so. However attractive such discretion is, one's soul profits from it more than does one's paper.

On paper, such display of scruples pushes a work of fiction toward the genre of biography, this last bastion of realism (which explains this genre's popularity far more than the uniqueness of its subjects). In the end, every tragedy is a biographical event, one way or another. As such, it tends to exacerbate the Aristotelian art-to-life proximity, to the point of reducing it to a synonym. The common view of prose as being made in the likeness of speech doesn't help matters much either. The sad truth about this equating art to life is that it's always done at the expense of art. Had a tragic experience been a guarantee of a masterpiece, readers would be a dismal minority vis-à-vis illustrious multitudes inhabiting ruined and freshly erected pantheons. Were ethics and aesthetics synonymous, literature would be the province of cherubs, not of mortals. Luckily, though, it's the other way around: cherubs, in all likelihood, wouldn't bother inventing the stream of consciousness, being more interested in the *steam* of it.

For prose is, apart from anything, an artifice, a bag of tricks. As artifice, it has its own pedigree, its own dynamics, its own laws, and its own logic. Perhaps more than ever, this sort of thing has been made apparent by the endeavors of modernism, whose standards play a great role in today's assessment of the work of the writer. For modernism is but a logical consequence—compression and concision—of things classical. (And this is why one is hesitant to add to the list of modernism's properties its own ethics. This is also why it's not altogether futile to ask history those questions. For, contrary to popular belief, history answers: by means of today, of the present; and that's what perhaps is the present's main charm, if not its sole justification.) At any rate, if these standards of modernism have any psychological significance, it is that the degree of their mastery indicates the degree of a writer's independence from his material or, more broadly, the degree of primacy of an individual over his own or his nation's predicament.

It can be argued, in other words, that stylistically at least, art has outlived tragedy, and, with it, so has the artist. That the issue to an artist is to tell the story not on its own but on his own terms. Because the artist stands for an individual, a hero of his own time: not of time past. His sensibility owes more to the aforesaid dynamics, logic, and laws of his artifice than to his actual historical experience, which is nearly always redundant. The artist's job vis-à-vis his society is to project, to offer this sensibility to the audience as perhaps the only available route of departure from the known, captive self. If art teaches men anything, it is to become like art: not like other men. Indeed, if there is a chance for men to become anything but victims or villains of their time, it lies in their prompt response to those last two lines from Rilke's "Torso of Apollo" that say:

> . . . *this torso shouts at you with its every muscle:*
> *"Do change your life!"*

And this is precisely where the Russian prose of this century fails. Hypnotized by the scope of the tragedy that befell the nation, it keeps scratching its wounds, unable to transcend the experience either philosophically or stylistically. No matter how devastating one's indictment of the political system may be, its delivery always comes wrapped in the sprawling cadences of *fin de siècle* religious humanist rhetoric. No matter how poisonously sarcastic one gets, the target of such sarcasm is always external: the system and the powers-that-be. The human being is always extolled, his innate goodness is always regarded as the guarantee of the ultimate defeat of evil. Resignation is always a virtue and a welcome subject, if only because of the infinity of its examples.

In the age that read Proust, Kafka, Joyce, Musil, Svevo, Faulkner, Beckett, etc., it's precisely these characteristics that make a yawning and disdainful Russian grab a detective novel or a book by a foreign author: a Czech, a Pole, a Hungarian, an Englishman, an Indian. Yet these same characteristics gratify many a Western literary pundit bewailing the sorry state of the novel in his own language and darkly or transparently hinting at the aspects of suffering beneficial to the art of letters. It may sound like a paradox, but, for a variety of reasons—chief of which is the low cultural diet on which the nation has been kept for more than half a century—the reading tastes of the Russian public are far less conservative than those of the spokesmen for their Western counterparts. For the latter, oversaturated presumably with modernist detachment, experimentation, absurdity, and so forth, the Russian prose of this century, especially that of the postwar period, is a respite, a breather, and they rave about and expand on the subject of the Russian soul, of the traditional values of Russian fiction, of the surviving legacy of the nineteenth century's religious humanism and all the good that it brought to Russian letters, of—should I quote—the severe spirit of Russian Orthodoxy. (As opposed, no doubt, to the laxness of Roman Catholicism.)

Whatever ax, and whomsoever with, people of this sort want to grind, the real point is that religious humanism is indeed a legacy. But it is a legacy not so much of the nineteenth century in particular as of the general spirit of consolation, of justifying the existential order on the highest, preferably ecclesiastical, plane, pertinent to the Russian sensibility and to the Russian cultural endeavor as such. To say the least, no writer in Russian history is exempt from this attitude, ascribing to Divine Providence the most dismal occurrences and making them automatically subject to human forgiveness. The trouble with this otherwise appealing attitude is that it's fully shared by the secret police as well, and could be cited by its employees on Judgment Day as a sound excuse for their practices.

Practical aspects aside, one thing is clear: this sort of ecclesiastical relativism (which is what the grounded flight of religious humanism boils down to on paper) naturally results in a heightened attention to detail, elsewhere called realism. Guided by this world view, a writer and a policeman rival each other in precision, and, depending on who is gaining the upper hand in a society, supply this realism with its eventual epithet. Which goes to show that the transition of Russian fiction from Dostoevsky to its present state hasn't occurred overnight, and that it wasn't exactly a transition either, because, even for his own time, Dostoevsky was an isolated, autonomous phenomenon. The sad truth about the whole matter is that Russian prose has been in a metaphysical slump for quite some time, ever since it produced Tolstoy, who took the idea of art reflecting reality a bit too literally and in whose shadow the subordinate clauses of Russian prose are writhing indolently till this day.

This may sound like a gross simplification, for indeed, by itself, Tolstoy's mimetic avalanche would be of a limited stylistic significance were it not for its timing: it hit the Russian readership almost simultaneously with Dostoevsky. Surely for an average Western reader, this sort of distinction between Dostoevsky and Tolstoy is of limited or exotic consequence, if any. Reading both of them in translation, he regards them as one great Russian writer, and the fact that they both were translated by the same hand, Constance Garnett's, is of no help. (Even today, it must be noted, the same translator can be assigned to do *Notes from the House of the Dead* and *The Death of Ivan Ilyich*—presumably because the Dead and Death are perceived as enough of a common denominator.) Hence, the pundits' speculation about the traditional values of Russian literature; hence, too, the popular belief in the coherent unity of Russian prose in the nineteenth century and the subsequent expectations of its similar show in the twentieth century. All that is quite far from reality; and, frankly, the proximity of Dostoevsky and Tolstoy in time was the unhappiest coincidence in the history of Russian literature. The consequences of it were such that perhaps the only way Providence can defend itself against charges of playing tricks with the spiritual makeup of a great nation is by saying that this way it prevented the Russians from getting too close to its secrets. Because who knows better than Providence that whoever follows a great writer is bound to pick things up precisely where the great man left them. And Dostoevsky went perhaps too high for Providence's liking. So it sends in a Tolstoy as if to ensure that Dostoevsky in Russia gets no continuum.

2

It worked; there was none. Save for Lev Shestov, a literary critic and philosopher, Russian prose went with Tolstoy, only too glad to spare itself climbing the heights of Dostoevsky's spiritual pitch. It went down the winding, well-trodden path of mimetic writing, and at several removes—via Chekhov, Korolenko, Kuprin, Bunin, Gorky, Leonid Andreev, Gladkov—has reached the pits of socialist realism. The Tolstoy mountain cast a long shadow, to emerge from which one had to either outdo Tolstoy in precision or offer a qualitatively new linguistic content. Even those who took the second route and fought that engulfing shadow of descriptive fiction most valiantly—authors like Pilnyak, Zamyatin, Babel, and a few others—were paralyzed by it into a telegraph-style tongue-twitching that, for a while, would pass for an avant-garde art. Still, however generously these men were endowed with talent, spiritually they were but products of the aforementioned ecclesiastical relativism; the pressures of the new social order easily reduced them to outright cynicism, and their works to tantalizing hors d'oeuvres on the empty table of a lean nation.

The reason Russian prose went with Tolstoy lies of course in his stylistic idiom, with its open invitation to imitate it. Hence, an impression that one can beat him; hence, too, a promise of security, since even by losing to him one winds up with a substantial—recognizable!—product. Nothing of the sort emanated from Dostoevsky. Quite apart from the nonexistent chances of beating him in the game, the pure aping of his style was out of the question. In a sense, Tolstoy was inevitable because Dostoevsky was unique. Neither his spiritual quest nor his "means of transportation" offered any possibility of repetition. The latter especially, with its plots evolving according to the immanent logic of scandal, with its feverishly accelerating sentences conglomerating in their rapid progress, bureaucratese, ecclesiastical terminology, *lumpen* argot, French utopists' mumbo-jumbo, the classical cadences of gentry prose —anything! all the layers of contemporary diction—the latter especially constituted an unthinkable act to follow.

In many ways, he was our first writer to trust the intuition of language more than his own—and more than intimations of his system of belief or those of his personal philosophy. And language repaid him a hundredfold. Its subordinate clauses often carried him much farther than his original intentions or insights would have allowed him to travel. In other words, he treated the language not so much as a novelist but as a poet—or as a biblical prophet demanding from his audience not imitation but conversion. A born metaphysician, he instinctively realized that for probing infinity, whether an ecclesiastical one or that of the human psyche, there was no tool more far-reaching than his highly inflected mother tongue, with its convoluted syntax. His art was anything but mimetic: it wasn't imitating reality; it was creating, or better still, reaching for one. In this vector of his he was effectively straying from Orthodoxy (or for that matter from any creed). He simply felt that art is not about life, if only because life is not about life. For Dostoevsky, art, like life, is about what man exists for. Like biblical parables, his novels are vehicles to obtain the answer and not goals unto themselves.

There are, roughly, two kinds of men and, correspondingly, two kinds of writers. The first kind, undoubtedly a majority, regards life as the one and only available reality. Turned writer, such a person will reproduce this reality in its minutest detail; he'll give you a conversation in the bedroom, a battlefield scene, the texture of upholstery, scents and tangs, with a precision rivaling your senses and the lenses of your camera; rivaling perhaps reality itself. Closing his book is like the end of a movie: the lights go up and you walk out into the street admiring Technicolor and the performance of this or that star whom you may even try to imitate subsequently in accent or deportment. The second kind, a minority, perceives his, and anyone else's, life as a test tube for certain human qualities, the retention of which under extreme duress is crucial for either an ecclesiastical or an anthropological version of the species' arrival. As a writer, such a man won't give you much in the way of detail; instead, he'll describe his characters' states and twists of psyche with such thoroughness that you feel grateful for not having met him in person. Closing his book is like waking up with a changed face.

One certainly should decide for oneself with whom to go; and Russian fiction obviously flocked to the former, prodded in that direction, we shouldn't forget, by history and her ironclad agent: the *Polizeistaat*. And normally it would be unjustifiable to pass judgment on such a choice, made under such circumstances, were it not for several exceptions, the main one being the career of Andrei Platonov. But before getting to him, it would be only prudent to emphasize once more that at the turn of the century, Russian prose was indeed at a crossroads, at a fork, and that one of those two roads wasn't taken. Presumably too many things were happening on the outside to waste that famous mirror of Stendhal's on scrutinizing the contortions of one's psyche. The vast, corpse-strewn, treachery-ridden historical vistas, whose very air turned solid with howls of ubiquitous grief, called for an epic touch, not for insidious questioning —never mind that that questioning could have prevented this epic sight.

If anything, this idea of a fork, of a road not taken, can be somewhat helpful to an average reader in his distinguishing between two great Russian writers, in putting him on alert whenever he hears about the "traditional values" of the Russian literature of the nineteenth century. The main point, though, is that the road not taken was the road that led to modernism, as is evidenced by the influence of Dostoevsky on every major writer in this century, from Kafka on. The road taken led to the literature of socialist realism. To put it differently, in terms of guarding its secrets, Providence suffered some setbacks in the West but it won in Russia. However, even knowing as little as we do about Providence's ways, we have a reason to assume that it may be not entirely happy with its victory. That is at least one explanation for its gift to Russian literature of Andrei Platonov.

3

If I refrain from stating here that Platonov is a greater writer than Joyce or Musil or Kafka, it's not because such ratings are in poor taste or because of his essential unavailability through existing translations. The trouble with such ratings is not poor taste (when was that ever a deterrent to an admirer?) but the vagueness of hierarchy that such a notion of superiority implies. As for the inadequacy of available translations, they are that way through no fault of the translators; the guilty party here is Platonov himself, or rather, the stylistic extremism of his language. It's the latter, along with the extreme character of the human predicament that Platonov is concerned with, that makes one refrain from this sort of hierarchical judgment, for the above-mentioned writers were not exposed to either extreme. He definitely belongs to this echelon of literature; yet, on those heights there is no hierarchy.

Platonov was born in 1899 and died in 1951 of tuberculosis, which he contracted from his son, whose release from prison he had eventually won, only to have his child die in his arms. From a photograph, a lean face with features as simple as a rural landscape looks at you patiently and as though prepared to take in anything. By education a civil engineer (he worked for several years on various irrigation projects), he began to write rather early, in his twenties, which coincided with the twenties of this century. He fought in the civil war, worked for various newspapers, and, although reluctantly published, achieved a great reputation in the thirties. Then came the arrest of his son on charges of anti-Soviet conspiracy, then came the first signs of official ostracism, then came World War II, during which he was in the army working for the army newspaper. After the war he was silenced; a short story of his published in 1946 invited a full-page pogrom by the top critic of *Literaturnaya Gazeta*, and that was it. After that he was allowed only occasional freelance ghost-writing jobs, such as editing some fairy tales for children; beyond that, nothing. But then his tuberculosis worsened and he couldn't do much anyway. He and his wife and their daughter lived on his wife's salary as an editor; he'd moonlight as a street sweeper or a stagehand in a theater nearby.

He wasn't arrested, although that review in *Literaturnaya Gazeta* was a clear sign that his days as a writer were numbered. But they were numbered anyway; the top honcho in the Writers' Union administration even refused to endorse the secret police's case against Platonov, both because of his grudging admiration for the man and because he knew that the man was ill. Regaining consciousness after a bout with his illness, Platonov would often see by his bedside a couple of men gazing at him very keenly: the state security was monitoring the progress of his illness to determine whether they should bother with this character, and whether the Writers' Union official's stubbornness was justified. So Platonov died of natural causes.

All of this, or most of it, you'll no doubt find in various encyclopedias, forewords, afterwords, in dissertations about his work. By the standards of the time and the place, it was a normal life, if not an idyllic one. However, by the standards of the work Platonov did, his life was a miracle. That the author of *The Foundation Pit* and *Chevengur* was allowed to die in his own bed can be attributed only to divine intervention, if only in the guise of a fraction of scruples surviving in the men from the administration of the Writers' Union. Another explanation could be that neither novel had ever been in circulation, since both were presumably, in Platonov's view, works in progress, temporarily abandoned, much in the same way as Musil's *The Man without Qualities*. Still, the reasons for which they were temporarily abandoned also should be regarded as divine intervention.

Chevengur is some six hundred pages long; *The Founda-*

tion Pit is one hundred and sixty. The first is about a man who, in the middle of the civil war, gets it into his head that there is a possibility that socialism has already emerged somewhere in a natural, elemental way; so he mounts his horse, which is named Rosa Luxemburg, and sets off to discover whether or not that is the case. *The Foundation Pit* takes place during collectivization, in some provincial landscape where for quite some time the entire population has been engaged in digging a vast foundation pit for the subsequent erection of a many-storied brightly lit building called "socialism." If from this idiotically simpleminded description one concludes that we are talking about yet another anti-Soviet satirical writer, with perhaps a surrealistic bent, one should blame the description's author, as well as the necessity for making the description; the main thing one should know is that one is wrong.

For these books are indescribable. The power of devastation they inflict upon their subject matter exceeds by far any demands of social criticism and should be measured in units that have very little to do with literature as such. These books never were published in Soviet Russia and they never will be published there, for they come closest to doing to the system what it has done to its subjects. One wonders whether they will ever be published in Russia, for apart from concrete social evil, their real target is the sensibility of language that has brought that evil about. The whole point about Andrei Platonov is that he is a millenarian writer if only because he attacks the very carrier of millenarian sensibility in Russian society: the language itself—or, to put it in a more graspable fashion, the revolutionary eschatology embedded in the language.

The roots of Russian millenarianism are essentially not

very different from those of other nations. This sort of thing always has to do with this or that religious community's anticipation of its oncoming peril (less frequently, but as well, with the presence of a real one) and with that community's limited literacy. The few who read, and the still fewer who write, normally get to run the show, suggesting as a rule an alternative interpretation of Holy Writ. On the mental horizon of every millenarian movement there is always a version of a New Jerusalem, the proximity to which is determined by the intensity of sentiment. The idea of God's City being within reach is in direct proportion to the religious fervor in which the entire journey originates. The variations on this theme include also a version of an apocalypse, ideas of a change of the entire world order, and a vague, but all the more appealing because of that, notion of a new time, in terms of both chronology and quality. (Naturally, transgressions committed in the name of getting to a New Jerusalem fast are justified by the beauty of the destination.) When such a movement succeeds, it results in a new creed. If it fails, then, with the passage of time and the spread of literacy, it degenerates into utopias, to peter out completely in the dry sands of political science and the pages of science fiction. However, there are several things that may somewhat rekindle soot-covered embers. It's either severe oppression of the population, a real, most likely military peril, a sweeping epidemic, or some substantial chronological event, like the end of a millennium or the beginning of a new century.

If only because the species' eschatological capacity is always one and the same, there is not much point in going on about the roots of Russian millenarianism in great detail. Its fruits, too, were not of such great variety, except for their volume and for the influence their volume exerted on the language of the epoch in which Platonov happened to live. Still, talking about Platonov and that epoch, we should bear in mind certain peculiarities of the period that directly preceded the arrival of this epoch in Russia, as well as elsewhere.

The period—the turn of the century—was indeed a peculiar one because of its climate of mass agitation fueled by the incoherent symbolism with which this chronological non-event—the turn of the century—was invested by a variety of technological and scientific breakthroughs, by the spread of means of communication, causing a qualitative leap in the masses' self-awareness. It was the period of great political activization: in Russia alone by the time of the Revolution there were more political parties than in today's America or Great Britain. Along with that, it was the period of a great upsurge in philosophical writing and in science fiction with strong utopian or social-engineering overtones. The air was filled with expectations and prophecies of a big change, of a new order of things coming, of restructuring the world. On the horizon there was Halley's comet, threatening to hit the globe; in the news, military defeat at the hands of the yellow race; and in an undemocratic society it's usually one step from a czar to a messiah or, for that matter, to the Antichrist. The period, to say the least, was a bit on the hysterical side. So it's indeed small wonder that when revolution came, many took it for what they had been looking for.

Platonov writes in the language of the "qualitative change," in the language of a greater proximity to New Jerusalem. More precisely, in the language of paradise's builders—or, as in the case with *The Foundation Pit*, of paradise's diggers. Now, the idea of paradise is the logical end of human thought in the sense that it, that thought, goes no further; for beyond paradise there is nothing else, nothing else happens. It can safely be said, therefore, that paradise is a dead end; it's the last vision of space, the end of things, the summit of the mountain, the peak from which there is nowhere to step—except into pure Chronos; hence the introduction of the concept of eternal life. The same actually applies to hell; structurally at least, these two things have a lot in common.

Existence in the dead end is not limited by anything, and if one can conceive that even there "circumstances condition consciousness" and engender their own psychology, then it is above all in language that this psychology is expressed. In general, it should be noted that the first casualty of any discourse about utopia—desired or already attained—is grammar; for language, unable to keep up with this sort of thought, begins to gasp in the subjunctive mood and starts to gravitate toward categories and constructions of a rather timeless denomination. As a consequence of this, the ground starts to slip out from under even the simplest nouns, and they gradually get enveloped in an aura of arbitrariness.

This is the sort of thing that is happening nonstop in Platonov's prose. It can safely be said about this writer that his every sentence drives the Russian language into a semantic dead end or, more precisely, reveals a proclivity for dead ends, a blind-alley mentality in the language itself. What he does on the page is approximately as follows: he starts a sentence in a way familiar enough that you almost anticipate the tenor of the rest. However, each word that he uses is qualified either by epithet or intonation, or by its incorrect position within the context, to the extent that the rest of the sentence gives you not so much a sense of surprise as the sense that you have compromised yourself by knowing anything about the tenor of speech in general and about how to place these words in particular. You find yourself locked in, marooned in blinding proximity to the meaninglessness of the phenomenon this or that word denotes, and you realize that you have got yourself into this predicament through your own verbal carelessness, through trusting too much your own ear and the words themselves. Reading Platonov, one gets a sense of the relentless, implacable absurdity built into the language and that with each new—anyone's—utterance, that absurdity deepens. And that there is no way out of that blind alley but to retreat back into the very language that brought one in.

This is perhaps a too laborious—and not terribly accurate or exhaustive (far from that!)—attempt to describe Platonov's writing technique. Perhaps, too, effects of this sort can be created in the Russian language only, although the presence of the absurd in grammar says something not just about a particular linguistic drama but about the human race as a whole. All I have tried to do is to highlight one of Platonov's stylistic aspects that happens to be not so much even a stylistic one. He simply had a tendency to see his words to their logical—that is absurd, that is totally paralyzing—end. In other words, like no other Russian writer before or after him, Platonov was able to reveal a self-destructive, eschatological element within the language itself, and that, in turn, was of extremely revealing consequence to the revolutionary eschatology with which history supplied him as his subject matter.

In casting a sort of myopic, estranged glance at any page

of this writer, one gets a feeling of looking at a cuneiform tablet: so densely is it packed with those semantic blind alleys. Or else his pages look like a great department store with its apparel items turned inside out. This by no means suggests that Platonov was the enemy of this utopia, of this socialism, of the regime, collectivization, etc.; not at all. It's just that what he was doing with the language went far beyond the framework of that specific utopia. But then this is what every language inevitably does: it goes beyond history. However, what's interesting about Platonov's style is that he appears to have deliberately and completely subordinated himself to the vocabulary of his utopia—with all its cumbersome neologisms, abbreviations, acronyms, bureaucratese, sloganeering, militarized imperatives, and the like. Apart from the writer's instinct, this willingness, not to say abandon, with which he went for newspeak, indicates, it would seem, his sharing of some beliefs in the promises the new society was so generous with.

It would be false as well as unnecessary to try to divorce Platonov from his epoch; the language was to do this anyway, if only because epochs are finite. In a sense, one can see this writer as an embodiment of language temporarily occupying a piece of time and reporting from within. The essence of his message is LANGUAGE IS A MILLENARIAN DEVICE, HISTORY ISN'T, and coming from him that would be appropriate. Of course, to get into excavating the genealogy of Platonov's style, one has inevitably to mention the "plaiting of words" of centuries of Russian hagiography, Nikolai Leskov with his tendency to highly individualized narrative (so-called "*skaz*"—sort of "yarn-ing"), Gogol's satirical epic sway, Dostoevsky with his snowballing, feverishly choking conglomeration of dictions. But with

Platonov the issue is not lines of succession or tradition in Russian literature but the writer's dependence on the synthesizing (or, more precisely, supra-analytical) essence of the Russian language itself, conditioning—at times by means of purely phonetic allusions—the emergence of concepts totally devoid of any real content. His main tool was inversion; and as he wrote in a totally inverted, highly inflected language, he was able to put an equals sign between "language" and "inversion." "Version"—the normal word order—came more and more to play a service role.

Again, very much after Dostoevsky's fashion, this treatment of language was more befitting a poet than a novelist. And, indeed, Platonov, like Dostoevsky, wrote some poetry. But if Dostoevsky, for his Captain Lebyadkin poem about the cockroach in *The Possessed*, can be considered the first writer of the absurd, Platonov's verses earn him a niche in no pantheon. But then scenes such as the one in *The Foundation Pit* where the bear-apprentice at some village's smithy is enforcing collectivization and is more politically orthodox than his master put Platonov somewhat beyond the status of a novelist as well. Of course, it could be said that he was our first properly surrealist writer, except that his surrealism wasn't a literary category tied in our mind with an individualistic world view but a product of philosophical madness, a product of blind-alley psychology on a mass scale. Platonov wasn't an individualist; quite the contrary: his consciousness was determined precisely by the mass scale and both the impersonal and the depersonalizing character of what was happening. His novels depict not a hero against a background but rather that background itself devouring a hero. And that's why his surrealism, in its turn, is impersonal, folkloric, and, to a certain degree, akin to ancient—or for that matter any—mythology, which, in all fairness, should be regarded as the classical form of surrealism.

It's not egocentric individualists whom both the Almighty and literary tradition automatically endow with a crisis-prone sensibility but traditionally inanimate masses that express in Platonov's works the philosophy of the absurd; and it is due to the numerical vastness of its carriers that this philosophy becomes far more convincing and utterly unbearable in its magnitude. Unlike Kafka, Joyce, and, let's say, Beckett, who narrate quite natural tragedies of their "alter egos," Platonov speaks of a nation which in a sense has become the victim of its own language; or, to put it more accurately, he tells a story about this very language, which turns out to be capable of generating a fictitious world, and then falls into grammatical dependence on it.

Because of all this, Platonov seems to be quite untranslatable, and, in one sense, that's a good thing: for the language into which he cannot be translated. Still, the body of his work is very substantial and relatively diverse. *Chevengur* and *The Foundation Pit* were written, respectively, toward the end of the twenties and in the beginning of the thirties; Platonov remained operational for quite some time after that. In this sense, his case could be regarded as that of Joyce in reverse: he produced his *Portrait of the Artist* and *Dubliners* AFTER *Finnegans Wake* and *Ulysses*. (And, as we are at this moment on this subject of translation, it is worth recalling that sometime in the late thirties one of Platonov's short stories was published in the United States and that Hemingway was extolling it. So it is not entirely hopeless, although the story was very third-rate Platonov; I think it was his "The Third Son.")

Like every living creature, a writer is a universe unto himself, only more so. There is always more in him that separates him from his colleagues than vice versa. To talk about his pedigree, trying to fit him into this or that tradition of literature is, essentially, to move in a direction exactly opposite to the one in which he himself was moving. In general, this temptation of seeing a literature as a coherent whole is always stronger when it's viewed very much from the outside. In this sense, perhaps, literary criticism indeed resembles astronomy; one wonders, though, if this resemblance is really flattering.

If there is any tradition of Russian literature, Platonov represents a radical departure from it. I, for one, don't see either his predecessors, save perhaps some passages in *The Life of Archpriest Avvakum*, or his successors. There is a sense of terrific autonomy to this man, and much though I'd like to link him to Dostoevsky, with whom he perhaps has more in common than with anyone else in Russian literature, I'd rather refrain from doing so: it would illuminate nothing. Of course, what screams to be pointed out is that both *Chevengur* and *The Foundation Pit* thematically, at least, can be regarded as sequels to Dostoevsky's *The Possessed* because they represent the realization of Dostoevsky's prophecy. But then again, this realization was supplied by history, by reality; it wasn't a writer's conjecture. For that matter, one can see in *Chevengur*, with its central character's passage through the lands in his search for the organically emerged socialism, and with his long soliloquies to a horse called Rosa Luxemburg, an echo of *Don*

Quixote or *Dead Souls*. But these echoes reveal nothing either—except the size of the wilderness in which one cries.

Platonov was very much on his own, and in a big way. His autonomy is the autonomy of an idiosyncratic metaphysician, a materialist, essentially, who tries to comprehend the universe independently, from his vantage—or disadvantage—point of a small muddy provincial town lost like a comma in the infinite book of a vast, sprawling continent. His pages are studded with people of this sort: provincial teachers, engineers, mechanics, who in their godforsaken places entertain their huge homemade ideas about world order, ideas that are as mind-boggling and fantastic as these men's own isolation.

I have gone on about Platonov at such length partly because he is not very well known in this country, but mainly in order to suggest that the mental plane of regard of contemporary Russian prose is somewhat different from the rustic view of it generally entertained in the West. The uniformity of the social order doesn't guarantee that of mental operation; an individual's aesthetics never completely surrenders to either personal or national tragedy, no more than it surrenders to either version of happiness. If there is any tradition in Russian prose, it is one of searching for a greater thought, for a more exhaustive analysis of the human condition than is at present available, of looking for a better resource to ladle from to endure the siege of reality. But in all that, Russian prose is not that different from the vectors of other Western and Eastern literatures: it's a part of Christian civilization's culture, and neither the best nor most exotic part at that. To regard it otherwise amounts to racism in reverse, to patting the poor relation on the shoulder for his decent conduct, and that should somehow be stopped: if only because this attitude encourages sloppy translations.

4

Perhaps the most troublesome aspect of Platonov is that the quality of his work makes it hard to sustain an engaged discourse about his contemporaries and those who came after him. This may even be cited by the powers-that-be as a reason for suppressing both *Chevengur* and *The Foundation Pit.* On the other hand, it's precisely the suppression of these two books, resulting in a lack of awareness of their existence, that has allowed a great number of writers—both his and our contemporaries—to go on with their production. There are crimes the forgiving of which is a crime also, and this is one of them. Suppression of Platonov's two novels not only set back the entire literature some fifty years; it also hampered the development of the national psyche as such by the same number of years. Burning books, after all, is just a gesture; not publishing them is a falsification of time. But then again, that is precisely the goal of the system: to issue its own version of the future.

Now this future has arrived, and although it's not exactly what the system bet on, in terms of Russian prose it's far less than it should have been. It's a good prose all right, but both stylistically and philosophically, it's far less enterprising than the prose of the twenties and thirties. It's conservative enough to enable one to talk about "traditions of Russian prose," of course, but it knows in what century it lives. For the latest in that knowledge it has to go, unfortunately, to foreign authors, most of whom still have less to offer than that same Platonov. In the sixties the best of modern Russian writers were taking their cues from Hemingway, Heinrich Böll, Salinger, and, to a lesser extent, from Camus and Sartre. The seventies were the decade of Nabokov, who is to Platonov what a tightrope walker is to a Chomolungma climber. The sixties also saw the first selection in Russian of writings by Kafka, and that mattered a lot. Then Borges came out, and on the horizon looms the Russian translation of Robert Musil's great masterpiece.

There are a great many other foreign authors of lesser stature who, one way or another, today teach Russian writers a lesson in modernism, from Cortázar to Iris Murdoch; but as has already been said, it's only the best of them who are willing to learn this lesson. The ones who really learn this lesson properly are the readers, and today an average Russian reader is much smarter than a promising Russian writer. Also, the trouble with the best is that they are writers of mainly satirical bent, and they face from the outset obstacles of such magnitude that they have to go easy even on that acquired knowledge. Apart from this, in the last decade there has been emerging in the country a largely unpalatable, strong tendency toward nationalistic self-appreciation, and many a writer, consciously or unwittingly, caters to that tendency, which often has the attraction of asserting the national identity in the face of the depersonalizing mass of the state. Natural and commendable as such an aspiration may be, for literature it beats a stylistic and aesthetic retreat and means recoiling without firing a destructive salvo, sequestering oneself in narcissistic self-pity because of having curbed one's own metaphysical ability. I am talking here obviously of the "peasant prose," which, in its Antaeus-like desire to touch the ground, went a bit too far and took root.

Neither in invention nor in overall world view does the Russian prose of today offer anything qualitatively new. Its most profound perception to date is that the world is radically evil, and the state is but that evil's blind, if not necessarily blunt, instrument. Its most avant-garde device is stream of consciousness; its most burning ambition is to admit eroticism and foul language into print: not, alas, for the sake of the print, but to further the cause of realism. Thoroughly fundamentalist in its values, it employs stylistic devices whose chief attraction lies in their familiar solidity. The name of the game is, in short, classical standards. But here is the rub.

What underlies this concept—classical standards—is the idea of man being the measure of all things. To tie them to a particular historical past, say, to the Victorian era, amounts to the dismissal of the species' psychological development. To say the least, it's like believing that a seventeenth-century man felt hunger more than his modern counterpart. Thus by harping on the traditional values of Russian fiction, on its "severe spirit of Orthodoxy," and whatnot, the critical profession invites us to judge this fiction by standards which are not so much classical as those of yesterday. A work of art is always a product of its time, and it should be judged by this time's standards, by the standards of its century to say the least (especially if that century is about to be over). It is precisely because Russia produced such great prose in the nineteenth century that there is no need for special provisions in evaluation of its contemporary fiction.

As in everything else, in the way of prose this century has seen a lot. What it has come to value, it seems, apart from popular-at-all-times straight storytelling, is a stylistic invention as such, a structural device—montage, hopscotch, whatever. In other words, it has come to like a display of self-awareness, manifested by the narrator's distancing himself from the narrative. That, after all, is time's own posture toward existence. In still other words, in art, this century (alias time) has come to like itself, the reflection of its own features: fragmentation, incoherence, an absence of content, a dimmed or a bird's-eye view of the human predicament, of suffering, of ethics, of art itself. For lack of a better name, the compendium of these features is commonly called today "modernism," and it is of "modernism" that contemporary Russian fiction, both published and underground, falls markedly short.

By and large, it still clings to an extensive, conventional narrative with an emphasis on a central character and his development, along the lines of a *Bildungsroman* technique, hoping—and not without good reason—that, by reproducing reality in its minute detail, it may produce a sufficiently surrealistic or absurdist effect. The grounds for such hope, of course, are solid: the quality of the reality of the country; oddly, though, that turns out to be not enough. What thwarts these hopes is precisely the stylistic conventionality of the means of depiction, which hark back to the psychological atmosphere of these means' noble origins, i.e., to the nineteenth century, i.e., to irreality.

There was one particular moment, for instance, in Solzhenitsyn's *Cancer Ward*, when Russian prose, as well as the writer himself, came within a two- or three-paragraph distance of a decisive breakthrough. Solzhenitsyn describes in one chapter the daily grind of a woman doctor. The description's flatness and monotony definitely matches the list of her tasks, epic in their length and idiocy, yet this list lasts longer than anyone's ability to sustain a dispassionate tone recording it: a reader expects an explosion: it is too unbearable. And this is exactly where the author stops. Had he gone on for two or three paragraphs more with this disproportion—of tone and content—we might have gotten a new literature; we might have gotten a real absurdity, engendered not by the stylistic endeavor of a writer but by the very reality of things.

So why did Solzhenitsyn stop? Why didn't he go on with those two or three paragraphs? Didn't he feel at the moment that he was on the verge of something? Perhaps he did, although I doubt it. The point is that he had no material to stuff those two more paragraphs with, no other tasks to mention. Why, then, one would ask, didn't he invent some? The answer is at the same time noble and sad: because he is a realist and inventing things would be untrue: both to the facts and to his nature as a writer. A realist, he had a different set of instincts from those that nudge you to make things up when you see an opening. It's for this reason that I doubt that he felt he was on the verge of something: he simply couldn't sense the opening, wasn't poised enough to see it. So the chapter ends on a moralizing, see-how-bad-things-are note. I remember reading it with my fingers almost trembling: "Now, now, now it's going to happen." It did not.

This episode in *Cancer Ward* is all the more symptomatic since Solzhenitsyn qualifies as both a published and an underground writer. Among many other things that these two categories have in common are their flaws. Unless he has completely crossed over to the experimental side, an underground writer can be distinguished from his colleagues in the establishment mainly by his subject matter, much less so by his diction. On the other hand, an experimentalist tends to go about his experimentation with a real vengeance: having no prospects of being published, he is usually quick to give up didactic concerns altogether, which eventually costs him even his limited audience of a few cognoscenti. Frequently, his only solace is a bottle, his only hope, to be compared by a scholar in some West German magazine to Uwe Johnson. In part because his work is utterly untranslatable, in part because he is usually employed by an institution doing some classified scientific research with military applications, he doesn't entertain thoughts about emigrating. Eventually, he abandons his artistic pursuits.

This is the way it goes, for the middle ground claimed in countries with a better political system by somebody like Michel Butor, Leonardo Sciascia, Günther Grass, or Walker Percy simply doesn't exist in Russia. It's an either/or situation in which even publishing abroad is not of decisive help, if only because it's invariably detrimental to the author's physical well-being. To produce a work of lasting consequence under these circumstances requires an amount of personal integrity more frequently possessed by tragic heroes than by the authors of those tragedies. Naturally, in this predicament prose fares worse than other forms of art, not only because the process of creating it is of a less mercurial nature, but also because, thanks to prose's didactic nature, it's been watched very closely indeed. The moment the prose watcher loses the author, it's curtains for the work; yet efforts to keep the work accessible to its watchdog render it properly sheepish. As for writing "for the drawer," "for the attic," which an established writer sometimes undertakes to clear his conscience, it too fails to bring him a stylistic cure—which became evident during the last decade, which saw almost the entire attic prose swept clean to the West and published there.

A great writer is one who elongates the perspective of human sensibility, who shows a man at the end of his wits an opening, a pattern to follow. After Platonov, the closest that Russian prose came to producing such a writer were Nadezhda Mandelstam with her memoirs and, to a somewhat lesser degree, Alexander Solzhenitsyn with his novels and documentary prose. I permit myself to put this great man second largely because of his apparent inability to discern behind the cruelest political system in the history of Christendom the human failure, if not the failure of the creed itself (so much for the severe spirit of Orthodoxy!). Given the magnitude of the historical nightmare he describes, this inability in itself is spectacular enough to suspect a dependence between aesthetic conservatism and resistance to the notion of man being radically bad. Quite apart from the stylistic consequence for one's writing, the refusal to accept this notion is pregnant with the recurrence of this nightmare in broad daylight—anytime.

Aside from these two names, Russian prose for the moment has very little to offer to a man at the end of his wits. There are a few isolated works which in their heartbreaking honesty or eccentricity approximate masterpieces. All they can supply our man with is either a momentary catharsis or comic relief. Though ultimately furthering one's subordination to the status quo, this is one of prose's better services; and it's better if the reading public in this country knows the names of Yury Dombrovsky, Vasily Grossman, Venedikt Erofeev, Andrei Bitov, Vasily Shukshin, Fazil Iskander, Yury Miloslavsky, Yevgeny Popov. Some of them authored only one or two books, some of them are already dead; but, together with the somewhat better-known Sergei Dovlatov, Vladimir Voinovich, Vladimir Maximov, Andrei Sinyavsky, Vladimir Maramzin, Igor Efimov, Eduard Limonov, Vasily Aksyonov, Sasha Sokolov, they constitute a reality with which everybody for whom Russian literature and things Russian are of any consequence sooner or later will have to reckon.

Each one of these men deserves a discussion of no lesser length than this lecture already is. Some of them happen to be my friends, some are quite the contrary. Squeezing them into one sentence is like listing air-crash victims; but then that's precisely where a catastrophe has occurred: in the air, in the world of ideas. The best works of these authors should be regarded as this catastrophe's survivors. If asked to name one or two books that stand to outlast their authors and the present generation of readers, I for one would name Voinovich's *In Plain Russian* and any selection of short stories by Yury Miloslavsky. However, the work that faces, in my view, a really incalculable future is Yuz Aleshkovsky's *Kangaroo*, soon to come out in English. (God help its translator!)

Kangaroo is a novel of the most devastating, the most terrifying hilarity. It belongs in the genre of satire; however, its net effect is neither revulsion at the system nor comic relief, but pure metaphysical terror. This effect has a lot less to do with the author's rather apocalyptical world view as such than with the quality of his ear. Aleshkovsky, whose reputation in Russia as a songwriter is extremely high (in fact, some of his songs are a part of national folklore), hears the language like a prodigy. The hero of *Kangaroo* is a professional pickpocket whose career spans the entire history of Soviet Russia, and the novel is an epic yarn spun out in the foulest of language, for which either "slang" or "argot" fails as a definition. Much like a private philosophy or set of beliefs for an intellectual, foul language in the mouths of the masses serves as an antidote to the predominantly positive, obtrusive monologue of authority. In *Kangaroo*, very much as in everyday Russian discourse, the volume of this antidote overshoots its curative purpose by a margin capable of accommodating yet another universe. While in terms of its plot and structure this book may bear a resemblance to something like *The Good Soldier Schweik* or *Tristram Shandy*, linguistically it is absolutely Rabelaisian. It is a monologue, nasty, morbid, frightful, rampant with a cadence resembling biblical verse. To drop yet another name, this book sounds like Jeremiah: laughing. For a man at the end of his wits that's already something. However, it is not exactly concern for that anonymous yet ubiquitous man that makes one appreciate this particular work, but its overall stylistic thrust in a direction unfamiliar to the Russian prose of today. It goes where the vernacular goes; that is, beyond the finality of a content, idea, or belief: toward the next phrase, the next utterance: into the infinity of speech. To say the least, it strays from the genre of the ideological novel of whatever denomination, absorbing the condemnation of the social order but spilling over it as over a cup too small to contain the flood of language.

Starting with the authors mentioned above, some may find these notes maximalist and biased; most likely they will ascribe these flaws to their author's own métier. Still others may find the view of things expressed here too schematic to be true. True: it's schematic, narrow, superficial. At best, it will be called subjective or elitist. That would be fair enough except that we should bear in mind that art is not a democratic enterprise, even the art of prose, which has an air about it of everybody being able to master it as well as to judge it.

The point, however, is that the democratic principle so welcome in nearly all spheres of human endeavor has no application in at least two of them: in art and in science. In these two spheres, the application of the democratic principle results in equating masterpiece with garbage and discovery with ignorance. The resistance to such an equation is synonymous with recognition of prose as an art; and it's precisely this recognition that forces one to discriminate in the most cruel fashion.

Whether one likes it or not, art is a linear process. To prevent itself from recoiling, art has the concept of cliché. Art's history is that of addition and refinement, of extending the perspective of human sensibility, of enriching, or more often condensing, the means of expression. Every new psychological or aesthetic reality introduced in art becomes instantly old for its next practitioner. An author disregarding this rule, somewhat differently phrased by Hegel, automatically destines his work—no matter what good press it gets in the marketplace—to assume the status of pulp.

But if it were only the fate of his work, or his own, that wouldn't be too bad. And the fact that supply of pulp creates a demand for pulp isn't too bad either; to art as such it's not dangerous: it always takes care of its own kind, as the poor or those in the animal kingdom do. The bad thing about prose which is not art is that it compromises the life it describes and plays a reductionist role in the development of the individual. This sort of prose offers one finalities where art would have offered infinities, comfort instead of challenge, consolation instead of a verdict. In short, it betrays man to his metaphysical or social enemies, whose name in either case is legion.

Heartless as it may sound in many ways, the condition Russian prose finds itself in today is of its own doing; the sad thing is that it keeps perpetuating this condition by being the way it is. Taking politics into consideration is therefore an oxymoron, or rather a vicious circle, for politics fills the vacuum left in people's minds and hearts precisely by art. There must be some lesson for other literatures in the plight of Russian prose in this century, for it's still a little bit more forgivable for Russian writers to operate the way they do, with Platonov dead, than for their counterparts in this country to court banalities, with Beckett alive.

1984

On "September 1, 1939" by W. H. Auden[*]

The poem in front of you has ninety-nine lines, and time permitting, we'll be going over each one of them. It may seem, and indeed be, tedious; but by doing so we have a better chance to learn something about its author as well as about the strategy of a lyrical poem in general. For this is a lyrical poem, its subject matter notwithstanding.

Because every work of art, be it a poem or a cupola, is understandably a self-portrait of its author, we won't strain ourselves too hard trying to distinguish between the author's persona and the poem's lyrical hero. As a rule, such distinctions are quite meaningless, if only because a lyrical hero is invariably an author's self-projection.

The author of this poem, as you already know, having been made to memorize it, is a critic of his century; but he is a part of this century also. So his criticism of it nearly

* This lecture was delivered as a part of a course in modern lyric poetry at the Writing Division of the School of the Arts at Columbia University. It was taped and transcribed by Miss Helen Handley and Ann Sherrill Pyne, students in the program.

always is self-criticism as well, and this is what imparts to his voice in this poem its lyrical poise. If you think that there are other recipes for successful poetic operation, you are in for oblivion.

We are going to examine this poem's linguistic content, since vocabulary is what distinguishes one writer from another. We will also pay attention to the ideas the poet puts forth, as well as to his rhyme schemes, for it's the latter that supply the former with a sense of inevitability. A rhyme turns an idea into law; and, in a sense, each poem is a linguistic codex.

As some of you have observed, there is a great deal of irony in Auden, and in this poem in particular. I hope we'll proceed in a fashion thorough enough for you to realize that this irony, this light touch, is the mark of a most profound despair; which is frequently the case with irony anyway. In general, I hope that by the end of this session, you'll develop the same sentiment toward this poem as the one that prompted it into existence—one of love.

2

This poem, whose title, I hope, is self-explanatory, was written shortly after our poet settled on these shores. His departure caused considerable uproar at home; he was charged with desertion, with abandoning his country in a time of peril. Well, the peril indeed came, but some time after the poet left England. Besides, he was precisely the one who, for about a decade, kept issuing warnings about its—the peril's—progress. The thing with perils, though, is that no matter how clairvoyant one is, there is no way to time their arrival. And the bulk of his accusers were precisely those who saw no peril coming: the left, the right, the pacifists, etc. What's more, his decision to move to the United States had very little to do with world politics: the reasons for the move were of a more private nature. We'll talk about that somewhat later, I hope. Presently what matters is that our poet finds himself at the outbreak of war on new shores, and therefore has a minimum of two audiences to address: those at home and those right in front of him. Let's see what effect this fact has upon his diction. Now, on with this thing . . .

I sit in one of the dives
On Fifty-second Street
Uncertain and afraid
As the clever hopes expire
Of a low dishonest decade:
Waves of anger and fear
Circulate over the bright
And darkened lands of the earth,
Obsessing our private lives;
The unmentionable odour of death
Offends the September night.

Let's start with the first two lines: "I sit in one of the dives/ On Fifty-second Street . . ." Why, in your view, does the poem start in this way? Why, for instance, this precision of "Fifty-second Street"? And how precise is it? Well, it's precise in that Fifty-second Street indicates a place that can't be somewhere in Europe. Good enough. And I think what Auden wants to play here a bit is the role of a journalist, of a war correspondent, if you wish. This opening has a distinct air of reporting. The poet says something like "your correspondent reports to you from . . ."; he is a newsman reporting to his people back in England. And here we are getting into something very interesting.

Watch that word "dive." It's not exactly a British word, right? Nor is "Fifty-second Street." For his posture of reporter they are obviously of immediate benefit: both things are equally exotic to his home audience. And this introduces you to one aspect of Auden with which we are going to deal for some time: the encroachment of American diction, a fascination with which was, I think, among the reasons for his move here. This poem was written in 1939, and for the five subsequent years his lines became literally strewn with Americanisms. He almost revels in incorporating them into his predominantly British diction, whose texture—the texture of English verse in general—gets considerably animated by the likes of "dives" and "raw towns." And we'll be going over them one by one because words and the way they sound are more important for a poet than ideas and convictions. When it comes to a poem, in the beginning there is still the word.

And in the beginning of this particular poem there is this "dive," and it's quite likely that this dive is responsible for the rest of it. He surely likes this word if only because he never used it before. But then again he thinks, "Humph, back there in England they might think that I am just kind of slumming, in the sense of language; that I am simply rolling these new American morsels over my tongue." So then, first of all, he rhymes "dives" with "lives," which is in itself telling enough, apart from animating an old rhyme. Secondly, he qualifies the word by saying "one of the dives," thereby reducing the exoticism of "dives."

At the same time, "one of the" increases the humbling effect of being in a dive in the first place, and this humbling effect suits well his reporter's posture. For he positions himself fairly low here: physically low, which means in the midst of things. That alone boosts the sense of verisimilitude: the guy who speaks from the thick of things is more readily listened to. What makes the whole thing even more convincing is "Fifty-second Street," because numbers after all are seldom used in poetry. Most likely, his first impulse was to say, "I sit in one of the dives"; but then he decided that "dives" may be too linguistically emphatic for the crowd back home, and so he puts in "on Fifty-second Street." This somewhat lightens the matter, since Fifty-second Street between Fifth and Sixth Avenues was at the time the jazz strip of the universe. Hence, by the way, all that syncopation that reverberates in the half-rhymes of those trimeters.

Remember: it is the second, and not the first, line that shows where your poem is to go metrically. It also informs an experienced reader as to the identity of the author, i.e., whether he is American or British (an American second line, normally, is quite bold: it violates the preconceived music of the meter with its linguistic content; a Briton, normally, tends to sustain the tonal predictability of the second line, introducing his own diction only in the third or, more likely, in the fourth line. Compare the tetrametric—or even pentametric—jobs of Thomas Hardy with E. A. Robinson, or better still, with Robert Frost). More importantly, though, the second line is the line that introduces the rhyme scheme.

"On Fifty-second Street" performs all these jobs. It tells you that it's going to be a poem in trimeters, that the author is hard-hitting enough to qualify as a native; that the rhyme is to be irregular, most likely assonant ("afraid" coming after "street"), with a tendency to expand (for it is "bright" that in fact rhymes with "street" via "afraid," which widens into "decade"). To Auden's British audience, the poem starts in earnest right here, with this amusing yet very matter-of-fact air that "Fifty-second Street" creates, in a fairly unexpected fashion. But the point is that by now our author isn't dealing only with Britons; not anymore. And the beauty is that this opening cuts both ways, since "dives" and "Fifty-second Street" inform his American public that he speaks its language as well. If one bears in mind the immediate aim of the poem, this choice of diction is not surprising at all.

Some twenty years later, in a poem written in memory of Louis MacNeice, Auden expresses a desire to "become, if possible, a minor Atlantic Goethe." This is an extremely significant admission, and the crucial word here is, believe it or not, not Goethe but Atlantic. Because what Auden had in mind from the very outset of his poetic career was the sense that the language in which he wrote was transatlantic or, better still, imperial: not in the sense of the British Raj but in the sense that it is the language that made an empire. For empires are held together by neither political nor military forces but by languages. Take Rome, for instance, or better still, Hellenic Greece, which began to disintegrate immediately after Alexander the Great's own demise (and he died very young). What held them for centuries, after their political centers collapsed, were *magna lingua Grecae* and Latin. Empires are, first and foremost, cultural entities; and it's language that does the job, not legions. So if you want to write in English, you ought to master all its idioms, from Fresno to Kuala Lumpur, so to speak. Other than that, the importance of what you are saying may not go far beyond your little parish, which is perfectly commendable, of course; what's more, there is that famous "drop of water" (which reflects the entire universe) approach to comfort you. That's fine. And yet there is every chance for you to become citizens of the Great English Language.

Well, this is, perhaps, demagoguery; but it won't hurt. To get back to Auden, I think, one way or another, the above considerations played their role in his decision to leave England. Also, his reputation at home was already very high and presumably the prospect facing him was to join the literary establishment: for in a carefully stratified society there is nowhere else to go, and nothing beyond. So he hit the road, and the language extended it. In any case, for him that empire was stretched not only in space but in time as well, and he was ladling from every source, level, and period of English. Naturally, a man who was so frequently charged with fishing out of the *OED* very old, obscure, dated words hardly could ignore the safari America was offering.

At any rate, "Fifty-second Street" rings enough of a bell on both sides of the Atlantic to make people listen. In the beginning of every poem, a poet has to dispel that air of art and artifice that clouds the public's attitude to poetry. He has to be convincing, plain—the way, presumably, the public itself is. He has to speak with a public voice, and all the more so if it is a public subject that he deals with.

"I sit in one of the dives / On Fifty-second Street" answers those requirements. What we get here is the level, confident voice of one of us, of a reporter who speaks to us in our own tones. And just as we are prepared for him to continue in this reassuring fashion, just as we've recognized this public voice and have been lulled into regularity by his trimeters, the poet plummets us into the very private diction of "Uncertain and afraid." Now, this is not the way reporters talk; this is the voice of a scared child rather than of a seasoned, trench-coated newsman. "Uncertain and afraid" denotes what?—doubt. And this is precisely where this poem—indeed poetry in general, art in general—starts for real: in, or with, doubt. All of a sudden the certitude of that Fifty-second Street dive is gone and you get the feeling that perhaps it was displayed there in the first place because he was "uncertain and afraid" in the very beginning: that's why he clung to their concreteness. But now the preliminaries are over, and we are in business indeed.

As we go line by line, we should examine not only their content and function in the overall design of a poem but also their individual independence and stability; for if a poem is there to last, it better have decent bricks. In that light, the first line is a bit shaky, if only because the meter is just introduced and the poet knows it. It has an air of natural speech and is quite relaxed and humble because of the activity it describes. The main thing is that it doesn't prepare you for the next line; neither metrically nor in terms of content. After "I sit in one of the dives" everything is possible: pentameter, hexameter, a couplet rhyme, you name it. "On Fifty-second Street," therefore, has a greater significance than its content suggests, for it locks the poem into the meter.

The three stresses of "On Fifty-second Street" render it as solid and straight as Fifty-second Street itself. Although sitting "in one of the dives" doesn't jibe with a traditional poetic posture, its novelty is rather provisional, as is everything that has to do with the pronoun "I." "On Fifty-second Street," on the other hand, is permanent because it is impersonal and also because of its number. The combination of these two aspects reinforced by the regularity of the stress gives the reader a sense of confidence and legitimizes whatever may follow.

Because of this, "Uncertain and afraid" strikes you all the more with its absence of anything concrete: no nouns, not even numbers; just two adjectives like two little fountains of panic surging in your stomach. The shift of diction from public to private is quite abrupt, and those open vowels in the beginning of this line's only two words leave you breathless and alone against the concrete stability of the world whose length doesn't stop at Fifty-second Street. The state that this line denotes isn't one of mind, obviously. The poet, however, tries to produce a rationale having, presumably, no desire to slip into whatever abyss his homelessness may invite him to glance at. This line could just as well have been dictated by the sense of his incongruity with the immediate surroundings (by the sense of one's flesh's incongruity with *any* surroundings, if you like). I would even venture to suggest that this sense was permanently present in this poet; it's simply his personal or, as is the case with this poem, historical circumstances that were making it more acute.

So he is quite right here to grope for a rationale for the described state. And the whole poem grows out of these gropings. Well, let's watch what is going on:

As the clever hopes expire
Of a low dishonest decade . . .

To begin with, a considerable portion of his English audience gets it in the neck here. "The clever hopes" stands here for a lot of things: for pacifism, appeasement, Spain, Munich—for all those events that paved the road to Fascism in Europe more or less in the same fashion as the road to Communism is paved there in our time by Hungary, Czechoslovakia, Afghanistan, Poland. Speaking of the last, September 1, 1939, which gave our poem its title, is the day when the German troops invaded Poland and World War II began. (Well, a little bit of history shouldn't hurt, should it?) The war, you see, began over the British guarantees of Polish independence. That was the *casus belli.* Now it's 1981, and where is that Polish independence today, forty years later? So, strictly, legally speaking, World War II was in vain. But I'm digressing . . . At any rate, these guarantees were British, and this epithet still meant something to Auden. To say the least, it could still imply home, and hence the lucidity and harshness of his attitude toward "clever hopes."

Still, the main role of this conjunction is the hero's attempt to quell the panic by rationalization. And that would do were it not for "clever hopes" being a contradiction in terms: it is too late for a hope if it is clever. The only quelling aspect of this expression comes from the word "hope" itself, since it implies a future invariably associated with improvement. The net result of this oxymoron is clearly satirical. And yet under the circumstances, satire is, on one hand, almost unethical and, on the other hand, not enough. So the author lowers his fist with "Of a low dishonest decade," which spans all those aforementioned instances of yielding to brute force. But before we get into this line, note the epigrammatic quality of "dishonest decade": thanks to the similarity of stresses and the common opening consonant, "dishonest" constitutes a sort of mental rhyme for "decade." Well, this is perhaps watching things too closely for their own good.

Now, why do you think Auden says "low dishonest decade"? Well, partly because the decade indeed had sunk very low—because as the apprehension about Hitler grew, so did the argument, especially on the Continent, that somehow everything was going to work out all right. After all, all those nations rubbed shoulders too long, not to mention the carnage of World War I still fresh in their memories, to conceive the possibility of yet another shooting session. To many of them that would have seemed sheer tautology. This is the type of mentality best described by the great Polish wit Stanislaw Jerzy Lec (whose *Unkempt Thoughts* Auden adored greatly) in the following observation: "A hero who survived tragedy isn't a tragic hero." Cute as it may sound, the sick thing is that a hero often survives one tragedy to die in another. Hence, in any case, those "clever hopes."

By adding "low dishonest decade" Auden produces the effect of being deliberately judgmental. In general, when a noun gets more than one adjective, especially on paper, we become slightly suspicious. Normally, this sort of thing is done for emphasis, but the doer knows it is risky. This, by the way, raises a parenthetical comment: in a poem, you should try to reduce the number of adjectives to a minimum. So that if somebody covers your poem with a magic cloth that removes adjectives, the page will still be black enough because of nouns, adverbs, and verbs. When that cloth is little, your best friends are nouns. Also, never rhyme the same parts of speech. Nouns you can, verbs you shouldn't, and rhyming adjectives is taboo.

By 1939 Auden is enough of an old hand to know this thing about two or more adjectives and yet he does exactly this with these epithets which, on top of everything else, are both pejorative. Why, do you think? In order to condemn the decade? But "dishonest" would have been enough. Besides, righteousness wasn't in Auden's character, nor would it escape him that he was a part of that decade himself. A man like him wouldn't employ a negative epithet without sensing a touch of self-portrayal in it. In other words, whenever you are about to use something pejorative, try to apply it to yourself to get the full measure of the word. Other than that, your criticism may amount simply to getting unpleasant things out of your system. Like nearly every self-therapy, it cures little . . . No, I think the reason for using the adjectives in a row was the poet's desire to supply the rational revulsion with physical gravity. He simply wants to seal this line for good, and the heavy, one-syllabled "low" does it. The trimeter is employed here in hammer-like fashion. He could have said "sick" or "bad"; "low," however, is more stable and it also reverberates with the seediness of the dive. We deal here not only with the ethical but also with the actual urban topography, as the poet wants to keep the whole thing on street level.

Waves of anger and fear
Circulate over the bright
And darkened lands of the earth,
Obsessing our private lives . . .

The "waves" are obviously those of radio broadcasts, although the position of the word—right after "dishonest decade" and at the beginning of a new sentence—promises you relief, a change of pitch; so originally a reader is inclined to take "waves" in a romantic key. Well, because a poem sits in the very middle of the page surrounded by the enormity of white margins, each word of it, each comma carries an enormous—i.e., proportionate to the abundance of unused space—burden of allusions and significances. Its words are simply overloaded, especially those at the beginning and at the end of the line. It ain't prose. It's like a plane in a white sky, and each bolt and rivet matter greatly. And that's why we are going over each one of them . . . Anyhow, "anger and fear" are presumably the substance of those broadcasts: the German invasion of Poland and the world's reaction to it, including the British declaration of war against Germany. It could be precisely the contrast of those reports with the American scene that made our poet assume his newsman posture here. In any case, it's this allusion to the press that is responsible for the choice of the verb "circulate" in the next line; but only partly.

The party more directly responsible for this verb is the word "fear" at the end of the previous line, and not only because of the generally recurring nature of this sensation but because of the incoherence associated with it. "Waves of anger and fear" is pitched a bit too high above the controlled, level diction of the previous lines, and the poet decides to undercut himself with this technical or bureaucratic, at any rate dispassionate, "circulate." And because of this impersonal, technical verb, he can safely—i.e., without risking an air of emotional superficiality—employ those allusion-laden epithets "bright and darkened," which depict both the actual and the political physiognomy of the globe.

"Waves of anger and fear" clearly echoes the poet's own state of mind in "uncertain and afraid." In any case, it is the latter that conditions the former, as well as "obsessing our private lives." The key word in this line obviously is "obsessing" because apart from conveying the importance of those news broadcasts/rustling tabloids, it introduces a sense of shame that runs through the entire stanza and casts its hissing sibilant shadow upon "our private lives" before we catch the meaning of the statement. Thus the posture of a reporter who speaks to us and about us conceals a self-disgusted moralist, and "our private lives" becomes a euphemism for something quite unspeakable; for something that bears responsibility for the stanza's last two lines:

> *The unmentionable odour of death*
> *Offends the September night.*

Here we sense once again British diction, something that smacks of a drawing room: "unmentionable odour." The poet, as it were, gives us two euphemisms in a row: an epithet and an object, and we almost see a wriggled nose. The same goes for "offends." Euphemism, generally, is inertia of terror. What makes these lines doubly horrid is the mixture of the poet's real fear with a roundabout locution, aping his audience's reluctance to call a spade a spade. The disgust that you detect in these two lines has much less to do with the "odour of death" as such and its proximity to our nostrils than with the sensibility that used to render it "unmentionable."

On the whole, this stanza's most important admission, "uncertain and afraid," has at the source not so much the outbreak of war as the sensibility that precipitated it and whose diction the last two lines emulate. Don't make the mistake of regarding them as a parody: not at all. They simply do their job in the author's drive to bring everybody and everything into the focus of collective guilt. He simply tries to show what that civilized, euphemistic, detached diction and everything that is associated with it result in, which is carrion. Now, this is of course a bit too strong a sentiment to end a stanza with, and the poet decides to give you a bit of breathing space; hence that "September night."

And although this "September night" has gone somewhat astray because of what's been done to it, it's still a September night and, as such, it evokes rather tolerable allusions. At this point, the poet's strategy is—apart from his overall desire to be historically precise—to pave the road for the next stanza: we shouldn't forget about considerations like this. So he gives us here a mixture of naturalism and high lyricism that stabs you both in the heart and in the plexus. The last thing in the stanza, however, is the voice of the heart, albeit a wounded one: "the September night." It doesn't constitute a great deal of relief: still, one senses that there is someplace to go. Let's see, then, where it is that our poet is taking us, after reminding us with "September night" that what we are reading is a poem.

3

The second stanza starts with a deliberate, I'd say pedantic surprise of "Accurate scholarship can/Unearth the whole offence/From Luther until now/. . ." Surely you expected anything but this: after "September night." You see, Auden is the most unpredictable poet. In music, his counterpart would be Joseph Haydn. With Auden, you don't foresee the next line even if the meter is the most conventional. And that's the way to do the job . . . Anyway, why do you think he starts here with "accurate scholarship"?

Well, he begins a new stanza, and his immediate concern and purpose is to change the pitch, in order to escape the monotony which the repetition of structural design always promises. Secondly, and more importantly, he is fully aware of the preceding sentence's gravity, of its effectiveness, and he doesn't want to continue in that authoritative fashion: he is simply mindful of the authority of a poet who, in the eyes of the audience, is *a priori* right. So what he tries to demonstrate here is his capacity for objective, dispassionate discourse. "Accurate scholarship" is evoked here to dispel any possibility of a romantic, poetic shadow supposedly cast by the first stanza's diction over the ethical argument in progress.

This pressure for objectivity, dryness of tone, etc., has been both the curse and the blessing of modern poetry. It choked quite a lot of throats; Mr. Eliot's would be one, although the same force made him a superb critic. What's good about Auden, among other things, is that he proved to be capable of manipulating this pressure to suit his lyrical ends. Here he is, for instance, speaking in this cool, pedantic voice: "Accurate scholarship can/Unearth the whole offence . . ." and yet you sense under the mask of objectivity the badly controlled anger. That is, the objectivity here is the result of controlled anger. Note that. And note also the pause after "can" that sits at the end of this line and rhymes rather faintly with "done," which is too far away to reckon with. After this pause, "unearth" comes as a false emphatic verb; it's a bit too elevated and casts considerable doubt over this scholarship's ability to unearth anything.

The metronome-like distribution of stresses in both lines reinforces the absence of emotion peculiar to scholastic undertakings, but a keen ear pricks up at "the whole offence": the dismissal here isn't exactly academic. Perhaps it's done to offset the aforesaid aloofness of "unearth," though I doubt it. The poet resorts to this colloquial dismissive intonation most likely to convey not so much the possible imprecision of this scholarship's findings as its gentlemanly, detached posture, which has very little to do with its very subject; neither with Luther nor with "now." By this time, the entire conceit—Oh yeah, we can be logical—that sustains this stanza starts to get on the author's nerves, and in "has driven a culture mad" Auden finally lets himself go and releases the word that twitched for too long on the tip of his tongue: "mad."

My hunch is that he loved this word dearly. As everyone whose mother tongue is English should: this word covers a lot of ground—if not all of it. Also, "mad" is very much English-schoolboy diction, which, for Auden, was a sort of *sancta sanctorum*; not so much because of his "happy childhood" or his experience as schoolmaster as due to every poet's craving for laconism. Apart from being apt in denoting both the state of the world and that of the speaker's mind, "mad" heralds here the arrival of a diction fully deployed by the end of this stanza. But let's get to the next line.

"Find what occurred at Linz." I bet you know more about Luther than about what occurred at Linz. Well, Linz is the city in Austria where Adolf Hitler, known also as Adolf Schiklgruber, spent his childhood; i.e., went to school, got his ideas, and so forth. Actually he wanted to become a painter and applied to the Viennese Academy of Fine Arts but was turned down. Too bad for fine arts, considering this man's energy. So he became a Michelangelo in reverse. Well, we'll return to this business of war and painting later. Now let's watch the lexical content of this stanza: here we are on to something interesting.

Let's assume that what we've said about that high-school aspect of "mad" is accurate. The point is that "what occurred at Linz" also refers to a high-school experience: that of young Schiklgruber. Of course, we don't know what exactly did happen there, but by now we all have bought that notion of "formative years." The next two lines, as you probably see, are "What huge imago made/A psychopathic god." Now, "imago" comes straight out of psychoanalytic lingo. It means an image of a father-figure that a child fashions for himself in the absence of the real father—which was young Adolf's case—and that conditions a child's subsequent development. In other words, here our poet grinds scholarship into the fine dust of psychoanalysis which we inhale nowadays unwittingly. Note also the beauty of this triple rhyme connecting "mad" and "god" via the assonant "made." Very subtly but relentlessly the poet is paving the road to the last four lines of this stanza, which every living person has to tattoo in his/her brain.

The whole idea of the stanza is to pit "accurate scholarship" (which is yet another version of "clever hopes") against the plain ethics of "Those to whom evil is done/Do evil in return." These basics are public knowledge: it's something that even schoolchildren know; i.e., it's something that belongs in the subconscious. In order to hammer this into the heads of his audience, he has to offset one diction with another since contrast is what we comprehend most. So he plays the manifest sophistication of Linz/Luther/imago versus the breathtaking simplicity of the last two lines. By the time he gets to "a psychopathic god," he is somewhat exasperated with his effort to be fair to the opposite side's argument as well as with the necessity of containing the actual sentiment. And so he breaks into this oratorical "I and the public know," unleashing the vowels and bringing in the word that explains everything: schoolchildren.

No, he isn't juxtaposing cunning and innocence here. Nor does he practice analysis without a license. Of course he knew the works of Freud (as a matter of fact, he read them quite early, before he entered Oxford). He is simply introducing the common denominator that binds us to Hitler, for his audience—or his patient—is not a faceless authority but all of us to whom this or that evil was, at some point, done. Hitler, according to Auden, is a human phenomenon: not just a political one. Therefore he uses the Freudian approach, as it promises a shortcut to the root of the problem, to its origin. Auden, you see, is a poet who is interested most of all in cause-and-effect interplay, and Freudianism for him is but a means of transportation: not destination. Also, if not primarily, this doctrine like any other simply expands his vocabulary: he ladles from every puddle. What he achieves here then is more than just a snipe at "accurate scholarship's" ability to explain human evil: he tells us that we all are quite evil, for we empathize with these four lines, don't we? And do you know why? Because this quatrain sounds, after all, like a most coherent rendition of the concept of Original Sin.

But there is something else to these four lines. For, by suggesting that we all are capable of becoming Hitlers, they steal somewhat from our resolve to condemn him (or the Germans). There is almost an air, however faint, of "who are we to judge?"—do you sense it? Or is it just my nostrils? And yet I think it is there. And if it is there, how would you explain this air?

Well, first of all, it's only September 1, 1939, and most of the enterprise hasn't yet taken place. Also, the poet could have been hypnotized enough by the effectiveness of those four lines (they also give an impression of having come off easily) to overlook the nuance. But Auden wasn't that kind of a poet, and on the other hand, he knew what modern warfare is like, having been to Spain. The most plausible explanation is that, after Oxford, Auden spent quite a lot of time in Germany. He traveled there several times, and some of his sojourns were long and happy.

The Germany he visited was the Germany of the Weimar Republic—the best Germany there ever was in this century, as far as your teacher is concerned. It was quite unlike England in terms of both misery and vivacity, for the population consisted of those who—defeated, crippled, impoverished, orphaned—survived the Great War, whose first casualty was the old imperial order. The entire social fabric, not to mention economy, was completely undone, and the political climate was that of high volatility. To say the least, it was unlike England, as regards its atmosphere of permissiveness, as regards the phenomenon loosely called decadence; especially as regards the visual arts. It was the period of the great outburst of Expressionism: the "ism" of which the German artists of the period are considered the founding fathers. Indeed, speaking of Expressionist art, whose chief visual characteristics are broken lines, nervous, grotesque deformity of objects and figures, lurid and cruel vividness of colors, one can't help thinking of World War II as its greatest show. One feels as though the canvases of those artists had wandered out of their frames and projected themselves across the land mass of Eurasia. German was also the language of Freud, and it was in Berlin that Auden got to deal with that great doctrine at close range. Well, to make a long story short, I'd recommend to you Christopher Isherwood's *Berlin Stories*, for they capture the atmosphere of both the place and the period a lot better than any movies you might have seen.

Hitler's rise to power, to be sure, spelled an end to nearly all that. In the eyes of European intellectuals, his advent was, at the time, not so much a triumph of will as a triumph of vulgarity. For Auden, who was a homosexual and who originally went to Berlin, I think, simply for boys, the Third Reich was also something like a rape of those youths. The boys were to become soldiers and kill or get killed. Or else they would be ostracized, incarcerated, and so forth. In a sense, I think, he took Nazism personally: as something totally hostile to sensuality, to subtlety. Needless to say he was right. The cause-and-effect man, he was quick to realize that in order to produce evil, the ground must be fertilized. His perception of the German developments was sharpened and aggravated by his firsthand knowledge that the evil had already been done to all those people before any Nazis ever surfaced. By that I suppose he means the peace of Versailles and that these boys were themselves children of war who had suffered its consequences: poverty, deprivation, neglect. And he knew them all too well to be surprised at them behaving nastily, with or without the uniform; he knew them well enough not to be taken aback by their "evil in return," provided there were congenial circumstances in which to do that evil.

Schoolchildren, you see, are the most menacing lot; and both the army and the *Polizeistaat* repeat the structure of a school. The point is that for this poet school was not only the "formative experience." It was the only social structure he ever went through (as a pupil and as a teacher); therefore it became for him the metaphor for existence. Once a boy, I suppose, always a boy; especially if you are English. That's why Germany was so clear to him, and that's why on September 1, 1939, he doesn't feel like condemning the Germans in blanket fashion. Besides, every poet is a bit of a Führer himself: he wants to rule minds, for he is tempted to think that he knows better—which is only a step away from thinking that you *are* better. To condemn is to imply superiority; given this opportunity, Auden chooses to express grief rather than to pass judgment.

These reservations, based in part on offended sensuality, reveal a despairing moralist whose only means of self-control is the iambic trimeter; and this trimeter pays him back with the reticent dignity it contains. Now, one doesn't choose one's meter; it's the other way around, for meters have been around longer than any poet. They start to hum in one's head—partly because they have been used by somebody one has just read; mostly, however, because they are themselves equivalents of certain mental states (which include ethical states)—or they contain a possibility of curbing a certain state.

If you are any good, you try to modify them formally by, say, playing with a stanzaic design or shifting a caesura around—or through the unpredictability of the content; by what you are going to stuff these familiar lines with. A lesser poet would repeat the meter more slavishly, a better one would try to animate it if only by giving it a jolt. It is possible that what set Auden's pen in motion here was W. B. Yeats's "Easter 1916," especially because of the similarity in subject matter. But it's equally possible that Auden had just reread Swinburne's "In the Garden of Proserpine": one may like tunes in spite of their lyrics, and great men are not necessarily influenced by their equals only. In any case, if Yeats used this meter to express his sentiments, Auden sought to control them by the same means. Hence, for you, not the hierarchy of poets but the realization that this meter is capable of both jobs. And of a lot more. Of practically everything.

Well, back to the mines. Why do you think the third stanza starts this way:

4

Exiled Thucydides knew
All that a speech can say
About Democracy . . .

A stanza, you see, is a self-generating device: the end of one spells the necessity of another. This necessity is first of all purely acoustical and, only then, didactical (although one shouldn't try to divorce them, especially for the sake of analysis). The danger here is that the preconceived music of a recurrent stanzaic pattern tends to dominate or even determine the content. And it's extremely hard for a poet to fight the dictates of the tune.

The eleven-line-long stanza of "September 1, 1939," is, as far as I can tell, Auden's own invention, and the irregularity of its rhyme pattern functions as its built-in anti-fatigue device. Note that. All the same, the quantitative effect of an eleven-line-long stanza is such that the first thing on the writer's mind as he starts a new one is to escape from the musical predicament of the preceding lines. Auden, it should be noted, must work here exceptionally hard precisely because of the tight, epigrammatic, spellbinding beauty of the previous quatrain. And so he brings in Thucydides—the name you are least prepared to encounter, right? This is more or less the same technique as putting "accurate scholarship" next to "the September night." But let's examine this line a bit closer.

"Exiled" is a pretty loaded word, isn't it? It's high-pitched not only because of what it describes but in terms of its vowels also. Yet because it comes right after a distinctly sprung preceding line and because it opens the line which, we expect, is to return the meter its regular breath, "exiled" arrived here in a lower key . . . Now, what in your opinion makes our poet think of Thucydides and of what this Thucydides "knew"? Well, my guess is that it has to do with the poet's own attempts at playing historian for his own Athens; all the more so because they are also endangered and because of his realization that no matter how eloquent his message—especially the last four lines—he, too, is doomed to be ignored. Hence this air of fatigue that pervades the line, and hence this exhaling feeling in "exiled"—which he could apply to his own physical situation as well, but only in a minor key, for this adjective is loaded with a possibility of self-aggrandizement.

We find another clue to this line in Humphrey Carpenter's splendid biography of Auden, where its author mentions the fact that our poet was rereading Thucydides' history of the Peloponnesian War about this time. And the main thing about the Peloponnesian War, of course, is that it spelled the end for what we know as classical Greece. The change wrought by that war was indeed a drastic one: in a sense, it was the real end of Athens and all it stood for. And Pericles, in whose mouth Thucydides puts the most heartbreaking speech about democracy you will ever read—he speaks there as though democracy has no tomorrow, which in the Greek sense of the word it really hadn't—that Pericles is being replaced in the public mind, almost overnight—by whom? By Socrates. The emphasis shifts from identification with community, with the *polis*, to individualism—and it is not such a bad shift, except that it paves the road to subsequent atomization of society, with all the attendant ills . . . So our poet, who has at least geographical reasons to identify with Thucydides, also realizes what change for the world, for our Athens, if you will, looms on the horizon. In other words, he also speaks here on the eve of war but, unlike Thucydides, not with the benefit of hindsight but in real anticipation of the shape of things—their ruins, rather— to come.

"All that a speech can say" is, in its wistfulness, a self-contained line. It sustains the fatigue-laden personal link with Thucydides, for speech can be disdained only by those who master it: by poets or historians. I'd even add that every poet is a historian of speech, although I'd resent having to clarify this remark. At any rate, in "speech" we have obviously a reference to the funeral oration that Thucydides put in the mouth of Pericles. On the other hand, of course, a poem itself is a speech, and the poet tries to compromise his enterprise before someone else—a critic or events—would do that. That is, the poet steals from your "so what" reaction to his work by saying this himself before the poem is over. This is not a safeguarding job, though; it's indicative neither of his cunning nor of his self-awareness but of humility, and is prompted by the minor key of the first two lines. Auden is indeed the most humble poet of the English language; next to him even Edward Thomas comes off as haughty. For his virtues are dictated not by his conscience alone but by prosody, whose voice is more convincing.

Watch for that "About Democracy," though! How reductive this line is! The emphasis here is of course on the limited—or doomed—ability of speech as such: an idea that Auden has dealt with in a thorough fashion already in his "In Memory of W. B. Yeats," where he states that ". . . poetry makes nothing happen." But thanks to this reductive, off-hand treatment of the line, the doom spreads onto "democracy" as well. And this "democracy," on top of everything, rhymes both as consonants and visually with "say." In other words, the hopelessness of a "a speech" is compounded by the hopelessness of its subject, be it "democracy" or "what dictators do."

What's interesting in this line about "dictators" is its more vigorous—by comparison with "about Democracy"—distribution of stresses, which, however, highlights less the author's resentment of dictators than his attempt to overcome the gravity of increasing fatigue. Watch also this technique of understatement in "dictators do." The euphemistic nature of this conjunction gets exposed through the almost unbearable syllabic superiority of the noun (dictators) over the verb (do). You sense here the great variety of things a dictator is capable of, and it's not for nothing that "do" (which plays here the role of "unmentionable" in the first stanza) rhymes with "knew."

"The elderly rubbish they talk/To an apathetic grave . . ." is certainly a reference to the aforesaid funeral oration of Pericles. Yet it's a bit more worrisome here because the distinction between the historian's (and by the same token, the poet's) speech and what's delivered by tyrants is blurred. And what blurs the distinction is "apathetic," an epithet more suitable for a crowd than for a grave. On second thought, it's suitable for both. On third, it equates "crowd" with "grave." "An apathetic grave" is, of course, your vintage Auden with his definitions' blinding proximity to an object. It's not the futility of dictators, therefore, that the poet is concerned with here but the destination of speech par excellence.

Such an attitude to one's own craft could again, of course, be explained by the author's humility, by his self-effacing posture. But you shouldn't forget that Auden landed in New York just eight months earlier, on December 23, 1938, the very date the Spanish Republic fell. The sense of helplessness which presumably overcame this poet (who had issued by that time more and better warnings against the onslaught of Fascism than anyone else in the field) on this September night simply seeks solace in the parallel with the Greek historian who dealt with the phenomenon at hand no less extensively, two millennia ago. In other words, if Thucydides failed to convince his Greeks, what chance is there for a modern poet, with his weaker voice and bigger crowd?

The very list of things "analyzed" in Thucydides' book, i.e., the very way in which Auden renders them, suggests a historical perspective: from an old-fashioned "enlightenment" via "habit-forming pain" and down to this very contemporary "mismanagement." As for "habit-forming pain," this expression, of course, isn't of the poet's own coinage (though it sounds remarkably like being one): he simply lifted it from psychoanalytical lingo. He did this often—and so should you. This is what these lingos are for. They save you a trip and often suggest a more imaginative treatment of the proper language. Also, Auden used this compound epithet as a sort of homage to Thucydides: because of Homer, classical Greece is associated with hyphenated definitions . . . Well, at any rate, the succession of these items shows that the poet is tracing the present malaise to its origins: a process that, like every retrospection, renders one's voice elegiac.

Yet there is a more loaded reason for this succession, since "September 1, 1939," is a transitional poem for Auden; i.e., what you've heard about our poet's so-called three stages—Freudian, Marxist, religious—is presented here in a nutshell of two lines. For while "habit-forming pain" clearly harks back to the Viennese doctor and "mismanagement" to political economy, the monosyllabic "grief" in which the entire succession results, nay, culminates, is straight out of King James and shows, as they say, our man's real drift. And the reasons for that drift, for the emergence of that third, religious stage which this "grief" heralds, are as much personal for this poet as they are historical. Under the circumstances the poem describes, an honest man wouldn't bother to distinguish between the two.

That Thucydides appears here not only because Auden was reading him at the moment, but because of the dilemma's own familiarity, is, I hope, clear. Nazi Germany indeed had begun to resemble a sort of Sparta, especially in the light of the Prussian military tradition. Under the circumstances the civilized world would thus have amounted to Athens, as it was duly threatened. The new dictator, too, was talkative. If this world was ripe for anything, it was retrospection.

But there is a peculiarity. Once you set the apparatus of retrospection into motion, you get yourself into a jumble of things possessing different degrees of remoteness, since all of them are past. How, and on what basis, does one choose? Emotional affinity with this or that tendency or event? Rationalization about its significance? Pure acoustic pleasure of a word or a name? Why, for instance, does Auden pick up "enlightenment"? Because it stands for civilization, cultural and political refinement associated with "Democracy"? In order to pave the road for the impact of "habit-forming pain"? And what is it in "enlightenment's" allusive powers that paves that road? Or maybe it has to do with the very act of retrospection: with its purpose as well as with its reason?

I think that he picked this word because it is enlightenment with a capital "E" that houses the origins of the malaise in question, not Sparta. To put it more aptly, what it seems to me was going through the poet's mind or, if you will, through his subconscious (although writing, let me repeat, is a very rational operation that exploits the subconscious to its own ends and not vice versa), was a search, in several directions, for those origins. And the closest thing in sight was Jean-Jacques Rousseau's idea of a "noble savage" ruined by imperfect institutions. Hence, obviously, the necessity of improving those institutions, hence, then, the concept of the Ideal State. And hence an array of social utopias, bloodshed in order to bring them about, and their logical conclusion, a *Polizeistaat*.

Because they are so remote, the Greeks are always of an archetypal denomination to us, and this goes for their historians too. And in a didactic poem, one is more successful with one's audience if one throws it an archetype to munch. Auden knew this, and that's why he does not mention Mr. Rousseau here by name, although this man is almost solely responsible for the concept of an ideal ruler, i.e., in this instance Herr Hitler. Also, under the circumstances, the poet most likely didn't feel like debunking even this sort of Frenchman. Finally, an Auden poem always tries to establish a more general pattern of human behavior, and for that, history and psychoanalysis are more suitable than their side products. I simply think that the Enlightenment was very much on the poet's mind as he was pondering the situation, and it wandered into the poem in the lower case, the way it wandered into history.

I'd like to allow myself one more digression, though, now that we are on this subject of the "noble savage." The very expression, I suppose, went into circulation because of all those world voyages of the Age of Discovery. I guess the great navigators—people like Magellan, La Pérouse, Bougainville, et al., were the ones who coined it. They simply had in mind the inhabitants of all those newly discovered tropical islands who presumably greatly impressed them by not eating the visitors alive. This is of course a joke, and in bad taste; literally so, I must add.

The appeal the concept of the "noble savage" enjoyed among the literati and, subsequently, with the rest of society had clearly to do with a very vulgar public notion of paradise, i.e., with a generally garbled reading of the Bible. It was simply based on the notion that Adam, too, was naked, as well as on the rejection of Original Sin (in this, of course, the ladies and gentlemen of the Enlightenment weren't the first; nor were they the last). Both attitudes—especially the latter—were presumably a reaction against the omnipresence and redundancy of the Catholic Church. In France, more particularly, it was a reaction against Protestantism.

But whatever its pedigree, the idea was shallow, if only because it flattered man. Flattery, as you know, doesn't take you too far. At best, it simply shifts the emphasis—i.e., guilt—by telling man that he is inherently good and that it's the institutions which are bad. That is, if things are rotten, it's not your fault but someone else's. The truth is, alas, that both men and institutions are good for nothing, since the latter, to say the least, are the product of the former. Still, each epoch—indeed, each generation—discovers this lovely species, the noble savage, for itself and lavishes it with its political and economic theories. As in the days of world voyages, the noble savage of today is mostly of a swarthy shade and dwells in the tropics. At present we call it the Third World and refuse to admit that our enthusiasm to apply there the formulas that failed in our parts is but an obverse form of racism. Having done all it could in the temperate zones, the great French idea in a sense has returned to its source: to breed tyrants al fresco.

Well, so much for "noble savages." Note other rhymes in this stanza which are no less suggestive than "knew–do" and "say–democracy–away": "talk–book," "grave–grief," and finally this "again" enhancing the habit-forming aspect of "pain." Also, I hope you've been able to appreciate the self-contained character of "mismanagement and grief": here you have that enormous distance between cause and effect covered in one line. Just as math preaches how to do it.

5

Why do you think he starts this stanza by mentioning "this neutral air" and why is this air neutral? Well, first of all, he does it in order to disengage his voice from the emotionally charged preceding line; any version of neutrality therefore is welcome. It also supports the notion of the poet's objectivity. Mainly, however, "this neutral air" is here because this is a poem about the outbreak of the war and America as yet is neutral; i.e., it hasn't yet entered the war. By the way, how many of you remember when it did? Well, never mind. Finally, "this neutral air" is here because there is no better epithet for air. What could be more apt? Every poet, as you probably know, tries to grapple with this problem: how to describe an element. Of the four, only the earth yields a handful of adjectives. It's worse with fire, desperate with water, and out of the question with air. And I don't think the poet would be able to pull it off here were it not for politics. Note that.

What do you think this stanza is all about, anyway? At

least, the first half of it? Well, to begin with, the author here shifts the focus from past history to the present. As a matter of fact, he went this way already in the last two lines of the previous stanza: "Mismanagement and grief:/ We must suffer them all again." This is the way the past closes. Here's how the present opens, and it's a bit ominous:

> *Into this neutral air*
> *Where blind skyscrapers use*
> *Their full height to proclaim*
> *The strength of Collective Man* . . .

First of all, why are skyscrapers blind? Paradoxically enough, precisely because of their glass, because of their windows; i.e., they are blind in direct proportion to the number of their "eyes." Argus-like, if you wish. Next, right after these more terrifying than majestic blind skyscrapers comes the verb "use," which, apart from everything else, reveals the reason they've been erected. And it comes too soon and too abruptly, in all its inanimate power. And you are fully aware of what "blind skyscrapers" are capable of if they "use." However, they don't use anything or anybody but "their full height." You get here a terrific sense of redundant self-reliance very much pertinent to these structures. This description hits you not by its invention but by stealing from your expectations.

For you expect skyscrapers to be animated, presumably in a nasty way, as is the fashion in poetry. This mindless, dildo-display-like "use/Their full height," however, suggests that they do not act on the outside: presumably on account of their blindness. Blindness, mind you, is, in its turn, a form of neutrality. As a result, you sense the tautology of this air and these buildings, an equation neither part of which is responsible for the other.

The poet here, you see, is painting a cityscape, the New York skyline, as it were. Partly for the purposes of the poem, but mostly because of the keenness of his eye, he renders it as a *paysage moralisé* (or *démoralisé*, in this case). The air here is qualified by buildings that jut into it as well as by the politics of their builders and dwellers. Conversely, it qualifies buildings by reflecting on their windows and rendering them blind, neutral. After all, it's literally a tall order: to describe a skyscraper. The only successful job that comes to my mind is that famous line by Lorca about the "gray sponge." Auden is giving you here a psychological equivalent of post-Cubism, for, in fact, what the "full height" of these structures proclaims is not "the strength of Collective Man" but the magnitude of his indifference, which, for Collective Man, is the only possible emotional state. Keep in mind that this sight is new for the author, and keep in mind also that description and itemization are forms of cognition, indeed of philosophy. Well, there is no other way to explain epic poetry.

This inanimate "strength of Collective Man" in a state of frightful passivity is the poet's main concern throughout the poem and surely in this stanza. Much as he appreciates the solidity of this republic (Collective Man, I take it, means this as well) into whose "neutral air" "Each language pours its vain/Competitive excuse," he recognizes in it the features of things that brought the whole tragedy about. These lines just as well could have been written on the other side of the Atlantic. "Competitive excuse" for doing nothing to stop Herr Hitler is, among other things, a snipe at the business world, although what prompts them as well as "Out of the mirror they stare / Imperialism's face / And the international wrong" is rather a terminological inertia that harks back to his Marxonian (from Marx and Oxford) period; more so than the conviction that he has found real culprits. In any case, "Out of the mirror they stare" suggests not so much those looming monstrosities as those who can meet their glances in the mirror. And this means not so much "them," whom it's customary to blame, as "us," who are, after all, not even so smug in this "euphoric dream," which we can afford, having erected these invincible structures that grew out of the Depression.

"September 1, 1939" is first and foremost a poem about shame. The poet himself, as you remember, is under some pressure for having left England. This is what helps him to discern the aforesaid faces in that mirror: he sees there his own. The speaker now is no longer a reporter; we hear in this stanza a voice shot through with the lucidity of despair over everyone's complicity in the events this date unleashed, and over the speaker's own impotence to make that Collective Man act. On top of that, Auden, a newcomer to American shores, probably must have felt uncertain as to his moral right to urge the natives to act. Curiously enough, toward the second part of this particular stanza, the rhymes are getting somewhat shabby, less assertive, and the whole tone becomes neither personal nor impersonal, but rhetorical. What began as a majestic vision dwindles to the aesthetics of John Heartfield's photo-montages, and I think the poet senses it. Hence the deft, muffled lyricism of the opening lines of the next stanza, of this love song for the interior.

6

Faces along the bar
Cling to their average day:
The lights must never go out,
The music must always play,
All the conventions conspire
To make this fort assume
The furniture of home;
Lest we should see where we are,
Lost in a haunted wood,
Children afraid of the night
Who have never been happy or good.

It's a real morsel, this stanza; a terrific verbal photograph: not Heartfield but Cartier-Bresson. "Out of the mirror they stare" paves the road to "Faces along the bar," because you can see those faces only in a bar mirror. In contrast with the public-placard diction in the last lines of the preceding stanza, this is a private voice: for this is a private, an intimate world that doesn't require explanations. An enclosure, an epitome of security: a fort indeed. Someone said about Auden that whatever he was writing about, he always kept an eye on civilization. Well, it would be more accurate to say that he always kept an eye on whether it's safe where he or his subjects are, whether the ground's firm. For every ground is a ground for suspicion, so to speak. And if this stanza is beautiful, it's beautiful because of the underlying uncertainty.

Uncertainty, you see, is the mother of beauty, one of whose definitions is that it's something which isn't yours. At least, this is one of the most frequent sensations accompanying beauty. Therefore, when uncertainty is evoked, then you sense beauty's proximity. Uncertainty is simply a more alert state than certitude, and thus it creates a better lyrical climate. Because beauty is something obtained always from without, not from within. And this is precisely what's going on in this stanza.

For every description is an externalization of the object: a step aside so as to see it. That's why the comfort that the poet describes in the first lines of this stanza is all but gone by its end. "Faces along the bar / Cling to their average day" is quite safe, perhaps with the exception of the verb "cling," but it sits at the beginning of the second line, far away from any emphatic position, so we let it go at that. "The lights must never go out, / The music must always play" are soothing too, except that those two "musts" alert you to a possibility that too much is taken for granted. In "The lights must never go out" one detects not so much a conviction that bars should stay open all night as a fidgeting hope that there won't be military blackouts. "The music must always play," through its combination of understatement and naïveté, tries to obscure that uncertainty, to prevent it from developing into anxiety that threatens to become audible in the self-conscious, faltering tone of "conventions conspire"—for the piling up of these two lengthy Latinate words indicates too much rationalization for the cozy place that this bar is.

The next line's job is to bring things under control and restore the original, appropriately relaxed atmosphere of the stanza; and the ironic "this fort" does the job very nicely. Actually, what's interesting here is the way the poet arrives at the intended statement that the bar is "home," disheartening as its accuracy may be. It takes him six lines, whose every word makes its hesitant contribution to the erection of the short verb "is" which is required for the emergence of that disheartening notion. This tells you about the complexity behind every "is" as well as about the author's reluctance to admit this equation. Also, you should pay attention to the deliberate assonance of "assume" and "home" as well as to the quiet desperation behind the word "furniture," which is our synonym for "home," isn't it? For this construction, "the furniture of home" in itself is a picture of the ruin. The moment the job is done, the moment you are lulled by this mixture of predictable meter and recognizable detail, this whole quest for solace goes up in smoke with "Lest we should see where we are," whose rather Victorian "lest" sweetens the rest of the line's pill. And this Victorian echo takes you into "a haunted wood," where it's audible enough to justify the "never" of "Who have never been happy or good"—which, in its own right, echoes those schoolchildren at the end of the second stanza. This second echo simply reverberates the theme of the subconscious, and very timely so, because this theme is pertinent to the next stanza's understanding. On our way there, however, let's note the fairy-tale-like, distinctly English character of the last two lines, which not only reinforces the admission of human imperfection but helps that echo to fade into the opening of the next stanza. Well, let's have it.

7

The windiest militant trash
Important Persons shout
Is not so crude as our wish:
What mad Nijinsky wrote
About Diaghilev
Is true of the normal heart;
For the error bred in the bone
Of each woman and each man
Craves what it cannot have,
Not universal love
But to be loved alone.

"Windiest" is a very English expression here. But the old-country diction also steals in in the old-country notion of autumn which, to me, is responsible for this line's content, at least in part. Because September in New York, as you all know, is a hot and muggy time. In England, and in English poetic tradition, however, the name of this month is the very synonym of autumn. Only October could be better. The poet, of course, has in mind the political climate, but he sets out to describe it in terms of the actual—for the old country as well as for the rest of the realm in question, i.e., Europe—weather. Somehow this opening reminds me of Richard Wilbur's first stanza in his "After the Last Bulletins," with its description of the trash blown along the big city's streets by the cold wind. I may be wrong about this line because there is this "militant" that would be hard to fit into my reading of it. Still, something tells me to take this "windiest" first of all literally and only then in its derogatory function.

With "Important Persons shout" we are on the safer ground of externalizing our discontent. Together with "The windiest militant trash," this line, because of its vigorous subordinate clause, contains the always welcome promise of laying the blame on somebody else, on authority. But just when we are ready to fully enjoy its deriding air comes:

Is not so crude as our wish . . .

which not only robs us of a scapegoat and states our own responsibility for the rotten state of affairs but tells us that we are worse than those we blame to the extent that "wish" assonates with "trash," failing to comfort us even with the equation of an exact rhyme. The next two lines usher in the most crucial statement made by the poet in this poem, and for all he saw in this era. "What mad Nijinsky wrote/About Diaghilev . . ." Well, in this city of ours, where ballet is a highbrow cum bourgeois equivalent of a ball game, it is, I presume, unnecessary to go into who is who here. Still, Nijinsky was the star of the legendary Ballet Russe in Paris in the teens and the twenties of the century, and that troupe was run by Sergei Diaghilev, a famous impresario responsible for a variety of breakthroughs in modern art, a sort of Renaissance man with a very strong personality, but first of all an aesthete. Nijinsky, whom he discovered, was his lover. Subsequently, Nijinsky got married and Diaghilev had his contract discontinued. Shortly afterward Nijinsky went mad. I am telling you all this not for its juiciness but in order to explain the pedigree of one word—actually of one consonant—farther down in the stanza. Actually there were several versions of why Diaghilev fired Nijinsky: because of dissatisfaction with the quality of his dancing, because there were signs of Nijinsky going mad earlier, because his very marriage illustrated that, and so forth. I simply don't want you holding a simplistic view of Diaghilev: partly because of the role his name plays in the poem, mostly because he was a unique man. For the same reasons, I don't want you to simplify Nijinsky either, if only because it's from his diary, which he wrote in a state close to madness, that Auden quotes verbatim at the end of this stanza. I recommend that diary to you very strongly—this book has the Gospels' pitch and intensity. That's why it is important "What mad Nijinsky wrote/About Diaghilev."

So much for our who-is-who game. What madmen say about sane ones is usually of interest and often valid. "Is true" in "Is true of the normal heart" shows that Auden applies here, albeit unwittingly, the holy-fool principle: i.e., the idea that the holy fool is right. Nijinsky, after all, qualifies for a "fool" because he is a performer; for "holiness" we have here his madness as manifested in his writing, which indeed has a strong religious bent. The poet here, as you know, is not free of the latter himself: "the error bred in the bone/Of each woman and each man" denotes not only the subconscious effects of upbringing but also echoes the Bible; "each woman and each man" both confirms and obfuscates that echo. Concreteness here fights allusion. What adds to the validity of Nijinsky's statement, however, is his "foolishness" rather than his "holiness": for, as a performer, he is, technically speaking, an agent of "universal love." I suggest you see Auden's "Ballad of St. Barnaby," where he expands on this subject; it's very late Auden.

The error is of course selfishness that is very deep-seated

in each one of us. The poet tries to zero in on the source of the tragedy, you understand, and his argument moves camera-like from the peripheral (politics) to the central (subconscious, instinct), where he encounters this craving not for "universal love / But to be loved alone." The distinction here is not so much between Christian and heathen or spiritual and carnal as between generous and selfish; i.e., between giving and taking; in a word, between Nijinsky and Diaghilev. Better still, between loving and having.

And watch what Auden is doing here. He comes up with the unthinkable: with a new rhyme for love: he rhymes "love" and "Diaghilev"! Now, let's see how it happens. I bet he had this rhyme in mind for a while. The point is, though, that it's easier if "love" comes first and "Diaghilev" comes second. The content, however, forces the poet to put "Diaghilev" first, which presents several problems. One of them is that the name is foreign, and the reader may misplace the stress. So Auden puts a very short, reductive line, "About Diaghilev," after the regularly stressed "What mad Nijinsky wrote." Apart from the regularity of its beat, this line also acquaints the reader with the possibility of a foreign name and allows him to distribute stresses here whichever way he likes. This liberty paves the road to the trochaic arbitrariness of the next line, where "Diaghilev" goes virtually stressless. A reader then is quite likely to put the stress on the last syllable, which suits the author just fine, for it will amount to rhyming "lev" and "love": what could be better?

However, the name contains that strange to an English ear, or eye, sound *gh*, which somehow should be taken care of. The culprit of its strangeness is the position of *h* after *g*.

So it appears that the poet should find a rhyme not for "lev" only but for "ghilev" or, rather, "hilev" as well. And so he does, and it is "have" in "Craves what it cannot have." Terrific line, that: the energy of "Craves" hits head-on the wall of "what it cannot have." It's of the same pattern as "For the error bred in the bone," which is awfully strong. Then the author momentarily relaxes his reader in "Of each woman and each man." Then he makes you pay for that relaxation with this monosyllabic "Craves what it cannot have," whose syntax is so tough it's almost strained; i.e., it's shorter than natural speech, *shorter than its thought*, or more final. Anyway, let's get back to "have," for it has far-reaching consequences.

You see, to rhyme "Diaghilev" with "love" straight would mean to equate them, about which both the poet and the reader could have some qualms. By interjecting "have" Auden scores a terrific hit. For now the rhyme scheme itself becomes a statement: "Diaghilev-have-love" or rather, "Diaghilev cannot have love." And "Diaghilev," mind you, stands here for art. So the net result is that "Diaghilev" gets equated with "love," but only via being equated with "have," and "having," as we know, is opposite to "loving," which is, as we remember, Nijinsky, which is "giving." Well, the implications of this rhyme scheme are profound enough to give you vertigo, and we've spent too much time on this stanza already. I wish, though, that at home you'd analyze this rhyme on your own: it may yield, perhaps, more than the poet himself had in mind to reveal while using it. I don't mean to whet your appetite, nor do I intend to suggest in the first place that Auden was doing all this consciously. On the contrary, he went for this rhyme scheme instinctively or, if you like this word better, subconsciously. But this is precisely what makes it so interesting to look into: not because you are getting into someone's subconscious (which in the case of a poet barely exists, being absorbed or badly exploited by the conscious) or his instincts: it simply shows you to what extent a writer is the tool of his language and how his ethical notions are the sharper, the keener his ear is.

On the whole, the role of this stanza is to finish the job of the previous one, i.e., to trace the malaise to its origins, and indeed Auden reaches the marrow.

Naturally enough, after this, one needs a break, and the break comes in the form of the next stanza, which employs less pointed thinking and a more general, more public level of diction.

8

From the conservative dark
Into the ethical life
The dense commuters come,
Repeating their morning vow;
"*I will be true to the wife,*
I'll concentrate more on my work,"
And helpless governors wake
To resume their compulsory game:
Who can release them now,
Who can reach the deaf,
Who can speak for the dumb?

This is, perhaps, the least interesting stanza in the poem, but it is not without its own jewels. Its most attractive job is the two opening lines describing the journey from the subconscious to the rational, i.e., ethical, existence, from sleep to action, from "dark" not to light but to "life." As for its rhymes, the most suggestive here is "dark–work–wake," which is quite functional considering the stanza's content. It's the assonant rhyme all along, and it shows you the possibilities this sort of rhyming contains, for as you arrive at "wake" after "dark," you realize that you can develop "wake" into something else as well. For example, you can go "wait–waste–west," and so on. As for the purely didactic aspect of this "dark–work–wake," the "dark–work" bit is more interesting because of "dark's" probable double significance. This reminds me of a couplet in Auden's "Letter to Lord Byron":

Man is no center of the Universe,
And working in an office makes it worse.

Which—I mean the "Letter"—is your only chance to be "happy" if not "good."

Metrically, the first six lines of this stanza are doing a lovely job of conveying the sense of train movement: you have a very smooth ride in the first four of them, and then you are getting jolted first by "will" and again by "more," which reveal the origins of each emphasis as well as the likelihood of delivering on these promises. With "And helpless governors wake," the meter regains equilibrium, and after the wallowing "To resume their compulsory game" the stanza is slowed down by three rhetorical questions, the last of which brings that train to a complete halt: "Who can release them now, / Who can reach the deaf, / Who can speak for the dumb?"

Now "The dense commuters" are presumably what "to be loved alone" results in: a herd. As for "conservative" applied here to "dark," this is yet another example of the typical, for Auden, blinding proximity of definition, like "neutral air" a couple of stanzas before, or "necessary murder" in an absolutely marvelous poem of this period called "Spain." These juxtapositions of his are effective and memorable because of merciless light—or rather dark—their parts normally cast upon one another; i.e., it's not only murder that is necessary, but necessity itself is murderous, and so is conservativeness dark. Therefore the next line's "ethical life" emerges as a double put-down: because you expect "ethical light." The standard positive locution all of a sudden is defamiliarized by apprehension: "life" is a leftover of "light." On the whole the stanza depicts a dispirited mechanical existence where "governors" are not in any way superior to the governed and neither are able to escape the enveloping gloom which they spun themselves.

And what do you think is the source, the root of all these conjunctions of his? Of things like that "necessary murder," "artificial wilderness" in "The Shield of Achilles," "important failure" in the "Musée des Beaux Arts," and so forth, and so forth? Yes, it is an intensity of attention, of course; but we are all endowed with this ability, aren't we? To yield results like these, this ability clearly should be enhanced by something. And what does enhance it in a poet, and in this poet in particular? It is the principle of rhyme. What is responsible for these blinding proximities is the same mechanism of instinct that allows one to see or to hear that "Diaghilev" and "love" do rhyme. Once that mechanism is set in motion, there is nothing to stop it, it becomes an instinct. It shapes your mental operation, to say the least, in more ways than one; it becomes your mode of cognition. And this is what makes the whole enterprise of poetry so valuable for our species. For it is the principle of rhyme that enables one to sense that proximity between seemingly disparate entities. All these conjunctions of his ring so true because they *are* rhymes. This closeness between objects, ideas, concepts, causes, and effects—this closeness, in itself, *is a rhyme*: at times, a perfect one, more frequently an assonance; or just a visual one. Having developed an instinct for these, you may have a better time with reality.

9

By now the poem is seventy-seven lines long, and apart from the content, its mass itself requires a resolution. That is, depiction of a world becomes, in its own turn, a world. So when the poet here says "All I have is a voice," it cuts many ways and doesn't just offer a lyrical relaxation to the ethical tension. The seventy-eighth line reflects not only the author's despair over the human condition as it is depicted but his sense of the futility of depiction. Despair alone would be more palatable, for there is always a chance to resolve it through anger or resignation, which are both promising avenues for a poet; well, anger especially. The same holds for futility also, for, by itself, it may be just as rewarding if treated with irony or sobriety.

Stephen Spender once wrote about Auden that good as he was at providing a diagnosis, he'd never presume to offer a cure. Well, "All I have is a voice" cures, because by changing tonality, the poet changes here the plane of regard. This line simply is higher pitched than all its predecessors. In poetry, as you know, tonality *is* content, or content's result. As pitches go, altitude determines attitude.

The important thing about the seventy-eighth line is the shift from impersonal objectivity of description to highly personal, subjective note. After all, this is the second and basically last time that the author employs "I." And this "I" is no longer wrapped in a newsman's trench coat: what you hear in this voice is incurable sorrow, for all its stoical timbre. This "I" is sharp and is echoed in a somewhat muffled way by "lie" in the next line's end. Still, remember that both high-pitched *i*'s come immediately after the "deaf" and "dumb" of the previous stanza, and this creates a considerable acoustic contrast.

The only thing that controls that sorrow here is the beat; and "sorrow controlled by meter" may do for you as a provisional definition of humility, if not of the entire art of poetry. As a rule, stoicism and obstinacy in poets are results not so much of their personal philosophies and preferences as of their experiences in prosody, which is the name of the cure. This stanza, as well as this whole poem, is a search for a reliable virtue which in the end brings the searching party to itself.

This, however, is jumping a bit ahead. Let's proceed in a proper fashion. Well, as far as rhymes are concerned, this stanza is not so spectacular. "Voice–choice–police" and "lie (authority)–sky–die" are all right; a better job is done by the poet in "brain–alone," which is suggestive enough. What's more suggestive, though, is "folded lie / The romantic lie in the brain." Both "folded" and "lie" are used twice within the space of two lines. Now, this is obviously done for emphasis; the only question is what's emphasized here. "Folded" of course suggests "paper" and "lie" therefore is the lie of a printed word, most likely the one of a tabloid. But then we are given a qualifier in "the romantic lie in the brain." What's qualified here is not the "lie" itself, although we have here a different epithet preceding it, but the brain that lies in folds.

It is rather sobriety, of course, and its by-products that are audible in "All I have is a voice" than the irony which is, nonetheless, discernible in the controlled anger of "the folded lie." Still, the seventy-eighth line's value lies neither in despair's and futility's separate effects, nor in their interplay; what we hear in this line most clearly is the voice of humility, which has, in the given context, stoic overtones. Auden isn't just punning here; no. These two lines simply paraphrase that "error bred in the bone / Of each woman and each man." In a sense, he opens the bone and shows us that lie (error) inside. Why does he do this here? Because he wants to drive home the idea of "universal love" versus "to be loved alone." "The sensual man-in-the-street" as well as "Authority" and "the citizen" or "the police" are simply elaborations of the "each woman and each man" theme, as well as spin-offs of the argument for the United States' isolationist posture at the time. "Hunger allows no choice / To the citizen or the police" is simply a commonsense way of arguing the existence of the common denominator among people, and it is placed appropriately low. Auden goes here for a typically English no-nonsense locution—precisely because the point he tries to make is of a very elevated nature; i.e., he appears to think that you can argue things like "universal love" best if you use down-to-earth logic. Apart from that, he, I believe, enjoys the deadpan, no-exit state of mind whose blinding proximity to the truth creates such a statement. (Actually, hunger allows a choice: to get hungrier; but that's beside the point.) At any rate, this hunger business offsets possible ecclesiastical association of the next, most crucial for the entire argument, line: "We must love one another or die."

Well, this is the line because of which the author subsequently scrapped the whole poem from his corpus. According to various sources, he did so because he found the line presumptuous and untrue. Because, he said, we must die anyway. He tried to change it but all he could come up with was "We must love one another *and* die," which would be a platitude with a misleading air of profundity. So he scrapped it from his postwar *Collected*, and if we have it now in front of our eyes, it's because of his literary executor, Edward Mendelson, who compiled a posthumous Viking edition and whose introduction to it is the best piece on Auden I've ever seen.

Was Auden right about this line? Well, yes and no. He was obviously extremely conscientious, and to be conscientious in English is to be literal. Also, we should consider the benefit of hindsight in his revising this line: after the carnage of World War II, either version would sound a bit macabre. Poetry isn't reportage, and its news should be of a permanent significance. In a sense, it could be argued that Auden pays a price here for his posture at the beginning of the poem. Still, I must say that if this line seemed to him untrue, it was through no fault of his own.

For the actual meaning of the line at the time was, of course, "We must love one another or kill." Or "we'll be killing one another in no time." Since—after all, all he had was a voice and this wasn't heard or heeded—what followed was exactly what he predicted: killing. But again, given

World War II's volume of carnage, one could hardly enjoy proving oneself a prophet. So the poet chooses to threat this "or die" literally. Presumably because he felt he was responsible for failing to avert what had happened, since the whole point of writing this poem was to influence public opinion.

10

This, after all, wasn't the benefit of hindsight only. The evidence that he didn't feel very secure about this line's prescription is felt in the opening of the next stanza: "Defenceless under the night . . ." Paired with "Our world in stupor lies," this is tantamount to an admission of failure to persuade. At the same time, "Defenceless under the night" is the most lyrical-sounding line in the poem and surpasses in the height of its pitch even "All I have is a voice." In both cases, the lyricism stems from the feeling of what he terms in "In Memory of W. B. Yeats" "human unsuccess," from his own "rapture of distress" here in the first place.

Coming right after "We must love one another or die," this line has a sharper personal air and leaps from the level of rationalization to that of pure emotional exposure, into the domain of revelations. Technically speaking, "We must love another or die" is the end of the mental road. After this, there is only a prayer, and "Defenceless under the night" climbs there in its tonality if not yet in its diction. And as though sensing that things may slip from under his control, that the pitch approaches a vibration of wailing, the poet undercuts himself with "Our world in stupor lies."

Yet no matter how hard he tries to pull his voice down in this as well as in the subsequent four lines, the spell cast by "We must love one another or die" gets reinforced almost against his own will by "Defenceless under the night" and won't go away. On the contrary, it penetrates his defenses at the rate at which he builds them. The spell, as we know it, is an ecclesiastical one, i.e., imbued with a sense of infinity; and words like "everywhere," "light," "just," thanks to their generic nature, echo that sense unwittingly and in spite of reductive qualifiers like "dotted" and "harmonic." And when the poet comes closest to having his voice completely harnessed, that spell breaks through with full lyrical force in this breathtaking cross between plea and prayer:

> *May I, composed like them*
> *Of Eros and of dust,*
> *Beleaguered by the same*
> *Negation and despair,*
> *Show an affirming flame.*

Well, what we have here, apart from everything else, is a self-portrait that strays into the definition of the species. And that definition, I must say, comes from the tenor of "May I" rather than from the precision of the next three lines. For it's their sum that produces "May I." What we have here, in other words, is truth resulting in lyricism or, better still, lyricism becoming truth; what we have here is a stoic who prays. This may not be the species' definition as yet, but this is surely its goal.

At any rate, this is the direction in which this poet went. You may, of course, find this ending a bit sanctimonious and wonder who are "the Just"—the fabled thirty-six or somebody in particular—or what does this "affirming flame" look like? But you don't dissect a bird to find the origins of its song: what should be dissected is your ear. In either case, however, you'll be dodging the alternative of "We must love one another or die," and I don't think you can afford to.

1984

To Please a Shadow

When a writer resorts to a language other than his mother tongue, he does so either out of necessity, like Conrad, or because of burning ambition, like Nabokov, or for the sake of greater estrangement, like Beckett. Belonging to a different league, in the summer of 1977, in New York, after living in this country for five years, I purchased in a small typewriter shop on Sixth Avenue a portable "Lettera 22" and set out to write (essays, translations, occasionally a poem) in English for a reason that had very little to do with the above. My sole purpose then, as it is now, was to find myself in closer proximity to the man whom I considered the greatest mind of the twentieth century: Wystan Hugh Auden.

I was, of course, perfectly aware of the futility of my undertaking, not so much because I was born in Russia and into its language (which I am never to abandon—and I hope vice versa) as because of this poet's intelligence, which in my view has no equal. I was aware of the futility of this effort, moreover, because Auden had been dead four years then. Yet to my mind, writing in English was the best way to get near him, to work on his terms, to be judged, if not by his code of conscience, then by whatever it is in the English language that made this code of conscience possible.

These words, the very structure of these sentences, all show anyone who has read a single stanza or a single paragraph of Auden's how I fail. To me, though, a failure by his standards is preferable to a success by others'. Besides, I knew from the outset that I was bound to fail; whether this sort of sobriety was my own or has been borrowed from his writing, I can no longer tell. All I hope for while writing in his tongue is that I won't lower his level of mental operation, his plane of regard. This is as much as one can do for a better man: to continue in his vein; this, I think, is what civilizations are all about.

I knew that by temperament and otherwise, I was a different man, and that in the best case possible I'd be regarded as his imitator. Still, for me that would be a compliment. Also I had a second line of defense: I could always pull back to my writing in Russian, of which I was pretty confident and which even he, had he known the language, probably would have liked. My desire to write in English had nothing to do with any sense of confidence, contentment, or comfort; it was simply a desire to please a shadow. Of course, where he was by then, linguistic barriers hardly mattered, but somehow I thought that he might like it better if I made myself clear to him in English. (Although when I tried, on the green grass at Kirchstetten eleven years ago now, it didn't work; the English I had at that time was better for reading and listening than for speaking. Perhaps just as well.)

To put it differently, unable to return the full amount of what has been given, one tries to pay back at least in the same coin. After all, he did so himself, borrowing the "Don Juan" stanza for his "Letter to Lord Byron" or hexameters for his "Shield of Achilles." Courtship always requires a degree of self-sacrifice and assimilation, all the more so if one is courting a pure spirit. While in the flesh, this man did so much that belief in the immortality of his soul becomes somehow unavoidable. What he left us with amounts to a gospel which is both brought about by and filled with love that's anything but finite—with love, that is, which can in no way all be harbored by human flesh and which therefore needs words. If there were no churches, one could easily have built one upon this poet, and its main precept would run something like his

If equal affection cannot be,
Let the more loving one be me.

2

If a poet has any obligation toward society, it is to write well. Being in the minority, he has no other choice. Failing this duty, he sinks into oblivion. Society, on the other hand, has no obligation toward the poet. A majority by definition, society thinks of itself as having other options than reading verses, no matter how well written. Its failure to do so results in its sinking to that level of locution at which society falls easy prey to a demagogue or a tyrant. This is society's own equivalent of oblivion; a tyrant, of course, may try to save his subjects from it by some spectacular bloodbath.

I first read Auden some twenty years ago in Russia in rather limp and listless translations that I found in an anthology of contemporary English poetry subtitled "From Browning to Our Days." "Our Days" were those of 1937, when the volume was published. Needless to say, almost the entire body of its translators along with its editor, M. Gutner, were arrested soon afterward, and many of them perished. Needless to say, for the next forty years no other anthology of contemporary English poetry was published in Russia, and the said volume became something of a collector's item.

One line of Auden in that anthology, however, caught my eye. It was, as I learned later, from the last stanza of his early poem "No Change of Place," which described a somewhat claustrophobic landscape where "no one goes / Further than railhead or the ends of piers, / Will neither go nor send his son . . ." This last bit, "Will neither go nor send his son . . ." struck me with its mixture of negative extension and common sense. Having been brought up on an essentially emphatic and self-asserting diet of Russian verse, I was quick to register this recipe whose main component was self-restraint. Still, poetic lines have a knack of straying from the context into universal significance, and the threatening touch of absurdity contained in "Will neither go nor send his son" would start vibrating in the back of my mind whenever I'd set out to do something on paper.

This is, I suppose, what they call an influence, except that the sense of the absurd is never an invention of the poet but is a reflection of reality; inventions are seldom recognizable. What one may owe here to the poet is not the sentiment itself but its treatment: quiet, unemphatic, without any pedal, almost *en passant*. This treatment was especially significant to me precisely because I came across this line in the early sixties, when the Theater of the Absurd was in full swing. Against that background, Auden's handling of the subject stood out not only because he had beaten a lot of people to the punch but because of a considerably different ethical message. The way he handled the line was telling, at least to me: something like "Don't cry wolf" even though the wolf's at the door. (Even though, I would add, it looks exactly like you. Especially because of that, don't cry wolf.)

Although for a writer to mention his penal experiences —or for that matter, any kind of hardship—is like dropping names for normal folk, it so happened that my next opportunity to pay a closer look at Auden occurred while I was doing my own time in the North, in a small village lost among swamps and forests, near the polar circle. This time the anthology that I had was in English, sent to me by a friend from Moscow. It had quite a lot of Yeats, whom I then found a bit too oratorical and sloppy with meters, and Eliot, who in those days reigned supreme in Eastern Europe. I was intending to read Eliot.

But by pure chance the book opened to Auden's "In Memory of W. B. Yeats." I was young then and therefore particularly keen on elegies as a genre, having nobody around dying to write one for. So I read them perhaps more avidly than anything else, and I frequently thought that the most interesting feature of the genre was the authors' unwitting attempts at self-portrayal with which nearly every poem "in memoriam" is strewn—or soiled. Understandable though this tendency is, it often turns such a poem into the author's ruminations on the subject of death, from which we learn more about him than about the deceased. The Auden poem had none of this; what's more, I soon realized that even its structure was designed to pay tribute to the dead poet, imitating in reverse order the great Irishman's own modes of stylistic development, all the way down to his earliest: the tetrameters of the poem's third—last—part.

It's because of these tetrameters, in particular because of eight lines from this third part, that I understood what kind of poet I was reading. These lines overshadowed for me that astonishing description of "the dark cold day," Yeats's last, with its shuddering

The mercury sank in the mouth of the dying day.

They overshadowed that unforgettable rendition of the stricken body as a city whose suburbs and squares are gradually emptying as if after a crushed rebellion. They overshadowed even that statement of the era

. . . *poetry makes nothing happen* . . .

They, those eight lines in tetrameter that made this third part of the poem sound like a cross between a Salvation Army hymn, a funeral dirge, and a nursery rhyme, went like this:

Time that is intolerant
Of the brave and innocent,
And indifferent in a week
To a beautiful physique,

Worships language and forgives
Everyone by whom it lives;
Pardons cowardice, conceit,
Lays its honours at their feet.

I remember sitting there in the small wooden shack, peering through the square porthole-size window at the wet, muddy, dirt road with a few stray chickens on it, half believing what I'd just read, half wondering whether my grasp of English wasn't playing tricks on me. I had there a veritable boulder of an English-Russian dictionary, and I went through its pages time and again, checking every word, every allusion, hoping that they might spare me the meaning that stared at me from the page. I guess I was simply refusing to believe that way back in 1939 an English poet had said, "Time . . . worships language," and yet the world around was still what it was.

But for once the dictionary didn't overrule me. Auden had indeed said that time (not *the* time) worships language, and the train of thought that statement set in motion in me is still trundling to this day. For "worship" is an attitude of the lesser toward the greater. If time worships language, it means that language is greater, or older, than time, which is, in its turn, older and greater than space. That was how I was taught, and I indeed felt that way. So if time—which is synonymous with, nay, even absorbs deity—worships language, where then does language come from? For the gift is always smaller than the giver. And then isn't language a repository of time? And isn't this why time worships it? And isn't a song, or a poem, or indeed a speech itself, with its caesuras, pauses, spondees, and so forth, a game language plays to restructure time? And aren't those by whom language "lives" those by whom time does too? And if time "forgives" them, does it do so out of generosity or out of necessity? And isn't generosity a necessity anyhow?

Short and horizontal as those lines were, they seemed to

me incredibly vertical. They were also very much offhand, almost chatty: metaphysics disguised as common sense, common sense disguised as nursery-rhyme couplets. These layers of disguise alone were telling me what language is, and I realized that I was reading a poet who spoke the truth—or through whom the truth made itself audible. At least it felt more like truth than anything else I managed to figure out in that anthology. And perhaps it felt that way precisely because of the touch of irrelevance that I sensed in the falling intonation of "forgives / Everyone by whom it lives; / Pardons cowardice, conceit, / Lays its honours at their feet." These words were there, I thought, simply to offset the upward gravity of "Time . . . worships language."

I could go on and on about these lines, but I could do so only now. Then and there I was simply stunned. Among other things, what became clear to me was that one should watch out when Auden makes his witty comments and observations, keeping an eye on civilization no matter what his immediate subject (or condition) is. I felt that I was dealing with a new kind of metaphysical poet, a man of terrific lyrical gifts, who disguised himself as an observer of public mores. And my suspicion was that this choice of mask, the choice of this idiom, had to do less with matters of style and tradition than with the personal humility imposed on him not so much by a particular creed as by his sense of the nature of language. Humility is never chosen.

I had yet to read my Auden. Still, after "In Memory of W. B. Yeats," I knew that I was facing an author more humble than Yeats or Eliot, with a soul less petulant than either, while, I was afraid, no less tragic. With the benefit of hindsight I may say now that I wasn't altogether wrong, and that if there was ever any drama in Auden's voice, it wasn't his own personal drama but a public or existential one. He'd never put himself in the center of the tragic picture; at best he'd acknowledge his presence at the scene. I had yet to hear from his very mouth that "J. S. Bach was terribly lucky. When he wanted to praise the Lord, he'd write a chorale or a cantata addressing the Almighty directly. Today, if a poet wishes to do the same thing, he has to employ indirect speech." The same, presumably, would apply to prayer.

3

As I write these notes, I notice the first person singular popping its ugly head up with alarming frequency. But man is what he reads; in other words, spotting this pronoun, I detect Auden more than anybody else: the aberration simply reflects the proportion of my reading of this poet. Old dogs, of course, won't learn new tricks; dog owners, though, end up resembling their dogs. Critics, and especially biographers, of writers with a distinctive style often adopt, however unconsciously, their subjects' mode of expression. To put it simply, one is changed by what one loves, sometimes to the point of losing one's entire identity. I am not trying to say that this is what happened to me; all I seek to suggest is that these otherwise tawdry I's and me's are, in their own turn, forms of indirect speech whose object is Auden.

For those of my generation who were interested in poetry in English—and I can't claim there were too many of those—the sixties was the era of anthologies. On their way home, foreign students and scholars who'd come to Russia on academic exchange programs would understandably try to rid themselves of extra weight, and books of poetry were the first to go. They'd sell them, almost for nothing, to secondhand bookstores, which subsequently would charge extraordinary sums if you wanted to buy them. The rationale behind these prices was quite simple: to deter the locals from purchasing these Western items; as for the foreigner himself, he would obviously be gone and unable to see the disparity.

Still, if you knew a salesperson, as one who frequents a place inevitably does, you could strike the sort of deal every book-hunting person is familiar with: you'd trade one thing for another, or two or three books for one, or you'd buy a book, read it, and return it to the store and get your money back. Besides, by the time I was released and returned to my hometown, I'd gotten myself some sort of reputation, and in several bookstores they treated me rather nicely. Because of this reputation, students from the exchange programs would sometimes visit me, and as one is not supposed to cross a strange threshold empty-handed, they'd bring books. With some of these visitors I struck up close friendships, because of which my bookshelves gained considerably.

I liked them very much, these anthologies, and not for their contents only but also for the sweetish smell of their bindings and their pages edged in yellow. They felt so American and were indeed pocket-size. You could pull them out of your pocket in a streetcar or in a public garden, and even though the text would be only a half or a third comprehensible, they'd instantly obliterate the local reality. My favorites, though, were Louis Untermeyer's and Oscar Williams's—because they had pictures of their contributors that fired up one's imagination in no less a way than the lines themselves. For hours on end I would sit scrutinizing a smallish black-and-white box with this or that poet's features, trying to figure out what kind of person he was, trying to animate him, to match the face with his half- or a third-understood lines. Later on, in the company of friends we would exchange our wild surmises and the snatches of gossip that occasionally came our way and, having developed a common denominator, pronounce our verdict. Again with the benefit of hindsight, I must say that frequently our divinations were not too far off.

That was how I first saw Auden's face. It was a terribly reduced photograph—a bit studied, with a too didactic handling of shadow: it said more about the photographer than about his model. From that picture, one would have to conclude either that the former was a naïve aesthete or the latter's features were too neutral for his occupation. I preferred the second version, partly because neutrality of tone was very much a feature of Auden's poetry, partly because anti-heroic posture was the *idée fixe* of our generation. The idea was to look like everybody else: plain shoes, workman's cap, jacket and tie, preferably gray, no beards or mustaches. Wystan was recognizable.

Also recognizable to the point of giving one the shivers were the lines in "September 1, 1939" ostensibly explaining the origins of the war that had cradled my generation but in effect depicting our very selves as well, like a black-and-white snapshot in its own right.

I and the public know
What all schoolchildren learn,
Those to whom evil is done
Do evil in return.

This four-liner indeed was straying out of context, equating victors to victims, and I think it should be tattooed by the federal government on the chest of every newborn, not because of its message alone, but because of its intonation. The only acceptable argument against such a procedure would be that there are better lines by Auden. What would you do with:

Faces along the bar
Cling to their average day:
The lights must never go out,
The music must always play,
All the conventions conspire
To make this fort assume
The furniture of home;
Lest we should see where we are,
Lost in a haunted wood,
Children afraid of the night
Who have never been happy or good.

Or if you think this is too much New York, too American, then how about this couplet from "The Shield of Achilles," which, to me at least, sounds a bit like a Dantesque epitaph to a handful of East European nations:

. . . they lost their pride
And died as men before their bodies died.

Or if you are still against such a barbarity, if you want to spare the tender skin this hurt, there are seven other lines in the same poem that should be carved on the gates of every existing state, indeed on the gates of our whole world:

A ragged urchin, aimless and alone,
Loitered about that vacancy, a bird
Flew up to safety from his well-aimed stone:
That girls are raped, that two boys knife a third,
Were axioms to him, who'd never heard
Of any world where promises were kept.
Or one could weep because another wept.

This way the new arrival won't be deceived as to this world's nature; this way the world's dweller won't take demagogues for demigods.

One doesn't have to be a gypsy or a Lombroso to believe in the relation between an individual's appearance and his deeds: this is what our sense of beauty is based on, after all. Yet how should a poet look who wrote:

Altogether elsewhere, vast
Herds of reindeer move across
Miles and miles of golden moss,
Silently and very fast.

How should a man look who was as fond of translating metaphysical verities into the pedestrian of common sense as he was of spotting the former in the latter? How should one look who, by going very thoroughly about creation, tells you more about the Creator than any impertinent agonist shortcutting through the spheres? Shouldn't a sensibility unique in its combination of honesty, clinical detachment, and controlled lyricism result if not in a unique arrangement of facial features then at least in a specific, uncommon expression? And could such features or such an expression be captured by a brush? registered by a camera?

I liked the process of extrapolating from that stamp-size picture very much. One always gropes for a face, one always wants an ideal to materialize, and Auden was very close at the time to amounting to an ideal. (Two others were Beckett and Frost, yet I knew the way they looked; however terrifying, the correspondence between their façades and their deeds was obvious.) Later, of course, I saw other photographs of Auden: in a smuggled magazine or in other anthologies. Still they added nothing; the man eluded lenses, or they lagged behind the man. I began to wonder whether one form of art was capable of depicting another, whether the visual could apprehend the semantic.

Then one day—I think it was in the winter of 1968 or 1969—in Moscow, Nadezhda Mandelstam, whom I was visiting there, handed me yet another anthology of modern poetry, a very handsome book generously illustrated with large black-and-white photographs done by, if I remember correctly, Rollie McKenna. I found what I was looking for. A couple of months later, somebody borrowed that book from me and I never saw the photograph again; still, I remember it rather clearly.

The picture was taken somewhere in New York, it seemed, on some overpass—either the one near Grand Central or the one at Columbia University that spans Amsterdam Avenue. Auden stood there looking as though he were caught unawares, in passage, eyebrows lifted in bewilderment. The eyes themselves, however, were terribly calm and keen. The time was, presumably, the late forties or the beginning of the fifties, before the famous wrinkled—"unkempt bed"—stage took over his features. Everything, or almost everything, became clear to me.

The contrast or, better still, the degree of disparity between those eyebrows risen in formal bewilderment and the keenness of his gaze, to my mind, directly corresponded to the formal aspects of his lines (two lifted eyebrows = two rhymes) and to the blinding precision of their content. What stared at me from the page was the facial equivalent of a couplet, of truth that's better known by heart. The features were regular, even plain. There was nothing specifically poetic about this face, nothing Byronic, demonic, ironic, hawkish, aquiline, romantic, wounded, etc. Rather, it was the face of a physician who is interested in your story though he knows you are ill. A face well prepared for everything, a sum total of a face.

It was a result. Its blank stare was a direct product of that blinding proximity of face to object which produced expressions like "voluntary errands," "necessary murder," "conservative dark," "artificial wilderness," or "triviality of the sand." It felt like when a myopic person takes off his glasses, except that the keensightedness of this pair of eyes had to do with neither myopia nor the smallness of objects but with their deep-seated threats. It was the stare of a man who knew that he wouldn't be able to weed those threats out, yet who was bent on describing for you the symptoms as well as the malaise itself. That wasn't what's called "social criticism"—if only because the malaise wasn't social: it was existential.

In general, I think this man was terribly mistaken for a social commentator, or a diagnostician, or some such thing. The most frequent charge that's been leveled against him was that he didn't offer a cure. I guess in a way he asked for that by resorting to Freudian, then Marxist, then ecclesiastical terminology. The cure, though, lay precisely in his employing these terminologies, for they are simply different dialects in which one can speak about one and the same thing, which is love. It is the intonation with which one talks to the sick that cures. This poet went among the world's grave, often terminal cases not as a surgeon but as a nurse, and every patient knows that it's nurses and not incisions that eventually put one back on one's feet. It's the voice of a nurse, that is, of love, that one hears in the final speech of Alonso to Ferdinand in "The Sea and the Mirror":

But should you fail to keep your kingdom
And, like your father before you, come
Where thought accuses and feeling mocks,
Believe your pain . . .

Neither physician nor angel, nor—least of all—your beloved or relative will say this at the moment of your final defeat: only a nurse or a poet, out of experience as well as out of love.

And I marveled at that love. I knew nothing about Auden's life: neither about his being homosexual nor about his marriage of convenience (for her) to Erika Mann, etc. —nothing. One thing I sensed quite clearly was that this love would overshoot its object. In my mind—better, in my imagination—it was love expanded or accelerated by language, by the necessity of expressing it; and language—that much I already knew—has its own dynamics and is prone, especially in poetry, to use its self-generating devices: meters and stanzas that take the poet far beyond his original destination. And the other truth about love in poetry that one gleans from reading it is that a writer's sentiments inevitably subordinate themselves to the linear and unrecoiling progression of art. This sort of thing secures, in art, a higher degree of lyricism; in life, an equivalent in isolation. If only because of his stylistic versatility, this man should have known an uncommon degree of despair, as many of his most delightful, most mesmerizing lyrics do demonstrate. For in art lightness of touch more often than not comes from the darkness of its very absence.

And yet it was love all the same, perpetuated by language, oblivious—because the language was English—to gender, and intensified by a deep agony, because agony, too, may, in the end, have to be articulated. Language, after all, is self-conscious by definition, and it wants to get the hang of every new situation. As I looked at Rollie McKenna's picture, I felt pleased that the face there revealed neither neurotic nor any other sort of strain; that it was pale, ordinary, not expressing but instead absorbing whatever it was that was going on in front of his eyes. How marvelous it would be, I thought, to have those features, and I tried to ape the grimace in the mirror. I obviously failed, but I knew that I would fail, because such a face was bound to be one of a kind. There was no need to imitate it: it already existed in the world, and the world seemed somehow more palatable to me because this face was somewhere out there.

Strange things they are, faces of poets. In theory, authors' looks should be of no consequence to their readers: reading is not a narcissistic activity, neither is writing, yet the moment one likes a sufficient amount of a poet's verse one starts to wonder about the appearance of the writer. This, presumably, has to do with one's suspicion that to like a work of art is to recognize the truth, or the degree of it, that art expresses. Insecure by nature, we want to see the artist, whom we identify with his work, so that the next time around we might know what truth looks like in reality. Only the authors of antiquity escape this scrutiny, which is why, in part, they are regarded as classics, and their generalized marble features that dot niches in libraries are in direct relation to the absolute archetypal significance of their oeuvre. But when you read

. . . To visit
The grave of a friend, to make an ugly scene,
To count the loves one has grown out of,
Is not nice, but to chirp like a tearless bird,
As though no one dies in particular

And gossip were never true, unthinkable . . .

you begin to feel that behind these lines there stands not a blond, brunette, pale, swarthy, wrinkled, or smooth-faced concrete author but life itself; and *that* you would like to meet; *that* you would like to find yourself in human proximity to. Behind this wish lies not vanity but certain human physics that pull a small particle toward a big magnet, even though you may end up echoing Auden's own: "I have known three great poets, each one a prize son of a bitch." I: "Who?" He: "Yeats, Frost, Bert Brecht." (Now about Brecht he was wrong: Brecht wasn't a great poet.)

4

On June 6, 1972, some forty-eight hours after I had left Russia on very short notice, I stood with my friend Carl

Proffer, a professor of Russian literature at the University of Michigan (who'd flown to Vienna to meet me), in front of Auden's summer house in the small village of Kirchstetten, explaining to its owner the reasons for our being there. This meeting almost didn't happen.

There are three Kirchstettens in northern Austria, and we had passed through all three and were about to turn back when the car rolled into a quiet, narrow country lane and we saw a wooden arrow saying "Audenstrasse." It was called previously (if I remember accurately) "Hinterholz" because behind the woods the lane led to the local cemetery. Renaming it had presumably as much to do with the villagers' readiness to get rid of this "memento mori" as with their respect for the great poet living in their midst. The poet regarded the situation with a mixture of pride and embarrassment. He had a clearer sentiment, though, toward the local priest, whose name was Schicklgruber: Auden couldn't resist the pleasure of addressing him as "Father Schicklgruber."

All that I would learn later. Meanwhile, Carl Proffer was trying to explain the reasons for our being there to a stocky, heavily perspiring man in a red shirt and broad suspenders, jacket over his arm, a pile of books underneath it. The man had just come by train from Vienna and, having climbed the hill, was short of breath and not disposed to conversation. We were about to give up when he suddenly grasped what Carl Proffer was saying, cried "Impossible!" and invited us into the house. It was Wystan Auden, and it was less than two years before he died.

Let me attempt to clarify how all this had come about. Back in 1969, George L. Kline, a professor of philosophy at Bryn Mawr, had visited me in Leningrad. Professor Kline was translating my poems into English for the Penguin edition and, as we were going over the content of the future book, he asked me whom I would ideally prefer to write the introduction. I suggested Auden—because England and Auden were then synonymous in my mind. But, then, the whole prospect of my book being published in England was quite unreal. The only thing that imparted a semblance of reality to this venture was its sheer illegality under Soviet law.

All the same, things were set in motion. Auden was given the manuscript to read and liked it enough to write an introduction. So when I reached Vienna, I was carrying with me Auden's address in Kirchstetten. Looking back and thinking about the conversations we had during the subsequent three weeks in Austria and later in London and in Oxford, I hear his voice more than mine, although, I must say, I grilled him quite extensively on the subject of contemporary poetry, especially about the poets themselves. Still, this was quite understandable because the only English phrase I knew I wasn't making a mistake in was "Mr. Auden, what do you think about . . ."—and the name would follow.

Perhaps it was just as well, for what could I tell him that he didn't already know one way or another? I could have told him, of course, how I had translated several poems of his into Russian and took them to a magazine in Moscow; but the year happened to be 1968, the Soviets invaded Czechoslovakia, and one night the BBC broadcast his "The Ogre does what ogres can . . ." and that was the end of this venture. (The story would perhaps have endeared me to him, but I didn't have a very high opinion of those translations anyway.) That I'd never read a successful translation of his work into any language I had some idea of? He knew that himself, perhaps all too well. That I was overjoyed to learn one day about his devotion to the Kierkegaardian triad, which for many of us too was the key to the human species? But I worried I wouldn't be able to articulate it.

It was better to listen. Because I was Russian, he'd go on about Russian writers. "I wouldn't like to live with Dostoevsky under the same roof," he would declare. Or, "The best Russian writer is Chekhov"—"Why?" "He's the only one of your people who's got common sense." Or he would ask about the matter that seemed to perplex him most about my homeland: "I was told that the Russians always steal windshield wipers from parked cars. Why?" But my answer —because there were no spare parts—wouldn't satisfy him: he obviously had in mind a more inscrutable reason, and, having read him, I almost began to see one myself. Then he offered to translate some of my poems. This shook me considerably. Who was I to be translated by Auden? I knew that because of his translations some of my compatriots had profited more than their lines deserved; yet somehow I couldn't allow myself the thought of *him* working for *me*. So I said, "Mr. Auden, what do you think about . . . Robert Lowell?" "I don't like men," came the answer, "who leave behind them a smoking trail of weeping women."

During those weeks in Austria he looked after my affairs with the diligence of a good mother hen. To begin with, telegrams and other mail inexplicably began to arrive for me "c/o W. H. Auden." Then he wrote to the Academy of American Poets requesting that they provide me with some financial support. This was how I got my first American money—$1,000 to be precise—and it lasted me all the way to my first payday at the University of Michigan. He'd recommend me to his agent, instruct me on whom to meet and whom to avoid, introduce me to friends, shield me from journalists, and speak ruefully about having given up his flat on St. Mark's Place—as though I were planning to settle in his New York. "It would be good for you. If only because there is an Armenian church nearby, and the Mass is better when you don't understand the words. You don't know Armenian, do you?" I didn't.

Then from London came—c/o W. H. Auden—an invitation for me to participate in the Poetry International in Queen Elizabeth Hall, and we booked the same flight by British European Airways. At this point an opportunity arose for me to pay him back a little in kind. It so happened that during my stay in Vienna I had been befriended by the Razumovsky family (descendants of the Count Razumovsky of Beethoven's Quartets). One member of that family, Olga Razumovsky, was working then for the Austrian airlines. Having learned about W. H. Auden and myself taking the same flight to London, she called BEA and suggested they give these two passengers the royal treatment. Which we indeed received. Auden was pleased, and I was proud.

On several occasions during that time, he urged me to call him by his Christian name. Naturally I resisted—and not only because of how I felt about him as a poet but also because of the difference in our ages: Russians are terribly mindful of such things. Finally in London he said, "It won't do. Either you are going to call me Wystan, or I'll have to address you as Mr. Brodsky." This prospect sounded so grotesque to me that I gave up. "Yes, Wystan," I said. "Anything you say, Wystan." Afterward we went to the reading. He leaned on the lectern, and for a good half hour he filled the room with the lines he knew by heart. If I ever wished for time to stop, it was then, inside that large dark room on the south bank of the Thames. Unfortunately, it didn't. Although a year later, three months before he died in an Austrian hotel, we did read together again. In the same room.

5

By that time he was almost sixty-six. "I *had* to move to Oxford. I am in good health, but I have to have somebody to look after me." As far as I could see, visiting him there in January 1973, he was looked after only by the four walls of the sixteenth-century cottage given him by the college, and by the maid. In the dining hall the members of the faculty jostled him away from the food board. I supposed that was just English school manners, boys being boys. Looking at them, however, I couldn't help recalling one more of those blinding approximations of Wystan's: "triviality of the sand."

This foolery was simply a variation on the theme of society having no obligation to a poet, especially to an old poet. That is, society would listen to a politician of comparable age, or even older, but not to a poet. There is a variety of reasons for this, ranging from anthropologic ones to the sycophantic. But the conclusion is plain and unavoidable: society has no right to complain if a politician does it in. For, as Auden once put it in his "Rimbaud":

But in that child the rhetorician's lie
Burst like a pipe: the cold had made a poet.

If the lie explodes this way in "that child," what happens to it in the old man who feels the cold more acutely? Presumptuous as it may sound coming from a foreigner, the tragic achievement of Auden as a poet was precisely that he had dehydrated his verse of any sort of deception, be it a rhetorician's or a bardic one. This sort of thing alienates one not only from faculty members but also from one's fellows in the field, for in every one of us sits that red-pimpled youth thirsting for the incoherence of elevation.

Turning critic, this apotheosis of pimples would regard the absence of elevation as slackness, sloppiness, chatter, decay. It wouldn't occur to his sort that an aging poet has the right to write worse—if indeed he does—that there's nothing less palatable than unbecoming old age "discovering love" and monkey-gland transplants. Between boisterous and wise, the public will always choose the former (and not because such a choice reflects its demographic makeup or because of poets' own "romantic" habit of dying young, but because of the species' innate unwillingness to think about old age, let alone its consequences). The sad thing about this clinging to immaturity is that the condition itself is far from being permanent. Ah, if it only were! Then everything could be explained by the species' fear of death. Then all those "Selected Poems" of so many a poet would be as innocuous as the citizens of Kirchstetten rechristening their "Hinterholz." If it were only fear of death, readers and the appreciative critics especially should have been doing away with themselves nonstop, following the example of their beloved young authors. But that doesn't happen.

The real story behind our species' clinging to immaturity is much sadder. It has to do not with man's reluctance to know about death but with his not wanting to hear about life. Yet innocence is the last thing that can be sustained naturally. That's why poets—especially those who lasted long—must be read in their entirety, not in selections. The beginning makes sense only insofar as there is an end. For unlike fiction writers, poets tell us the whole story: not only in terms of their actual experiences and sentiments but—and that's what's most pertinent to us—in terms of language itself, in terms of the words they finally choose.

An aging man, if he still holds a pen, has a choice: to write memoirs or to keep a diary. By the very nature of their craft, poets are diarists. Often against their own will, they keep the most honest track of what's happening (a) to their souls, be it the expansion of a soul or—more frequently—its shrinkage and (b) to their sense of language, for they are the first ones for whom words become compromised or devalued. Whether we like it or not, we are here to learn not just what time does to man but what language does to time. And poets, let us not forget, are the ones "by whom it [language] lives." It is this law that teaches a poet a greater rectitude than any creed is capable of.

That's why one can build a lot upon W. H. Auden. Not only because he died at twice the age of Christ or because of Kierkegaard's "principle of repetition." He simply served an infinity greater than we normally reckon with, and he bears good witness to its availability; what's more, he made it feel hospitable. To say the least, every individual ought to know at least one poet from cover to cover: if not as a guide through the world, then as a yardstick for the language. W. H. Auden would do very well on both counts, if only because of their respective resemblances to hell and Limbo.

He was a great poet (the only thing that's wrong with this sentence is its tense, as the nature of language puts one's achievements within it invariably into the present), and I consider myself immensely lucky to have met him. But had I not met him at all, there would still be the reality of his work. One should feel grateful to fate for having been exposed to this reality, for the lavishing of these gifts, all the more priceless since they were not designated for anybody in particular. One may call this a generosity of the spirit, except that the spirit needs a man to refract itself through. It's not the man who becomes sacred because of this refraction: it's the spirit that becomes human and comprehensible. This—and the fact that men are finite—is enough for one to worship this poet.

Whatever the reasons for which he crossed the Atlantic and became American, the result was that he fused both idioms of English and became—to paraphrase one of his own lines—our transatlantic Horace. One way or another, all the journeys he took—through lands, caves of the psyche, doctrines, creeds—served not so much to improve his argument as to expand his diction. If poetry ever was for him a matter of ambition, he lived long enough for it to become simply a means of existence. Hence his autonomy, sanity, equipoise, irony, detachment—in short, wisdom. Whatever it is, reading him is one of the very few ways (if not the only one) available for feeling decent. I wonder, though, if that was his purpose.

I saw him last in July 1973, at a supper at Stephen Spender's place in London. Wystan was sitting there at the table, a cigarette in his right hand, a goblet in his left, holding forth on the subject of cold salmon. The chair being too low, two disheveled volumes of the OED were put under him by the mistress of the house. I thought then that I was seeing the only man who had the right to use those volumes as his seat.

1983

A Commencement Address

Ladies and gentlemen of the Class of 1984:

No matter how daring or cautious you may choose to be, in the course of your life you are bound to come into direct physical contact with what's known as Evil. I mean here not a property of the gothic novel but, to say the least, a palpable social reality that you in no way can control. No amount of good nature or cunning calculations will prevent this encounter. In fact, the more calculating, the more cautious you are, the greater is the likelihood of this rendezvous, the harder its impact. Such is the structure of life that what we regard as Evil is capable of a fairly ubiquitous presence if only because it tends to appear in the guise of good. You never see it crossing your threshold announcing itself: "Hi, I'm Evil!" That, of course, indicates its secondary nature, but the comfort one may derive from this observation gets dulled by its frequency.

A prudent thing to do, therefore, would be to subject your notions of good to the closest possible scrutiny, to go, so to speak, through your entire wardrobe checking which of your clothes may fit a stranger. That, of course, may turn into a full-time occupation, and well it should. You'll be surprised how many things you considered your own and good can easily fit, without much adjustment, your enemy. You may even start to wonder whether he is not your mirror image, for the most interesting thing about Evil is that it is wholly human. To put it mildly, nothing can be turned and worn inside out with greater ease than one's notion of social justice, civic conscience, a better future, etc. One of the surest signs of danger here is the number of those who share your views, not so much because unanimity has the knack of degenerating into uniformity as because of the probability—implicit in great numbers—that noble sentiment is being faked.

By the same token, the surest defense against Evil is extreme individualism, originality of thinking, whimsicality, even—if you will—eccentricity. That is, something that can't be feigned, faked, imitated; something even a seasoned impostor couldn't be happy with. Something, in other words, that can't be shared, like your own skin: not even by a minority. Evil is a sucker for solidity. It always goes for big numbers, for confident granite, for ideological purity, for drilled armies and balanced sheets. Its proclivity for such things has to do presumably with its innate insecurity, but this realization, again, is of small comfort when Evil triumphs.

Which it does: in so many parts of the world and inside ourselves. Given its volume and intensity, given, especially, the fatigue of those who oppose it, Evil today may be regarded not as an ethical category but as a physical phenomenon no longer measured in particles but mapped geographically. Therefore the reason I am talking to you about all this has nothing to do with your being young, fresh, and facing a clean slate. No, the slate is dark with dirt and it is hard to believe in either your ability or your will to clean it. The purpose of my talk is simply to suggest to you a mode of resistance which may come in handy to you one day; a mode that may help you to emerge from the encounter with Evil perhaps less soiled, if not necessarily more triumphant than your precursors. What I have in mind, of course, is the famous business of turning the other cheek.

I assume that one way or another you have heard about the interpretations of this verse from the Sermon on the Mount by Leo Tolstoy, Mahatma Gandhi, Martin Luther King, Jr., and many others. In other words, I assume that you are familiar with the concept of nonviolent, or passive, resistance, whose main principle is returning good for evil, that is, not responding in kind. The fact that the world today is what it is suggests, to say the least, that this concept is far from being cherished universally. The reasons for its unpopularity are twofold. First, what is required for this concept to be put into effect is a margin of democracy. This is precisely what 86 percent of the globe lacks. Second, it is common sense that tells a victim that his only gain in turning the other cheek and not responding in kind yields, at best, a moral victory, i.e., something quite immaterial. The natural reluctance to expose yet another part of your body to a blow is justified by a suspicion that this sort of conduct only agitates and enhances Evil; that a moral victory can be mistaken by the adversary for his impunity.

There are other, graver reasons to be suspicious. If the first blow hasn't knocked all the wits out of the victim's head, he may realize that turning the other cheek amounts to manipulation of the offender's sense of guilt, not to speak of his karma. The moral victory itself may not be so moral after all, not only because suffering often has a narcissistic aspect to it, but also because it renders the victim superior, that is, better than his enemy. Yet no matter how evil your enemy is, the crucial thing is that he is human; and although incapable of loving another like ourselves, we nonetheless know that evil takes root when one man starts to think that he is better than another. (This is why you've been hit on your right cheek in the first place.) At best, therefore, what one can get from turning the other cheek to one's enemy is the satisfaction of alerting the latter to the futility of his action. "Look," the other cheek says, "what you are hitting is just flesh. It's not me. You can't crush my soul." The trouble, of course, with this kind of attitude is that the enemy may just accept the challenge.

Twenty years ago the following scene took place in one of the numerous prison yards of northern Russia. At seven o'clock in the morning the door of a cell was flung open and on its threshold stood a prison guard, who addressed its inmates: "Citizens! The collective of this prison's guards challenges you, the inmates, to socialist competition in chopping the lumber amassed in our yard." In those parts there is no central heating, and the local police, in a manner of speaking, tax all the nearby lumber companies for one-tenth of their produce. By the time I am describing, the prison yard looked like a veritable lumberyard: the piles were two to three stories high, dwarfing the one-storied quadrangle of the prison itself. The need for chopping was evident, although socialist competitions of this sort had happened before. "And what if I refuse to take part in this?" inquired one of the inmates. "Well, in that case no meals for you," replied the guard.

Then axes were issued to inmates, and the cutting

started. Both prisoners and guards worked in earnest, and by noon all of them, especially the always underfed prisoners, were exhausted. A break was announced and people sat down to eat: except the fellow who asked the question. He kept swinging his ax. Both prisoners and guards exchanged jokes about him, something about Jews being normally regarded as smart people whereas this man . . . and so forth. After the break they resumed the work, although in a somewhat more flagging manner. By four o'clock the guards quit, since for them it was the end of their shift; a bit later the inmates stopped too. The man's ax still kept swinging. Several times he was urged to stop, by both parties, but he paid no attention. It seemed as though he had acquired a certain rhythm he was unwilling to break; or was it a rhythm that possessed him?

To the others, he looked like an automaton. By five o'clock, by six o'clock, the ax was still going up and down. Both guards and inmates were now watching him keenly, and the sardonic expression on their faces gradually gave way first to one of bewilderment and then to one of terror. By seven-thirty the man stopped, staggered into his cell, and fell asleep. For the rest of his stay in that prison, no call for socialist competition between guards and inmates was issued again, although the wood kept piling up.

I suppose the fellow could do this—twelve hours of straight chopping—because at the time he was quite young. In fact, he was then twenty-four. Only a little older than you are. However, I think there could have been another reason for his behavior that day. It's quite possible that the young man—precisely because he was young—remembered the text of the Sermon on the Mount better than Tolstoy and

Gandhi did. Because the Son of Man was in the habit of speaking in triads, the young man could have recalled that the relevant verse doesn't stop at

> *but whosoever shall smite thee on thy right cheek, turn to him the other also*

but continues without either period or comma:

> *And if any man will sue thee at the law, and take away thy coat, let him have* thy *cloak also.*
> *And whosoever shall compel thee to go a mile, go with him twain.*

Quoted in full, these verses have in fact very little to do with nonviolent or passive resistance, with the principles of not responding in kind and returning good for evil. The meaning of these lines is anything but passive, for it suggests that evil can be made absurd through excess; it suggests rendering evil absurd through dwarfing its demands with the volume of your compliance, which devalues the harm. This sort of thing puts a victim into a very active position, into the position of a mental aggressor. The victory that is possible here is not a moral but an existential one. The other cheek here sets in motion not the enemy's sense of guilt (which he is perfectly capable of quelling) but exposes his senses and faculties to the meaninglessness of the whole enterprise: the way every form of mass production does.

Let me remind you that we are not talking here about a situation involving a fair fight. We are talking about situations where one finds oneself in a hopelessly inferior position from the very outset, where one has no chance of fighting back, where the odds are overwhelmingly against one. In other words, we are talking about the very dark hours in one's life, when one's sense of moral superiority over the enemy offers no solace, when this enemy is too far gone to be shamed or made nostalgic for abandoned scruples, when one has at one's disposal only one's face, coat, cloak, and a pair of feet that are still capable of walking a mile or two.

In this situation there is very little room for tactical maneuver. So turning the other cheek should be your conscious, cold, deliberate decision. Your chances of winning, however dismal they are, all depend on whether or not you know what you are doing. Thrusting forward your face with the cheek toward the enemy, you should know that this is just the beginning of your ordeal as well as that of the verse—and you should be able to see yourself through the entire sequence, through all three verses from the Sermon on the Mount. Otherwise, a line taken out of context will leave you crippled.

To base ethics on a faultily quoted verse is to invite doom, or else to end up becoming a mental bourgeois enjoying the ultimate comfort: that of his convictions. In either case (of which the latter with its membership in well-intentioned movements and nonprofit organizations is the least palatable) it results in yielding ground to Evil, in delaying the comprehension of its weaknesses. For Evil, may I remind you, is only human.

Ethics based on this faultily quoted verse have changed nothing in post-Gandhi India, save the color of its administration. From a hungry man's point of view, though, it's all the same who makes him hungry. I submit that he may even prefer a white man to be responsible for his sorry state if only because this way social evil may appear to come from elsewhere and may perhaps be less efficient than the suffering at the hand of his own kind. With an alien in charge, there is still room for hope, for fantasy.

Similarly in post-Tolstoy Russia, ethics based on this misquoted verse undermined a great deal of the nation's resolve in confronting the police state. What has followed is known all too well: six decades of turning the other cheek transformed the face of the nation into one big bruise, so that the state today, weary of its violence, simply spits at that face. As well as at the face of the world. In other words, if you want to secularize Christianity, if you want to translate Christ's teachings into political terms, you need something more than modern political mumbo-jumbo: you need to have the original—in your mind at least if it hasn't found room in your heart. Since He was less a good man than a divine spirit, it's fatal to harp on His goodness at the expense of His metaphysics.

I must admit that I feel somewhat uneasy talking about these things: because turning or not turning that other cheek is, after all, an extremely intimate affair. The encounter always occurs on a one-to-one basis. It's always your skin, your coat and cloak, and it is your limbs that will have to do the walking. To advise, let alone to urge, anyone about the use of these properties is, if not entirely wrong, indecent. All I aspire to do here is to erase from your minds a cliché that harmed so many and yielded so little. I also would like to instill in you the idea that as long as you have your skin, coat, cloak, and limbs, you are not yet defeated, whatever the odds are.

There is, however, a greater reason for one to feel uneasy

about discussing these matters in public; and it's not only your own natural reluctance to regard your young selves as potential victims. No, it's rather mere sobriety, which makes one anticipate among you potential villains as well, and it is a bad strategy to divulge the secrets of resistance in front of the potential enemy. What perhaps relieves one from a charge of treason or, worse still, of projecting the tactical status quo into the future, is the hope that the victim will always be more inventive, more original in his thinking, more enterprising than the villain. Hence the chance that the victim may triumph.

Williams College, 1984

Flight from Byzantium

To Véronique Schiltz

Bearing in mind that every observation suffers from the observer's personal traits—that is, it too often reflects his psychological state rather than that of the reality under observation—I suggest that what follows be treated with a due measure of skepticism, if not with total disbelief. The only thing the observer may claim by way of justification is that he, too, possesses a modicum of reality, inferior in extent, perhaps, but conceding nothing in quality to the subject under scrutiny. A semblance of objectivity might be achieved, no doubt, by way of a complete self-awareness at the moment of observation. I do not think I am capable of this; in any event, I did not aspire to it. All the same, I hope that something of the sort took place.

2

My desire to get to Istanbul was never a genuine one. I am not even sure whether such a word—"desire"—should be used here. On the other hand, it could hardly be called a mere whim or a subconscious urge. Let it be a desire, then, and let's note that it came about partly as the result of a promise I made to myself in 1972, on leaving my hometown, that of Leningrad, for good—to circumnavigate the inhabited world along the latitude and along the longitude (i.e., the Pulkovo meridian) on which Leningrad is situated. By now, the latitude has been more or less taken care of; as to the longitude, the situation is anything but satisfactory. Istanbul, though, lies only a couple of degrees west of that meridian.

The aforementioned motive is only marginally more fanciful than the serious—indeed, the chief—reason, about which I will say something a bit later, or than a handful of totally frivolous secondary or tertiary ones, which I'll broach at once, it being now or never with such trivia: (a) it was in this city that my favorite poet, Constantine Cavafy, spent three momentous years at the turn of the century; (b) I always felt, for some reason, that here, in apartments, shops, and coffeehouses, I should find intact an atmosphere that at present seems to have totally vanished everywhere else; (c) I hoped to hear in Istanbul, on the outskirts of history, that "overseas creak of a Turkish mattress" which I thought I discerned one night some twenty years ago in the Crimea; (d) I wanted to find myself addressed as "effendi"; (e)—But I'm afraid the alphabet isn't long enough to accommodate all these ridiculous notions (though perhaps it's better if you are set in motion precisely by some such nonsense, for it makes final disappointment so much easier to bear). So let us get on to the promised "chief" reason, even though to many it may seem deserving of at best the "f" in my catalogue of bêtises.

This "chief" reason represents the pinnacle of fancifulness. It has to do with the fact that several years ago, while I was talking to a friend of mine, an American Byzantinist, it occurred to me that the cross that Constantine beheld in his dream on the eve of his victory over Maxentius—the cross that bore the legend "In this sign, conquer"—was not in fact a Christian cross but an urban one, the basic element of any Roman settlement. According to Eusebius and others, Constantine, inspired by his vision, at once set off for the East. First at Troy and then, having abruptly abandoned Troy, at Byzantium he founded the new capital of the Roman Empire—that is, the Second Rome. The consequences of this move of his were so momentous that, whether I was right or wrong, I felt an urge to see this place. After all, I spent thirty-two years in what is known as the Third Rome, about a year and a half in the First. Consequently, I needed the Second, if only for my collection.

But let us handle all this in an orderly fashion, so far as this is feasible.

3

I arrived in Istanbul, and left it, by air, having thus isolated it in my mind like some virus under a microscope. If one considers the infectious nature of any culture, the comparison does not seem irresponsible. Writing this note in the Hotel Aegean in the little place called Sounion—at the southeast corner of Attica, forty miles from Athens, where I landed four hours ago—I feel like the carrier of a specific infection, despite constant inoculations of the "classical rose" of the late Vladislav Khodasevich, to which I have subjected myself for the greater part of my life. I really do feel feverish from what I have seen; hence a certain incoherence in all that follows. I believe that my famous namesake experienced something of the sort as he strove to interpret the pharaoh's dreams—though it's one thing to bandy interpretations of sacred signs when the trail is hot (or warm, rather) and quite another a thousand and a half years later.

4

About dreams. This morning, in the wee hours, in Istanbul's Pera Palace, I, too, beheld something—something utterly monstrous. The scene was the Department of Philology of Leningrad University, and I was coming downstairs with someone I took to be Professor D. E. Maximov, except that he looked more like Lee Marvin. I can't recall what we were talking about, but that's not the point. My attention was caught by a scene of furious activity in a dark corner of the landing where the ceiling came down extremely low. I saw there three cats fighting with an enormous rat, which quite dwarfed them. Glancing over my shoulder, I noticed one of the cats ripped apart by the rat and writhing convulsively in agony on the floor. I chose not to watch the battle's outcome—I recall only that the cat became still—and, exchanging remarks with Marvin-Maximov, I kept going down the staircase. I woke up before I reached the hall.

To begin with, I adore cats. Then it should be added that I can't abide low ceilings; that the place only seemed like the Department of Philology, which is just two stories high anyway; that its grubby gray-brown color was that of the façades and interiors of Istanbul, especially the offices I had visited in the last few days; that the streets there are crooked, filthy, dreadfully cobbled, and piled up with refuse, which is constantly rummaged through by ravenous local cats; that the city, and everything in it, strongly smells of Astrakhan and Samarkand; and that the night before I had made up my mind to leave— But of that later. There was enough, in short, to pollute one's subconscious.

5

Constantine was, first and foremost, a Roman emperor—in charge of the Western part of the Empire—and for him "In this sign, conquer" was bound to signify, above all, an extension of his own rule, of his control over the whole empire. There is nothing novel about divining the most immediate future by roosters' innards, or about enlisting a deity as your own captain. Nor is the gulf between absolute ambition and utmost piety so vast. But even if he had been a true and zealous believer (a matter on which various doubts have been cast, especially in view of his conduct toward his children and in-laws), "conquer" must have had for him not only the military, sword-crossing meaning but also an administrative one—that is, settlements and cities. And the plan of any Roman settlement is precisely a cross: a central highway running north and south (like the Corso in Rome) intersects a similar road running east and west. From Leptis Magna to Castricum, an imperial citizen always knew where he was in relation to the capital.

Even if the cross of which Constantine spoke to Eusebius was that of the Redeemer, a constituent part of it in his dream was, un- or subconsciously, the principle of settlement planning. Besides, in the fourth century the symbol of the Redeemer was not the cross at all; it was the fish, a Greek acrostic for the name of Christ. And as for the Cross of the Crucifixion itself, it resembled the Russian (and Latin) capital T, rather than what Bernini depicted on that staircase in St. Peter's, or what we nowadays imagine it to have been. Whatever Constantine may or may not have had in mind, the execution of the instructions he received in a dream took the form in the first place of a territorial expansion toward the East, and the emergence of a Second Rome was a perfectly logical consequence of this eastward expansion. Possessing, by all accounts, a dynamic personality, he considered a forward policy perfectly natural. The more so if he was in actual fact a true believer.

Was he or wasn't he? Whatever the answer might be, it is the genetic code that laughed the last laugh. For his nephew happened to be no one else than Julian the Apostate.

6

Any movement along a plane surface which is not dictated by physical necessity is a spatial form of self-assertion, be it empire-building or tourism. In this sense, my reason for going to Istanbul differed only slightly from Constantine's. Especially if he really did become a Christian—that is, ceased to be a Roman. I have, however, rather more grounds for reproaching myself with superficiality; besides, the results of my displacements are of far less consequence. I don't even leave behind photographs taken "in front of" walls, let alone a set of walls themselves. In this sense, I am inferior even to the almost proverbial Japanese. (There is nothing more appalling to me than to think about the family album of the average Japanese: smiling and stocky, he/she/both against a backdrop of everything vertical the world contains—statues, fountains, cathedrals, towers, mosques, ancient temples, etc. Least of all, I presume, Buddhas and pagodas.) *Cogito ergo sum* gives way to *Kodak ergo sum*, just as *cogito* in its day triumphed over "I create." In other words, the ephemeral nature of my presence and my motives is no less absolute than the physical tangibility of Constantine's activities and his thoughts, real or supposed.

7

The Roman elegiac poets of the end of the first century B.C. —especially Propertius and Ovid—openly mock their great contemporary Virgil and his *Aeneid*. This may be explicable in terms of personal rivalry or professional jealousy or opposition of their idea of poetry as a personal, private art to a conception of it as something civic, as a form of state propaganda. (This last may ring true, but it is a far cry from the truth, nonetheless, since Virgil was the author not only of the *Aeneid* but also of the *Bucolics* and the *Georgics*.) There may also have been considerations of a purely stylistic nature. It is quite possible that from the elegists' point of view, the epic—any epic, including Virgil's—was a retrograde phenomenon. The elegists, all of them, were disciples of the Alexandrian school of poetry, which had given birth to a tradition of short lyric verse such as we are familiar with in poetry today. The Alexandrian preference for brevity, terseness, compression, concreteness, erudition, didacticism, and a preoccupation with the personal was, it seems, the reaction of the Greek art of letters against the surplus forms of Greek literature in the Archaic period: against the epic, the drama; against mythologizing, not to say mythmaking itself. A reaction, if one thinks about it—though it's best not to—against Aristotle. The Alexandrian tradition absorbed all these things and fitted them to the confines of the elegy or the eclogue: to the almost hieroglyphic dialogue in the latter, to an illustrative function of myth (*exempla*) in the former. In other words, we find a certain tendency toward miniaturization and condensation (as a means of survival for poetry in a world less and less inclined to pay it heed, if not as a more direct, more immediate means of influencing the hearts and minds of readers and listeners) when, lo and behold, Virgil appears with his hexameters and gigantic "social order."

I would add here that the elegists, almost without exception, were using the elegiac distich, a couplet combining dactylic hexameter and dactylic pentameter; also, that they, again almost without exception, came to poetry from the schools of rhetoric, where they had been trained for a juridical profession (as advocates: arguers in the modern sense). Nothing corresponds better to the rhetorical system of thought than the elegiac distich, which provided a means of expressing, at a minimum, two points of view, not to mention a whole palette of intonational coloring permitted by the contrasting meters.

All this, however, is in parentheses. Outside the parentheses lie the elegists' reproaches directed at Virgil on ethical rather than metrical grounds. Especially interesting in this regard is Ovid, in no way inferior to the author of the *Aeneid* in descriptive skills, and psychologically infinitely more subtle. In "Dido to Aeneas," one of his *Heroides*—a collection of made-up correspondence from love poetry's standard heroines to their either perished or unfaithful beloveds—the Carthaginian queen, rebuking Aeneas for abandoning her, does so in approximately the following fashion: "I could have understood if you had left me because you had resolved to return home, to your own kinfolk. But you are setting out for unknown lands, a new goal, a new, as yet unfounded city, in order, it seems, to break yet another heart." And so on. She even hints that Aeneas is leaving her pregnant and that one of the reasons for her suicide is the fear of disgrace. But this is not germane to the matter in hand. What matters here is that in Virgil's eyes Aeneas is a hero, directed by the gods. In Ovid's eyes, he is an unprincipled scoundrel, attributing his mode of conduct —his movement along a plane surface—to Divine Providence. (As for Providence, Dido has her own teleological explanations as well, but that is of small consequence, as is our all too eager assumption of Ovid's anti-civic posture.)

8

The Alexandrian tradition was a Grecian tradition: one of order (the cosmos), of proportion, of harmony, of the tautology of cause and effect (the Oedipus cycle)—a tradition of symmetry and the closed circle, *of return to the origin.* And it is Virgil's concept of linear movement, his linear model of existence, that the elegists find so exasperating in him. The Greeks should not be idealized overmuch, but one cannot deny them their cosmic principle, informing celestial bodies and kitchen utensils alike.

Virgil, it appears, was the first—in literature, at least—to apply the linear principle: his hero never returns; he always departs. Possibly, this was in the air; more likely, it was dictated by the expansion of the Empire, which had reached a scale in which human displacement had indeed become irreversible. This is precisely why the *Aeneid* is unfinished: it must not—indeed, could not—be completed. And the linear principle has nothing to do with the "feminine" character of Hellenism or with the "masculinity" of Roman culture—or with Virgil's own sexual tastes. The point is that the linear principle, detecting in itself a certain irresponsibility vis-à-vis the past—irresponsibility linked with the linear idea of existence—tends to balance this with a detailed projection of the future. The result is either a "retroactive prophecy," like Anchises' conversations in the *Aeneid,* or social utopianism or the idea of eternal life—i.e., Christianity. There is not much difference between these. In fact, it is their similarity, and not the "messianic" Fourth Eclogue, that practically allows one to consider Virgil the first Christian poet. Had I been writing *The Divine Comedy,* I would have placed this Roman in Paradise: for outstanding services to the linear principle, into its logical conclusion.

9

The delirium and horror of the East. The dusty catastrophe of Asia. Green only on the banner of the Prophet. Nothing grows here except mustaches. A black-eyed, overgrown-with-stubble-before-supper part of the world. Bonfire embers doused with urine. That smell! A mixture of foul tobacco and sweaty soap and the underthings wrapped around loins like another turban. Racism? But isn't it only a form of misanthropy? And that ubiquitous grit flying in your muzzle even in the city, poking the world out of your eyes—and yet one feels grateful even for that. Ubiquitous concrete, with the texture of turd and the color of an upturned grave. Ah, all that nearsighted scum—Corbusier, Mondrian, Gropius—who mutilated the world more effectively than any Luftwaffe! Snobbery? But it's only a form of despair. The local population in a state of total stupor whiling its time away in squalid snack bars, tilting its heads as in a *namaz* in reverse toward the television screen, where somebody is permanently beating somebody else up. Or else they're dealing out cards, whose jacks and nines are the sole accessible abstraction, the single means of concentration. Misanthropy? Despair? Yet what else could be expected from one who has outlived the apotheosis of the linear principle? From a man who has nowhere to go back to? From a great turdologist, sacrophage, and the possible author of *Sadomachia*?

10

A child of his age—that is, the fourth century A.D., or, better, P.V. (Post-Virgil)—Constantine, a man of action, if only because he was emperor, could regard himself as not only the embodiment but also the instrument of the linear principle of existence. Byzantium was for him not only symbolically but literally a cross, an intersection of trade routes, caravan roads, etc.—both from east to west and from north to south. This alone might have drawn his attention to the place, which had given to the world (in the seventh century B.C.) something that in all tongues means the same: money.

Money certainly interested Constantine exceedingly. If he did possess a measure of greatness, it was most likely financial. A pupil of Diocletian, having failed to learn his tutor's high art of delegating authority, he nonetheless succeeded in a by no means inferior art: to use the modern term, he stabilized the currency. The Roman solidus, introduced in his reign, played the role of our dollar for over seven centuries. In this sense, the transfer of the capital to Byzantium was a movement of the bank to the mint.

One should perhaps also bear in mind that the philanthropy of the Christian Church at this time was, if not an alternative to the state economy, then at least a recourse for a considerable part of the population, the have-nots. To a large extent, the popularity of Christianity was based not so much on the idea of the equality of souls before the Lord as on the tangible—for the have-nots—fruits of an organized system of mutual assistance. It was in its way a combination of food stamps and the Red Cross. Neither

Neoplatonism nor the cult of Isis organized anything of the kind. In this, frankly, lay their mistake.

One may muse at length on what went on in Constantine's heart and mind with regard to the Christian faith, but as an emperor he could not fail to appreciate the organizational and economic effectiveness of this particular church. Besides, the transference of the capital to the extreme rim of the Empire transforms that rim into the center, as it were, and implies an equally extensive space on the other side. On the map, this is equivalent to India: the object of all imperial dreams known to us, before and after the birth of Christ.

11

Dust! This weird substance, driving into your face! It merits attention; it should not be concealed behind the word "dust." Is it just agitated dirt, incapable of finding its own place but constituting the very essence of this part of the world? Or is it the earth striving to rise into the air, detaching itself from itself, like mind from body, like the body yielding itself to the heat? Rain betrays the nature of this substance when brown-black rivulets of it go snaking beneath your feet, beaten back to the cobbles and away down the undulating arteries of this primeval *kişlak*, and yet unable to amass themselves enough to form puddles, because of the countless splashing wheels, numerically superior to the faces of the inhabitants, that bear this substance off, to the sound of blaring horns, across the bridge into Asia, Anatolia, Ionia, to Trebizond and Smyrna.

As everywhere in the East, there are vast numbers of shoeshiners here of all ages, with their exquisite brassbound boxes housing their kit of boot creams in round, thinnest-of-copper containers with cupola lids. Like little mosques without the minarets. The ubiquity of the profession is explained by the dirt, by that dust which covers your dazzling, reflecting-the-entire-universe-just-five-minutes-ago loafer with a gray, impenetrable powder. Like all shoeshiners, these people are great philosophers. Or, better, all philosophers are but shiners of great shoes. For this reason, it isn't all that important whether you know Turkish.

12

Who these days really examines maps, studies contours, reckons distances? Nobody, except perhaps vacationers or drivers. Since the invention of the pushbutton, even the military don't do it anymore. Who writes letters listing the sights he has seen and analyzing the feelings he had while doing so? And who reads such letters? After us, nothing will remain that is worthy of the name of correspondence. Even young people, seemingly with plenty of time, make do with postcards. People of my age usually resort to those either in a moment of despair in some alien spot or just to kill time. Yet there are places examination of which on a map makes you feel for a brief moment akin to Providence.

13

There are places where history is inescapable, like a highway accident—places where geography provokes history.

Such is Istanbul, alias Constantinople, alias Byzantium. A traffic light gone haywire, with all three colors flaring up at once. Not red-amber-green but white-amber-brown. Also, of course, blue: for the water, for the Bosporus-Marmara-Dardanelles, which separates Europe from Asia—or does it? Ah, all these natural frontiers, these straits and Urals of ours! How little they have ever meant to armies or cultures, and even less to non-cultures—though for nomads they may actually have signified a bit more than for princes inspired by the linear principle and justified in advance by an entrancing vision of the future.

Did not Christianity triumph precisely because it provided an end that justified the means, because it temporarily —i.e., for the whole of one's life—absolved one from responsibility? Because the next step, any step at all, in any direction, was becoming logical? Wasn't it—in the spiritual sense, at least, Christianity—an anthropological echo of nomadic existence, its metastasis in the psychology of man the settler? Or, better still, hasn't it simply coincided with purely imperial needs? Pay alone could hardly be enough to stir a legionary (whose career's meaning lay precisely in a long-service bonus, demobilization, and getting a farm plot) from the spot. He should be inspired, too; otherwise, the legions turn into that wolf which only Tiberius could haul back by the ears.

14

A consequence can rarely look back at its cause with anything like approval. Still less can it suspect the cause of anything. The relations between effect and cause lack, as a rule, the rational, analytic element. As a rule, they are tautological and, at best, tinged with the incoherent enthusiasm the latter feels for the former.

It should not be forgotten, therefore, that the belief system called Christianity came from the East, and, for the same reason, it shouldn't be forgotten that one of the ideas that overpowered Constantine after the victory over Maxentius and the vision of the cross was the desire to come at least physically closer to the source of that victory and that vision: to the East. I have no clear notion of what was going on in Judea at that time, but it is obvious, at least, that if Constantine had set off by land to go there he would have encountered a good many obstacles. In any event, to found a capital overseas would have contradicted plain common sense. Also, one shouldn't rule out a dislike of Jews, quite possible on Constantine's part.

There is something amusing, and even a bit alarming, isn't there, in the idea that the East is actually the metaphysical center of mankind? Christianity had been only one of a considerable number of sects within the Empire—though, admittedly, the most active. By Constantine's reign, the Roman Empire, in no small measure because of its sheer size, had been a veritable country fair or bazaar of creeds. With the exception of the Copts and the cult of Isis, however, the source of all the belief systems on offer was in fact the East.

The West was offering nothing. Essentially, the West was a customer. Let us treat the West with tenderness, then, precisely for its lack of this sort of inventiveness, for which it has paid quite heavily, that pay including the reproaches of excessive rationality one hears to this day. Is this not the way a vender inflates the price of his wares? And where will he go once his coffers are overflowing?

15

If the Roman elegists reflected the outlook of their public in any way at all, one might suppose that by Constantine's reign—i.e., four centuries after the elegists—arguments like "The motherland is in danger" or "Pax Romana" had lost their spell and cogency. And if Eusebius' assertions are correct then Constantine turns out to be neither more nor less than the first Crusader. One should not lose sight of the fact that the Rome of Constantine was no longer the Rome of Augustus, or even that of the Antonines. It was, generally speaking, not ancient Rome anymore: it was Christian Rome. What Constantine brought to Byzantium no longer denoted classical culture: it was already the culture of a new age, brewed in the concept of monotheism, which now relegated polytheism—i.e., its own past, with all its spirit of law, and so forth—to the status of idolatry. This, to be sure, was already progress.

16

Here I should like to admit that my ideas concerning antiquity seem somewhat wild even to me. I understand polytheism in a simple, and therefore no doubt incorrect, fashion. For me, it is a system of spiritual existence in which every form of human activity, from fishing to contemplating the constellations, is sanctified by specific deities. An individual possessing appropriate will and imagination is thus able to discern in his activity its metaphysical, infinite lining. Alternatively, one or another god may, as the whim takes him, appear to a man at any time and possess him for a period. The only thing required of the latter, should he wish this to happen, is for him to "purify" himself, so as to enable the visit to take place. This process of purification (catharsis) varies a great deal and has an individual character (sacrifice, pilgrimage, a vow of some kind) or a public one (theater, sporting contests). The hearth is no different from the amphitheater, the stadium from the altar, the statue from the stewing pan.

A world view of this kind can exist, I suppose, only in settled conditions: when the god knows your address. It is not surprising that the culture we call Greek arose on islands. It is no surprise, either, that its fruits hypnotized for a millennium the entire Mediterranean, including Rome. And it is not surprising again that, as its Empire grew, Rome—which was not an island—fled from that culture. The flight began, in fact, with the Caesars and with the idea of absolute power, since in that intensely political sphere polytheism was synonymous with democracy. Absolute power—autocracy—was synonymous, alas, with monotheism. If one can imagine an unprejudiced man, then polytheism must seem far more attractive to him than monotheism, if only because of the instinct of self-preservation.

But there is no such person; even Diogenes, with his lamp, would fail to find him in broad daylight. Bearing in mind the culture we call ancient or classical, rather than the instinct of self-preservation, I can only say that the longer I live the more this idol worship appeals to me, and the more dangerous seems to me monotheism in its pure form. There's little point, I suppose, in laboring the matter, in calling the spade the spade, but the democratic state is in fact the historical triumph of idolatry over Christianity.

17

Naturally, Constantine could not know this. I assume he intuited that Rome was no more. The Christian in him combined with the ruler in a natural and, I am afraid, prophetic manner. In that very "In this sign, conquer" of his, one's ear discerns the ambition of power. And it was "conquer" indeed—more even than he imagined, since Christianity in Byzantium lasted ten centuries. But this victory was, I am sorry to say, a Pyrrhic one. The nature of this victory was what compelled the Western Church to detach itself from the Eastern. That is to say, the geographical Rome from the projected one, from Byzantium. The Church the bride of Christ from the Church the spouse of the state. And it is quite possible that in his drive eastward Constantine was in fact guided by the East's political climate—by its despotism without any experience of democracy, congenial to his own predicament. The geographical Rome, one way or another, still retained some memories of the role of the senate. Byzantium had no such memory.

18

Today, I am forty-five years old. I am sitting stripped to the waist in the Lykabettos Hotel in Athens, bathed in sweat, absorbing vast quantities of Coca-Cola. In this city, I don't know a soul. In the evening, when I went out looking for a place to have supper, I found myself in the thick of a highly excited throng shouting something unintelligible. As far as I can make out, elections are imminent. I was shuffling along some endless main street blocked by people and vehicles, with car horns wailing in my ears, not understanding a word, and it suddenly dawned on me that this, essentially, is the afterlife—that life had ended but movement was still continuing; that this is what eternity is all about.

Forty-five years ago, my mother gave me life. She died the year before last. Last year, my father died. I, their only child, am walking along the evening streets in Athens, streets they never saw and never will. The fruit of their love, their poverty, their slavery in which they lived and died—their son walks free. Since he doesn't bump into them in the crowd, he realizes that he is wrong, that this is not eternity.

19

What did Constantine see and not see as he looked at the map of Byzantium? He saw, to put it mildly, a *tabula rasa*. An imperial province settled by Greeks, Jews, Persians, and such—a population he was used to dealing with, typical subjects of the eastern part of his empire. The language was Greek, but for an educated Roman this was like French for a nineteenth-century Russian nobleman. Constantine saw a town jutting out into the Sea of Marmara, a town that would be easy to defend if a wall was just thrown around it. He saw the hills of this city, somewhat reminiscent of Rome's, and if he pondered erecting, say, a palace or a church, he knew that the view from the windows would be really smashing: on all Asia. And all Asia would gape at the crosses that would crown that church. One may also imagine him toying with the idea of controlling the access of those Romans he had dropped behind him. They would be compelled to trail across the whole of Attica to get here, or to sail around the Peloponnesus. "This one I'll let in, that one I won't." In these terms, no doubt, he thought of his version of the earthly Paradise. Ah, all these excise man's dreams! And he saw, too, Byzantium acclaiming him as her protector against the Sassanids and against our—your and my, ladies and comrades—ancestors from that side of the Danube. And he saw a Byzantium kissing the cross.

What he did not see was that he was dealing with the East. To wage wars against the East—or even to liberate the East—and actually to live there are very different things. For all its Greekness, Byzantium belonged to a world with totally different ideas about the value of human existence from those current in the West: in—however pagan it was—Rome. For Byzantium, Persia, for example, was far more real than Hellas, if only in a military sense. And the differences in degree of this reality could not fail to be reflected in the outlook of these future subjects of their Christian lord. Though in Athens Socrates could be judged in open court and could make whole speeches—three of them!—in his defense, in Isfahan, say, or Baghdad, such a Socrates would simply have been impaled on the spot, or flayed, and there the matter would have ended. There would have been no Platonic dialogues, no Neoplatonism, nothing: as there wasn't. There would have been only the monologue of the Koran: as there was. Byzantium was a bridge into Asia, but the traffic across it flowed in the opposite direction. Of course, Byzantium accepted Christianity, but there this faith was fated to become Orientalized. In this, too, to no small degree lies the root of the subsequent hostility of the Roman Church toward the Eastern. Certainly Christianity nominally lasted a thousand years in Byzantium, but what kind of Christianity it was and what sort of Christians these were is another matter.

Oh, I am afraid I am going to say that all the Byzantine scholastics, all Byzantium's scholarship and ecclesiastical ardor, its Caesaro-papism, its theological and administrative assertiveness, all those triumphs of Photius and his twenty anathemas—all these came from the place's inferiority complex, from the youngest patriarchy grappling with its own ethnic incoherence. Which, in the far end where I find myself standing, has spawned its dark-haired, leveling victory over that incredibly high-pitched spiritual quest which took place here, and reduced it to a matter of wistful yet reluctant mental archeology. And—oh, again—I am afraid I am going to add that it is for this reason, and not just because of mean, vengeful memory, that Rome, which doctored the history of our civilization anyway, deleted the Byzantine millennium from the record. Which is why I find myself standing here in the first place. And the dust stuffs my nostrils.

20

How dated everything is here! Not old, ancient, antique, or even old-fashioned, but dated. This is where old cars come to die, and instead become *dolmuşlar*, public taxis; a ride in one is cheap, bumpy, and nostalgic to the point of making you feel that you are moving in the wrong, unintended direction—in part, because the drivers rarely speak English. The United States naval base here presumably sold all these Dodges and Plymouths of the fifties to some local entrepreneur, and now they prowl the mud roads of Asia Minor, rattling, throttling, and wheezing in evident disbelief in this so taxing afterlife. So far from Dearborn; so far from the promised junkyard!

21

And also Constantine did not see—or, more precisely, did not foresee—that the impression produced on him by the geographical position of Byzantium was a natural one. That if Eastern potentates should also glance at a map they were bound to be similarly impressed. As, indeed, was the case—more than once—with consequences grievous enough for Christianity. Up until the seventh century, friction between East and West in Byzantium was of a standard, I'll-skin-you-alive military sort and was resolved by force of arms, usually in the West's favor. If this did not increase the popularity of the cross in the East, at all events it inspired respect for it. But by the seventh century what had risen over the entire East and started to dominate it was the crescent of Islam. Thereafter, the military encounters between East and West, whatever their outcome, resulted in a gradual but steady erosion of the cross and in a growing relativism of the Byzantine outlook as a consequence of too close and too frequent contact between the two sacred signs. (Who knows whether the eventual defeat of iconoclasm shouldn't be explained by a sense of the inadequacy of the cross as a symbol and by the necessity for some visual competition with the anti-figurative art of Islam? Whether it wasn't the nightmarish Arabic lace that was spurring John Damascene?)

Constantine did not foresee that the anti-individualism of Islam would find the soil of Byzantium so welcoming that by the ninth century Christianity would be more than ready to flee to the north. He, of course, would have said that it was not flight but, rather, the expansion of Christianity which he had—in theory, at least—dreamed of. And many would nod to this in agreement: yes, an expansion. Yet the Christianity that was received by Rus from Byzantium in the ninth century already had absolutely nothing in common with Rome. For, on its way to Rus, Christianity dropped behind it not only togas and statues but also Justinian's Civil Code. No doubt in order to facilitate the journey.

22

Having decided to leave Istanbul, I set about finding a steamship company serving the route from Istanbul to Athens or, better still, from Istanbul to Venice. I did the rounds of various offices, but, as always happens in the East, the nearer you get to the goal, the more obscure become the means of its attainment. In the end, I realized that I couldn't sail from either Istanbul or Smyrna for two more weeks, whether by passenger ship, freighter, or tanker. In one of the agencies, a corpulent Turkish lady, puffing a frightful cigarette like an ocean liner, advised me to try a company bearing the Australian—as I at first imagined—name

Boomerang. Boomerang turned out to be a grubby office smelling of stale tobacco, with two tables, one telephone, a map of—naturally—the World on the wall, and six stocky, pensive, dark-haired men, torpid from idleness. The only thing I managed to extract from the one sitting nearest the door was that Boomerang dealt with Soviet cruises in the Black Sea and the Mediterranean, but that that week there were no sailings. I wonder where that young Lubyanka lieutenant who dreamed up that name came from. Tula? Chelyabinsk?

23

Dreading a repetition, I will nonetheless state again that if Byzantine soil turned out to be so favorable for Islam it was most likely because of its ethnic texture—a mixture of races and nationalities that had neither local nor, moreover, overall memory of any kind of coherent tradition of individualism. Dreading generalizations, I will add that the East means, first of all, a tradition of obedience, of hierarchy, of profit, of trade, of adaptability: a tradition, that is, drastically alien to the principles of a moral absolute, whose role —I mean the intensity of the sentiment—is fulfilled here by the idea of kinship, of family. I foresee objections, and am even willing to accept them, in whole or in part. But no matter what extreme of idealization of the East we may entertain, we'll never be able to ascribe to it the least semblance of democracy.

And I am speaking here of Byzantium before the Turkish domination: of the Byzantium of Constantine, Justinian, Theodora—of Christian Byzantium, anyway. Still, Michael

Psellus, the eleventh-century Byzantine historian, describing in his *Chronographia* the reign of Basil II, tells us about Basil's prime minister, also Basil, who was the Emperor's illegitimate stepbrother and, because of that, was simply castrated in childhood to eliminate any possible claim to the throne. "A natural precaution," comments the historian, "since as a eunuch he would not attempt to usurp the throne from the legitimate heir." Psellus adds, "He was completely reconciled to his fate, and was sincerely dedicated to the ruling house. After all, it was his family." Let's make a note that this was written at the time of the reign of Basil II (A.D. 976–1025), and that Psellus mentions the incident very much in passing, as a routine affair—as, indeed, it was—at the Byzantine court. If this was A.D., what, then, of B.C.?

24

And how do we measure an age? And is an age susceptible to measurement? We should also note that what Psellus describes takes place before the arrival of the Turks. There are no Bajazet-Muhammad-Suleimans about, none of that. For the time being, we are still interpreting sacred texts, warring against heresy, gathering at universal councils, erecting cathedrals, composing tracts. That's with one hand. With the other we are castrating a bastard, so that when he grows up there will be no extra claim to the throne. That, indeed, is the Eastern attitude toward things—toward the human body in particular—and whatever era or millennium it is is irrelevant. So it is hardly surprising that the Roman Church turned its nose away from Byzantium.

But something needs to be said here about that church, too. It was natural for it to shun Byzantium, both for the reasons given above and because Byzantium—this new Rome—had abandoned Rome proper completely. With the exception of Justinian's short-lived efforts to restore imperial coherence, Rome was left solely to its own devices and to its fate, which meant to the Visigoths, the Vandals, and whoever else felt inclined to settle old and new scores with the former capital. One can understand Constantine: he was born, and spent his entire childhood, in the Eastern empire, at Diocletian's court. In this sense, Roman though he was, he wasn't a Westerner, except in his administrative designation or through his mother. (Believed to be born in Britain, she was the one who was interested in Christianity first—to the extent that she traveled later in her life to Jerusalem and discovered there the True Cross. In other words, in that family it was the mom who was a believer. And although there is ample reason to regard Constantine as a true mama's boy, let's avoid the temptation—let's leave it to the psychiatrists, as we don't hold a license.) One, let's repeat, can understand Constantine.

As for the attitude of the subsequent Byzantine emperors toward the genuine Rome, it is more complex and rather less explicable. Surely, they had their fill of problems right there in the East, both with their subjects and with their immediate neighbors. Yet the title of Roman emperor, it would seem, should have implied certain geographical obligations. The whole point, of course, was that the Roman emperors after Justinian came for the most part from provinces farther and farther East, from the Empire's traditional recruiting grounds: Syria, Armenia, and so on. Rome was for them, at best, an idea. Several of them, like the majority of their subjects, knew no word of Latin and had never set foot in the city that even by then was quite Eternal. And yet they all regarded themselves as Romans, called themselves so and signed themselves as such. (Something of the sort may be observed even today in the many and varied dominions of the British Empire, or let's recall—so that we don't twist our necks looking for examples—the Evenki, who are Soviet citizens.)

In other words, Rome was left to itself, as was the Roman Church. It would be too lengthy a haul to describe the relations between the Eastern and Western Churches. It may be noted, however, that in general the abandonment of Rome was to a certain degree to the Roman Church's advantage, but not entirely to its advantage.

25

I did not expect this note on my trip to Istanbul to expand so much, and I am beginning to feel irritated both with myself and with the material. On the other hand, I am aware that I won't have another chance to discuss all these matters, or if I do I will consciously miss it. From now on, I do promise myself and anyone who has got this far a greater compression—though what I would like to do right now is drop the whole business.

If one must resort to prose, a procedure utterly hateful to the author of these lines, for the very reason that it lacks any form of discipline aside from that generated in the process—if one must use prose, it would be better to concentrate on details, descriptions of places and character: i.e., on things the reader presumably may not have a chance to come across. For the bulk of the aforesaid, as well as everything that follows, is sooner or later bound to occur to anybody, since we are all, one way or another, dependent on history.

26

The advantage of the Roman Church's isolation lay above all in the natural benefits to be derived from any form of autonomy. There was almost nothing and nobody, with the exception of the Roman Church itself, to prevent its developing into a defined, fixed system. Which is what indeed took place. The combination of Roman law, reckoned with more seriously in Rome than in Byzantium, and the specific logic of the Roman Church's inner development evolved into the ethico-political system that lies at the heart of the so-called Western conception of the state and of individual being. Like almost all divorces, the one between Byzantium and Rome was by no means total; a great deal of property stayed shared. But in general one can insist that this Western conception drew around itself a kind of circle, which the East, in a purely conceptual sense, never crossed, and within whose ample bounds was elaborated what we term, or understand as, Western Christianity and the world view it implies.

The drawback of any system, even a perfect one, is that it is a system—i.e., that it must by definition exclude certain things, regard them as alien to it, and as far as possible relegate them to the nonexistent. The drawback of the system that was worked out in Rome—the drawback of

Western Christianity—was the unwitting reduction of its notions of evil. Any notions about anything are based on experience. For Western Christianity, the experience of evil was the experience reflected in the Roman law, with the addition of firsthand knowledge of the persecution of Christians by the emperors before Constantine. That's a lot, of course, but it is a long way from exhausting the reality of evil. By divorcing Byzantium, Western Christianity consigned the East to nonexistence, and thus reduced its own notion of human negative potential to a considerable, perhaps even a perilous, degree.

Today, if a young man climbs up a university tower with an automatic rifle and starts spraying passersby, a judge—this is assuming, of course, that the young man has been disarmed and brought to court—will class him as mentally disturbed and lock him up in a mental institution. Yet in essence the behavior of that young man cannot be distinguished from the castration of the royal by-blow as related by Psellus. Nor can it be told apart from the Iranian Imam's butchering tens of thousands of his subjects in order to confirm his version of the will of the Prophet. Or from Dzhugashvili's maxim, uttered in the course of the Great Terror, that "with us, no one is irreplaceable." The common denominator of all these deeds is the anti-individualistic notion that human life is essentially nothing—i.e., the absence of the idea that human life is sacred, if only because each life is unique.

I am far from asserting that the absence of this concept is a purely Eastern phenomenon; it is not, and that is what's indeed scary. But Western Christianity, along with developing all its ensuing ideas about the world, law, order, the norms of human behavior, and so forth, made the unforgivable error of neglecting, for the sake of its own growth and eventual triumph, the experience supplied by Byzantium. After all, that was a shortcut. Hence all these daily—by now—occurrences that surprise us so much; hence that inability on the part of states and individuals to react to them adequately, which shows itself in their dubbing the aforementioned phenomena mental illness, religious fanaticism, and whatnot.

27

In Topkapi, the former palace of the sultans, which has been turned into a museum, are now displayed in a special chamber the objects, most sacred to every Muslim's heart, associated with the life of the Prophet. Exquisitely encrusted caskets preserve the Prophet's tooth, locks from the Prophet's head. Visitors are asked to be quiet, to keep their voices down. All about hang swords of all kinds, daggers, the moldering pelt of some animal bearing the discernible letters of the Prophet's missive to some real historical character, along with other sacred texts. Contemplating these, one feels like thanking fate for one's ignorance of the language. For me, I thought, Russian will do. In the center of the room, inside a gold-rimmed cube of glass, lies a dark-brown object, which I was unable to identify without the assistance of the label. This, in bronze inlay, read, in Turkish and English, "Impress of the Prophet's footprint." Size 18 shoe minimum, I thought as I stared at the exhibit. And then I shuddered: Yeti!

28

Byzantium was renamed Constantinople during Constantine's lifetime, if I am not mistaken. So far as simplicity of vowels and consonants goes, the new name was presumably more popular among the Seljuk Turks than Byzantium had been. But Istanbul also sounds reasonably Turkish—to the Russian ear, at any rate. The fact is, however, that Istanbul is a Greek name, deriving, as any guidebook will tell you, from the Greek *stin poli*, which means simply town. *Stin*? *Poli*? A Russian ear? Who here hears whom? Here, where *bardak* (brothel in Russian) means glass, where *durak* (fool) means stop. *Bir bardak çay*—one glass of tea; *otobüs durağı*—a bus stop. Good thing "*otobüs*," at least, is only half Greek.

29

For anyone suffering from shortness of breath, there's nothing to do here—unless he hires a taxi for the day. For anyone coming to Istanbul from the West, the city is remarkably cheap. With the price converted into dollars, marks, or francs, several things here actually cost nothing at all. Those shoeshiners again, for example, or tea. It's an odd sensation to watch human activity that has no monetary expression: it cannot be evaluated. It feels like a sort of heaven, an Ur-world; it's probably this otherworldliness that constitutes that celebrated "fascination" of the East for the northern Scrooge.

Ah, this battle cry of the graying blonde: "Bargain!"

Doesn't it sound guttural, too, even to an English ear? And, ah, this "Isn't that cute, dearie?" in a minimum of three European languages, and the rustle of worthless banknotes under the scrutiny of dark, apprehensive eyes, otherwise doomed to the TV set's interference and the voluminous family. Ah, this middle age dispatched all over the world by its suburban mantelpieces! And yet, for all its vulgarity and crassness, this quest is markedly more innocent, and of better consequence for the locals, than that of some talkative smart-ass Parisienne, or of the spiritual lumpen fatigued by yoga, Buddhism, or Mao and now digging into the depths of Sufi, Sunni, Shia "secret" Islam, etc. No money changes hands here, of course. Between the actual and the mental bourgeois, one is better off with the former.

30

What happened next everybody knows: from out of who knows where appeared the Turks. There seems to be no clear answer to where they actually came from; obviously, a very long way off. What drew them to the shores of the Bosporus is also not terribly clear. Horses, I guess. The Turks—more precisely, *tuyrks*—were nomads, so we were taught at school. The Bosporus, of course, turned out to be an obstacle, and here, all of a sudden, the Turks made up their minds not to wander back the way they had come but, instead, to settle. All this sounds rather unconvincing, but let's leave it the way we got it. What they wanted from Byzantium-Constantinople-Istanbul is, at any rate, beyond argument: they wanted to be in Constantinople—i.e., more or less the same thing that Constantine himself wanted. Before the eleventh century, the Turks had no shared symbol. Then it appeared. As we know, it was the crescent.

In Constantinople, however, there were Christians; the city churches were crowned with the cross. The *tuyrks'*—gradually becoming the Turks'—love affair with Byzantium lasted approximately three centuries. Persistence brought its rewards, and in the fifteenth century the cross surrendered its cupolas to the crescent. The rest is well documented, and there is no need to expand upon it. What is worth noting, however, is the striking similarity between "the way it was" and "the way it became." For the meaning of history lies in the essence of structures, not in the character of décor.

31

The meaning of history! How, in what way, can the pen cope with this aggregation of races, tongues, creeds: with the vegetative—nay, zoological—pace of the crumbling-down of the tower of Babel, at the end of which one fine day, among the teeming ruins, an individual catches himself gazing in terror and alienation at his own hand or at his procreative organ, not in Wittgensteinian fashion but possessed, rather, by a sensation that these things don't belong to him at all, that they are but components of some do-it-yourself toy set: details, shards in a kaleidoscope through which it is not the cause that peers at the effect but blind chance squinting at the daylight. Unobscured by the blowing dust.

32

The difference between spiritual and secular power in Christian Byzantium wasn't terribly striking. Nominally, the Emperor was obliged to take the views of the Patriarch into account, and, indeed, this often happened. On the other hand, the Emperor frequently appointed the Patriarch and on occasion was, or had grounds for supposing himself to be, a superior Christian vis-à-vis the Patriarch. And, of course, we need not mention the concept of the Lord's anointed, which of itself could relieve the Emperor of the necessity of reckoning with anyone's metaphysics at all. This also happened, and, in conjunction with certain mechanical marvels, of which Theophilus was greatly enamored, played a decisive role in the adoption of Eastern Christianity by Rus in the ninth century. (Incidentally, these marvels—the throne ascending into the air, the metal nightingale, the roaring lions of the same material, and so on—were borrowed by the Byzantine ruler, with minor modifications, from his Persian neighbors.)

Something very similar also occurred with the Sublime Porte, which is to say the Ottoman Empire, alias Muslim Byzantium. Once again, we have an autocracy, heavily militarized and somewhat more despotic. The absolute head of the state was the Padishah, or Sultan. Alongside him, however, existed the Grand Mufti, a position combining—indeed, equating—spiritual and administrative authority. The whole state was run by a vastly complex hierarchical system, in which the religious—or, to put it more conveniently, staunchly ideological—element predominated.

In purely structural terms, the difference between the

Second Rome and the Ottoman Empire is accessible only in units of time. What is it, then? The spirit of place? Its evil genius? The spirit of bad spells—*porcha* in Russian? Where, incidentally, do we get this word *porcha* from? Might it not derive from *porte*? It doesn't matter. It's enough that both Christianity and *bardak* with *durak* came down to us from this place where people were becoming converted to Christianity in the fifth century with the same ease with which they went over to Islam in the fifteenth (even though after the fall of Constantinople the Turks did not persecute the Christians in any way). The reason for both conversions was the same: pragmatism. Not that this is connected with the place, however; this has to do with the species.

33

Oh, all these countless Osmans, Muhammads, Murads, Bajazets, Ibrahims, Selims, and Suleimans slaughtering their predecessors, rivals, brothers, parents, and offspring—in the case of Murad II, or III (who cares?), eighteen brothers in a row—with the regularity of a man shaving in front of a mirror. Oh, all these endless, uninterrupted wars: against the infidel, against their own but Shiite Muslims, to extend the Empire, to avenge a wrong, for no reason at all, and in self-defense. And, oh, those Janissaries, the élite of the army, dedicated at first to the Sultan, then gradually turning into a separate caste, with only its own interests at heart. How familiar it all, including the slaughter, is! All these turbans and beards, that uniform for heads possessed by one idea only—massacre—and because of that, and not at all because of Islam's ban on the depiction of anyone or anything living, totally indistinguishable from one another! And perhaps "massacre" precisely because all are so much alike that there is no way to detect a loss. "I massacre, therefore I exist."

And, broadly speaking, what, indeed, could be nearer to the heart of yesterday's nomad than the linear principle, than movement across a surface, in whatever direction? Didn't one of them, another Selim, say during the conquest of Egypt that he, as Lord of Constantinople, was heir to the Roman Empire and therefore had a right to all the lands that had ever belonged to it? Do these words sound like justification or do they sound like prophecy, or both? And does not the same note ring four hundred years later in the voice of Ustryalov and the Third Rome's latter-day Slavophiles, whose scarlet, Janissary's-cloaklike banner neatly combined a star and the crescent of Islam? And that hammer, isn't it a modified cross?

These non-stop, lasting-a-thousand-years wars, these endless tracts of scholastic interpretation of the art of archery—might not these be responsible for the development in this part of the world of a fusion between army and state, for the concept of politics as the continuation of war by other means, and for the phantasmagoric, though ballistically feasible, fantasies of Konstantin Tsiolkovsky, the grandfather of the missile?

A man with imagination, especially an impatient one, may be sorely tempted to answer these questions in the affirmative. But perhaps one shouldn't rush; perhaps one should pause and give them the chance to turn into "accursed" ones, even if that may take several centuries. Ah, these centuries, history's favorite unit, relieving the individual of the necessity of personally evaluating the past, and awarding him the honorable status of victim of history.

34

Unlike the Ice Age, civilizations, of whatever sort, move from south to north, as if to fill up the vacuum created by the retreating glacier. The tropical forest is gradually ousting the conifers and mixed woodland—if not through foliage, then by way of architecture. One sometimes gets the feeling that baroque, rococo, and even the Schinkel style are simply a species' unconscious yearning for its equatorial past. Fernlike pagodas also fit this idea.

As for latitudes, it's only nomads who move along them, and usually from east to west. The nomadic migration makes sense only within a distinct climatic zone. The Eskimos glide within the Arctic Circle, the Tartars and Mongols in the confines of the black-earth zone. The cupolas of yurts and igloos, the cones of tents and tepees.

I have seen the mosques of Central Asia, of Samarkand, Bukhara, Khiva: genuine pearls of Muslim architecture. As Lenin didn't say, I know nothing better than the Shah-i-Zinda, on whose floor I passed several nights, having nowhere else to lay my head. I was nineteen then, but I retain tender memories of these mosques not at all for that reason. They are masterpieces of scale and color; they bear witness to the lyricism of Islam. Their glaze, their emerald and cobalt get imprinted on your retina, not least because of the contrast with the yellow-brown hues of the surrounding landscape. This contrast, this memory of a coloristic (at least) alternative to the real world, may also have been the main pretext for their birth. One does, indeed, sense in them an idiosyncrasy, a self-absorption, a striving to accomplish, to perfect themselves. Like lamps in the darkness. Better: like corals in the desert.

35

Whereas Istanbul's mosques are Islam triumphant. There is no greater contradiction than a triumphant church—or greater tastelessness, either. St. Peter's in Rome suffers from this as well. But the Istanbul mosques! These enormous toads in frozen stone, squatting on the earth, unable to stir. Only the minarets, resembling more than anything (prophetically, alas) ground-to-air batteries—only they indicate the direction the soul was once about to take. Their shallow domes, reminiscent of saucepan lids or cast-iron kettles, are unable to conceive what they are to do with the sky: they preserve what they contain, rather than encourage one to set eyes on high. Ah, this tent complex! Of spreading on the ground. Of *namaz*.

Silhouetted against the sunset, on the hilltops, they create a powerful impression: the hand reaches for the camera, like that of a spy spotting a military installation. There is, indeed, something menacing about them—eerie, otherworldly, galactic, totally hermetic, shell-like. And all this in a dirty-gray color, like most of the buildings in Istanbul, and all set against the turquoise of the Bosporus.

And if one's pen does not poise to chide their nameless true-believing builders for being aesthetically dumb it is because the tone for these ground-hugging, toad- and crablike constructions was set by the Hagia Sophia, an edifice in the utmost degree Christian. Constantine, it is asserted, laid the foundations; it was erected, though, in the reign of Justinian. From the outside, there is no way to tell it from the mosques, or them from it, for fate has played a cruel (or was it cruel?) joke on the Hagia Sophia. Under Sultan Whatever-His-Redundant-Name-Was, our Hagia Sophia was turned into a mosque.

As transformations go, this one didn't require a great deal of effort: all the Muslims had to do was to erect four minarets on each side of the cathedral. Which they did; and it became impossible to tell the Hagia Sophia from a mosque. That is, the architectural standard of Byzantium was taken to its logical end, for it was exactly the squat grandeur of this Christian shrine that the builders of Bajazet, Suleiman, and the Blue Mosque, not to mention their lesser brethren, sought to emulate. And yet they shouldn't be reproached for that, partly because by the time of their arrival in Constantinople it was the Hagia Sophia that loomed largest over the entire landscape; mainly, however, because in itself the Hagia Sophia was not a Roman creation. It was an Eastern—or, more precisely, Sassanid—product. And, similarly, there is no point in blaming that Sultan What's-His-Name—was it Murad?—for converting a Christian church into a mosque. This transformation reflected something that one may, without giving the matter much thought, take for profound Eastern indifference to problems of a metaphysical nature. In reality, though, what stood behind this, and stands now, in much the same way as the Hagia Sophia, with her minarets and with her Christian-Muslim decor inside, is a sensation, instilled by both history and the Arabic lace, that everything in this life intertwines—that everything is, in a sense, but a pattern in a carpet. Trodden underfoot.

36

It is a monstrous idea, but not without a measure of truth. So let us try to grapple with it. At its source lies the Eastern principle of ornamentation, whose basic element is a verse from the Koran, a quotation from the Prophet: sewn, engraved, carved in stone or wood, and graphically coincident with this very process of sewing, engraving, carving if one bears in mind the Arabic form of writing. In other words, we are dealing with the decorative aspect of calligraphy, the decorative use of sentences, words, letters—with a purely visual attitude to them. Let us, disregarding here the unacceptability of this attitude toward words (and letters, too), point out only the inevitability of a literally spatial—because conveyed by distinctly spatial means—perception of any sacred locution. Let us note the dependence of this ornament on the length of the line and on the didactic character of the locution, often ornamental enough in itself. Let us remind ourselves: the unit of Eastern ornament is the sentence, the word, the letter.

The unit—the main element—of ornamentation that arose in the West was the notch, the tally, recording the passage of days. Such ornament, in other words, is temporal. Hence its rhythm, its tendency toward symmetry, its essentially abstract character, subordinating graphic expression to a rhythmic sense. Its extreme non-antididacticism. Its persistence—by means of rhythm, or repetition—in abstracting from its unit, from that which has already been once expressed. In short, its dynamism.

I would also remark that the unit of this ornamentation—the day, or the idea of the day—absorbs into itself any experience, including that of the sacred locution. From this follows the suggestion that the natty little bordure on a Grecian urn is superior to a pattern in a carpet. Which, in turn, leads us to consider who is more the nomad, the one who wanders in space or the one who migrates in time. However overwhelming (literally, too) the notion that all is interwoven, that everything is merely a pattern in a carpet, trodden underfoot, it frankly yields to the idea that everything gets left behind—the carpet and one's own foot upon it included.

37

Oh, I foresee objections! I see an art historian or an ethnologist preparing to wage battle, figures or potsherds in his hands, over everything stated above. I can see a bespectacled someone carrying in an Indian or a Chinese vase with a meander or an epistyle just like the natty little Greek bordure and exclaiming, "Well, what about this? Isn't India (or China) the East?" Worse still, that vase or dish may turn out to be from Egypt or elsewhere in Africa, from Patagonia, or from Central America. Then out will gush a downpour of proofs and incontrovertible facts that pre-Islamic culture was figurative, that, thus, in this area the West simply lags behind the East, that ornament is by definition non-functional, and that space is greater than time. Or that I, for no doubt political reasons, am substituting anthropology for history. Something like that, or worse.

What can I say to this? And need I say anything? I'm not sure, but all the same, I will point out that if I hadn't foreseen these objections I wouldn't have taken up my pen—that space to me is, indeed, both lesser and less dear than time. Not because it is lesser but because it is a thing, while time is an idea about a thing. In choosing between a thing and an idea, the latter is always to be preferred, say I.

And I also foresee that there will be no vase, no potsherds, no dish, or bespectacled someone. That no objections will be issued, that silence will reign supreme. Less as a sign of assent than as one of indifference. So let us nastify our conclusion somewhat and add that an awareness of time is a profoundly individualistic experience. That in the course of his life every person sooner or later finds himself in the position of Robinson Crusoe, carving notches and, having counted, say, seven of them, or ten, crossing them out. Such is the origin of ornament, regardless of preceding civilizations, or of that to which this given person belongs. And these notches are a profoundly solitary activity, isolating the individual and forcing him toward an understanding, if not of his uniqueness, then at least of the autonomy of his existence in the world. That is what the basis of our civilization is, and that is what Constantine walked away from to the East. To the carpet.

38

A normal hot, dusty, perspiring summer day in Istanbul. Moreover, it is Sunday. A human herd loitering about under the vaults of the Hagia Sophia. Up there aloft, inaccessible to the sight, are mosaics representing either kings or saints. Lower down, accessible to the eye, yet not to the mind, are circular metallic-looking shields with lacelike quotations from the Prophet in gold against dark-green enamel. Monumental cameos with coiling characters, evoking shadows of Jackson Pollock or Kandinsky. And now I become aware of a slipperiness: the cathedral is sweating. Not only the floor but the marble of the walls as well. The stone is sweating. I inquire, and am told it is because of the sharp jump in temperature. I decide it is because of my presence, and leave.

39

To get a good picture of one's native realm, one needs either to get outside its walls or to spread out a map. But, as has been remarked before, who looks at maps nowadays?

If civilizations—of whatever sort they are—do indeed spread like vegetation in the opposite direction to the glacier, from south to north, where could Rus, given her geographical position, possibly tuck herself away from Byzantium? Not just Kievan Rus, but Muscovite Rus as well, and then all the rest of it between the Donets and the Urals. And one should, frankly, thank Tamerlane and Genghis Khan for retarding the process somewhat, by somewhat freezing—or, rather, trampling—the flowers of Byzantium. It is not true that Rus played a shielding role for Europe, preserving the West from the Mongol yoke. It was Constantinople, then still the bulwark of Christendom, that played that role. (In 1402, incidentally, a situation developed under the walls of Constantinople which pretty nearly turned into a total catastrophe for Christianity and, indeed, for the whole of the then known world: Tamerlane encountered Bajazet. Luckily, they turned their arms against each other: interracial rivalry, it would seem, made itself known. Had they joined forces against the West—that is, in the direction both were moving—we would now be looking at the map with an almond-shaped, predominantly hazel eye.)

There was nowhere for Rus to go to get away from Byzantium—any more than for the West to get away from Rome. And, just as the West in age after age became overgrown with Roman colonnades and legality, Rus happened to become the natural geographical prey of Byzantium. If in the way of the former stood the Alps, the latter was impeded only by the Black Sea—a deep but, in the final analysis, flat thing. Rus received, or took, from Byzantium hands everything: not only the Christian liturgy but also the Christian-Turkish system of statecraft (gradually more and more Turkish, less vulnerable, more militarily ideological), not to mention a significant part of its vocabulary. The only thing Byzantium shed on its way north was its remarkable heresies—its Monophysites, its Arians, its Neoplatonists, and so on—which had constituted the very essence of its literary and spiritual life. But then its northward expansion took place at a time of growing domination by the crescent, and the purely physical power of the Sublime Porte hypnotized the North in far greater measure than the theological polemics of dying-out scholiasts.

Still, in the end Neoplatonism triumphed in art, didn't it? We know where our icons are from, we know the same about our onion-domed churches. We also know that there is nothing easier for a state than to adapt to its own ends

Plotinus' maxim that an artist's task must be the interpretation of ideas rather than the imitation of nature. As for ideas, in what way does the late M. Suslov, or whoever is now scraping the ideological dish, differ from the Grand Mufti? What distinguishes the General Secretary from the Padishah—or, indeed, the Emperor? And who appoints the Patriarch, the Grand Vizier, the Mufti, or the Caliph? What distinguishes the Politburo from the Great Divan? And isn't it only one step from a divan to an ottoman?

Isn't my native realm an Ottoman Empire now—in extent, in military might, in its threat to the Western world? Aren't we now by the walls of Vienna? And is not its threat the greater in that it proceeds from the Easternized, to the point of unrecognizability—no, recognizability!—Christianity? Is it not greater because it is more seductive? And what do we hear in that howl of the late Milyukov under the cupola of the short-lived Duma: "The Dardenelles will be ours!" An echo of Cato? The yearning of a Christian for his holy place? Or still the voice of Bajazet, Tamerlane, Selim, Muhammad? And if it comes to this, if we are quoting and interpreting, what do we discern in that falsetto of Konstantin Leontiev, the falsetto that pierced the air precisely in Istanbul, where he served in the Czarist embassy: "Russia must rule shamelessly"? What do we hear in this putrid, prophetic exclamation? The spirit of the age? The spirit of the nation? Or the spirit of the place?

40

God forbid we delve any further into the Turkish-Russian dictionary. Let us take the word "*çay*," meaning "tea" in both languages, whatever its origins. The tea in Turkey is wonderful—better than the coffee—and, like the shoeshining, costs almost nothing in any known currency. It's strong, the color of transparent brick, but it has no overstimulating effect, because it is served in a *bardak*, a fifty-gram glass, no more. Of all things I came across in this mixture of Astrakhan and Stalinabad, it's the best item. Tea—and the sight of Constantine's wall, which I would not have seen if I hadn't struck it lucky and got a rogue taxi driver who, instead of going straight to Topkapi, bowled around the whole city.

You can judge the seriousness of the builder's intent by the wall's height and width and the quality of the masonry. Constantine was thus extremely serious: the ruins where gypsies, goats, and young people trading in their tender parts may be found could withstand even today any army, given a positional war. On the other hand, if civilizations are granted vegetative—in other words, ideological—character, the erection of the wall was a sheer waste of time. Against anti-individualism, to say the least, against the spirit of relativism and obedience, neither wall nor sea offers a protection.

When I finally reached Topkapi and, having surveyed a good part of its contents—predominantly the caftans of the Sultans, which correspond linguistically and visually to the wardrobe of the Muscovite rulers—headed toward the object of my pilgrimage, the seraglio, I was greeted, sadly, at the door of this most important establishment in the world by a notice in Turkish and English: CLOSED FOR RESTORATION. "Oh, if only!" I exclaimed inwardly, trying to control my disappointment.

41

The quality of reality always leads to a search for a culprit—more accurately, for a scapegoat. Whose flocks graze in the mental fields of history. Yet, a son of a geographer, I believe that Urania is older than Clio; among Mnemosyne's daughters, I think, she is the oldest. So, born by the Baltic, in the place regarded as a window on Europe, I always felt something like a vested interest in this window on Asia with which we shared a meridian. On grounds perhaps less than sufficient, we regarded ourselves as Europeans. By the same token, I thought of the dwellers of Constantinople as Asians. Of these two assumptions, it's only the first that proved to be arguable. I should also admit, perhaps, that East and West vaguely corresponded in my mind to the past and the future.

Unless one is born by the water—and at the edge of an empire at that—one is seldom bothered by this sort of distinction. Of all people, somebody like me should be the first to regard Constantine as the carrier of the West to the East, as someone on a par with Peter the Great: the way he is regarded by the Church itself. If I had stayed longer at that meridian, I would. Yet I didn't, and I don't.

To me, Constantine's endeavor is but an episode in the general pull of the East westward, a pull motivated neither by the attraction of one part of the world for another nor by the desire of the past to absorb the future—although at times and in some places, of which Istanbul is one, it seems that way. This pull, I am afraid, is magnetic, evolutionary; it has to do, presumably, with the direction in which this planet rotates on its axis. It takes the forms of an attraction to a creed, of nomadic thrusts, wars, migration, and the flow of money. The Galata Bridge is not the first to be built over the Bosporus, as your guidebook would claim; the first one was built by Darius. A nomad always rides into a sunset.

Or else he swims. The strait is about a mile wide, and what could be done by a "blond cow" escaping the wrath of Jupiter's spouse could surely have been managed by the dusky son of the steppes. Or by lovesick Leander or by sick-of-love Lord Byron splashing across the Dardanelles. Bosporus! Well-worn strip of water, the only cloth that is properly Urania's, no matter how hard Clio tries to put it on. It stays wrinkled, and on gray days, especially, no one would say that it has been stained by history. Its surface current washes itself off Constantinople in the north—and that's why, perhaps, that sea is called Black. Then it somersaults to the bottom and, in the form of a deep current, escapes back into Marmara—the Marble Sea—presumably to get itself bleached. The net result is that dusted-bottle-green color: the color of time itself. The child of the Baltic can't fail to recognize it, can't rid himself of the old sensation that this rolling, non-stop, lapping substance itself is time, or that this is what time would look like had it been condensed or photographed. This is what, he thinks, separates Europe and Asia. And the patriot in him wishes the stretch were wider.

42

Time to wrap it up. As I said, there were no steamers from Istanbul or Smyrna. I boarded a plane and, after less than two hours' flight over the Aegean, through air that at one time was no less inhabited than the archipelago down below, landed in Athens.

Forty miles from Athens, in Sounion, at the top of a cliff plummeting to the sea, stands a temple to Poseidon, built almost simultaneously—a difference of some fifty years—with the Parthenon in Athens. It has stood here for two and a half thousand years.

It is ten times smaller than the Parthenon. How many times more beautiful it is would be hard to say; it is not clear what should be considered the unit of perfection. It has no roof.

There is not a soul about. Sounion is a fishing village with a couple of modern hotels now, and lies far below. There, on the crest of the dark cliff, the shrine looks from a distance as if it had been gently lowered from heaven rather than been erected on earth. Marble has more in common with the clouds than with the ground.

Fifteen white columns connected by a white marble base stand evenly spaced. Between them and the earth, between them and the sea, between them and the blue sky of Hellas, there is no one and nothing.

As practically everywhere else in Europe, here, too, Byron incised his name on the base of one of the columns. In his footsteps, the bus brings tourists; later it takes them away. The erosion that is clearly affecting the surface of the columns has nothing to do with weathering. It is a pox of stares, lenses, flashes.

Then twilight descends, and it gets darker. Fifteen columns, fifteen vertical white bodies evenly spaced at the top of the cliff, meet the night under the open skies.

If they counted days, there would have been a million such days. From a distance, in the evening haze, their white vertical bodies resemble an ornament, thanks to the equal intervals between them.

An idea of order? The principle of symmetry? Sense of rhythm? Idolatry?

43

Presumably, it would have been wiser to take letters of recommendation, to jot down two or three telephone numbers at least, before going to Istanbul. I didn't do that. Presumably, it would have made sense to make friends with someone, get into contact, look at the life of the place from the inside, instead of dismissing the local population as an alien crowd, instead of regarding people as so much psychological dust in one's eyes.

Who knows? Perhaps my attitude toward people has in its own right a whiff of the East about it, too. When it comes down to it, where am I from? Still, at a certain age a man gets tired of his own kind, weary of cluttering up his conscious and subconscious. One more, or ten more, tales of cruelty? Another ten, or hundred, examples of human baseness, stupidity, valor? Misanthropy, after all, should also have its limits.

It's enough, therefore, to glance in the dictionary and find that *katorga* (forced labor) is a Turkish word, too. And it's enough to discover on a Turkish map, somewhere in Anatolia, or Ionia, a town called Niğde (Russian for nowhere).

44

I'm not a historian, or a journalist, or an ethnographer. At best, I'm a traveler, a victim of geography. Not of history, be it noted, but of geography. This is what still links me with the country where it was my fate to be born, with our famed Third Rome. So I'm not particularly interested in the politics of present-day Turkey, or in what happened to Atatürk, whose portrait adorns the greasy walls of every last coffeehouse as well as the Turkish lira, unconvertible and representing an unreal form of payment for real labor.

I came to Istanbul to look at the past, not at the future—since the latter doesn't exist here: whatever there was of it has gone north as well. Here there is only an unenviable, third-rate present of the people, industrious yet plundered by the intensity of the local history. Nothing will happen here anymore, apart perhaps from street disorders or an earthquake. Or perhaps they'll discover oil: there's a fearful stench of sulfureted hydrogen in the Golden Horn, crossing whose oily surface you get a splendid panorama of the city. Still, it's unlikely. The stench comes from oil seeping out of rusty, leaking, nearly hole-ridden tankers passing through the Strait. One might squeeze out a living from refining that alone.

A project like that, though, would probably strike a local as altogether too enterprising. The locals are rather conservative by nature, even if they are businessmen or dealers; as for the working class, it is locked, reluctantly but firmly, in a traditional, conservative mentality by the beggarly rates of pay. In his own element, a native finds himself only within the infinitely intertwining—in patterns akin to the carpet's or the mosque walls'—web-like, vaulted galleries of the local bazaar, which is the heart, mind, and soul of Istanbul. This is a city within a city; it, too, is built for the ages. It cannot be transported west, north, or even south. GUM, Bon Marché, Macy's, Harrods taken together and raised to the cube are but child's babble compared with these catacombs. In an odd way, thanks to the garlands of yellow hundred-watt bulbs and the endless wash of bronze, beads, bracelets, silver, and gold under glass, not to mention the very carpets and the icons, samovars, crucifixes, and so on, this bazaar in Istanbul produces the impression of—of all things—an Orthodox church, though convoluted and branching like a quotation from the Prophet. A laid-out version of the Hagia Sophia.

45

Civilizations move along meridians; nomads (including our modern warriors, since war is an echo of the nomadic instinct) along latitudes. This seems to be yet another version of the cross that Constantine saw. Both movements possess a natural (vegetable or animal) logic, considering which one easily finds oneself in the position of not being able to reproach anyone for anything. In the state known as melancholy—or, more exactly, fatalism. It can be blamed on age, or on the influence of the East, or, with an effort of the imagination, on Christian humility.

The advantages of this condition are obvious, since they are selfish ones. For it is, like all forms of humility, always achieved at the expense of the mute helplessness of the victims of history, past, present, and future; it is an echo of the helplessness of millions. And if you are not at an age when you can draw a sword from a scabbard or clamber up to a platform to roar to a sea of heads about your detestation of the past, the present, and what is to come; if there is no such platform or the sea has dried up, there still remain the face and the lips, which can accommodate your slight—provoked by the vista opening to both your inner and your naked eye—smile of contempt.

46

With it, with that smile on the lips, one may board the ferry and set off for a cup of tea in Asia. Twenty minutes later, one can disembark in Çengelköy, find a café on the very shore of the Bosporus, sit down and order tea, and, inhaling the smell of rotting seaweed, observe without changing the aforesaid facial expression the aircraft carriers of the Third Rome sailing slowly through the gates of the Second on their way to the First.

(Translated by Alan Myers and the author)
1985

In a Room and a Half

To L.K.

The room and a half (if such a space unit makes any sense in English) in which the three of us lived had a parquet floor, and my mother strongly objected to the men in her family, me in particular, walking around with our socks on. She insisted on us wearing shoes or slippers at all times. Admonishing me about this matter, she would evoke an old Russian superstition; it is an ill omen, she would say, it may bode a death in the family.

Of course, it might be that she simply regarded this habit as uncivilized, as plain bad manners. Men's feet smell, and that was the pre-deodorant era. Yet I thought that, indeed, one could easily slip and fall on a polished parquet, especially if one wore woolen socks. And that if one were old and frail, the consequences could be disastrous. The parquet's affinity with wood, earth, etc., thus extended in my mind to any ground under the feet of our close and distant relatives who lived in the same town. No matter what the distance, it was the same ground. Even living on the other side of the river, where I would subsequently rent an apartment or a room of my own, didn't constitute an excuse, for there were too many rivers and canals in that town. And although some of them were deep enough for the passage of seagoing ships, death, I thought, would find them shallow, or else, in its standard underground fashion, it could creep across under their bottoms.

Now my mother and my father are dead. I stand on the Atlantic seaboard: there is a great deal of water separating me from two surviving aunts and my cousins: a real chasm, big enough to confuse even death. Now I can walk around in my socks to my heart's content, for I have no relatives on this continent. The only death in the family I can now incur is presumably my own, although that would mean mixing up transmitter with receiver. The odds of that merger are small, and that's what distinguishes electronics from superstition. Still, if I don't tread these broad Canadian-maple floorboards in my socks, it's neither because of this certitude nor out of an instinct for self-preservation, but because my mother wouldn't approve of it. I guess I want to keep things the way they were in our family, now that I am what's left of it.

2

There were three of us in that room and a half of ours: my father, my mother, and I. A family, a typical Russian family of the time. The time was after the war, and very few people could afford more than one child. Some of them couldn't even afford to have the father alive or present: great terror and war took their toll in big cities, in my hometown especially. So we should have considered ourselves lucky, especially since we were Jews. All three of us survived the war (and I say "all three" because I, too, was born before it, in 1940); my parents, however, survived the thirties also.

I guess they considered themselves lucky, although they never said as much. In general, they were not terribly self-aware, except when they grew old and malaises began to beset them. Even then, they wouldn't talk about themselves and death in that way that terrifies a listener or prods him to compassion. They would simply grumble, or complain addresslessly about their aches, or discuss at length some medicine or other. The closest my mother would ever come to uttering something of the sort would be while pointing at an extremely delicate set of china, saying: This will become yours when you get married or when . . . and she would interrupt herself. And, once, I remember her on the phone talking to some distant friend of hers who I was told was ill: I remember my mother emerging from the telephone booth on the street, where I was waiting for her, with a somewhat unfamiliar look in her so familiar eyes, behind her tortoiseshell-rimmed glasses. I leaned toward her (I was already a good deal taller) and asked what the woman had said, and my mother replied, staring aimlessly ahead: "She knows that she is dying and was crying into the phone."

They took everything as a matter of course: the system, their powerlessness, their poverty, their wayward son. They simply tried to make the best of everything: to keep food on the table—and whatever that food was, to turn it into morsels; to make ends meet—and although we always lived from payday to payday, to stash away a few rubles for the kid's movies, museum trips, books, dainties. What dishes, utensils, clothes, linen we had were always clean, polished, ironed, patched, starched. The tablecloth was always spotless and crisp, the lampshade above it dusted, the parquet shining and swept.

The amazing thing is that they were never bored. Tired, yes, but not bored. Most of their time at home, they were on their feet: cooking, washing, circulating between the communal kitchen of our apartment and our room and a half, fiddling with this or that item of the household. When they were seated, it was of course for meals, but mainly I remember my mother in a chair, bent over her manual-cum-pedal Singer sewing machine, fixing our clothes, turning old shirt collars inside out, repairing or readjusting old coats. As for my father, his only time in a chair was when he was reading the paper, or else at his desk. Sometimes in the evening they would watch a movie or a concert on our 1952 TV set. Then they would also be seated . . . This way, seated in a chair in the empty room and a half, a neighbor found my father dead a year ago.

3

He had outlived his wife by thirteen months. Out of seventy-eight years of her life and eighty of his, I've spent only thirty-two years with them. I know almost nothing about how they met, about their courtship; I don't even know in what year they were married. Nor do I know the way they lived the last eleven or twelve years of their lives, the years without me. Since I am never to learn it, I'd better assume that the routine was the usual, that perhaps they were even better off without me: in terms both of money and of not having to worry about my being rearrested.

Except that I couldn't help them in their old age; except that I wasn't there when they were dying. I am saying this not so much out of a sense of guilt as because of the rather egotistical desire of a child to follow his parents through all the stages of their life; for every child, one way or another, repeats his parents' progress. I could argue that, after all, one wants to learn from one's parents about one's own future, one's own aging; one wants to learn from them also the ultimate lesson: how to die. Even if one doesn't want any of these, one knows that one learns from them, however unwittingly. "Shall I look this way when I am old, too? Is this cardiac—or any other—problem hereditary?"

I don't and I never will know how they felt during those last years of their life. How many times they were scared, how many times they felt prepared to die, how they felt then, reprieved, how they would resume hoping that the three of us would get together again. "Son," my mother would say over the telephone, "the only thing I want from this life is to see you again. That's the only thing that keeps me going." And a minute later: "What were you doing five minutes ago, before you called?" "Actually, I was doing the dishes." "Oh, that's very good. It's a very good thing to do: the dishes. Sometimes it's awfully therapeutic."

4

Our room and a half was part of a huge enfilade, one-third of a block in length, on the northern side of a six-story building that faced three streets and a square at the same time. The building was one of those tremendous cakes in so-called Moorish style that in Northern Europe marked the turn of the century. Erected in 1903, the year of my father's birth, it was the architectural sensation of the St. Petersburg of that period, and Akhmatova once told me that her parents took her in a carriage to see this wonder. On its western side, facing one of the most famous avenues of Russian literature, Liteiny Prospect, Alexander Blok had an apartment at one time. As for our enfilade, it was occupied by the couple that dominated the pre-revolutionary Russian literary scene as well as the intellectual climate of Russian emigration in Paris later on, in the twenties and the thirties: by Dmitry Merezhkovsky and Zinaida Gippius. And it was from our room and a half's balcony that the larva-like Zinka shouted abuse to the revolutionary sailors.

After the Revolution, in accordance with the policy of "densening up" the bourgeoisie, the enfilade was cut up into pieces, with one family per room. Walls were erected between the rooms—at first of plywood. Subsequently, over the years, boards, brick, and stucco would promote these partitions to the status of architectural norm. If there is an infinite aspect to space, it is not its expansion but its reduction. If only because the reduction of space, oddly enough, is always more coherent. It's better structured and has more names: a cell, a closet, a grave. Expanses have only a broad gesture.

In the U.S.S.R., the living quarters' minimum per person is 9 square meters. We should have considered ourselves lucky, because due to the oddity of our portion of the enfilade, the three of us wound up with a total of 40 meters. That excess had to do also with the fact that we had obtained this place as the result of my parents' giving up the two separate rooms in different parts of town in which they had lived before they got married. This concept of exchange —or, better still, swap (because of the finality of such exchange)—is something there is no way to convey to an outsider, to a foreigner. Property laws are arcane everywhere, but some of them are more arcane than others, especially when your landlord is the state. Money has nothing to do with it, for instance, since in a totalitarian state income brackets are of no great variety—in other words, every person is as poor as the next. You don't buy your living quarters: at best, you are entitled to the square equivalent of what you had before. If there are two of you, and you decide to live together, you are therefore entitled to an equivalent of the square sum total of your previous residencies. And it is the clerks in the borough property office who decide what you are going to get. Bribery is of no use, since the hierarchy of those clerks is, in its own turn, terribly arcane and their initial impulse is to give you less. The swaps take years, and your only ally is fatigue; i.e., you may hope to wear them down by refusing to move into something quantitatively inferior to what you previously had. Apart from pure arithmetic, what goes into their decision is a vast variety of assumptions never articulated in law, about your age, nationality, race, occupation, the age and sex of your child, social and territorial origins, not to mention the personal impression you make, etc. Only the clerks know what is available, only they judge the equivalence and can give or take a few square meters here and there. And what a difference those few square meters make! They can accommodate a bookshelf, or, better yet, a desk.

5

Apart from an excess of thirteen square meters, we were terribly lucky because the communal apartment we had moved into was very small. That is, the part of the enfilade that constituted it contained six rooms partitioned in such a way that they gave home to only four families. Including ourselves, only eleven people lived there. As communal apartments go, the dwellers can easily amount to a hundred. The average, though, is somewhere between twenty-five and fifty. Ours was almost tiny.

Of course, we all shared one toilet, one bathroom, and one kitchen. But the kitchen was fairly spacious, the toilet very decent and cozy. As for the bathroom, Russian hygienic habits are such that eleven people would seldom overlap when either taking a bath or doing their basic laundry. The latter hung in the two corridors that connected the rooms to the kitchen, and one knew the underwear of one's neighbors by heart.

The neighbors were good neighbors, both as individuals and because all of them were working and thus absent for the better part of the day. Save one, they didn't inform to the police; that was a good percentage for a communal apartment. But even she, a squat, waistless woman, a surgeon in the nearby polyclinic, would occasionally give you medical advice, take your place in the queue for some scarce food item, keep an eye on your boiling soup. How does that line in Frost's "The Star-Splitter" go? "For to be social is to be forgiving"?

For all the despicable aspects of this mode of existence, a communal apartment has perhaps its redeeming side as well. It bares life to its basics: it strips off any illusions about human nature. By the volume of the fart, you can tell who occupies the toilet, you know what he/she had for supper as well as for breakfast. You know the sounds they make in bed and when the women have their periods. It's often you in whom your neighbor confides his or her grief, and it is he or she who calls for an ambulance should you have an angina attack or something worse. It is he or she who one day may find you dead in a chair, if you live alone, or vice versa.

What barbs or medical and culinary advice, what tips about goods suddenly available in this or that store are traded in the communal kitchen in the evening when the wives cook their meals! This is where one learns life's essentials: by the rim of one's ear, with the corner of one's eye. What silent dramas unfurl there when somebody is all of a sudden not on speaking terms with someone else! What a school of mimics it is! What depths of emotion can be conveyed by a stiff, resentful vertebra or by a frozen profile! What smells, aromas, and odors float in the air around a hundred-watt yellow tear hanging on a plait-like tangled electric cord. There is something tribal about this dimly lit cave, something primordial—evolutionary, if you will; and the pots and pans hang over the gas stoves like would-be tom-toms.

6

I recall these not out of nostalgia but because this was where my mother spent one-fourth of her life. Family people seldom eat out; in Russia almost never. I don't recall either her or my father across the table in a restaurant, or for that matter in a cafeteria. She was the best cook I ever knew, with the exception, perhaps, of Chester Kallman; but then he had more ingredients. I recall her most frequently in the kitchen, in her apron, face reddened and eyeglasses a bit steamy, shooing me away from the stove as I try to fish this or that item from the burner. Her upper lip glistens with sweat; her short, cropped, dyed-red but otherwise gray hair curls disorderedly. "Go away!" she exclaims. "What impatience!" I won't hear that anymore.

Nor shall I see the door opening (how did she do it with both her hands holding a casserole or two big pans? By lowering them onto the latch and applying their weight to it?) and her sailing in with our dinner/supper/tea/dessert. My father would be reading the paper, I would not move from my book unless told to do so, and she knew that any help she could expect from us would be delayed and clumsy anyway. The men in her family *knew* more about courtesy than they themselves could master. Even when they were hungry. "Are you reading your Dos Passos again?" she would remark, setting the table. "Who is going to read Turgenev?" "What do you expect from him?" my father would echo, folding the paper. "Loafer is the word."

7

How is it possible that I see myself in this scene? And yet, I do; as clearly as I see them. Again, it is not nostalgia for my youth, for the old country. No, it is more likely that, now that they are dead, I see their life as it was then; and then their life included me. This is what they would remember about me as well, unless they now have the gift of omniscience and observe me at present, sitting in the kitchen of the apartment that I rent from my school, writing this in a language they didn't understand, although now they should be *pan-glot*. This is their only chance to see me and America. This is the only way for me to see them and our room.

8

Our ceiling was some fourteen, if not more, feet high, adorned with the same Moorish-style plaster ornamentation, which, combined with cracks and stains from occasionally bursting pipes upstairs, turned it into a highly detailed map of some nonexisting superpower or archipelago. There were three very tall arched windows through which we could see nothing except a high school across the street, were it not for the central window, which also served as a door to the balcony. From this balcony we could view the entire length of the street, whose typically Petersburgian, impeccable perspective ended up with the silhouette of the cupola of St. Panteleimon's Church, or—if one looked to the right—the big square, in the center of which sat the Cathedral of the Savior of Her Imperial Majesty's Transfiguration Battalion.

By the time we moved into this Moorish wonder, the street already bore the name of Pestel, the executed leader of the Decembrists. Originally, though, it was named after that church that loomed at its far end: Panteleimonovskaya. There, at the far end, the street would fling around the church and run to the Fontanka River, cross over the Police Bridge, and take you into the Summer Garden. Pushkin once lived on that part of the street, and somewhere in a letter to his wife he says that "every morning, in nightgown and slippers I go across the bridge for a stroll in the Summer Garden. The entire Summer Garden is my orchard . . ."

His was Number 11, I think; ours was Number 27, and that was at the end of the street, which flowed into the cathedral square. Yet, since our building was at the street's intersection with the fabled Liteiny Prospect, our postal address read: Liteiny Pr. #24, Apt. 28. This is where we received our mail; this is what I wrote on the envelopes addressed to my parents. I am mentioning it here not because it has any specific significance but because my pen, presumably, will never write this address again.

9

Oddly, the furniture we had matched the exterior and the interior of the building. It was as busy with curves, and as monumental as the stucco molding on the façade or the panels and pilasters protruding from the walls inside, skeined with plaster garlands of some geometrical fruits. Both the outside and the inner decor were of a light-brown, cocoa-cum-milk shade. Our two huge, cathedral-like chests of drawers, however, were of black varnished oak; yet they belonged to the same period, the turn of the century, as did the building itself. This was what perhaps favorably disposed the neighbors toward us from the outset, albeit unwittingly. And this was why, perhaps, after barely a year in that building, we felt we had lived there forever. The sensation that the chests had found their home, or the other way around, somehow made us realize that we, too, were settled, that we were not to move again.

Those ten-foot-high, two-story chests (you'd have to take off the corniced top from the elephant-footed bottom when moving) housed nearly everything our family had amassed in the course of its existence. The role played elsewhere by the attic or the basement, in our case was performed by the chests. My father's various cameras, developing and printing paraphernalia, prints themselves, dishes, china, linen, tablecloths, shoe boxes with his shoes now too small for him yet still too large for me, tools, batteries, his old Navy tunics, binoculars, family albums, yellowed illustrated supplements, my mother's hats and scarves, some silver Solingen razor blades, defunct flashlights, his military decorations, her motley kimonos, their mutual correspondence, lorgnettes, fans, other memorabilia—all that was stored in the cavernous depths of these chests, yielding, when you'd open one of their doors, a bouquet of mothballs, old leather, and dust. On the top of the lower part, as if on a mantelpiece, sat two crystal carafes containing liqueurs, and a glazed porcelain figurine of two tipsy Chinese fishermen dragging their catch. My mother would wipe the dust off them twice a week.

With hindsight, the content of these chests could be compared to our joined, collective subconscious; at the time, this thought wouldn't have crossed my mind. To say the least, all these things were part of my parents' consciousness, tokens of their memory: of places and of times by and large preceding me; of their common and separate past, of their own youth and childhood, of a different era, almost of a different century. With the benefit of the same hindsight, I would add: of their freedom, for they were born and grew up free, before what the witless scum call the Revolution, but what for them, as for generations of others, meant slavery.

10

I write this in English because I want to grant them a margin of freedom: the margin whose width depends on the number of those who may be willing to read this. I want Maria Volpert and Alexander Brodsky to acquire reality under "a foreign code of conscience," I want English verbs of motion to describe their movements. This won't resurrect them, but English grammar may at least prove to be a better escape route from the chimneys of the state crematorium than the Russian. To write about them in Russian would be only to further their captivity, their reduction to insignificance, resulting in mechanical annihilation. I know that one shouldn't equate the state with language but it was in Russian that two old people, shuffling through numerous state chancelleries and ministries in the hope of obtaining a permit to go abroad for a visit to see their only son before they died, were told repeatedly, for twelve years in a row, that the state considers such a visit "unpurposeful." To say the least, the repetition of this utterance proves some familiarity of the state with the Russian language. Besides, even if I had written all this in Russian, these words wouldn't see the light of day under the Russian sky. Who would read them then? A handful of émigrés whose parents either have died or will die under similar circumstances? They know this story only too well. They know what it feels like not to be allowed to see their mothers or fathers on their deathbed; the silence that follows their request for an emergency visa to attend a relative's funeral. And then it's too late, and a man or a woman puts the receiver down and walks out of the door into the foreign afternoon feeling something neither language has words for, and for which no howl will suffice, either . . . What could I possibly tell them? In what way could I console them? No country has mastered the art of destroying its subjects' souls as well as Russia, and no man with a pen in his hand is up to mending them; no, this is a job for the Almighty only, this is what He has all that time of His for. May English then house my dead. In Russian I am prepared to read, write verses or letters. For Maria Volpert and Alexander Brodsky, though, English offers a better semblance of afterlife, maybe the only one there is, save my very self. And as far as the latter is concerned, writing this in this language is like doing those dishes: it's therapeutic.

11

My father was a journalist—a newspaper photographer, to be more precise—although he wrote articles as well. As he wrote mostly for small dailies that are never read anyway, most of his articles would start with "Heavy, storm-laden clouds hang over the Baltic . . . ," confident that the weather in our parts would make this opening newsworthy or pertinent. He held two degrees: in geography, from Leningrad University, and in journalism, from the School of Red Journalism. He enrolled in the latter when it was made clear to him that his chances to travel, especially abroad, weren't worth reckoning: as a Jew, a son of a print-shop owner, and a non-member of the Party.

Journalism (to a certain extent) and the war (substantially) restored the balance. He covered one-sixth of the earth's surface (the standard quantitative definition of the territory of the U.S.S.R.) and a great deal of water. Although he was assigned to the Navy, the war started for him in 1940, in Finland, and ended in 1948, in China, where he was sent with a bunch of military advisers to help Mao in his endeavors and from where those tipsy porcelain fishermen and the china sets my mother wanted me to have when I got married came from. In between, he was escorting the Allies' PQs in the Barents Sea, defending and losing Sevastopol on the Black Sea, joining—after his torpedo boat was sunk—the then Marines. During the siege of Leningrad, he was dispatched to the Leningrad front, took the best pictures I've seen in print of the city under siege, and participated in the siege's dislodging. (This part of the war, I believe, mattered to him most, since it was too close to his family, to his home. Still, for all his proximity, he lost his apartment and his only sister: to bombs and to hunger.) Afterward, he was sent back to the Black Sea, landed at the ill-famed Malaya Zemlya, and held it; then, as the front advanced westward, went with the first detachment of torpedo boats to Rumania, landed there, and, for a short time, was even the military governor of Constanza. "We liberated Rumania," he'd boast sometimes, and proceed to recall his encounters with King Michael. That was the only king he had ever seen; Mao, Chiang Kai-shek, not to mention Stalin, he regarded as upstarts.

12

Whatever monkey business he was up to while in China, our small pantry, our chests, and our walls profited from it considerably. What art objects the last displayed were of Chinese origin: the cork-cum-watercolor paintings, the samurai swords, little silk screens. The tipsy fishermen were the last of the lively population of porcelain figurines, dolls, and hat-wearing penguins that would only gradually disappear, victims of careless gestures or the need for birthday presents for various relatives. The swords, too, had to be surrendered to the state collections as potential weapons a regular citizen wasn't supposed to have. A reasonable caution, come to think of it, in light of the subsequent police invasions I brought upon our room and a half. As for the china sets, astonishingly exquisite even to my untrained eye—my mother wouldn't hear about a single beautiful saucer on *our* table. "These are not for slobs," she would explain patiently to us. "And you are slobs. You are very sloppy slobs." Besides, the dishes we were using were elegant enough, as well as sturdy.

I remember one dark cold November evening in 1948, in the small, sixteen-square-meter room where my mother and I lived during and right after the war. That evening Father was returning from China. I remember the doorbell ringing and my mother and I rushing to the dimly lit landing, suddenly dark with Navy uniforms: my father, his friend and colleague, Captain F.M., and a bunch of servicemen entering the corridor carrying three huge crates, with their China catch, splashed on all four sides with gigantic, octopuslike Chinese characters. And later on, Captain F.M.

and I sitting at the table, while my father unpacks the crates, my mother in her yellow-pink, crepe de chine dress, on high heels, clasping her hands and exclaiming "*Ach! oh wunderbar!*"—in German, the language of her Latvian childhood and present occupation—interpreter in a camp for German POWs—and Captain F.M., a tall wiry man in his dark-blue, unbuttoned tunic, pouring himself a glass from a carafe and winking at me as to a grownup. The belts with their anchor buckles and holstered Parabellums are on the windowsill, my mother gasps at the sight of a kimono. The war is over, it's peace, I am too small to wink back.

13

Now I am exactly the age my father was that November evening: I am forty-five, and again I see the scene with an unnatural, high-resolution-lens clarity, although all its participants save me are dead. I see it so well that I can wink back at Captain F.M. . . . Was it meant to be that way? Is there, in these winks over the space of nearly forty years, some meaning, some significance that eludes me? Is this what life is all about? If not, why this clarity, what is it for? The only answer that occurs to me is: So that this moment exists, so that it is not forgotten when the actors are gone, myself included. Maybe this way you understand indeed how precious it was: the arrival of peace. Into one family. And by the same token, in order to make it clear what moments *are*. Be they just a return of someone's father, an opening of a crate. Hence this mesmerizing clarity. Or maybe it's because you are a son of a photographer and your memory simply develops a film. Shot with your own two eyes, almost forty years ago. That's why you couldn't wink back then.

14

My father wore the Navy uniform for approximately two more years. And this is when my childhood started in earnest. He was the officer in charge of the photography department of the Navy Museum, located in the most beautiful building in the entire city. Which is to say, in the entire empire. The building was that of the former Stock Exchange: a far more Greek affair than any Parthenon, and far better situated as well, at the tip of Basil Island, which juts into the Neva River where it is at its widest.

On late afternoons, school over, I'd wade through the town to the river, cross the Palace Bridge, and run to the museum to pick up my father and walk home with him. The best times were when he was the evening duty officer, when the museum was already closed. He would emerge from the long, marbled corridor, in full splendor, with that blue-white-blue armband of the duty officer around his left arm, the holstered Parabellum on his right side, dangling from his belt, the Navy cap with its lacquered visor and gilded "salad" above covering his disconcertingly bald head. "Greetings, Commander," I would say, for such was his rank; he'd smirk back, and as his tour of duty wouldn't be over for another hour or so, he'd cut me loose to loiter about in the museum alone.

It is my profound conviction that apart from the literature of the last two centuries and, perhaps, the architecture of the former capital, the only other thing Russia can be proud of is its Navy's history. Not because of its spectacular victories, of which there have been rather few, but because of the nobility of spirit that has informed its enterprise. Call it idiosyncrasy or even psycho-fancy, but this brain child of the only visionary among Russian emperors, Peter the Great, seems to me indeed a cross between the aforementioned literature and architecture. Patterned after the British Navy, but less functional than decorative, informed more by the spirit of discovery than by that of expansion, prone rather to a heroic gesture and self-sacrifice than to survival at all costs, this Navy indeed was a vision: of a perfect, almost abstract order, borne upon the waters of the world's oceans, as it could not be attained anywhere on Russian soil.

A child is always first of all an aesthete: he responds to appearances, to surfaces, to shapes and forms. There is hardly anything that I've liked in my life more than those clean-shaven admirals, *en face* and in profile, in their gilded frames looming through a forest of masts on ship models that aspired to life size. In their eighteenth- and nineteenth-century uniforms, with those jabots or high-standing collars, burdock-like fringe epaulets, wigs and chest-crossing broad blue ribbons, they looked very much the instruments of a perfect, abstract ideal, no less precise than bronze-rimmed astrolabes, compasses, binnacles, and sextants glittering all about. They could compute one's place under the stars with a smaller margin of error than their masters! And one could only wish they ruled human waves as well: to be exposed to the rigors of their trigonometry rather than to a shoddy planimetry of ideologues, to be a figment of the vision, of a mirage perhaps, instead of a part of reality. To this day, I think that the country would do a hell of a lot better if it had for its national banner not that foul double-headed imperial fowl or the vaguely masonic hammer-and-sickle, but the flag of the Russian Navy: our glorious, incomparably beautiful flag of St. Andrew: the diagonal blue cross against a virgin-white background.

15

On the way home, my father and I would drop into stores, buy food or photographic materials (film, chemicals, paper), stop by shop windows. As we made our way through the center of town, he would tell me about this or that façade's history, about what was here or there before the war or before 1917. Who was the architect, who was the owner, who was the dweller, what happened to them, and, in his view, why. This six-foot-tall Navy commander knew quite a lot about civilian life, and gradually I began to regard his uniform as a disguise; more precisely, the idea of distinction between form and content began to take root in my schoolboy mind. His uniform had to do with this effect no less than the present content of the façades he was pointing at. In my schoolboy's mind this disparity would refract, of course, into an invitation to lie (not that I needed one); deep down, though, I think this taught me the principle of maintaining appearances no matter what is going on inside.

In Russia, the military seldom change into civvies, even at home. Partly, this is a matter of one's wardrobe, which is never too vast; mainly, though, this has to do with the notion of authority associated with uniform and thus with your social standing. Especially if you are an officer. Even the demobilized and retired tend to wear for quite some time, at home and in public, this or that part of their service attire: a tunic without epaulets, tall boots, a military cap, an overcoat, indicating to everybody (and reminding themselves of) the degree of their belonging: for once in charge, always in charge. It is like the Protestant clergy in these parts; and in the case of a Navy man, this similarity is all the stronger because of his white undercollar.

We had lots of those, plastic and cotton ones, in the chest's upper drawer; years later, when I was in the seventh grade and a uniform was introduced into school, my mother would cut and sew them to the standing collar of my rat-gray tunic. For that uniform, too, was semi-military: tunic, belt with a buckle, matching trousers, a cap with a lacquered visor. The earlier one starts to think of himself as a soldier, the better it is for the system. That was fine with me, and yet I resented the color, which suggested the infantry or, worse still, the police. In no way could it match my father's pitch-black overcoat with two rows of yellow buttons that suggested an avenue at night. And when he'd unbutton it, underneath you'd see the dark-blue tunic with yet another file of the same buttons: a dimly lit street in evening. "A street within an avenue"—this is how I thought about my father, looking askance at him as we walked home from the museum.

16

There are two crows in my backyard here in South Hadley. They are quite big, almost raven-size, and they are the first thing I see every time I drive to or leave the house. They appeared here one by one: the first, two years ago, when my mother died; the second, last year, right after my father died. Or else that's the way I noticed their presence. Now they always show up or flap away together, and they are too silent for crows. I try not to look at them; at least, I try not to watch them. Yet I've noticed that they tend to stay in the pine grove that starts at the end of my back yard and slopes for a quarter of a mile to a meadow that edges a small ravine with a couple of big boulders at the edge. I never walk there anymore because I expect to find them, the crows, dormant atop those two boulders in the sunlight. Nor did I try to find their nest. They are black, but I have noticed that the inside of their wings is the color of wet ash. The only time that I don't see them is when it's raining.

17

In 1950, I think, my father was demobilized in accordance with some Politburo ruling that people of Jewish origin should not hold high military rank. The ruling was initiated, if I am not mistaken, by Andrei Zhdanov, who was then in charge of ideological control over the armed forces. By that time my father was already forty-seven, and he had to, as it were, begin his life anew. He decided to return to journalism, to his photoreportage. To do so, however, he had to be employed by a magazine or a newspaper. That turned out to be quite difficult: the fifties were bad years for the Jews. The campaign against the "rootless cosmopolites" was in full swing; then, in 1953, came the "Doctors' Case," which didn't end in the usual bloodbath only because its instigator, Comrade Stalin himself, all of a sudden, at the case's nadir, kicked the bucket. But long before, and for some time after, the air was full of rumors of the Politburo's planned reprisals against the Jews, of relocating all those "paragraph five" creatures to Eastern Siberia, to the area called Birobidzhan, near the Chinese border. There was even a letter in circulation, signed by the most prominent "paragraph five" individuals—chess champions, composers, and writers—containing a plea to the Central Committee of the Party, and to Comrade Stalin personally, to permit us, the Jews, to redeem with hard labor in remote parts the great harm we had inflicted upon the Russian people. The letter was to appear any day now in *Pravda* as the pretext for our deportation.

What appeared in *Pravda*, however, was the announcement of Stalin's death, although by that time we were preparing to travel and had already sold our upright piano, which nobody in our family could play anyhow (notwithstanding the distant relative my mother invited to tutor me: I had no talent whatsoever, and even less in the way of patience). Still, in that atmosphere, the chances for a Jew and a non-Party member to be hired by a magazine or a paper were dismal; so my father hit the road.

For several years he freelanced all over the country under contract to the All-Union Agricultural Exhibit in Moscow. This way we occasionally would get some marvels on our table—four-pound tomatoes or apple-cum-pear hybrids; but the pay was less than meager, and the three of us existed solely on my mother's salary as a clerk in the borough's development council. Those were our very lean years, and it was then that my parents began to get ill. All the same, my father looked his gregarious self and he frequently would take me about town to see his Navy pals, now running a yacht club, minding old dockyards, training youngsters. There were quite a lot of those, and invariably they were pleased to see him (on the whole, I've never met anyone, man or woman, who held a grudge against him). One of them, the editor in chief of the newspaper for the regional branch of the Merchant Marine, a Jew who bore a Russian-sounding name, finally hired him, and until my father went into retirement he worked for that publication, in the Leningrad harbor.

It appears that most of his life was spent on foot ("Reporters, like wolves, live by their paws" was his frequent utterance), among ships, sailors, captains, cranes, cargo. In the background, there was always a rippled zinc sheet of water, masts, the black metal bulk of a stern with a few white first or last letters of the ship's home port. Except in winter, he always wore the black Navy cap with the lacquered visor. He liked to be near the water, he adored the sea. In that country, this is the closest one gets to freedom. Even looking at it is sometimes enough, and he looked at it, and photographed it, for most of his life.

18

To a varying degree, every child craves adulthood and yearns to get out of his house, out of his oppressive nest. Out! Into real life! Into the wide world. Into life on his own terms.

In time, he gets his wish. And for a while, he is absorbed with new vistas, absorbed with building his own nest, with manufacturing his own reality.

Then one day, when the new reality is mastered, when his own terms are implemented, he suddenly learns that his old nest is gone, that those who gave him life are dead.

On that day he feels like an effect suddenly without its cause. The enormity of the loss makes it incomprehensible. His mind, made naked by this loss, shrinks, and increases the magnitude of this loss even further.

He realizes that his youthful quest for "real life," his departure from the nest, have rendered that nest defenseless. This is bad enough; still, he can put the blame on nature.

What he can't blame on nature is the discovery that his achievement, the reality of his own manufacture, is less valid than the reality of his abandoned nest. That if there ever was anything real in his life, it was precisely that nest, oppressive and suffocating, from which he so badly wanted to flee. Because it was built by *others*, by those who gave him life, and not by him, who knows only too well the true worth of his own labor, who, as it were, just *uses* the given life.

He knows how willful, how intended and premeditated, everything that he has manufactured is. How, in the end, all of it is provisional. And even if it lasts, the best way he can put it to use is as evidence of his skill, which he may brag about.

Yet, for all his skill, he'll never be able to reconstruct that primitive, sturdy nest that heard his first cry of life. Nor will he be able to reconstruct those who put him there. An effect, he can't reconstruct his cause.

19

The biggest item of our furniture—or rather, the one that occupied the most space—was my parents' bed, to which I think I owe my life. It was a large, king-sized affair whose carvings, again, matched to a certain degree the rest, yet they were done in a more modern fashion. The same vegetation motif, of course, but the execution oscillated somewhere between Art Nouveau and the commercial version of Constructivism. This bed was the object of my mother's special pride, for she had bought it very cheaply in 1935, before she and my father got married, having spotted it and a matching dressing table with three mirrors in some second-rate carpenter shop. Most of our life gravitated toward this low-sitting bed, and the most momentous decisions in our family were made when the three of us gathered, not around the table, but on that vast surface, with myself at my parents' feet.

By Russian standards, this bed was a real luxury. I often thought that it was precisely this bed that persuaded my father to get married, for he loved to tarry in it more than anything else. Even when he and my mother were engaged in the bitterest possible mutual acrimony, mostly on the subject of our budget ("You are just hell-bent to dump all the cash at the grocer's!" comes his indignant voice over bookshelves separating my "half" from their "room." "I am poisoned, poisoned by thirty years of your stinginess!" replies my mother), even then he'd be reluctant to get out of it, especially in the morning. Several people offered us very good money for that bed, which indeed occupied too much space in our quarters. But no matter how insolvent we were, my parents never considered this option. The bed was clearly an excess, and I believe they liked it precisely for that.

I remember them sleeping in it on their sides, backs turned to each other, a gulf of crumpled blankets in between. I remember them reading there, talking, taking their pills, fighting this or that illness. The bed framed them for me at their most secure and most helpless. It was their very private lair, their ultimate island, their own inviolable, by no one except me, place in the universe. Wherever it stands now, it stands as a vacuum within the world order. A seven-by-five-foot vacuum. It was of light-brown polished maple, and it never creaked.

20

My half was connected to their room by two large, nearly-ceiling-high arches which I constantly tried to fill with various combinations of bookshelves and suitcases, in order to separate myself from my parents, in order to obtain a degree of privacy. One can speak only about degrees, because the height and the width of those two arches, plus the Moorish configuration of their upper edge, ruled out any notion of complete success. Unless, of course, one could fill them up with bricks or cover them with wooden boards. But that was against the law for this would result in our having two rooms instead of the one and a half that the borough housing order stated we were entitled to. Short of the fairly frequent inspections of our building's super, the neighbors, no matter how nice the terms we were on with them, would report us to the appropriate authorities in no time.

One had to design a palliative, and that was what I was busy at from the age of fifteen on. I went through all sorts of mind-boggling arrangements, and at one time even contemplated building-in a twelve-foot-high aquarium, which would have in the middle of it a door connecting my half with the room. Needless to say, that architectural feat was beyond my ken. The solution, then, was more and more bookshelves on my side, more and thicker layers of drapery on my parents'. Needless to say, they liked neither the solution nor the nature of the problem itself.

Girls and friends, however, grew in quantity more slowly than did the books; besides, the latter were there to stay. We had two armoires with full-length mirrors built into their doors and otherwise undistinguished. But they were rather tall, and they did half the job. Around and above them I built the shelves, leaving a narrow opening, through which my parents could squeeze into my half, and vice versa. My father resented the arrangement, particularly since at the farthest end of my half he had built himself a darkroom where he was doing his developing and printing, i.e., where the large part of our livelihood came from.

There was a door in that end of my half. When my father wasn't working in his darkroom, I would use that door for getting in and out. "So that I won't disturb you," I told my parents, but actually it was in order to avoid their scrutiny and the necessity of introducing my guests to them, or the other way around. To obfuscate the nature of those visits, I kept an electric gramophone, and my parents gradually grew to hate J. S. Bach.

Still later, when books and the need for privacy increased dramatically, I partitioned my half further by repositioning those armoires in such a way that they separated my bed and my desk from the darkroom. Between them, I squeezed a third one that was idling in the corridor. I tore its back wall out, leaving its door intact. The result was that a guest would have to enter my *Lebensraum* through two doors and one curtain. The first door was the one that led into the corridor; then you'd find yourself standing in my father's darkroom and removing a curtain; the next thing was to open the door of the former armoire. Atop the armoires, I piled all the suitcases we had. They were many; still, they failed to reach the ceiling. The net effect was that of a barricade; behind it, though, the gamin felt safe, and a Marianne could bare more than just her breast.

21

The dim view my mother and father took of these transformations brightened somewhat when they began to hear from behind the partition the clatter of my typewriter. The drapery muffled it considerably but not fully. The typewriter, with its Russian typeface, was also part of my father's China catch, little though he expected it to be put to use by his son. I had it on my desk, tucked into the niche created by the bricked-up former door once connecting our room and a half with the rest of the enfilade. That's when that extra foot came in handy! Since my neighbors had their piano on the opposite side of this door, I fortified my side against their daughter's "Chopsticks" with a walled bookcase that, resting on my desk, fit the niche perfectly.

Two mirrored armoires and the passage between them on one side; the tall draped window with the windowsill just two feet above my rather spacious brown cushionless couch on the other; the arch, filled up to its Moorish rim with bookshelves behind; the niche-filling bookcase and my desk with the Royal Underwood in front of my nose—that was my *Lebensraum*. My mother would clean it, my father would cross it on his way back and forth to his darkroom; occasionally he or she would come for refuge in my worn-out but deep armchair after yet another verbal skirmish. Other than that, these ten square meters were mine, and they were the best ten square meters I've ever known. If space has a mind of its own and generates its own distribution, there is a chance some of these square meters, too, may remember me fondly. Now especially, under a different foot.

22

I am prepared to believe that it is more difficult for Russians to accept the severance of ties than for anyone else. We are, after all, a very settled people, even more so than other Continentals (Germans or French), who move around a lot more, if only because they have cars and no borders to speak of. For us, an apartment is for life, the town is for life, the country is for life. The notions of permanence are therefore stronger; the sense of loss as well. Yet a nation that has lost in half a century nearly sixty million souls to its carnivorous state (which includes the twenty million killed in the war) surely was capable of upgrading its sense of stability. If only because those losses were incurred for the sake of the status quo.

So if one dwells on all this, it is not necessarily to comply with the native realm's psychological makeup. Perhaps what is responsible for this outpouring is exactly the opposite: the incompatibility of the present with what's remembered. Memory, I suppose, reflects the quality of one's reality no less than utopian thought. The reality I face bears no relation and no correspondence to the room and a half and its two inhabitants, across the ocean and now nonexistent. As alternatives go, I can't think of anything more drastic than where I am at. The difference is that between two hemispheres, between night and day, between a cityscape and a countryside, between the dead and the living. The only points in common are my own frame and a typewriter. Of a different make and with a different typeface.

I suppose that had I been around my parents for the last twelve years of their life, had I been around them when they were dying, the contrast between night and day or between a street in a Russian town and an American country lane would be less sharp; the onslaught of memory would yield to that of utopian thinking. The sheer wear and tear would have dulled the senses enough to perceive the tragedy as a natural one and leave it behind in a natural way. However, there are few things more futile than weighing one's options in retrospect; similarly, the good thing about an artificial tragedy is that it makes one pay attention to the artifice. The poor tend to utilize everything. I utilize my sense of guilt.

23

It is an easy sentiment to master. After all, every child feels guilty toward his parents, for somehow he knows that they will die before him. So all he needs to alleviate his guilt is to have them die of natural causes: of an illness, or old age, or both. Still, can one extend this sort of cop-out to the death of a slave? Of someone who was born free but whose freedom was altered?

I narrow this definition of a slave neither for academic reasons nor out of lack of generosity. I am willing to buy that a human being born in slavery knows about freedom either genetically or intellectually: through reading or just by hearsay. Yet I must add that his genetic craving for freedom is, like all cravings, to a certain degree incoherent. It is not the actual memory of his mind or limbs. Hence the cruelty and aimless violence of so many revolts. Hence, too, their defeats, alias tyrannies. Death to such a slave or to his kin may seem a liberation (the famous Martin Luther King, Jr.'s "Free! Free! Free at last").

But what about someone born free but dying a slave? Would he or she—and let's keep ecclesiastical notions out of this—think of it as a solace? Well, perhaps. More likely, they would think of it as the ultimate insult, the ultimate irreversible stealing of their freedom. Which is what their kin or their child would think, and which is what it is. The last theft.

I remember how once my mother went to buy a railroad ticket to the south, to the Mineral Waters Sanatorium. She had her twenty-one-day vacation after two straight years in her borough development's office, and she was going to that sanatorium because of her liver (she never learned it was cancer). In the city ticket office, in the long queue where she had already spent three hours, she discovered that her money for the ticket, four hundred rubles, had been stolen. She was inconsolable. She came home and stood in our communal kitchen and cried and cried. I led her to our room and a half; she lay on her bed and kept crying. The reason I remember this is that she never cried, except at funerals.

24

In the end my father and I came up with the money, and she went to the sanatorium. However, it wasn't the lost money she was crying about . . . Tears were infrequent in our family; the same goes to a certain extent for the whole of Russia. "Keep your tears for more grave occasions," she would tell me when I was small. And I am afraid I've succeeded more than she wanted me to.

I suppose she wouldn't approve of me writing all this, either. Nor would, of course, my father. He was a proud man. When something reprehensible or horrendous was drawing near him, his face assumed a sour yet at the same time a challenging expression. It was as if he were saying "Try me" to something that he knew from the threshold was mightier than he. "What else could you expect from this scum?" would be his remark on those occasions, a remark with which he would go into submission.

This was not some brand of stoicism. There was no room for any posture or philosophy, however minimalist, in the reality of that time, which compromised every conviction or scruple by demanding total submission to the sum of their opposites. (Only those who did not return from the camps could claim intransigence; those who did were every bit as pliable as the rest.) Yet that was no cynicism, either.

It was simply an attempt to keep one's back straight in a situation of complete dishonor; to keep one's eyes open. That's why tears were out of the question.

25

The men of that generation were the either/or men. To their children, much more adept in transactions with their conscience (very profitable at times), these men often seemed simpletons. As I said, they were not terribly self-aware. We, their children, were brought up—or rather brought ourselves up—to believe in the complexity of the world, in the significance of the nuance, of overtones, of gray areas, of the psychological aspects of this and that. Now, having reached the age that equates us to them, having acquired the same physical mass and wearing clothes their size, we see that the whole thing boils down precisely to either/or, to the yes/no principle. It took us nearly a lifetime to learn what they seemed to know from the outset: that the world is a very raw place and doesn't deserve better. That "yes" and "no" pretty well embrace, without anything left out, all that complexity which we were discovering and structuring with such relish, and which nearly cost us our willpower.

26

Had they looked for a motto for their existence, they could have taken a few lines from one of Akhmatova's "Northern Elegies":

Just like a river,
I was deflected by my stalwart era.
They swapped my life: into a different valley,
past different landscapes, it went rolling on.
And I don't know my banks or where they are.

They never told me much about their childhood, about the families they were from, about their parents or grandparents. I know only that one of my grandparents (on my mother's side) was a Singer sewing machine salesman in the Baltic provinces of the empire (Lithuania, Latvia, Poland) and that the other (on my father's side) was a print-shop owner in St. Petersburg. This reticence had less to do with amnesia than with the necessity of concealing their class origins during that potent era, in order to survive. Engaging raconteur that my father was, he would be quickly stopped in his reminiscing about his high-school endeavors by the warning shot of my mother's gray eyes. In her turn, she would not even blink at hearing an occasional French expression on a street or coming from some of my friends, although one day I found her with a French edition of my works. We looked at each other; then she silently put the book back on the shelf and left my *Lebensraum*.

A deflected river running to its alien, artificial estuary. Can anyone ascribe its disappearance at this estuary to natural causes? And if one can, what about its course? What about human potential, reduced and misdirected from the outside? Who is there to account for what it has been deflected from? Is there anyone? And while asking these questions, I am not losing sight of the fact that this limited or misdirected life may produce in its course yet another life, mine for instance, which, were it not precisely for that reduction of options, wouldn't have taken place to begin with, and no questions would be asked. No, I am aware of the law of probability. I don't wish that my parents had never met. I am asking these questions precisely because I am a tributary of a turned, deflected river. In the end, I suppose, I am talking to myself.

So when and where, I ask myself, does the transition from freedom to slavery acquire the status of inevitability? When does it become acceptable, especially to an innocent bystander? At what age is it most harmless to alter one's free state? At what age does this alteration register in one's memory least? At the age of twenty? Fifteen? Ten? Five? In the womb? Rhetorical questions, these, aren't they? Not really. A revolutionary or a conqueror at least should know the right answer. Genghis Khan, for instance, knew it. He just carved up everyone whose head was above a cart wheel's hub. Five, then. But on October 25, 1917, my father was already fourteen; my mother, twelve. She already knew some French; he, Latin. That's why I am asking these questions. That's why I am talking to myself.

27

On summer evenings all three of our tall windows were open, and the breeze from the river tried to acquire the rank of an object in the tulle curtains. The river wasn't far, just ten minutes' walk from our building. Nothing was too far: the Summer Garden, the Hermitage, the Field of Mars. Yet even when they were younger my parents seldom went for a stroll, together or separately. After a whole day on his feet, my father wasn't terribly keen on hitting the streets again. As for my mother, standing in queues after eight hours in the office produced the same results; besides, there were plenty of things she had to do at home. If they ventured out, it would be mostly to attend some relatives' gathering (a birthday or a wedding anniversary), or for a movie, very seldom for the theater.

Living near them all my life, I wasn't conscious of their aging. Now that my memory is shuttling between various decades, I see my mother watching from the balcony the shuffling figure of her husband down below and muttering under her breath, "A real oldster, aren't you. A real decided oldster." And I hear my father's "You're just bent on driving me into the grave," which concluded their quarrels in the sixties, instead of the door bang and receding sound of his steps a decade earlier. And I see, while shaving, his silver-gray stubble on my chin.

If my mind gravitates now to their images as old people, it has to do presumably with the knack of memory for retaining last impressions best. (Add to this our addiction to linear logic, to the principle of evolution—and the invention of photography is inevitable.) But I think my own getting there, to old age, also plays some role: one seldom dreams even about one's own youth, about, say, being twelve. If I have any notion of the future, it is made in their likeness. They are my "Kilroy was here" for the day after tomorrow, at least visually.

28

Like most males, I bear more resemblance to my father than to my mother. Yet as a child I spent more time with her—

partly because of the war, partly because of the subsequent nomadic life my father had to lead. She taught me how to read at the age of four; most of my gestures, intonations, and mannerisms are, I presume, hers. Some of the habits, too, including the one of smoking.

By Russian standards, she was fairly tall, five foot three, fair, and on the plump side. She had dishwater-blond hair, which she wore short all her life, and gray eyes. She was especially pleased that I inherited her straight, almost Roman nose, and not the arching majestic beak of my father, which she found absolutely fascinating. "Ah, this beak!" she would start, carefully punctuating her speech with pauses. "Such beaks"—pause—"are sold in the sky"—pause—"six rubles apiece." Although resembling one of the Sforza profiles by Piero della Francesca, the beak was clearly Jewish, and she had reasons for being glad that I didn't get it.

In spite of her maiden name (which she retained in marriage), the "fifth paragraph" played in her case a lesser role than usual: because of her looks. She was positively very attractive, in a general North European, I would say Baltic, way. In a sense, that was a blessing: she had no trouble getting employment. As a result, however, she had to work all her conscious life. Presumably having failed to disguise her petit bourgeois class origins, she had to give up her hopes for higher education, and spent her entire life in various offices, as either a secretary or an accountant. The war brought a change: she became an interpreter in a camp for German POWs and received the rank of junior lieutenant in the Interior Ministry forces. When Germany signed the surrender, she was offered a promotion and a career within that ministry's system. Not anxious to join the Party, she declined and returned to the graph sheets and abacus. "I don't intend to salute my husband first," she told her superior. "And I don't want to turn my wardrobe into an arsenal."

29

We called her "Marusya," "Manya," "Maneczka" (my father's and her sisters' diminutives for her), and "Masya" or "Keesa," which were my inventions. With the years, the last two acquired a greater currency, and even my father began to address her in this way. With the exception of "Keesa," all these nicknames were diminutive forms of her first name, Maria. "Keesa" is a slightly endearing form for a female cat, and she resisted being addressed in this way for quite some time. "Don't you dare call me that!" she would exclaim angrily. "And in general, stop using all these feline pet words of yours! Else you'll end up having cat brains!"

That meant my predilection as a boy to enunciate in a catlike fashion certain words whose vowels seemed to me to invite such treatment. "Meat" was one, and by the time I was fifteen, there was a great deal of meowing in our family. My father proved to be susceptible to this, and we began to address or refer to each other as "Big Cat" and "Little Cat." A "meow" or a "purrmeow," or a "purr-murr-meow," covered a substantial part of our emotional spectrum: approval, doubt, indifference, resignation, trust. Gradually, my mother started to use it, too, but mainly to denote detachment.

"Keesa," however, stuck to her, especially when she got really old. Rotund, wrapped in a couple of brown shawls, with her terribly kind, soft face, she looked very cuddly and very much self-contained. It seemed as if she might purr. Instead, she would say to my father: "Sasha, have you paid this month's electricity?" or to nobody in particular: "Next week is our turn for cleaning up the apartment." Which meant scrubbing and washing the floors in the corridors and the kitchen, as well as cleaning the bathroom and the john. She would address nobody in particular because she knew it was she who had to do it.

30

How they managed all those chores, cleanups especially, for the last twelve years, I have no idea. My departure, of course, meant one less mouth to fill, and they could hire someone from time to time to do these things. Still, knowing their budget (two meager pensions) and my mother's character, I doubt that they did. Besides, in communal apartments, this practice is rare: the natural sadism of neighbors, after all, needs some degree of satisfaction. A relative, perhaps, may be allowed, but not a hired hand.

Croesus though I became, with my university salary, they wouldn't hear of exchanging U.S. dollars into rubles. They regarded the official rate of exchange as a rip-off; and they were both fastidious and fearful of having anything to do with the black market. The last reason was perhaps the strongest: they remembered how their pensions had been revoked in 1964, when I received my five-year sentence, and they had to find work again. So it was mostly clothes and art books that I sent them, since the latter command very high prices with bibliophiles. They relished the clothes, especially my father, who was always quite a sharp dresser. As for the art books, they kept them for themselves. To look at after scrubbing the communal floor at the age of seventy-five.

31

Their reading tastes were very catholic, with my mother preferring Russian classics. Neither she nor my father held definite opinions about literature, music, art, although in their youth they knew personally a number of Leningrad writers, composers, painters (Zoshchenko, Zabolotsky, Shostakovich, Petrov-Vodkin). They were just readers—evening readers, to be more precise—and they were always careful to renew their library cards. Returning from work, my mother would invariably have in her string bag full of potatoes or cabbage a library book wrapped in a newspaper cover to prevent it from getting soiled.

It was she who suggested to me when I was sixteen and working at the factory that I register at the city public library; and I don't think she had in mind only to prevent me from loitering about in the streets in the evening. On the other hand, as far as I knew, she wanted me to become a painter. At any rate, the rooms and corridors of that former hospital on the right bank of the Fontanka River were the beginning of my undoing, and I remember the first book I asked for there, on my mother's advice. It was *Gulistan* (*The Garden of Roses*) by the Persian poet Saadi. My mother, it turned out, was fond of Persian poetry. The next thing that I asked for, on my own, was Maupassant's *La Maison Tellier*.

32

What memory has in common with art is the knack for selection, the taste for detail. Complimentary though this observation may seem to art (that of prose in particular), to memory it should appear insulting. The insult, however, is well deserved. Memory contains precisely details, not the whole picture; highlights, if you will, not the entire show. The conviction that we are somehow remembering the whole thing in a blanket fashion, the very conviction that allows the species to go on with its life, is groundless. More than anything, memory resembles a library in alphabetical disorder, and with no collected works by anyone.

33

The way other people mark the growth of their children with pencil notches on the kitchen wall, every year on my birthday my father took me out to our balcony and photographed me there. In the background lay a medium-size cobblestone square with the Cathedral of the Savior of Her Imperial Majesty's Transfiguration Battalion. In the war years its crypt was designated a local bomb shelter, and my mother kept me there during air raids, in a big box with remembrance notes. This is one thing that I owe to Orthodoxy, and it has to do with memory.

The cathedral, a six-story-tall classicistic affair, surrounded by a considerable garden full of oak, linden, and maple, was my playground in the postwar years, and I remember my mother collecting me there (she pulls, I stall and scream: an allegory of cross-purposes) and dragging me home to do homework. With similar clarity I see her, my grandfather, and my father, in one of this garden's narrow alleys, trying to teach me to ride a two-wheel bicycle (an allegory of common goal, or of motion). On the rear, eastern wall of the cathedral, there was, covered with thick glass, a large, dim icon depicting the Transfiguration: Christ floating in the air above a bunch of bodies reclined in fascination. Nobody could explain to me the significance of that picture; even now I am not sure I grasp it fully. There were a great many clouds in the icon, and somehow I associated them with the local climate.

34

The garden was surrounded by a black cast-iron fence held up by equally spaced groups of cannons standing upside-down, captured by the Transfiguration Battalion's soldiers from the British in the Crimean War. Adding to the decor of the fence, the cannon barrels (a threesome in each case, on a granite block) were linked by heavy cast-iron chains on which children swung wildly, enjoying both the danger of falling on the spikes below and the clang. Needless to say, that was strictly forbidden and the cathedral wardens chased us away all the time. Needless to say, the fence was far more interesting than the inside of the cathedral, with its smell of incense and much more static activity. "See those?" asks my father, pointing at the heavy chain links. "What do they remind you of?" I am in the second grade, and I say, "They are like figure eights." "Right," he says. "And do you know what the figure eight is a symbol of?" "Snakes?" "Almost. It is a symbol of infinity." "What's infinity?" "That you had better ask in there," says my father with a grin, his finger pointed at the cathedral.

35

Yet it was he who, having bumped into me on the street in broad daylight when I was skipping school, demanded an explanation, and, being told that I was suffering from an awful toothache, took me straight to the dental clinic, so that I paid for my lies with two hours of straight terror. And yet again it was he who took my side at the Pedagogical Council when I was about to be expelled from my school for disciplinary problems. "How dare you! You who wear the uniform of our Army!" "Navy, madam," said my father. "And I defend him because I am his father. There is nothing surprising about it. Even animals defend their young. Even Brehm says so." "Brehm? Brehm? I . . . I will inform the Party organization of your outfit." Which she, of course, did.

36

"On your birthday and on the New Year you must always put on something absolutely new. At least, socks"—this is the voice of my mother. "Always eat before going to see somebody superior: your boss or your officer. That way you'll have some edge." (This is my father speaking.) "If you've just left your house and have to return because you forgot something, take a look in the mirror before you leave the house again. Else you may encounter trouble." (She again.) "Never think how much you've spent. Think how much you can make." (That's him.) "Don't you ever walk in town without a jacket." "It's good that you are red-haired, no matter what they say. I was a brunette, and brunettes are a better target."

I hear these admonitions and instructions, but they are fragments, details. Memory betrays everybody, especially those whom we knew best. It is an ally of oblivion, it is an ally of death. It is a fishnet with a very small catch, and with the water gone. You can't use it to reconstruct anybody, even on paper. What's the matter with those reputed millions of cells in our brain? What's the matter with Pasternak's "Great god of love, great god of details"? On what number of details must one be prepared to settle?

37

I see their faces, his and hers, with great clarity, in the variety of their expressions—but these are fragments also: moments, instances. These are better than photographs with their unbearable laughter, and yet they are as scattered. At times, I begin to suspect my mind of trying to produce a cumulative, generalized image of my parents: a sign, a formula, a recognizable sketch; of trying to make me settle for these. I suppose I could, and I fully realize how absurd the grounds of my resistance are: these fragments' lack of continuum. One shouldn't expect so much from memory; one shouldn't expect a film shot in the dark to develop new images. Of course not. Still, one can reproach a film shot in the daylight of one's life for missing frames.

38

Presumably the whole point is that there should be no continuum: of anything. That failures of memory are but a proof of a living organism's subordination to the laws of nature. No life is meant to be preserved. Unless one is a pharaoh, one doesn't aspire to become a mummy. Granted the objects of one's recollection possess this sort of sobriety; this may reconcile one to the quality of one's memory. A normal man doesn't expect anything to continue; he expects no continuity even for himself or his works. A normal man doesn't remember what he had for breakfast. Things of a routine, repetitive nature are meant to be forgotten. Breakfast is one; the loved ones is another. The best thing to do is to attribute this to economy of space.

And one can use those prudently saved brain cells for pondering whether failures of memory are not just a mute voice of one's suspicion that we are all but strangers to one another. That our sense of autonomy is far stronger than that of unity, let alone of causality. That a child doesn't remember his parents because he is always outbound, poised for the future. He, too, presumably, saves his brain cells for future use. The shorter your memory, the longer you live, says a proverb. Alternatively, the longer your future, the shorter your memory. That's one way of determining one's prospects for longevity, of telling the future patriarch. The drawback, though, is that patriarchs or not, autonomous or linked, we, too, are repetitive, and a Big Somebody saves His brain cells on us.

39

It is neither aversion to this sort of metaphysics nor dislike of the future, evidently guaranteed by the quality of my memory, that keeps me poring over it in spite of meager returns. The self-delusions of a writer, or the fear of facing the charge of conspiring with the laws of nature at the expense of my father and mother, have very little to do with this also. I simply think that natural laws denying continuum to anyone in concert with (or in the guise of) deficient memory serve the interests of the state. As far as I am concerned, I am unwilling to work for their advancement.

Of course, twelve years of dashed, rekindled, and dashed-again hopes, leading a very old couple over the thresholds of numerous offices and chancelleries to the furnace of the state crematorium, are repetitive in themselves, considering not only their duration but the number of similar cases as well. Yet I am less concerned with sparing my brain cells this monotony than the Supreme Being is with His. Mine are quite polluted, anyway. Besides, remembering even mere details, fragments, not to mention remembering them in English, is not in the interests of the state. That alone can keep me going.

40

Also, these two crows get a bit too brazen. Now they have landed on my porch and loiter about its old woodpile. They are pitch-black, and although I avoid looking at them, I notice they differ in size somewhat from each other. One is shorter than the other, the way my mother was up to my father's shoulder; their beaks, however, are identical. I am no ornithologist, but I believe crows live long; at least ravens do. Although I can't make out their age, they seem to be an old couple. On an outing. I don't have it in me to shoo them away, nor can I communicate with them in any fashion. I also seem to remember that crows do not migrate. If the origins of mythology are fear and isolation, I am isolated all right. And I wonder how many things will remind me of my parents from now on. That is to say, with this sort of visitor, who needs a good memory?

41

A mark of its deficiency is that it retains odd items. Like our first, then a five-digit, phone number, which we had right after the war. It was 265–39, and I suppose I still remember it because the phone was installed when I was memorizing the multiplication table in school. It is of no use to me now: in the same way as our last number, in our room and a half, is of no use anymore. I don't remember it, the last one, although for the past twelve years I called it almost every week. Letters wouldn't go through, so we settled for the telephone: it is evidently easier to monitor a phone call than to perlustrate and then deliver a letter. Ah, those weekly calls to the U.S.S.R.! ITT never had it so good.

We couldn't say much during those exchanges, we had to be either reticent or oblique and euphemistic. It was mostly about weather or health, no names, a great deal of dietetic advice. The main thing was hearing each other's voice, assuring ourselves in this animal way of our respective existences. It was mostly non-semantic, and small wonder that I remember no particulars except Father's reply on the third day of my mother's being in the hospital. "How is Masya?" I asked. "Well, Masya is no more, you know," he said. The "you know" was there because on this occasion, too, he tried to be euphemistic.

42

Or else a key is thrown up to the surface of my mind: a longish, stainless-steel key which was awkward to carry in our pockets, yet which fit easily in my mother's purse. This key would open our tall white door, and I don't understand why I recall it now, for that place doesn't exist. I doubt that there is any erotic symbolism to it, for among us we had three replicated versions. For that matter, I don't understand why I recall the wrinkles on my father's forehead, and under his chin, or the reddish, slightly inflamed left cheek of my mother's (she called it "vegetative neurosis"), for neither those marks nor the rest of their bearers exist any longer either. Only their voices somehow survive in my conscience: presumably because my own blends them the way my features must blend theirs. The rest—their flesh, their clothes, the telephone, the key, our possessions, the furniture—is gone, and never to be found, as if our room and a half had been hit by a bomb. Not by a neutron bomb, which at least leaves the furniture intact, but by a time bomb, which splinters even one's memory. The building still stands, but the place is wiped out clean, and new tenants, no, troops, move in to occupy it: that's what a time bomb is all about. For this is a time war.

43

They liked opera arias, tenors, and the movie stars of their youth, didn't care very much for painting, had a notion of "classical" art, enjoyed solving crossword puzzles, and were bewildered and upset by my literary pursuits. They thought me wrong, worried about the way I was going, but supported me as much as they could, because I was their child. Later on, when I managed to print something here and there, they felt pleased, and at times even proud; but I know that should I have turned out to be simply a graphomaniac and a failure, their attitude toward me wouldn't have been any different. They loved me more than themselves, and most likely wouldn't understand my guilt feelings toward them at all. The main issues were bread on the table, clean clothes, and staying healthy. Those were their synonyms for love, and they were better than mine.

As for that time war, they fought it valiantly. They knew that a bomb was going to explode, but they never changed their tactics. As long as they were vertical, they were moving about, buying and delivering food to their bedridden friends, relatives; giving clothes, what money they could spare, or refuge to those who now and then happened to be worse off. They were that way always, for as long as I remember them; and not because deep down they thought that if they were kind to some people, it would somehow be registered on high and they would be treated one day in kind. No, this was the natural and uncalculated generosity of extroverts, which perhaps became all the more palpable to others now that I, its main object, was gone. And this is what ultimately may help me to come to terms with the quality of my memory.

That they wanted to see me before they died had nothing to do with a desire or an attempt to dodge that explosion. They didn't want to emigrate, to live their last days in America. They felt too old for any sort of change, and at best, America for them was just the name of the place where they could meet their son. It was real for them only in terms of their doubt whether they could manage the trip should they be allowed to travel. And yet what games these two old, frail people tried to play with all that scum in charge of granting permission! My mother would apply for a visa alone to indicate that she was not intending to defect to the United States, that her husband would stay behind as a hostage, as the guarantee of her return. Then they would reverse roles. Then they wouldn't apply for a while, pretending that they had lost interest, or showing the authorities that they understood how difficult it was for them to make a decision under this or that climate in U.S.–Soviet relations. Then they would apply just for a one-week stay in the U.S., or for permission to travel to Finland or Poland. Then she would go to the capital, to seek an audience with what that country had for a President, and knock on all the doors of the foreign and internal ministries that there are. All was in vain: the system, from its top to its bottom, never made a single mistake. As systems go, it can be proud of itself. But then inhumanity is always easier to structure than anything else. For that job, Russia never had to import the know-how. In fact, the only way for that country to get rich is to export it.

44

And so it does, in ever-increasing volume. Yet one may derive some comfort, if not necessarily hope, from the fact that, if not the last laugh, then the last word belongs to one's genetic code. For I am grateful to my mother and my father not only for giving me life but also for failing to bring up their child as a slave. They tried the best they could—if only to safeguard me against the social reality I was born into—to turn me into the state's obedient, loyal member. That they didn't succeed, that they had to pay for it with their eyes being closed not by their son but by the anonymous hand of the state, testifies not to their laxness but to the quality of their genes, whose fusion produced a body the system found alien enough to eject. Come to think of it, what else could be expected from the combined strength of his and her ability to endure?

If this sounds like bragging, so be it. The mixture of their genes is worth bragging about, if only because it proved to be state-resistant. And not simply state but the First Socialist State in the History of Mankind, as it prefers to bill itself: the state specifically adept at gene splicing. That's why its hands are always awash in blood, because of its experiments in isolating and paralyzing the cell responsible for one's willpower. So, given that state's volume of export, today if one is to build a family, one should ask for more than just the partner's blood group or dowry: one should ask for her or his DNA. That's why, perhaps, certain peoples look askance at mixed marriages.

There are two pictures of my parents taken in their youth, in their twenties. He, on the deck of a steamer: a smiling, carefree face, a smokestack in the background; she, on a footboard of a railroad carriage, demurely waving her kid-gloved hand, the buttons of the train conductor's tunic behind. Neither of them is as yet aware of the other's existence; neither of them, of course, is me. Besides, it is impossible to perceive anyone existing objectively, physically outside your own skin, as a part of yourself. ". . . but Mom and Dad/Were not two other people" as Auden says. And although I can't relive their past, even as the smallest possible part of either one of them, what is there to prevent me, now that they are objectively nonexistent outside my skin, from regarding myself as their sum, as their future? This way, at least, they are as free as when they were born.

Should I brace myself then, thinking that I am hugging my mother and father? Should I settle for the contents of my skull as what's left of them on earth? Possibly. I am presumably capable of this solipsistic feat. And I suppose I may also not resist their shrinkage to the size of my, lesser than their, soul. Suppose I can do that. Am I then to meow to myself as well, after having said "Keesa"? And into which one of the three rooms I am now living in do I have to run to make this meowing sound convincing?

I am them, of course; I am now our family. Yet since nobody knows the future, I doubt that forty years ago, on some September night of 1939, it crossed their mind that they were conceiving their way out. At best, I suppose, they thought of having a child, of starting a family. Fairly young, and born free on top of that, they did not realize that in the country of their birth it is now the state which decides what kind of family one is to have, and whether one is to have a family at all. When they realized that, it was already too late for everything except hope. Which is what they did until they died: they hoped. Family-minded people, they couldn't do otherwise: they hoped, planned, tried.

45

For their sake, I would like to think that they didn't allow themselves to build up their hopes too high. Perhaps my mother did; but if so, that had to do with her own kindness, and my father didn't miss a chance to point this out to her. ("Nothing pays less, Marusya," he used to retort, "than self-projection.") As for him, I recall the two of us walking one sunny afternoon together in the Summer Garden when I was already twenty or perhaps nineteen. We'd stopped before the wooden pavilion in which the Marine Brass Band was playing old waltzes: he wanted to take some pictures of this band. White marble statues loomed here and there, smeared with leopard-cum-zebra patterns of shadows, people were shuffling along on the gravel, children shrieked by the pond, and we were talking about the war and the Germans. Staring at the brass band, I found myself asking him which concentration camps in his view were worse: the Nazis' or ours. "As for myself," came the reply, "I'd rather be burned at the stake at once than die a slow death and discover a meaning in the process." Then he proceeded to snap pictures.

1985